TACTICAL RECONNAISSANCE IN THE COLD WAR

Tactical Reconnaissance in the Cold War

1945 to Korea, Cuba, Vietnam and The Iron Curtain

Doug Gordon

Pen & Sword
AVIATION

First published in
Great Britain in 2006
By Pen & Sword Aviation
An imprint of Pen and Sword Books Ltd
47 Church Street
Barnsley
South Yorkshire
S70 2AS
England

Copyright © Doug Gordon, 2006

ISBN 1 84415 332 0

The right of Doug Gordon to be identified as the Authors of this Work has been asserted by him in accordance with the Copyright, Designs and Patents Act 1988.

A CIP record for this book is available from the British Library.

All rights reserved. No part of this book may be reproduced or transmitted in any form or by any means, electronic or mechanical including photocopying, recording or by any information storage and retrieval system, without permission from the Publisher in writing.

Typeset in the UK by Mac Style, Nafferton, E. Yorkshire.
Printed and bound in Singapore by Koyodo.

Pen & Sword Books Ltd incorporates the imprints of Pen & Sword Aviation, Pen & Sword Maritime, Pen & Sword Military, Wharncliffe Local History, Pen & Sword Select, Pen & Sword Military Classics and Leo Cooper.

For a complete list of Pen & Sword titles please contact
Pen & Sword Books Limited
47 Church Street, Barnsley, South Yorkshire, S70 2AS, England
E-mail: enquiries@pen-and-sword.co.uk
Website: www.pen-and-sword.co.uk

Contents

	Acknowledgements	7
I	Introduction	9
II	Korea	15
III	Haymakers, Heart Throbs and Slick Chicks	44
IV	USAFE	74
V	Back Home	152
VI	PACAF Between the Wars	191
VII	South-east Asia	214
Appendix I	The Aircraft	269
Appendix II	Aerial Photography	296
Appendix III	Glossary of Abbreviations	312
	Bibliography	314
	Web Sites	314
	Index	315

Dedication

'Recce Pukes' was a term used to describe the men who flew tactical reconnaissance by the drivers of the fighter and fighter-bomber squadrons whose job it was to fight air-to-air or deliver ordnance. It was a term of derision. Many of the tac recce pilots have taken the name and made it their own. Recce pilots took an enormous pride in their mission and the skills as pilots they had to attain in order to achieve it. Their motto was, 'Alone, Unarmed and Unafraid'. For the most part, the story of USAF Cold War Tactical Reconnaissance is the story of men and machines at the front line constantly practising and honing their skills; knowing that at any moment they may be called upon to exercise those skills in a hot war. In the hot wars in Korea and South-east Asia they truly did fly alone and unarmed into the very heart of the enemy's territory. Most will tell you that they were never unafraid and many died.

This book is for them and their families.

Acknowledgements

This volume has been a long time in gestation, and there are many people who, over the past few years, have helped with stories, advice, comments and illustrations. The book contains much primary evidence from people who were actually involved in the events that form the narrative. Their names appear in the text and it is unnecessary to repeat them here. To them I owe a special vote of thanks for taking so much time to share their memories with me and for allowing me to include these in the book. Most of our correspondence has been in the form of emails and letters. I have also had the privilege of attending reunions of tac recce pilots and aircrew in the USA and made transcripts of our conversations. Much of the primary evidence in the Chapter: Haymakers, Heart Throbs and Slick Chicks comes from transcripts of pilots' testimonies at the RF-86 pilots reunion in Arlington in September 1999; and contributions from pilots and aircrew to the Early Cold War Overflights Symposium held at the Defence Intelligence Agency in Washington in February 2001. I have been fortunate for many years to have had the opportunity of corresponding with many of the people who were involved in the symposium. My very special thanks to Cargill Hall who, as convener of the symposium and joint editor of the proceedings documents, has allowed me to use illustrations included in the text and to quote from it; also to Bob Archibald who kindly loaned me tapes of the Arlington reunion and other material related to the RF-86.

The Recce Reunion Association has been extremely helpful in providing support for the project. My special thanks to Bob Gould, editor of the *Recce Reader* for his help in publishing my many cries for help on a variety of recce subjects, both in the journal and by email. Jim Milam of the B-66 Destroyer Association has also given of his time in publicizing my requests for information. The Voodoo Pilots Association has also been very supportive and I have had the privilege of being invited to their reunions over the years. Also thanks to Dick Cathriner of the 38th TRS pilots' association. Dick has put me in touch with many 38th pilots and other personnel of the 10th TRW in the 1950s.

Many people have provided photographs for me to use. Their names appear with the photos they have shared. To them I also owe special thanks, not only for the permission to use the photos, but also trusting me with them, often for long periods of time.

The secondary evidence that I have referenced has been principally from official unit histories obtained as microfilm from the holdings at the Air Force Historical Research Agency at Maxwell AFB. I am indebted to Essie Roberts at the Archives section at the AFHRA for her help and assistance. Other works I have accessed are included in the Bibliography. Where a work has been specifically quoted, with the author's permission, a note appears in the text.

Thanks to Robbie Robinson for his superb colour profiles of the tac recce aircraft of the USAF as used in the Cold War.

There is one person, without whose help this book would probably not have been written. I am forever in the debt of Don Karges, ex Voodoo and Phantom pilot. Many years ago Don responded to a call for help for personal contacts to help with the writing of a magazine article on the 66th TRW RF-101s in USAFE. It was he who started me on this long path by putting me in touch with so many tac recce veterans.

Foreword
by
Major General Larry Garrison USAF (Ret)

The story of the Tactical Reconnaissance Mission and the pilots who flew it has been a neglected one. Over the decades, the 'Recce Puke' played second fiddle to the glamour boys of the Fighter Squadrons in the Hot and Cold War. In this book, Doug Gordon has attempted to redress the balance and place. Tac Recce is in the rightful place where it belongs, in the forefront of the History of the Air Force.

You will meet many of my friends and mentors, the pilots and aircrew who flew demanding missions over Korea, Lebanon, Cuba and Vietnam. You will also know the men who flew top secret clandestine reconnaissance flights over China and the USSR and its East European satellites in their RF-86's, RF-100's and the RB-57's. Much of our mission was routine: constant and rigourous training. Doug has captured this well in describing the deployments and exercises which comprised much of our flying time all over the world.

You will become acquainted with our aircraft as well. Each had its idiosyncracies and there were some which we were happier to take into combat than others. All however, continued to live in our affections to one degree or another.

In these pages, Doug Gordon has captured the spirit of Tactical Reconnaissance Missions at a time when the world lived under the threat of nuclear war. Through the narrative, the dedication, diligence and humor of the people shines through.

This book is a fitting tribute to them.

General Garrison enlisted in the Air Force in 1950 and entered Pilot Training with class 52H flying the T-6, T-33 and F-80 aircraft. Assigned as a Tac Recon Pilot he flew the RF-80 and F-86 prior to arrival in Korea. There he flew the RF-80 and the RF-86 with the 15th Tac Recon Sqdn from Kimpo Air Base.

When the unit moved to Japan in 1954, he participated in 'Top Secret' clandestine long-range Photo Missions over China and the USSR flying the latest model of the RF-86F.

From 1959 to 1963 General Garrison was a Flight Commander with the 17th Tac Recon Sqdn flying the RF-101 from Laon air Base France. After a tour as an Instructor in the Air Force ROTC Program at the University of North Carolina, he left for South East Asia with the 20th Tac Recon Sqdn flying the RF-101 from Tan Son Nhut Air Base Vietnam and Udorn Air Base Thailand. He completed 198 missions over North and South Vietnam and Laos.

In 1971 he assumed Command of the 32nd Tac Recon Sqdn flying the RF-4C from RAF Alconbury in the United Kingdom.

General Garrison's last flying assignment was as Commander of the 47th Flying Training Wing at Laughlin Air Force Base in Texas. He retired in 1987 with 36 great years and 10 months in the Air force and just under 5000 hours flying time, virtually all of it in Tac Recce.

CHAPTER ONE

Introduction

The United States Air Force identifies two distinct types of aerial reconnaissance: Strategic and Tactical. Strategic Reconnaissance is the responsibility of Strategic Air Command (SAC) and Tactical Reconnaissance is the responsibility of Tactical Air Command (TAC). This book seeks to tell the story of USAF Tactical Reconnaissance from the end of the Second World War to the mid 1970s; the period when the Cold War was at its coldest. It is also a period which saw two major conflicts involving the United States, both in Asia.

The primary function of Tactical Reconnaissance is to gather intelligence about the enemy's disposition, strength and technology in the confines of the battlefield and its environs. It differs from Strategic Reconnaissance which embraces the finding and pinpointing of targets for intercontinental warfare and indications and warnings of possible surprise attack. With the exception of the clandestine overflights involving tactical aircraft and pilots, this book does not deal with the reconnaissance carried out by Strategic Air Command aircraft or aircrews.

Since the Montgolfier Brothers invented the Hot Air Balloon and gave man the ability to fly, Tactical Reconnaissance has played a major part in warfare. Now it was possible to see behind the immediate front line and the intelligence brought back by the shallow incursions of foot patrols. The turmoil of military activity that extended beyond the horizon was no longer a secret or a mystery. Troop dispersals, tanks, gun emplacements were accessible and beyond them the complex of airfields, factories, railroads and roads which supported the fighting troops could be studied and assessed. The development of photography added yet another dimension. Now all aspects of the disposition and strength of the enemy could be recorded on film and analyzed at will.

The story of USAF Tactical Reconnaissance begins in the First World War when, in 1917, the 1st and 2nd Balloon Squadrons were activated and sent to France. Prior to this there had been some army aerial activity in the American Spanish War in 1916. It had not been until August 1916 that Congress even agreed to fund the fledging air force.

In France the 1st and 2nd Balloon Squadrons were attached to the American 1st Army Corps and the French Eighth Army. They spent the next two years moving through France: Lorraine, Aisne-Marne, Champagne, St Mihiel and Meuse Argonne. Their aircraft was the Type R Observation Balloon and they were responsible for front-line battlefield surveillance. After the Armistice in 1918 the two units moved to Germany with the 3rd Army Corps as part of the army of Occupation. At this time the 12th Aero Squadron flying the AR-2 and later the DH-4 was also attached to the American 1st Army Corps and the French VI Army Corps. The mission of the 12th was as an observation unit.

During the period between the wars the Army Air Corps, which had fought so hard to come into being in 1917, found itself once again on a downward spiral with poor funding and incompetent political management. The few reconnaissance units which did exist throughout this time were involved, in the main, in forest fire patrols and flood relief operations. At the time of the outbreak of war in Europe the Army Air Corps was as ill prepared for hostilities as it had been at the commencement of the First World War. The American aircraft industry was boosted by the demand from the United Kingdom, which could not produce enough aircraft to meet its needs in the conflict. It was not until the fall of France that the administration in the USA fully realized the desperate need for a massive expansion in its Armed Forces; not least in the Air Force. Hitler had demonstrated the necessity of a strong air arm very well! The attack on Pearl Harbor was the final incentive to the United States to enter the war in Europe as well as fight in the Far East.

Such was the development in the Army Air Force at this time that, by 1943, there were approximately seventy squadrons dedicated to Tactical Reconnaissance in both Europe and the Pacific. These squadrons flew a diverse number of airplanes; amongst them P-38s, P-39s, P-40s, P-51s and Spitfires; both in their fighter versions and, in the case of the P-38 and P-51, their specially modified recce versions: the F-4, F-5 and F-6. At the end of the war, with almost indecent haste, the majority of these units were deactivated.

By the end of 1946 there were just eleven squadrons with a tactical reconnaissance mission. They were the 4th TRS, 8th TRS, 11th TRS, 12th TRS, 22nd Reconnaissance Squadron (RS), 25th TRS, 82nd RS, 45th TRS, 160th RS, 161st RS and 162nd RS.

In the immediate post-war period the aircraft flown in the tactical reconnaissance squadrons were predominately the F-6 Mustang in the day-time role and the FA-26 in the night role. As we shall see, the FA-26, soon to be redesignated the RB-26, was to soldier on for some years; but the day-time role would soon be taken over by the FP-80, to be redesignated the RF-80. In June, 1946, the 12th TRS based at March AFB, California began equipping with the FP-80A. The 12th TRS was assigned to the 67th Reconnaissance Group and had previously been designated the 39th TRS flying the P-80A as part of the 412th Fighter Group. At approximately the same time, at Langley, the 160th and 161st TRS, attached to the 363rd Reconnaissance Group were also receiving the aircraft.

In April of 1946 the 10th Reconnaissance Group in West Germany became involved in a very special project. The 45th Reconnaissance Squadron, based at Furth, acquired some A-26 Invaders specially modified for a special project. At this time there was a restriction on reconnaissance aircraft flying in the military corridors. To overcome this and gain some valuable intelligence several A-26 aircraft were modified to carry a camera in the nose in the forward oblique position. The K-18 camera shot through a small hole in the nose, a hole so small that it would certainly not be identified as a recce modification.

Major Roger Rhodarmer was assigned to the project:

> We ended up with about fifteen or sixteen A-26s organized as the 45th Reconnaissance Squadron, 10th Reconnaissance Group. Except for a few guys, there was not anybody there who knew one end of the camera from the other. We checked out fast on the equipment and then during the Spring and Summer began flying at a fast and furious rate. I flew eighty to ninety hours a month and covered targets in Western Europe. We usually photographed industrial sites, bridges, tunnels and that sort of thing. We flew as low as we could go, and actually got pictures of railroad tunnels where you could see both ends of the tunnel!*

John Auer flew some of the more unusual Birdseye missions that approached very close to the borders of East Germany:

> We would climb an RB-26 equipped with a forward shooting (Dicing) 24 in camera to well above 10000 ft and dive towards the East German border shooting all the way. I never saw any of the photography I took due to my own lack of curiosity. I don't believe there was any censorship involved but I can't be sure. I have since wondered if the whole thing was a ruse to arouse the Russian radars so they could be located and mapped. The area involved was along the border from about 50 miles north of Nuremberg to about 50 miles south of Nuremberg.

---

* As quoted in *Early Cold War Overflights Symposium Proceedings* Ed. Cargill Hall and Clayton Laurie. The National Reconnaissance Office. 2003

These photos depict the camera installation in the A-26s of Project Birdseye. The aperture at the front of the nose was so small that the aircraft would never have been identified as photo recce birds. (Roger Rhodarmer, reproduced by kind permission of Cargill Hall editor of *Early Cold War Overflights Symposium* papers)

The 10th Reconnaissance Group returned to the USA in 1947 and resided at Pope Field until deactivated in 1948. The 45th RS remained in Europe until March 1949 when it was assigned to the 543rd Support Group in Japan.

In December, 1947, the 4th TRS, part of the Caribbean Air Command, converted to the FP-80A from the F-6. The aircraft were ferried in by TAC and arrived at France Field. Almost the whole base was out to greet them. Three officers, Captains Craig, Krug and Lieutenant Allen returned from Langley 'jet school' as Instructor Pilots (IPs) and began training the new pilots. For some time the FP-80s and F-6s worked side by side. On 6 January 1948 the squadron underwent a Combat Readiness Test in both visual and photo recce. Two FP-80s provided the photos and two F-6Ds the visual intelligence. The task was to reconnoitre a 5 mile wide strip of beach near Rio Hato. What was critical at this time was the shortage of jet fuel and this seriously affected FP-80 mission effectiveness. The primary role of the FP-80 was photographic reconnaissance. Training in this role was a high priority in the 4th TRS throughout 1948. The tests were stringent. On one test mission only ten minutes were allowed to fit cameras into three FP-80s. After the aircraft had landed only one hour was allowed for the films to be developed and prints made. The film was delivered to headquarters (HQ) at Albrook Field by L-5. In June, 1948, the squadron received three P-80s to augment the thirteen FP-80s already assigned.

On the 22nd July, 1948, the squadron overflew the USS *Sicily*, which was carrying the 36th Fighter Group to Europe.

In August the 4th moved to Howard Field in the Canal Zone. In September it was involved in two aerial reviews: at Albrook and France Fields. At Albrook their display included a three aircraft aerobatic display.

In December, 1948, the squadron played host to a detachment of the Chilean Air Force. On 16 December they treated their hosts to an air display involving a formation take-off of nine aircraft, a singleton aerobatic display and an FP-80 photo-run past the stands, giving the Chilean officers two copies of the resultant prints.

In March, 1949, shortly after entertaining some visiting Guatemalan officers to a similar display, the 4th TRS was deactivated.

Meanwhile, in Japan, at Johnson AB the 8th TRS of the 71st TRG was preparing for the arrival of the newly redesignated RF-80A. It seems likely that these were those relinquished by the 4th TRS. In the immediate post-war period, whilst attached to the 315th Composite Wing, the 8th PRS had had a night photo mission, flying RF-61C Black Widows. In reality they had a daylight role. They had been responsible for photo mapping a vast area of the Far East and Pacific, including South Korea and the Philippines. They were unique in that they were the only USAF unit to fly the reconnaissance version of the Black Widow.

FP-80A *Wee Stud* of the 4th TRS. This was the aircraft of the squadron commander, Colonel Bob Baselor. The 4th was one of the first squadrons to receive the FP-80 in 1947. (via Dave Menard)

This F-15A (later RF-61) Black Widow belongs to the 8th PRS (later TRS). One of the post-war responsibilities of the 8th was photo mapping a large area of the Pacific and Korea. (Via Dave Menard)

Another unit responsible for mapping in the immediate post-war years was the 25th TRS flying P-51Ds out of Itazuke and Itami in Japan. They, too, had a mapping responsibility, specifically in Japan and Korea. Tom Halfhill was with the 25th in 1946:

> The '51s were equipped with wing tanks for longer flights. The photo resolution was quite good for the time. I made contact with a Colonel about fifty years later. He transferred to a fighter unit and flew combat missions over Korea. He said that all the mapping that we had done was apparently lost as no one knew about it. He was issued with First World War Signals Corps maps!

In March, 1949, the first of the RF-80s for the 8th TRS arrived. They were involved in a variety of activities, including some classified photo missions in co-operation with the British and US

F-6 Mustangs of the 25th TRS at Itami in 1946. The 25th flew both the P-51 and the F-6 versions of the aircraft and were responsible with the 8th TRS for a lot of mapping work in post-war Asia. (Tom Halfhill)

These Mustangs, also photographed at Itami in 1946, belong to the 25th TRS. (Tom Halfhill)

Navy. One such mission in July, 1949, involved the RF-80s flying radar calibration missions in the company of HMS *Jamaica*. By November, 1949, the squadron had seventeen aircraft on its strength.

In March, 1949, the 67th TRG was deactivated and with it the 12th TRS. The 363rd followed suit in August, 1949, and in September of that year the 161st moved to Shaw AFB where it became attached to the 20th Fighter Wing; being redesignated the 18th TRS in October, 1950. At the outbreak of the Korean War there were only two photo jet-squadrons in the regular USAF: the 8th and the 161st TRS.

The 8th TRS converted to the RF-80A in 1949. This flight is seen over Mount Fuji, a favourite photo call venue for PACAF based units. (USAF via Bob Archibald)

CHAPTER TWO

Korea

On Sunday, 25 June, 1950, the North Korean People's Army invaded South Korea across the 38th Parallel. They captured the city of Kaesong on the road to Soeul, the capital of the south. The move wasn't entirely a surprise to Far East Air Force command headquartered in Japan. Their first thought was to evacuate US citizens and this commenced at once. The threat from the air force of the communist north to the evacuation strategy was considerable and the south had virtually no means of defence against the Il-10 attack aircraft and the Yak fighters which were bombing and strafing the airfields. General McArthur ordered US fighters to cover the evacuation and within days F-82 Twin Mustangs and F-80s engaged the enemy. On 27 June C-46s of the 374th Troop Carrier Wing out of Tachikawa, Japan, began the evacuation of US personnel from Kimpo airfield. F-82s of the 68th Fighter Squadron operating out of Itakuze, Japan, provided air cover. In the process they shot down three Yak fighters. From this moment the USAF and the air forces of the United Nations were committed to defend the territorial integrity of South Korea.

The only tactical reconnaissance assets that the USAF had in the Far East Theatre were the RF-80s of the 8th Tactical Reconnaissance Squadron, based at Yokota in Japan. On 27 June a detachment was sent to operate from Itazuke. On this day the first recce sortie of the war was flown by First Lieutenant Bryce Poe. Poe's mission was a weather recce and his report enabled the successful launching of the day's fighter and fighter-bomber strikes. All missions were flown out of Japan until September, 1950, when the squadron moved to Taegu, South Korea, on 30 September. Major Jean Woodyard and Lieutenant Ray Schrecengost made the first landing at K-2 following a combat mission over North Korea. At this time the 8th TRS was under the control of the 543rd Tactical Support Group. The variety of missions flown by the 8th TRS were many: supply dumps, airfields, bridges across the Yalu, pre- and post-fighter bomber strikes, troop movements and so on. One of the innovations made in the field was to enable the RF-80s to take forward oblique photos through the nose of the aircraft. The radio compass antenna was removed to make space for the camera, a K-18 with a 36 in lens. Needless to say, this was not a standard configuration. The loss of the radio compass did have implications for pilot survival! However, this installation did have many advantages for pre-strike photographs in particular, which gave clear and precise indications to the fighter-bomber pilots on the approaches to the target.

In August, 1950, the 162nd TRS arrived at Itazuke flying Douglas RB-26 Invaders. The 162nd included the 6166th Weather Flight. The missions flown by the 6166th were primarily regular routes observing and reporting the weather. This was valuable information passed on to the units destined to strike targets in the designated areas. These missions were flown by day and night. The night missions provided weather information for units that were conducting dawn strike missions.

In October, 1950, the 45th TRS was activated at Komaki, Japan. This unit was to receive the RF-51 Mustang, but these did not arrive until December. Clyde East was the Operations Officer of the 45th; transferred from the 8th TRS where he had completed some 60 combat missions over North Korea in the RF-80A. After intensive training the 45th was ordered to Taegu, arriving there on 28 December, 1950. Clyde East:

RB-26s of the 12th TRS, K2, 1951. The 12th TRS was activated at Taegu in February 1951 taking over the aircraft and personnel of the 162nd R (Ed Stoltz)

I flew the first combat mission on 29 December, with Lieutenant Bob Sweet as my wingman. Bob was one of our pilots with no previous Mustang time, but had flown over a hundred missions as a Mosquito pilot and knew the Pusan Perimeter like no one else! Although the 45th was seldom assigned missions in the Army front area (The T-6 Mosquitoes were still very much in operation) it was a big help to have someone of Bob Sweet's experience to give us an insight into operating with the ground forces.

Bob Sweet flew joined the 45th after a tour with the 6147th Tactical Control Group Mosquitoes flying T-6s. (Bob Sweet)

KOREA 17

 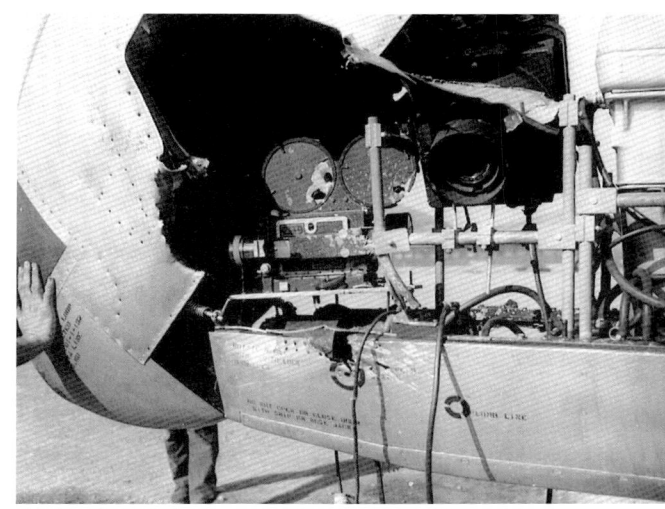

AAA damage occurred to RF-80A 44-85379 on the 19th January 1951 on its 40th mission. In the photo above right, the movie camera can be seen. This was not a standard fit but had been installed for a special project. In addition one vertical and one oblique were installed. (Ed Stoltz)

Major Horace Myers after parking battle-damaged RF-80A, 45-8472 in early 1951. 'Whitey' Myers became Missing in Action shortly after this flight. Photos right above and below detail the damage to his RF-80A. (Ed Stoltz)

F-51 Mustang of the 45th TRS. The Mustang was the principal workhorse of the 45th at K2 and K14 until the arrival of the RF-80. The fighter variant was used primarily for visual recce and the 45th suffered many losses including the 67th CO 'Pop' Polifka. (Ed Stoltz)

Both the 8th and the 45th TRS' sustained losses in those early days. The missions were invariably flown alone. For this reason it is often not known what fate befell the unfortunate pilots who went missing. Lieutenants Ben Raeder, Donald Drama and Captain 'Roho' Williams were such casualties in September, 1950. Lieutenant Bruce Shaw was luckier in November, 1950. Indications were that he had been downed by anti aircraft fire. He became a prisoner of war and was later released. AAA was believed to have accounted for Lieutenant J.B. Smith who was lost in the Pyongyang area. His RF-80 caught fire and he baled out. He was injured in the process and further abused by North Korean soldiers. However, thankfully he survived. Captain Horace Myers and Lieutenant Meizner were flying out of Taegu when they were lost; Myers to AAA in the Pyongyang area, and all that is known about Meizner's demise is that he was flying a mission near the Yalu. Cecil Rigsby flew with the 8th:

> Some of the pilots lost to AAA and small-arms fire were flying at altitudes below 200 ft using the Sonne Continuous Strip, six inch focal length camera. This camera was designed for very low altitude and produced an outstanding vertical image. Due to losses, use of the Sonne camera was discontinued when First Lieutenant Wes Brothers devised a twin K-22, 24-inch vertically mounted camera installation. Each camera would fire alternately permitting the pilot to fly at 5,000 ft altitude, above small arms fire, and achieving a large scale picture of 1 to 2,500 with overlapping photos.

The 45th TRS suffered the heaviest losses. Bob Sweet:

> By June Lieutenant Summerlin, Lieutenant Dolan, Captain Brown, Captain McCallum and Lieutenant Thatcher had been lost. Lieutenant Rice had been shot up, he baled out between the lines and was fortunate to be picked up by US Army troops. He had struck the tail of his aircraft and broke his leg. Rice always flew armed to the teeth as he had done as a Mosquito pilot. It did not do him much good this time as he ended up on the ground with the stock broken on his Thompson sub-machine gun and his handgun missing….. The 45th pilots felt that they were taking the vast majority of battle damage and aircrew losses. The number of missions to complete a tour were the same as for the 15th TRS and double the 12th TRS. Given that the RF-51s operated at low altitude for hours at a time rather than the shorter sorties of the jets it is not hard to understand why losses were high.

On 25 February, 1951, the 67th Tactical Reconnaissance Wing was activated and took over the assets of the 543rd Support Group at K-2. The 8th TRS became the 15th TRS and the wing was

RF-80A, 45-8447, 15th TRS, refuelling at K2 Taegu in 1951. Most missions in the RF-80s were flown alone. (Ed Stoltz)

joined by the 12th TRS flying the Douglas RB-26 Invader. The 12th had been activated to take over the assets of the 162nd TRS. Also, in this month the wing came under the command of Colonel Karl L. Polifka. Polifka was a veteran recce pilot of the Second World War and had served with distinction in the Far East and European theatres. He had commanded the 8th Photo Reconnaissance Squadron in the South-west Pacific and post war in Japan; flying Photo Recce P-38 Lightnings and was considered by most tac recce pilots at that time as an outstanding pilot and tactician, as well as the most respected voice in USAF reconnaissance. Clyde East, himself a Second World War ace, was pleased to see Polifka in command:

> Polifka was a very aggressive commander and spent much of his time at 5th Air Force HQ in downtown Taegu, promoting things for his wing and tutoring the 5th Operations Section and senior staff officers on how tac recce should be employed. He was very disturbed over the heavy losses of the 45th Sq. He suggested several tactics that probably reduced casualties and AAA damage somewhat, but the assignment of additional F/RF-51s to the 45th, and the increased sorties resulting, still gave the unit what was probably the highest loss and damage rate in 5th AF.

One of the most serious of the problems facing the 67th TRW was the shortage of experienced pilots. This was particularly acute in the 45th TRS, but was also evident in the 15th TRS. Clyde East:

> Upon activation of the 45th we were assigned several pilots who had been recalled, had never flown a fighter aircraft, and had little, or no, flying time to speak of since '45–'46. These assignments continued after we arrived in Korea. We were assigned a T-6 sometime in February, after impassioned pleas to Wing; allowing us to run a check-out programme there, in addition to our daily mission schedule. As we had no two seat '51s for check-out we had to assign a chase plane to assist and instruct. Of course it was not easy to get two Mustangs available for these check-outs, as we always had a heavy combat commitment. The 15th was not as strapped as we were since there was an RF-80 recce school at Shaw AFB, SC, turning out almost enough pilots to satisfy their requirements. The RB-26s had a school also, at Langley AFB, VA, that later moved to Shaw. The problem of properly trained crews was particularly serious in the 12th/15th Sqs in the Spring/Summer of '51, since by this time most of the experienced crews had completed their missions and were returning to the US. With the 45th, inexperience was a constant problem from it's activation forward.

In a review of pilot competence and experience held in the early summer of 1951 it was revealed that seven of the newly assigned pilots were recalled reserve pilots, many of whom had not flown for five years. Two of the pilots had no experience in the particular aircraft they were to fly, and no combat experience whatsoever! The 67th was not impressed! They requested that, in future,

Colonel Karl 'Pop' Polifka was the Commander of the 67th TRW at K-2. Polifka was an experienced and inspired champion of tactical reconnaissance. He was killed when the F-51 he was flying near Kaesong was hit by small arms fire. (USAF)

all assigned pilots should have at least nine months transition training in the USA before being posted to combat units. It was not the job of tactical squadrons at war to run a transition school!

However, in spite of the many problems facing the 67th, business had to go ahead as usual. Clyde East recalls the missions flown by the 45th out of Taegu:

> ... Except for a few special missions we flew singly. Since the fighters had no cameras we were unable to get photo confirmation of significant sightings, but the air force was willing to live with that and rely on visual sightings alone. Also they regularly increased the number of

Bridge down....or is it? All is not what it seems. This bridge can be raised at night and used as a supply route. (USAF via Jean Woodyard)

sorties scheduled, until it was impossible to fly them all! Of course we began to experience losses and, being alone, there was usually no way to determine how or where the loss occurred. Pleas to Wing were in vain, as we were flooding the system with loads of good information and the army was as pleased as they could be with the work of the 45th! We also coordinated fighter-bomber strikes on many of the targets sighted, sometimes within minutes of discovery.

The tactic which the 45th pilots developed for more efficient visual recce was known as the 'Circle 102'. The pilot would fly a 16 km radius circle around an area where 12th TRS RB-26s had identified enemy ground activity the night before. Each 45th Pilot was assigned a specific area with which he was required to be very familiar. He would fly round this area and look out for anything which was different from the day before, or anything which was out of place. If they found anything they would call in the fighter bombers to attack the hidden trucks or armour. This was not the only way in which day and night operations were mutually supportive. Jean Woodyard:

> ….the RB-26 aircraft at least on two occasions reported rail traffic over bridges that the RF-80s through photos proved were knocked out. Closer photos and interpreter's analysis identified that one end of the bridge was being lowered in the day time and pulled back into position at night. The fighters did a more complete job on the next air strikes.

It was not only the Mustangs that were required to fly alone in those early days. While the 15th TRS was at Taegu and prior to this in Japan as the 8th TRS, the vast majority of missions were flown without any escort and alone. This included missions into 'Mig Alley'. Ed Stoltz flew the RF-80 out of K2 and into 'Mig Alley':

> The majority of these missions were made without escort or top cover. Prior to my joining the 8th TRS attempts had been made to escort out of K2 with first the F-80Cs and later the F-84s. These efforts, in most cases, were a failure as neither fighter could defend against or compete with a Mig 15. A plus for the single RF-80 was that it offered a very

The debrief was an essential part of post mission routine. What the pilots saw was often as important as what they photographed. Ed Stoltz has returned from a mission to be debriefed by Mort Cameron. 'That's a map in front of me and Mort is putting down what I saw – then the information is sent to the fighter squadrons etc who do the dirty work'. (Ed Stoltz)

RF-80s on the flightline at K-14. The 67th TRW moved to this base near Soeul in August, 1951. (Bob Archibald)

F-51D *Linda and Bobby Jr* in company with RF-51s, F-51s and RB-26s at K-14. The buzz numbers of the recce Mustangs began with RF as opposed to FF. (Lieutenant Colonel Boardman C. Reed via Dave Menard)

An RB-26 of the 12th TRS waiting for the night at Kimpo 1952. (Boe Simpson)

small cross section to radar. An escort of fighters attracted a lot of attention…. I was fired on by MiG 15s once and by AAA several times. The MiG firing occurred in the area south-east of Sinuiju while on a straight and level 'strip' photo run at 20,000 ft. Although three or four Migs fired there were no hits. This was the most vulnerable period during a solo photo mission as it could be required from several seconds to minutes of wings-level flight.

Ed also belies the commonly held belief that the RF-80s flew in pairs during this period:

Flights scheduled for targets in the same general area would sometimes fly together to the target area. Once in the target area they would split up but remain in radio contact. Newly assigned pilots were often accompanied on their first mission. This was the extent of our 'two ship' flights.

The RF-80s endeavoured to have a long reach into north-eastern Korea. In working at the limit of its range the aircraft of the 15th TRS had to take their photos from a high level, 30,000 ft with a 36 in focal length camera. Ed Stoltz flew one such mission in the cold days of early 1951:

That was the coldest looking landscape, the longest flight, and certainly the loneliest flight while in Korea. Approaching the target area from above 40,000 ft the industrial steam and smoke at Vladivostok could be seen rising into what had to be the clearest, coldest sky ever.

On 1 July, 1951, the 67th TRW was dealt a devastating blow. Karl Polifka took off from Taegu in F-51D, 44-74638 of the 45th TRS on a visual reconnaissance mission in the Kaesong area, just south of the 38th Parallel. It was an area known to contain a lot of anti-aircraft artillery. He descended to taker a closer look at some enemy ground activity and in the process his aircraft was hit in the coolant system by small arms fire and spun out of control. He managed to exit the aircraft; but his parachute snagged on the tail and he went down with it. His body was recovered the next day. In the face of considerable opposition from his officers and staff he had wanted to see for himself what dangers the pilots of the 45th faced. The loss to the 67th was profound and Tactical Reconnaissance had lost one of it's staunchest proponents.

Meteors of 77 Sq Royal Australian Air Force at K-14. The Meteors would often escort the RF-80s on their photo missions. (Ed Stoltz)

Major Jean Woodyard, 1st Lieutenant Henry Ezell and Major Clyde East make final preparations for their historic in-flight refuelling mission on the 6th July 1951. (Clyde East)

The presence of ten Soviet TU4 bombers on an airfield at Mukden in northeast China gave rise to a great deal of concern to the US Forces in Korea. The presence of the bombers was confirmed by Jean Woodyard on 13 May, 1951:

> I flew an RF-80 out of Suwon and crossed the border into China above the Suiho reservoir while the F-86s mixed it with the Mig 15s out of Antung. Photographed the Mukden Airfields, four of them, and exited out over the Yellow Sea. The TU4s were there.

One of the outcomes of the discovery of the TU4s was an attempt to increase the radius of action of the RF-80 so that targets outside the normal range could be reached. Major Jean Woodyard and Lieutenant Ray Schrecengost were responsible for the tests on an air-to-air refuelling system in May, 1951. In July 1951 the first ever Air Refuelling Combat mission took place in the USAF. The mission was commanded by Major Jean K. Woodyard and together with First Lieutenant Henry E. Ezell and Major Clyde East and refuelling from a KB-29 of SAC, they flew their RF-80As along the North Korean, Manchurian and Soviet borders. Clyde East:

> We were temporarily assigned a KB-29 from SAC for the task. This was one of Polifka's ideas and initially was planned to cover numerous military airfields in Manchuria. However, due to the initiation of an 'Armistice feeler' by the North Koreans in late June, it was decided by Commander FEAF that such flights, if discovered, would cause serious political repercussions and would likely provide grounds for calling off the Armistice talks. In order to exercise the air refuelling training we had undergone, Polifka persuaded the FEAF Commander to allow us to cover targets in north-eastern Korea, along the North Korean, Soviet and Manchurian borders – areas the RF-80 was unable to reach from Taegu. He received approval for these three flights and Polifka was killed the next day. We didn't fly the missions until 6 July 1951. It was a complete success, although as everyone knew there were no militarily significant targets in the north-east corner of Korea!

The method of refuelling used was basically the probe and drogue still used today by some air forces. The 230 gallon wing-tip tanks of the RF-80s were fitted with probes. Jean Woodyard:

> The RF-80 pilot had to insert a probe 20 ft out on his wing tip into a 2 ft funnel-like drogue which was dancing in the wind. Once locked into the drogue, close formation flying was maintained while the fuel tank began to fill. The sequence was: plug in probe on right wing tank until half full. Break off, plug in left wing tank probe and receive full fuel. Break off, and replug in right wing tank for full fuel. This was not only time consuming but with asymmetric wing loading it took maximum formation flying skill and hard work involving several tries at plugging into the drogue. Radio silence was broken only once on the mission when Clyde said 'Shit!' after missing the drogue three or four times. My mission was visual 'recon' of the Russian/Manchurian border to detect resupply/reinforcement movements across the border. Much of this mission was flown below 100 ft to identify visually vehicle tracks, construction or anti-aircraft defences. Two small airfields over the border in Russia were checked. The runways were post holed with timbers. The North Koreans were not getting any support directly from Russia at this time.

One of the primary missions of the 67th in the early days was the Basic Cover project. This project was designed to provide adequate maps of Korea for the fighter and fighter-bomber wings. Because there was a lack of such maps these units could not designate targets accurately nor could they brief pilots efficiently. Basic Cover was the means by which all relevant areas of the country would be mapped in the form of 1:10,000 scale photographs. These maps would be made available to all 5th Air Force tactical units. The 8th Fighter Bomber Wing was the first recipient of the material in July, 1951.

On 21 August, 1951 the 67th TRW moved to K-14 at Kimpo. The base was ill prepared for their arrival. Parking areas were overcrowded, the runway, only 5000 ft long, was in need of repair and there were very short overruns. When the base had been evacuated in the face of the North Korean advance, the concrete runway had been cratered to prevent it's use by the enemy. When the area around Soeul had been reclaimed hasty repairs had been made, filling the craters and covering with a tarmacadam substance. On a hot August day a fully loaded aircraft could be felt dragging as it hit the softer repair areas. On hot days the RF-80s used the water injection system to provide additional thrust to get the fully loaded airplane off the ground.

The move to K-14 put the Wing much nearer to the action than they had ever been. This was evidenced by the aircraft and pilot toll in the few days following arrival. One RF-51 was destroyed by enemy action, one RF-80 was damaged by a Mig 15, and an RB-26 limped home from a mission after a mauling by flak, with crew members wounded. In September, 1951, enemy activity in Mig Alley increased markedly. The Chinese were pouring Mig 15s into the North and the bases to hold these aircraft were rapidly being built. It was one of the primary missions of the 67th to keep an eye on this construction and provide regular updates to 5th Air Force. In October, '51 Lieutenant Tex Hill of the 15th TRS discovered and photographed two new airfields of concrete construction at Namsi and Taechon. On 9 November a sortie revealed twenty-six Migs on a new airfield at Uiju, south of the Yalu. All RF-80 missions into the 'alley' were now obliged to have an escort. These escorts were usually 4th Fighter Interceptor Wing F-86s or 77 Sqdn Royal Australian Air Force Meteors which shared Kimpo with the 67th. Norman Duquette flew with the 15th TRS:

> We flew many missions to photograph the enemy's Mig bases. At times, the targets would be the North Korean airfields at Namsi, Taechon, Sinuiju, or Kunari. Other times the targets were Antung and Ta Tung Kao just north of the Yalu River on the Chinese side. When flying an airfield recce mission, I would break from my fighter escort just south of the target. After a rapid descent, I would point the nose of the airplane directly at the target, and begin my photo run. As I approached close in to the target, the entire airfield or target

An RB-26 Invader of the 12th TRS in transit from a maintenance facility in Japan. (Bill Martz)

would fill the camera lens. The photographs taken would reveal valuable intelligence for future UN Air Forces mission planning. Our escorts would continue to cover us until we completed our photo runs and then we would turn south and skeedaddle for home. We flew out as fast as our RF-80s could scoot until we got out of Mig range – on the deck or as close as we could get to the waters of the Yellow Sea.

The pilots of the 67th had specific orders not to overfly China. Cecil Rigsby flew with the 15th and recalls:

In covering the two airfields at Antung and Tatingkow (SP) with 40 in, K-22 cameras in the forward oblique position, the pilot was required to shoot across the river. More than once, in marginal weather, I found myself breaking out of clouds on the other side of these airfields and having to reposition the aircraft to provide coverage at the required angle. We were told not to fly into China unless ordered to do so. Photos from the opposite angle would prove that you violated that order.

In addition to the demands of the 5th Air Force for reconnaissance, the 67th aircraft regularly flew missions to provide intelligence for the 8th Army; in particular regular reviews of the front line.

Revetments at K-14 contain both RF-80As of the 15th TRS and F-86s of the 4th Fighter Wing. (Bill McMurray)

A single RF-80 flying at 20,000 ft, using a 24 in, K-38 camera and a 390 ft roll of film, would cover an area of 20 miles by 15 miles at a scale of 1: 10,000. The weather was a significant factor in mission success which required 80 per cent of the area to be satisfactorily covered. The army would request coverage of some areas of the front line more than others. Some were flown twice a week, others as little as once a month.

Regular sorties over the new airfields revealed every new development taking place there. Towards the end of 1951 it became evident that the communists were installing ever more sophisticated radar early-warning systems. An Electronic Countermeasures (ECM) programme was put in hand by the 12th TRS to find and photograph these sites. First it was necessary to identify areas in which equipment was being deployed using vertical photography from high altitude to pinpoint positions. Subsequently low-level trimetrogen photography would be flown by 15th TRS RF-80s. Then the installations could be attacked by the tactical fighter-bomber squadrons. The 12th TRS never got to grips with the ECM programme as they would have liked. Initially there was a shortage of suitable aircraft to do the job. In December, 1951, they only possessed one RB-26 which was capable of the work. When, in April 1952, they requested more aircraft to be modified so that they could undertake a search and destroy role, their request was turned down by 5th AF. In May, 1952, tacit approval was given for the squadron to have an enhanced electronic capability, but they would have to soldier on until September with only one aircraft. Another four would be made available then. In fact the first of the new aircraft did not arrive until November, 1952. By February, 1953, 112 ECM missions had been flown by the 12th TRS, but none were considered particularly satisfactory or productive. The role of the 12th TRS was under constant review throughout the war. There was some criticism in December, 1951, of the squadron fulfilling its night reconnaissance requirements. The altitude from which the unit could satisfactorily operate its RB-26s was cited as being one reason for operational deficiencies. Plans were laid to modify a K-37 camera with a 24 in focal length which would enable the aircraft to operate for above 15,000 ft by both day and night. By January 1952, the number of night targets being flown by the 12th TRS was twenty; compared to eight in December of 1951.

On the 12th TRS flightline at K-14 RB-26Cs wait to be loaded with flash bombs for the night missions, February 1953. (Davis Collection via Dave Menard)

The RB-26Cs of the 12th were modified to give them an increased maximum speed of approximately 425 mph. This entailed removing the upper and lower turrets from the rear of the fuselage, thus reducing weight and aerofoil resistance. Jere Moulton flew with the 12th TRS out of Kimpo and describes the recce suite:

> Two cameras were installed behind this compartment at an angle that would give you a stereo effect when the pictures were later viewed by technicians. Both cameras were triggered by one photo-electric cell. In addition; in the compartment itself a Short Range Navigation (SHORAN) set and a Long Range Navigation (LORAN) set were installed. The Bomb-Bays were rigged for Flares and Photo-Flood bombs or Photo Cartridge racks. The control panel for these munitions was also in the rear compartment. Since we did not carry any guns or other armament we were able to attain much greater speed than the Interdiction Aircraft

The routine missions of the RB-26s were usually on scheduled routes. Jere Moulton:

> We had an East Coast run that went up to where you could see the city lights and the airport rotating beacon at Vladivostok, Russia. The West Coast run was up to the mouth of the Yalu River. The Central run was up past P'yongyang into MIG Alley and again to the Yalu River. We had selected targets of Airfields, Military Bases and Marshalling Yards. We were to watch for targets of interest such as convoys, train movements, munition and supply storage areas, and troop concentrations. If we sighted train or convoy activity we would contact an interdiction aircraft from the 3rd or 17th Bomb Wing and vector them to our position. Then drop flares for them to light up the target. When they were finished we would go back in to take pictures for Bomb Damage Assessment (BDA) so they would get credit for destroying the targets.

The east coast run was also known as the 'Chonjin Sweep'. Bill Martz, a navigator with the 12th TRS, had an interesting experience on the one occasion that he flew this route out of Kimpo when the RB-26 he was flying was fired upon by 'friendly forces':

> On the way back we determined that our compass was malfunctioning almost 60 degrees which is probably why we strayed into US Navy territory. However our IFF (Identification Friend or Foe) was functioning. In our vernacular, 'our parrot was squawking the right channel.' They should have known we were friendly. Anyway, they didn't come close. Because our compass was out, I brought us home by referencing the North Star. Fortunately it was a clear night.

Significantly there were several RB-26 missions that the 12th TRS performed that were highly classified. One such took place one night in October, 1951 when a lone aircraft flew at low altitude over Vladivostok and, with the aid of flash bombs photographed the harbour.

The intensification of enemy action in Mig Alley proved frustrating for the pilots of the 67th TRW; not least the RF-80 drivers of the 15th TRS. They had worked hard to overcome the pilot training problem; and were now confronted by marked disadvantage in the performance characteristics of their penetration aircraft, when compared to the intercept capabilities of the Mig 15s, which were appearing in ever greater numbers. In November, 1951, 15th RF-80s were attacked eleven times by Mig 15s. Certain photo missions had to be flown several times in order to provide required coverage. Without doubt an aircraft was needed which would be more than a match for the Mig 15 in its performance and which would be capable of taking good photographs. There was only one aircraft in the USAF inventory which satisfied the first criteria; but how could you modify the F-86 to carry a camera or cameras? Far East Air Material Command (FEAMCOM) was adamant that it couldn't be done. Undaunted in the face of such opposition 15th TRS commander Major Ruffin Gray and Captain Joe Daly, Assistant Wing Operations

Officer began making regular visits to the 4th FIW crash dump on the other side of the airfield in the hope of coming across an airframe they could experiment with.

Meanwhile, all the RF-80 flights into Mig Alley continued to be escorted. The coverage of airfields received top priority as ever. Norman Duquette:

> My RF-80 chuffing along on a straight course at top speed, 600 mph, to enable the F-86s to keep their combat speed up. In effect they were making S-turns overhead and behind me, thus travelling a greater distance than I was, but at a faster rate of speed than I was travelling. The plan was for me to drop away from the escort over the next peninsula, a prominent land feature readily identifiable from high altitude, on the west coast just south of the mouth of the Yalu River, I have forgotten the name of the peninsula, but it had the common geographical reference of 'Long Dong' to all fighter Pilots. I think the actual name sounded similar to the nickname that it was given.
>
> So, from about 35,000 ft, above the contrail level, I began my straight ahead descent through the contrail level over 'Long Dong' as planned, to an altitude of about 10,000 ft, pointing the nose of my aircraft directly at Antung, really zinging along. My RF-80 was equipped with a 40 in focal length telescopic lens pointed straight out the front/nose camera window at an angle of about ten degrees below the horizon giving me photo coverage from about thirty degrees ahead/below the aircraft to almost the horizon straight ahead. All of that and a full roll of 360 ft of 9 in × 18 in film.
>
> I had been briefed not to cross the Yalu River into mainland China on my photo run. By the time I reached the south boundary of the Yalu, I was down to about 5000 ft, with camera running, clicking away. My flight plan called for me to make a straight-in run to Antung and then to make a hard left turn when I reached the north side of the river, fly parallel to the river for about a minute, then do a hard turn to the right, and to point the aircraft directly at Tatungkou for a straight-in run, which I did.
>
> I continued in my descent to about 2500 ft and to a distance of about a couple of miles from target, then another hard left turn and a descent to water level and on out to Sea, where I picked up a southerly heading as fast as my F-80 could scoot. The F-86s were engaged with Migs all the while I was in my photo run and escape route. I had apparently gone undetected by the Migs. At least, I did not see any in close proximity, and believe me, I was looking with my head on a complete 360 degree swivel.
>
> Again, as I approached Chinnampo Peninsula from the North flying at sea level, I proceeded back to an economic fuel consumption altitude for my return flight to Kimpo. The pictures came out great. With a forty inch lens, it brings a target up really close.

Regrettably, in January, 1952, Norman Duquette was shot down and became a prisoner of war until the truce.

Bill McMurray earned the DFC for his third escorted mission over the Yalu photographing the dam across the river at Sinuiju; very close to the the Mig base at Antung. His RF-80A was to be escorted by eight F-86s. Four of these would fly in close formation and the other four would fly top cover, about 10,000 ft higher. Take-off and trip to target were relatively uneventful. Then:

> A few seconds before the run began all hell broke loose. The whole sky was filled with flak. The close escort flight leader said, 'Recce, let's get the hell out of here and come back later.' I was taught that we never did that because when you return there will be a helluva lot more flak. I answered 'Negative' and continued the run shooting frames as fast as I thought the cameras could handle.
>
> Suddenly, in a flash, I found myself looking at the ground. The blue and the brown had swapped places so fast that I was not conscious of the roll. I instinctively got the blue and brown back in their places and what I then saw really gave me a scare. The flak was

This RB-26 44-35307 had to make a forced landing at K-14 in April 1953. (Davis Collection via Dave Menard)

extremely thick and stratified. It was as if I was looking at a big long asphalt runway and that, if I so desired, I could drop the gears and flaps and make the perfect landing. Unbeknown to me, a chunk of flak had penetrated the top of the left wing about two inches from the main wing fuel-tank. Evidently it had hit me while I was inverted.

How long this run lasted I have no concept. Back then it seemed like an eternity but I suspected it lasted less than two minutes. After the run, I added full power, started climbing and took the southerly heading for home. The close escort had already notified me that they were 'bingo' and heading for home.

Bill made it back to Kimpo. He obtained 100 per cent coverage of the target and some good pictures of the flak!

An RF-51D 44-14547 of the 45th TRS in need of repair at K-14. (Major General S. Newman via Dave Menard)

RF-51D 44-84778 *My Mimi* is prepared for another mission. The camera port can clearly be seen in the rear fuselage behind the wing. Note the 45th Polka Dots helmet on the wing. (USAF via Dave Menard)

Bill McMurray flew the RF-80 with the 45th TRS. He earned the DFC for a mission over the Yalu photographing the dam at Sinuiju. (Bill McMurray)

Aircraft 48-217 was the first of the Honeybucket RF-86As. Pilot Clyde Voss named the aircraft after his wife *Priss*. (Clyde Voss)

On 28 November, 1951, the 15th TRS received it's first F-86A for modification. Gray and Daly had succeeded in obtaining a suitable nose section from their colleagues in the 4th FIW and had successfully installed a camera in it with the cooperation of the 67th Maintenance Squadron. They requested permission to install the modification in two 4th FIW F-86As that were being returned to the Zone of the Interior. Subsequently, one of these aircraft, 48-217, was modified and flown into K-14 by Captain Daly on the 28th November, 1951. The project was named *Honeybucket*. Ruff Gray:

> We wanted to keep the development hush-hush so we kept the RF-86s painted identically to the 4th FIW fighters; kept them on the 4th Wing flight line. When we used them for a recce mission in Mig Alley one of our pilots flew lead on the third flight of four in the 4th Wing's fighter sweep and that flight just so happened to overfly the targets in North Korea that we wanted to photo. If the Migs came up and engaged the flight, the recce bird went over the water and the recce bird came home alone while the other three fighters of the flight got back into the hassle.

The second Honeybucket aircraft 48-187 taxies out for a test flight. The pilot is Frank Meyer. Frank had qualified on the F-86 before arriving in Korea. (Frank Meyer)

John Pell and Frank Meyer were two of the initial pilots to fly the Honeybucket aircraft in December, 1951. Both of them had prior time on the '86 before joining the 15th TRS. Frank Meyer:

> One day an RF-86 taxied onto our ramp and Ruff Gray said, 'You're gonna fly it' I said 'Great!' He said it was going to be camera tests. It was good flying the F-86 again. I went over to the 4th Fighter Group and got a re-check-out. The first mission was over Seoul taking all sorts of vertical shots. The camera tests weren't too good because there was so much vibration.

The second of the Honeybucket aircraft, 48-187 began to be tested in December, '51, and at this time the project was renamed Ashtray. There were to be five aircraft specially modified to Ashtray standard with a suite designed by the FEAMCOM and North American, which comprised a K-22 nose oblique camera and a K-22 vertical camera with a 36 in cone installed with the axis of the cone parallel to the axis of the wing; the photo obtained by shooting through a 45 degree mirror. The aircraft converted, in addition to the two Honeybucket aircraft, were 48-195, 48-246, 48, 257 and 48-196.

Necessity is the mother of invention and this is no more true than at a time of war. Throughout the conflict in Korea, the 67th TRW was involved in a number of projects. All had been initiated with the sole purpose of enhancing the war effort and developing strategies for increasing efficiency and thus ensuring ultimate victory. Trailer Camp evaluated the feasibility of a mobile photo lab. Highlight involved a modification of the front and rear bomb-bay and installation of S1 bomb racks to the bay and wings to increase the photoflash and parachute flare capability of the RB-26. Nightowl evaluated the use of a specially modified M9 bombsight fitted to the RB-26 to aid more accurate photoflash bomb drops. Vector evaluated the use of AN/APN-60 radars in both the RF-80 and the RB-26 in order to extend the range of AN/MPO 2 ground control stations. Pigeon was the evaluation of the AN/ARN 6 radar in the RF-80. Camera Pod consisted of the installation of external camera pods on the 45th's F-51s to upgrade these aircraft to RF-51 Standard. Shotgun evaluated the suitability of the A3 flash cartridge ejector system in conjunction with the A74 IWC film for night photography. Many of these developments and innovations were

The camera pod slung under the wing of an F-51D of the 45th TRS. This attempt to give the fighter a photo capability was abandoned when it was discovered that the modification caused considerable and dangerous instability in flight. (USAF)

In 1953 the 45th TRS The Polka Dots relinquished their RF-51s and converted to the RF-80 and RF-80C. Note the unusual RF buzz number on the nose of the RF-80C.(Lloyd Wooley)

successful and became standard air force practise for many years such as Highlight which was given the go ahead in early 1953. Others, such as Camera Pod, were abandoned because they were inefficient or even dangerous.

The failure of Camera Pod and its subsequent abandonment hastened the withdrawl from active service of all the 45th TRS F-51s and their replacement, by the end of 1951, with RF-51s of which twenty-one aircraft were assigned. The addition of the RF-51s gave the squadron a greatly enhanced photographic capability, which, together with the RF-80 sorties of the 15th TRS, increased material available to the fighter bomber units. However what was obviously required was the upgrading of the squadron to jet photo status at the earliest opportunity. Plans were put in hand at the commencement of 1952 to convert the 45th to RF-80s. They would also receive F-80Cs and RF-80Cs. The latter aircraft had been specially modified by the 67th Maintenance Squadron being fitted with a single camera instead of the guns. As early as July 1952 the 67th MS had modified one F-80C to test the feasibility of the project and the system had worked so well that forty of the aircraft had been scheduled for conversion. To all intents and purposes the RF-80Cs looked exactly like their fighter counterparts, even the gun ports being painted on. The 45th also flew a number of RF-80C-11-LO aircraft. These were created by the marriage of an RF-80A camera nose to the standard F-80C airframe. The F-80C fighter bombers played a major role in all combat missions. When a shortage of RF-80s and RF-51s had first become apparent in mid 1952; the fighter bombers were assigned to fly in the wing position on all missions requiring two ship flights. Since the wingman didn't take photos this scheme worked well.

Bill Neely of the 45th TRS flies RF-80C 424 on Bill McMurray's wing. The badge of the squadron can clearly be seen just behind the cockpit. (Bill McMurray)

An RF-80C 573 of the 45th TRS, K-14, 1953. (Bill McMurray)

An RF-86A 48-257, Mig Killer at Kimpo was one of five F-86A reconnaissance conversions carried out by FEAMCOM and North American. (Lloyd Wooley)

Ashtray was evaluated in terms of penetration capability and photographic capability. The RF-86 was expected to get to a target north of the Chong Chon River, take photos and get back home without an escort. In fact many of the missions were flown in pairs. In terms of the first of these requirements, the RF-86 proved itself more than capable. In the photographic area there were severe problems, so severe in fact that the 67th TRW was forced to the conclusion that the aircraft was, at best, a poor reconnaissance aircraft, its only assets being the ability to penetrate a heavily defended area and an excellent nose oblique installation, for which there was only a small requirement, only 3 per cent of the total mission of the wing. The problems in vertical photography lay in the use of the mirror, which not only produced a reversed print, but also vibrated to the extent that the quality of the photo was markedly impaired. It was okay for counting the number of Migs on an airfield or for seeing if the span of a bridge was down, but hopeless for fine detailed work such as identifying camouflaged gun positions.

The RF-86 however did all the nose oblique photography; one important asset being its speed, which reduced the possibility of being hit by ground fire. Unfortunately one of the original Honeybucket aircraft was brought down by ground fire in a mission over the hydroelectric plant at Wonsan. The pilot was the commander of the 15th TRS, Lieutenant Colonel Jack Williams. Cecil Rigsby was Operations Officer of the 15th TRS:

> As Operations Officer of the 15th TRS, I briefed him on the mission. We sent Clyde Voss to escort him because the day before I covered the same target in a single ship RF-86. On my mission I drew ground fire tracers from what appeared to be a single .50 calibre machine gun. Bullets were going over and under my aircraft but I held the heading until I was sure I had the photos. Both pilots knew the target was defended and that is why we sent two aircraft.

It was Lieutenant Colonel Williams' first mission in the RF-86 and sadly it was to be his last. Clyde Voss:

> He never once responded to radio calls. Finally there was fire coming out of every crack in the fuselage behind the cockpit and his airplane rolled fairly fast, into me. I was right

Generals Weyland and Twining visited K-14 to inspect the RF-86 project. The forward oblique 'dicing' camera can clearly be seen in the nose of the Sabre. (via Howard Peckham)

on his wing and had to push over hard to go under him. When I re-oriented myself to him, his seat had ejected and the plane was in its final dive. I saw his chute and took a forward oblique photo of the scene.

Clyde flew CAP over the site of the crash until relieved by some Marine Corsairs. Jack Griffis, also of the 15th TRS, flew up to the scene of the crash in an F-80 and was there to see Williams' body picked up by helicopter.

Ground fire also gave Lieutenant Jim Fosdick an uncomfortable ride home from a solo RF-86 mission in Mig Alley. He received a wound to his side from a portion of a bullet that further glanced off a rib and slid around to his back. He got back to K-14 safely and received medical treatment.

Many of the missions were routine for the RF-86 pilots. There were many, however, that were far from this. Regular penetration missions were flown as far north as Mukden and Harbin; well into China. The purpose of these flights was to establish whether or not the Russians had moved Ilyushin Il.28 bombers into Manchuria. Cecil undertook one such mission in the June of 1952:

Clyde Voss, who was Jack Williams wingman on that fateful day in June 1952, when RF-86A 48-217 went down near Wonsan to small arms fire, took this sequence of photos. The photos were taken with the nose oblique camera of Voss's RF-86. and clearly show 217 trailing smoke and, in Photo 4, Williams's descending parachute can be clearly seen. (Clyde Voss)

In June of 1952, we had a top secret order come down to send three RF-86s deep into China. The missions were to be escorted by 4th Fighter Wing F-86s. As 15th Tac Recon Squadron operations officer I selected First Lieutenant Edgar Hill to fly the penetration in the Antung area but the specific targets were kept from me. Because of his RF-86 experience, I selected Captain Tony Katauski to fly with me on double coverage of Chinese airfields deep into the central area. Ed hill and our mission were to be flown simultaneously.

When it came to the time to drop our wing tanks, one of Tony's tanks sheared off his pitot tube leaving him with no airspeed indicator. He returned to base with his single fighter escort. My escort and I continued on the mission. The weather was perfect and I had no trouble locating and photographing the two Chinese airfields using the split vertical, K-22, 24-in focal length cameras at 30,000 ft altitude. On the way out we were supposed to photograph an LOC (Line of Communication) but this target was a considerable distance off our course home. We were below Bingo fuel and my fighter said that he could not stay with me much longer. I decided not to risk the added miles required and to return to our base at K-14, Kimpo. As it was we had to climb to over 40,000 ft to conserve fuel and make it back to base.

There were Mig sightings by other aircraft and Bandit warnings but we saw no enemy fighters. While all reconnaissance pilots were glad to be escorted by armed, friendly fighters there were a couple of drawbacks, at least for me. Our F-86 escorts always wanted to use higher power settings, I'm sure for good reasons, than we used and these power settings cut down on range and fuel reserves. Also, there were far too many channel changes as they tried to stay in touch with other fighter formations. These were disruptive when you are trying to navigate and find your targets.

Headquarters considered these China penetrations very dangerous and authorized combat awards up to the Distinguished Service Cross. Ed Hill and I received the Silver Star and I assume our fighter escorts did also.

It was common practice for the RF-86s engaged on missions north of the Yalu to proceed with only a wingman, leaving the main escorting force to mix it with the Migs over the Yalu. One such flight was undertaken by Mele Vojdovich in late 1952, but he was to find himself alone:

I flew up to Harbin and back down the Yalu and I was just about approaching Mukden at 50,000 ft in my RF-86F-30, which was equipped at take-off with four wing tanks, moving along at mach 0.9 when I looked off my left wing and, lo and behold, there were four Mig 15s sitting there. I couldn't believe it. I thought, 'Here I am, 350 miles away from home base at Kimpo, low on fuel and I'm surrounded by the enemy. But they did not attack. They just flew along and looked at me and I looked at them. I did not move. I was just frozen at the stick. Next thing I knew the Migs popped their speed brakes, descended right beneath me and headed down to land in Mukden. I should have suspected something. About ten minutes later just as I made my turn to overfly Mukden I discovered about twenty-four friends on my tail. I think those first four Migs had been low on fuel. The pilots must have called in to their Air Defence Centre earlier and reported an F-86 lost. They probably could not figure out what I was doing, thinking I was crazy. So as I made the turn at Mukden to head back south to Antung, the rear view mirror revealed twenty-four 24 Migs closing on me at 55,000 ft, about 4,000 to 5,000 ft above and behind me. As I made that turn the Migs cut me off and I thought, 'Boy, this is going to be a desperation act. You'd better do something quick.' I rolled over Split-S in the RF-86, and, in the dive got terminal velocity at about Mach 1.05. I looked in the rear view mirror again and saw that the Migs were all out of control.

They were all trying to hit Mach 0.95 and were fishtailing and firing cannons like crazy. The good thing about being in a dog-fight with twenty-four aeroplanes is that only one can get on your tail at a a time and they were all behind me. I broke radio silence, yelling like a wounded eagle, screaming for help because I thought Blackjack Leader, who was the leader of the F-86s, would come to my rescue across the Yalu River. I dove to the deck and flew across Antung Air Base at about a hundred ft altitude right down a ramp. I'm sure all those Chinese fighter pilots were wondering what I was doing. I zipped across and headed south for the Yellow Sea which was only a short distance away because I knew that that was my only escape. If I had to punch out the US Navy would rescue me. The Migs dropped off as soon as we crossed the coast of the Yellow Sea. I climbed back to altitude on fumes, called up Kimpo airfield and told them I was flamed out. They said, 'You're number six in the flameout pattern.'

Vojdovich was met by Colonel Russell Berg, the 67th wing commander, who asked him where the heck he'd been! For this mission Vojdovich was awarded the DSC. He did find the Il-28s at Harbin.

In February, 1953, the go ahead was given for Highlight and by the 6th June six RB-26s had been modified. Also, at this time, on the 12th February, the 15th TRS received the first of two RF-86F aircraft to replace the war weary and ageing RF-86As. These new aircraft were still part of the Ashtray project and carried the same recce suite as the earlier Sabres; the fundamental difference being that they were built on better and more updated airframes with better flying controls: the F-86F-30. Some of the initial F models had the slatted wing whereas the later models did not. These aircraft were able to turn more tightly and at higher mach numbers and therefore were even more of a match for the Migs. The downside was that the hard wing RF-86F handled at low speeds very differently from the previous models. The stalling speed was increased from 128 to 144 mph. Regrettably this idiosyncrasy was later to claim the life of Lieutenant Elliot B. Sartain when his RF-86F stalled on take-off and hit machinery at the end of the runway on 3rd June, 1953.

For some time the 15th only had two RF-86Fs on strength. In June 1953, one of these 52-4330 had a 35mm movie camera temporarily installed in a wing mounted pod for the purposes of photographing F-84s and F-86s in fighter bomber sorties. Excessive vibration rendered the project untenable and it was abandoned.

In April 1953 the 12th TRS had two dedicated ECM aircraft assigned. These were capable of determining frequency, pulse shape, sweep rate and any unusual characteristics of enemy radar and could locate the position with reasonable accuracy. ECM routes covered the coastline of Korea and were flown at 10,000 ft thereby giving complete coverage of all radar in the North.

On the 17th February, 1953 the 45th TRS relinquished its last RF-51 and became an all jet squadron. Just prior to this, in January, the first of the F-80Cs for conversion had been received by the squadron. Altogether twenty conversions had been completed by the 10th March. In June 1953 the 45th had on strength: fifteen RF-80As, eleven RF-80Cs, two F-80Cs and a T-33. The F-80Cs carried a single K-22 in the vertical position. This camera was used primarily for confirmation photography as the F-80C had a largely visual recce role. Although it had a shorter range than the Mustang its speed enabled it to cover more territory in less time. It was also less vulnerable to ground fire which had been a serious problem for the RF-51.

The departure of the RF-51s placed an increasing demand on the Shooting Stars for visual reconnaissance. This still had a large part to play in the mission of the 67th TRW in spite of the ever developing sophistication of the recce systems carried in the aircraft. Regular surveillance of enemy and friendly ground forces provided vital information to the 8th Army. Certainly, a major ground push by the Communists in the Pukham River Valley region was prevented when RF-80 pilots spotted a large contingent of vehicles and equipment out in the open in daylight and called in fighter-bomber strikes. The photo jets remained on station to report on and photograph the area after the army had counter-attacked.

The signing of the armistice on 27 July, 1953, was preceded by a frenzy of activity in the 67th TRW. The demands of the 8th Army for forward oblique photography of the enemy forward

An RF-86F-30 Ashtray, 52-4330. This aircraft, here piloted by Captain LaVerne, was used to test the installation of a cine camera carried in a modified pod on the port wing. (LaVerne Griffin)

positions were considerable. In order to fulfil this request 191 sorties were flown. Unfortunately the limitations of the RF-80's 12 in cameras and the reconnaissance ceiling imposed by the 5th Air Force did not make for favourable results. Hastily, to overcome the problem, 15 RF-80As were fitted with K-22, 36 in forward looking cameras, and seven RF-80As and fifteen RF-80Cs with K-22, 24 in forward looking cameras. This did not help greatly as on any one day the number of aircraft in commission with the modification rarely exceeded six. Following the Armistice the Ground Liaison Section of the 67th reviewed the contribution of the wing to the operations of the 8th Army and concluded: Air Reconnaissance accounted for 44 per cent of all intelligence available to the ground units. Information obtained by air reconnaissance was sufficient and timely. Information obtained from air reconnaissance was instrumental in denying the element of surprise to the enemy. The only shortfall was found to be in the aforementioned photography of enemy forward positions due to aircraft limitations.

The last combat mission of the war was a night photo mission flown by an RB-26 of the 12th TRS. Which landed at 2201 hours on 27th July. Sadly for the 15th TRS the celebrations of the armistice were marred by the death in action of Captain James Howell, whose RF-80 was shot down while on a visual recce mission over enemy territory. The 45th TRS were entrusted with the task of declaring the truce to the world when on 27 July, a T-33, piloted by Major Edward Ellis and First Lieutenant Philip R. Howell delivered the first press release of the signing of the truce to Tokyo International Airport for dissemination to the world.

The day of the truce placed a very large requirement on all the squadrons of the wing to photograph enemy airfields in the north and China. The restrictions imposed by 5th Air Force often made recording the final order of battle difficult. An Air Buffer zone was imposed under radar control, and the ban on overflying the Demilitarised Zone (DMZ) made keeping a check on the enemy forward positions very difficult indeed. A 12th TRS RB-26 was equipped with a K-38 camera fitted in the oblique position and given the task of flying along the edge of the DMZ every 15 days and taking photos.

The RF-86s of the 15th TRS were kept extremely busy during the period before and after the truce. Because of their speed there is no doubt that many of their missions were in violation of the truce, but there was an urgent need to get pictures of the enemy order of battle. One of the terms of the truce was that neither side was to introduce into the theatre of operations new aircraft after the armistice had taken effect. Operations Officer of the 15th TRS Captain LaVerne 'Griff' Griffin was tasked on 27 July with a mission to photograph a power station at Kirin and some airfields at Harbin, both north of the Yalu in Manchuria. In the event he saw no Migs, much to the chagrin of his F-86 wingman who was looking for his fifth kill and status of ace.

> The weather cleared north of the Yalu. I could see miles of the Great Stone Wall and we continued on up to about 45,000 ft. I will say that this wingman was good; never had to look back to see him; he was always there, but I knew he was hoping like hell that we would see some Migs. Navigation was easy now and I photographed the power plant at Kirin and headed for some airfields in the Harbin area.
>
> Still we hadn't sighted any Migs which was okay by me, and I snapped pictures of the Harbin airfield by rolling 90 degrees left and then 90 degrees right until I could see half of the airfield on each roll, then counting 'one potato, two potato, three potato' turning on cameras as the runways passed under the nose. Heading for home now feeling on top of the world; all targets covered, no Migs, no sign of enemy activity anywhere. We crossed the Yalu, dropped the two 120s in Korea and climbed to 47,000 ft since fuel was somewhat of a consideration, although not critical enough to bite doughnut rings in the seat cushion.

Griff did get home but not without mishap. He suffered from a serious oxygen shortage. Only by judicious use of his bale-out bottle of oxygen and descent to 16,000 ft did he avoid having to bale-out and losing his precious film. He had succeeded in making the longest penetration flight over Chinese territory in the Korean conflict in a single-engine aircraft.

The ECM work of the 12th TRS continued to develop from those early inauspicious beginnings. Project Bird Dog was instituted to test the aircraft in determining the exact location of enemy radar sites by 'homing'. Electronic homing equipment was tested in conjunction with AN/APN-3 and AN/APA-54 Shoran equipment. This kit was fitted into RB-26 45-35231 and initially was unsuccessful because one operator, which was all the aircraft had, could simply not operate all the equipment at once. In August, permission was given to fit a second ECM operator's position in two aircraft: 44-35825A and 44-35909A. This doubled the capability of the systems and was adjudged a success.

In September, 1953 the 67th TRW received its dedicated ECM and Weather Reconnaissance Squadron when the 11th TRS was assigned. The 11th TRS had thirteen B-26 and two C-47 aircraft assigned. It consisted of two flights: Weather and Electronic Countermeasures. The weather flight flew unarmed B-26s over the Yellow Sea and the Bay of Korea. The ECM Flight flew B-26s and the C-47s on a variety of missions; their primary function being to pinpoint the location of enemy radar, and to determine the type of radar, type of antenna, and the pulse width and frequency of the output. Don White was assigned to the 11th TRS:

> Basically our ECM planes would fly towards North Korea to trigger their gun laying radar and then measure it for PPM (pulses per minute), and carrier frequency, 10 cm was common, and power. The spool of recording wire would be forwarded to Tokyo for further evaluation. Our mission was to fly two weather missions daily. We had one mission to fly due west into the Yellow Sea, about 200 miles. The second flight was approximately south-west, the same 200 miles. The idea was to arrive at that point just at daylight. Then weather observations were made, and pictures of clouds and sea were taken, then the plane turned for home and poured on the 'coal' to get back as soon as possible.

An RF-80A 049 receives a camera change on the 45th flightline at K-14. (Lloyd Wooley)

It was often written, and said by the Office of Information of the 67th Tactical Reconnaissance Wing during the Korean conflict, that the very hardest job that they had was to convince a watching world of the heroic, difficult and vital role played by the unit in the ongoing and ultimate victories of the whole campaign. The flyers of the RF-80s, RF-51s and RB-26s did not share in the glory and adulation accorded to their counterparts in the fighter and fighterbomber squadrons whose victories over the Migs were always newsworthy. The fact remains that the part played in bringing the war to a satisfactory conclusion was due in no small degree to the contribution of tactical reconnaissance.

An RF-80A 442 of 45th TRS at K-14 1953. (Bill McMurray)

A T-33 624 of the 45th TRS in its revetment at K-14 in 1952. In a T-33 Major Ed Ellis and First Lieutenant Phil Howell delivered the press release of the signing of the truce on 27 July 1953 to Tokyo Airport for dissemination to the world. (Bill McMurray)

An RF-80C of 590a at 45th TRS, K-14, 1953. (Bill McMurray)

CHAPTER THREE

Haymakers, Heart Throbs and Slick Chicks

It could be argued that what follows has no part in a history of Tactical Reconnaissance. The missions flown with the RF-86 Haymaker and with the RB-57 and the RF-100A under the auspices of the Heart Throb and Slick Chick projects were strategic in their design. The primary purpose of overflights of the Soviet Union and China and their allies was to provide the United States and NATO with intelligence about the communist military machine, and where to attack if and when hostilities broke out. Here was an enemy that was growing in strength and expanding its areas of influence. It was an enemy that possessed atomic weapons. It was also an enemy about which little was known. There was much conjecture about the disposition of its forces and it's military infrastructure. Little or nothing was known about the air force and it's defence capabilities. War between the Soviet Bloc and the US and its NATO allies was a distinct possibility in the 1950s. There were some who considered it inevitable. Some, indeed, would have considered it desirable! In the event of hostilities breaking out, an air force needs to be able to define significant targets and destroy them and in the process irrevocably damage the enemy's capability to defend itself and wage further war. Since the end of the Second World War Strategic Air Command had been conducting clandestine overflights of enemy territory in varying degrees in both Europe and the Far East.

Although the Haymaker, Heart Throb and Slick Chick missions were motivated by strategic requirements rather than tactical ones they are included here because they used what could be

Two RF-86F Haymaker aircraft over Japan in 1954: 52-4510 and 52-4860. The aircraft have different markings. 860 lacks the yellow fuselage band and 510 has the US Air Force legend on the tail and not the fuselage. (Bob Gould)

An RF-86F 52-4585 over Japan in 1954. The 'Mae West' camera blisters can clearly be seen. (Bob Gould)

deemed tactical aircraft flown by pilots who had a background in tactical reconnaissance flying single pilot recce missions. Many of these pilots came from and returned to regular tactical reconnaissance units following their tour

The stipulation of the Korean Truce that no new aircraft could be based in Korea was what had prompted the USAF to move the 15th TRS from K-14 to Komaki in the Spring of 1954. At that time the squadron was equipped with the RF-86F Ashtray Sabres and the RF-80. However, they were destined, in early 1954 to receive another variant of the RF-86F: the Haymaker. The squadron would fly this aircraft alongside its other Sabres and, for a time, its RF-80s. However a part of its mission with the Haymaker was to be radically different to anything the squadron had done before. It was to conduct overflights of the countries of the communist bloc in the Far East and photograph their military installations.

Once at Komaki the pilots of the 15th began to receive their new aircraft. Test flights were flown and long-range missions simulated to assess more accurately the aircraft's fuel capacity, endurance and flight characteristics. For maximum fuel load the aircraft would carry two

The camera windows under the front fuselage of this RF-86F can clearly be seen. (Don MacDonald)

Captain LaVerne Griffin of the 15th TRS mounts his Haymaker prior to a mission at Komaki in early 1954. Griffin was the Operations Officer for the 15th and one of the first pilots of the 15th to overfly the Soviet Union in an RF-86F. (LaVerne Griffin)

The seniors officers of the 15th TRS at Komaki: Captain LaVerne Griffin, Operations Officer; Lieutenant Colonel Ralph Newman, CO; Major George Saylor, Executive Officer; and Captain Louis Martin, Maintenance Officer. (LaVerne Griffin)

March 1954: Captain Griffin, Major Saylor and First Lieutenant Bill Bissett. All three pilots were involved in the first overflight mission. (LaVerne Griffin)

120 gallon tanks on the inboard station and two 200 gallon tanks on the outboard. The Operations Officer at this time was still Captain LaVerne Griffin and it was he who was destined to fly the first mission over the Soviet Union. The first mission, over Vladivostok was scheduled for 22nd March and to be led by LaVerne Griffin with First Lieutenant Bill Bissett on his wing. Major George Saylor and Lieutenant Larry Garrison were also to penetrate Russian airspace in a second flight. The two spares were First Lieutenant Sam Dickens and Lieutenant Pete Garrison.

Six aircraft took off from Komaki to K-55 at Osan. Because of the range of the RF-86 it was not possible to stage out of Komaki. It had to be Korea and under the noses of the nits! As soon as the aircraft landed they were towed away to hangars and the doors firmly closed. They were refuelled in the hangar and early the next morning they were towed out onto the ramp. Here the tanks were topped up with fuel until it ran out onto the ground. The pilots then got in and taxied to the end of the runway. The signal to go was a green light from the tower. There was no radio communication at all. The six aircraft were bound for Russia flying eastwards out of Osan over the Sea of Japan. Over the island of Ullung-do they turned northwards at approximately 25,000 ft. When the 200 gallon tanks were emptied they were dropped. All tanks dropped cleanly. This was the signal for the spares to turn back. La Verne Griffin:

> Four of us continued on in tactical formation, wingmen with their eyes on a swivel to detect possible MiG-15 interceptors. Once everyone had dropped their extra fuel tanks, we climbed to 42,000 ft, our cruising altitude to the target area. As we approached the coast near Vladivostok, the two elements split up as each had specific targets to photograph. It was shortly after this that I heard the transmission 'Alabama!'. This transmission brought a tingle down my spine. Alabama was the codeword of our companion element for pulling

On 22 March, 1954, the first overflight of the Soviet Union took place. Six pilots took off on that mission. Standing from left to right: First Lieutenant Sam Dickens, Second Lieutenant Pete Garrison, Captain LaVerne Griffin, Major George Saylor, First Lieutenant Bill Bissett, Second Lieutenant Larry Garrison. Kneeling: Major Red Morrison, and the 15th TRS Intelligence Officer. (LaVerne Griffin).

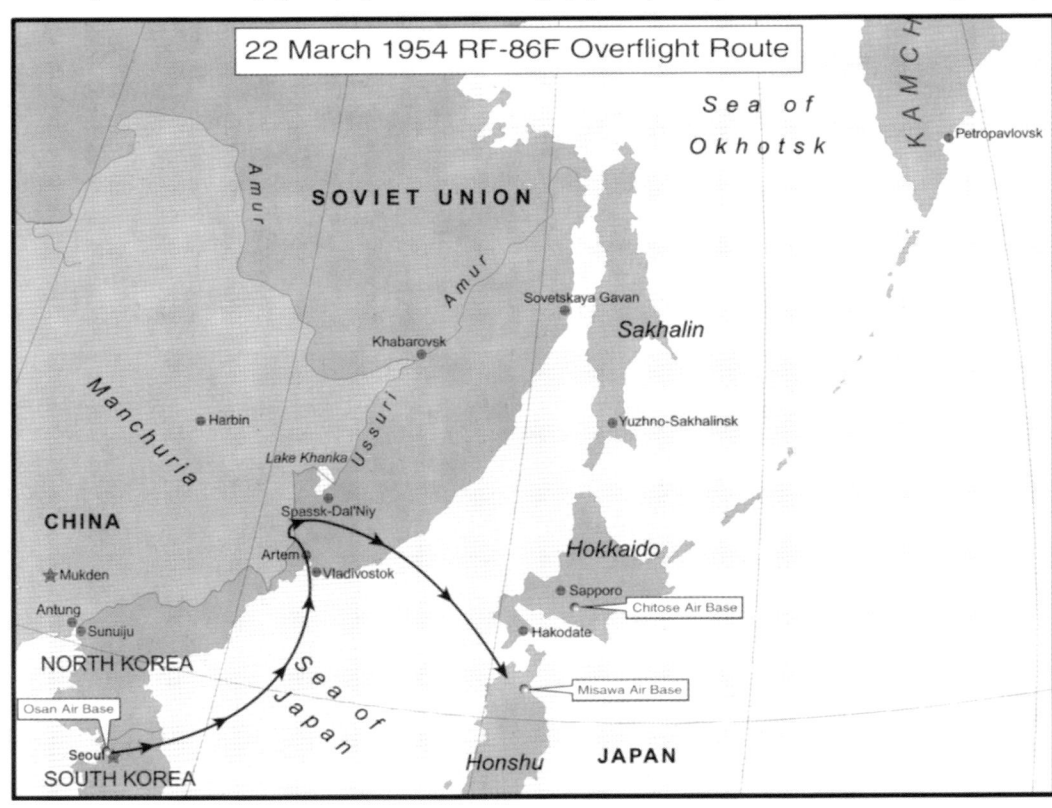

Map illustrating the route taken by the RF-86s on the first overflight on 22 March 1954. (Reproduced from the *Early Cold War Overflights Symposium Proceedings* papers by kind permission of Editor Cargill Hall)

HAYMAKERS, HEART THROBS AND SLICK CHICKS 49

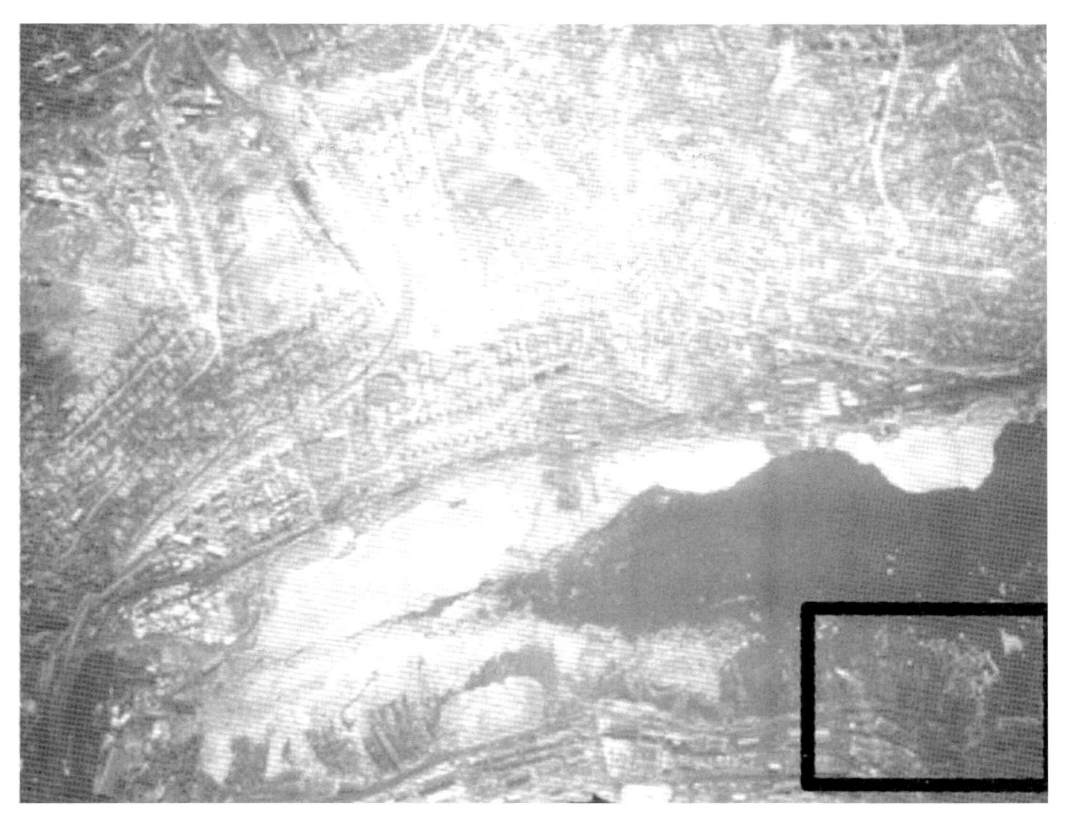

Photograph taken by LaVerne Griffin of Vladivostok Harbour on the 22 March 1954. (Reproduced from the *Early Cold War Overflights Symposium Proceedings* papers by kind permission of Editor Cargill Hall).

Detail of the above photograph showing Soviet ships in harbour. (Reproduced from the *Early Cold War Overflights Symposium Proceedings* papers by kind permission of Editor Cargill Hall)

contrails, which would be a dead giveaway to revealing our presence over the Soviet mainland. The codeword for our element was 'California' I looked at my wingman, Bissett and, as he was not pulling contrails, I continued to press on over the Vladivostok area, nervously, I might add. Forecasters had predicted little chance of contrails. I did not know it at the time, but the other element had aborted their mission and headed back for Misawa, Japan. We flew over the airfields at Vladivostok, proceeding as far as Artem and exposed over 90 frames of film on several airfields. Unknown to me at that time, my wingman's cameras had failed, so I was the only person on this mission that took any pictures.

When the mission was completed the aircraft returned to Misawa without incident. There the pilots accompanied the film to Tokyo in a C-47 for debriefing. Both Griffin and Bissett were awarded the DFC for that mission. Saylor and Garrison had indeed had to abort due to contrails after they had penetrated Russian airspace by some seventy-five miles. The second mission, on the 3rd April, was again over Vladivostok and Captain Sam Dickens was on LaVerne's wing. The two pilots photographed a number of targets north of Vladivostok including a number of airfields, one containing TU-4 bombers. The third mission, on the 21st April, with Frank Halstead, and was memorable for one particular reason. La Verne Griffin:

On the last mission we sighted two airborne Migs about 5000 ft below us as we were exiting the area and I managed to take pictures of them. Upon examining the film the photo interpreter rushed out of the lab and exclaimed, "Do you know what you've got on this film?" I said that I hoped I had gotten the targets and he said, "No, I mean the airplane." I said, "You mean the Mig 15 that flew under us." He said, "That is not a Mig 15. It is a Mig

Plotting chart for the overflight mission on 3 April. The aircraft entered Soviet airspace west of Vladivostok and flew due north up the valley toward Lake Khanka, turning approximately north east just south of the lake. The boxes record the exposures of the vertical cameras. (USAF via Bob Archibald)

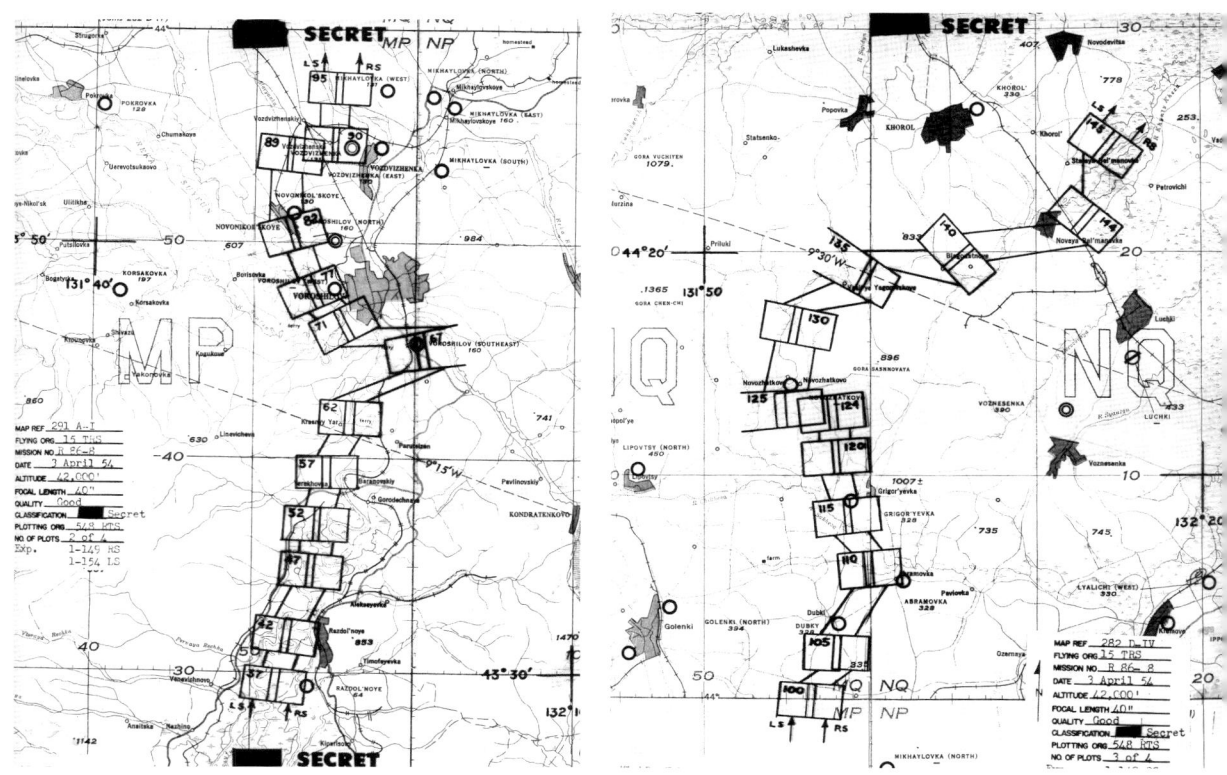

On the 3 April this small airfield at Novonikol was photographed just north of Voroshilov (now Ussuriysk). (USAF Via Bob Archibald)

17, and we didn't know they were deployed east of the Urals." And that is how a lucky strike extra picture became a valuable intelligence find.

At the end of May, 1954, LaVerne Griffin rotated back the United States. For each of his three overflight missions he had been awarded the DFC.

Communist China was considered as relevant a target as the Soviet Union for the clandestine overflights. On 1 May, Second Lieutenant Jerry Depew flew a mission to Dairen in China. The city provided a variety of targets, all of which would be encompassed by the large focal length K-22s. There were airfields and submarine pens in particular. The mission was staged out of Kunsan in Korea and Jerry's wingman was First Lieutenant Rudy Anderson. Jerry Depew:

> We levelled off at 35,000 ft and burned off the 200 gallon external tanks that were then jettisoned. We then climbed and levelled off at 43,000 ft to burn off and drop the two 120 gallon tanks. All jettisoned perfectly and we slowly climbed to 54,000 feet with our clean ships.
>
> For quite a long time we were over water with no land in sight, two specks of aluminium

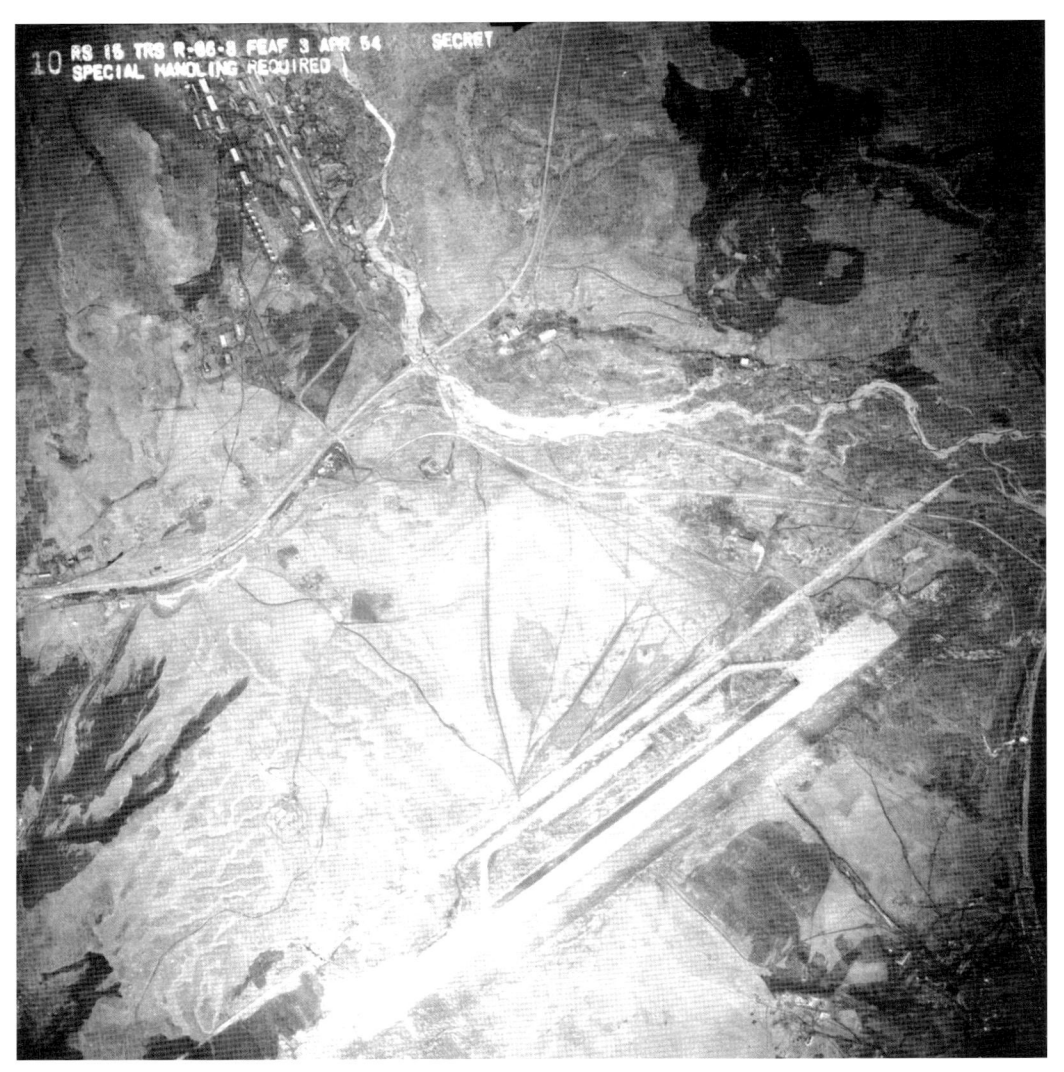

This vertical photograph shows the airfield at Rybalka Perevoznaya due west of Vladivostok on the other side of the bay. It was taken by an RF- 86F on the 3 April 1954.(USAF via Bob Archibald)

more than 10 miles above the earth. Things were very quiet, and very lonely. I kept a close watch on the instruments, scanned the air for Chinese or North Korean fighters and eagerly looked forward to locating Darien, taking the photos and getting the hell home.

We cracked the wing flaps slightly to bring down the nose of our fighters, which gave us a better forward vision, and helped to stabilize the ship in the rarefied air. Finally we sighted land ahead. We came to the right of our target, corrected our heading and turned on the cameras. The cameras were equipped with an intervalometer that automatically took pictures at the proper intervals compensating for the speed over the ground thereby relieving the pilots of that responsibility and ensuring properly spaced pictures for the use of Photo Interpreters later on. Dairen was in the clear as we flew over and did a wide 180 degree turn to the left in order to photograph Port Arthur. We saw no evidence of our being detected, such as fighters ascending through the contrail levels, which were about 34,000 ft, but we did not linger in the area. On our return we put the fighters into a shallow descent, picked up airspeed and made a quick return to Kunsan.

HAYMAKERS, HEART THROBS AND SLICK CHICKS 53

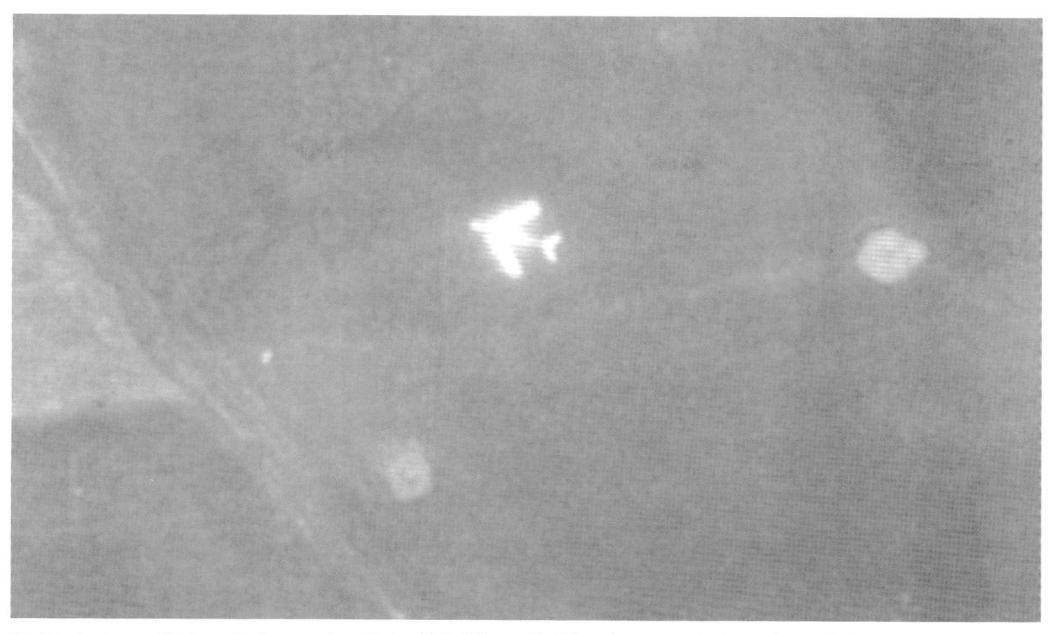

On his last overflight mission on the 22 April LaVerne Griffin photographed a Mig 17 flying underneath him. Up to this point the US Air Force didn't know that the aircraft was deployed east of the Urals. (LaVerne Griffin)

Depew and Anderson had succeeded in photographing submarine elements of the Chinese fleet in Dairen. Both the Russian and Chinese fleets came in for considerable attention from the Haymakers. First Lieutenant Larry Garrison overflew Vladivostok and in addition to photographing some previously unknown airfields he also brought home pictures of several ships in port, including a large battleship. The submarine pens in the Kurile Islands were also targeted on at least two occasions.

Flights were often very long and although it would be true to say that the pilots never felt threatened by the enemy, flying at heights that no enemy aircraft could reach; there were some anxious moments! Major 'Red' Morrison 15th TRS commander flew a long mission up to Khabarovsk, but while over the city he had to drop his remaining fuel tank over the city. It had become 'hung up.'

> The standard flight procedure at the time was to punch off our 200 gallon tanks when we had burned up the fuel and emptied them, and that

This detail from a photograph of Khorol Airfield taken on the 21 April, 1954, clearly shows TU-4 bombers on the ramps. (USAF via Bob Archibald)

An RF-86F-30 Haymaker, 52-4864. This aircraft was the mount of Lieutenant Tom Hagler and was named Pretty Billie. (Tom Hagler)

is what I did. Then you kept climbing and the idea was that you would jettison the 120 gallon tanks when you reached a mission altitude of between 43,000 and 48,000 ft. Thereafter you would fly on a full load of internal fuel. Anyway, as I approached Khabarovsk the 120s ran dry and I punched them off, but only one of them dropped. I kept working the mission assignment and taking pictures, rolling to the right to take a look, then rolling to the left to compare views, and then putting it down to take pictures. Well I did all that, and on the second roll the 120 tank that had hung up, dropped off and went straight down over Khabarovsk.

For most of the extended flights the pilots had perfected a method of 'packing' the fuel into the aircraft. The RF-86 would receive a full load of fuel and would taxi to the end of the runway. The forward fuel tank filler cap was marginally below the top of the tank. As the aircraft was stationary at the end of the runway fuel would be pumped from the rear tank into the forward tank above the filler level. This would leave room for a further few pounds of precious fuel to be added to the rear tank. Then the aircraft would take off on the mission.

Pretty Billie on the ground at Komaki. (Tom Hagler)

An RF-86F-30 Haymaker being refuelled at Komaki in 1954. (USAF via Bob Archibald)

Although many missions were target specific there were some that were undertaken for the purposes of finding something new. Often the intelligence people had a reason to believe that an airfield was in a particular place and the RF-86s were sent up in the approximate area to find it. Bill Semonin undertook such an overflight staging out of K-55 in 1955:

> We had one of these deeper airfields they didn't know was there and we found that one. As we were turning over the last target to come out we looked down the coast and there was a huge strip of concrete. We knew it wasn't a canal! In fact the most impressive thing

Two RF-86s of the 15th TRS 52-4767 and 52-4800 on the ramp at Komaki. (USAF via Bob Archibald)

An RF-86F 52-4864 at Komaki. The guy sitting on the wing is North American Technical Representative Ozzie Neicerman (USAF via Bob Archibald)

about it was it was probably a 15,000 ft long runway, but the thing was unbelievably wide and it looked disproportionate to its length, but we could see it way off. It was probably 75 to 80 miles, maybe even a 100 miles away. These guys did do a pretty good job in teaching us to actually fly the aeroplane so we bellied the aeroplane up with these split 40s in it and figured if we turned round I could get this airfield way off on the horizon in one of the pictures if we were lucky. Well, sure enough when we got back to Yokota this was one of the few times we got together with the Photo Interpreters. They wouldn't let us see the results of the fields we went over but they wanted us to identify the piece of concrete we had seen earlier. So, of course we identified it and I think, later on, a second mission was flown back to this particular airfield.

The 15th TRS wasn't alone in flying the RF-86F Sabre in the Far East and neither

On an overflight over North Korea on the 12 January 1955 this Haymaker was photographed by his wing man. (USAF)

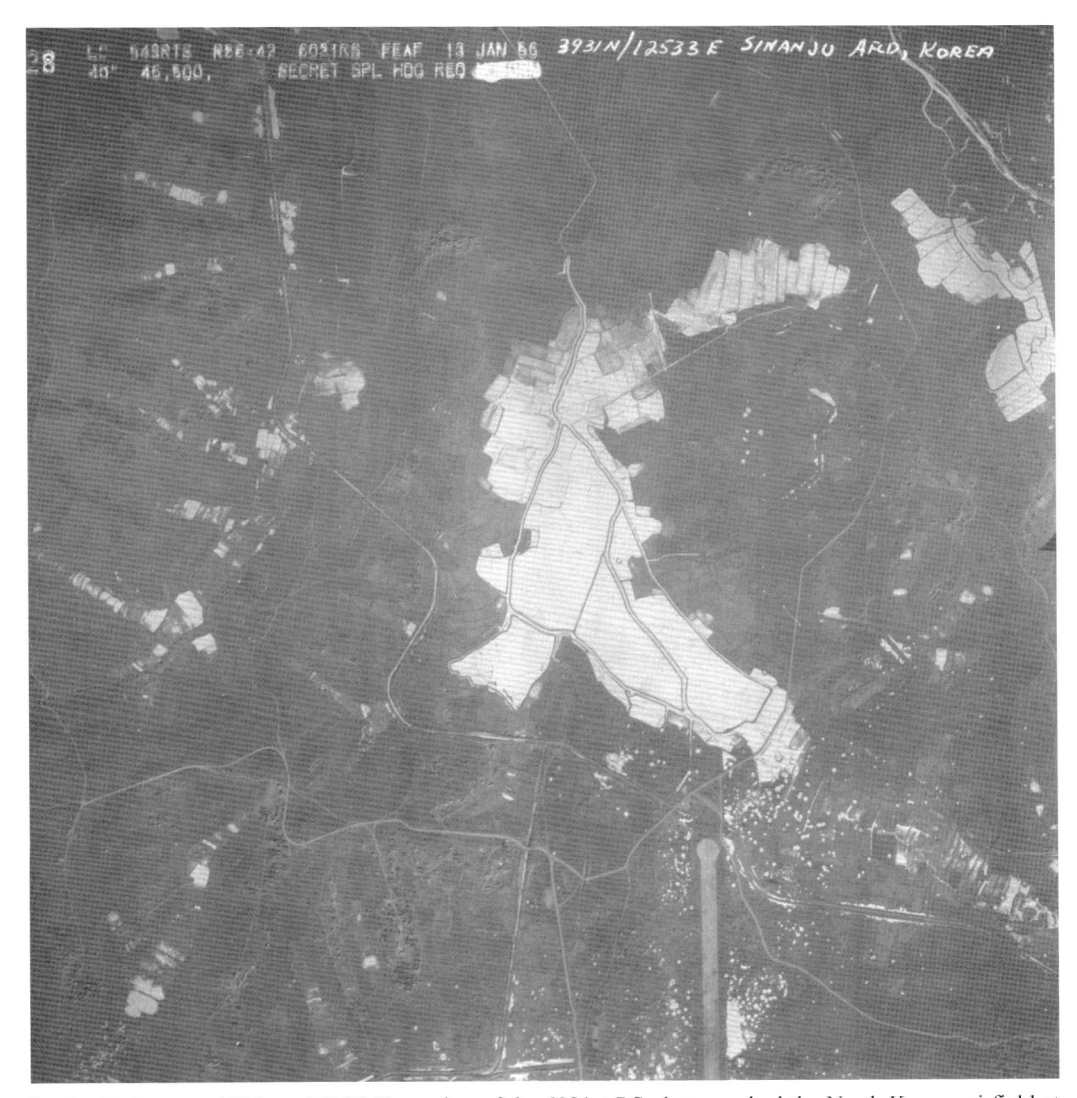

On the 13 January, 1956, an RF-86 Haymaker of the 6021st RS photographed the North Korean airfield at Sinuiju. (USAF)

was it alone in conducting secret flights over enemy territory. From December, 1954, the 6021st Reconnaissance Squadron (Composite) operated out of Yokota, Japan and pilots from the 15th were detached to this unit and conducted overflights under its auspices. In addition to the RF-86 the 6021st flew RB-57As under Operation Heart Throb and RF-100As under Operation Slick Chick. It also flew RB-45 Tornadoes.

Operation Heart Throb involved the deployment of specially modified RB-57A aircraft to two bases: Yokota in Japan and Rhein-Main in Germany. The mission was to undertake high altitude photo reconnaissance flights over the Soviet Far East, China and other countries of the Soviet Bloc in Eastern Europe. Captains Guthrie, Picciano, Bryant and Hines were destined for the Far East and Captains Bill Gafford, Gerry Cooke, Ralph Finlay, Robert Holladay, Robert Thorne and Kenneth Johnson for Europe. The Far East contingent was to be led by Joe Guthrie and the European contingent by Bill Gafford. All pilots were current on the B-57 with the exception of

58 TACTICAL RECONNAISSANCE IN THE COLD WAR

A formation of 6021st RS aircraft flies over Yokota, led by an RB-45C Tornado. (Bob Gould)

A line up of RB-57As at the Martin plant in 1955. The Heart Throb aircraft were modified from the basic RB-57A production model. (USAF via Mike Hooks)

One of the early production RB-57As takes off from the Martin factory. (USAF via Mike Hooks)

Robert Thorne who came from flying B-47s with SAC. Finlay, Holliday, Gafford and Johnson were experienced recce pilots with the 363rd TRW based at Shaw AFB.

The RB-57As were specially modified from the standard production models. The modifications were designed to reduce the weight of the aircraft thus enabling it to attain the heights necessary for it to undertake its clandestine mission. The navigator's seat was removed as was all the navigation equipment and armour. The rotating bomb-door and associated hydraulics and racks were removed and the bomb bay skinned over. An optical viewfinder was installed and pilot intervalometer controls for the cameras, for setting shutter speeds and time between picture exposures, thus producing the necessary picture overlap for the photo interpreters. Navigation was to be through pilotage aided by the viewfinder which looked through the nose, making positioning the aircraft on course and over targets easier. Because of the altitude the RB-57s were to operate at, a pressure suit ventilator system was installed. The recce suite installed within a pressurized camera compartment was: one T-11 vertical mapping camera and two K-38, 36 in focal length oblique cameras with 10–15 per cent overlap.

The pilots and aircraft were flown to their respective overseas bases. It had originally been planned to transport the Far East aircraft to Japan by carrier but Joe Guthrie had other ideas:

> It seemed such an inglorious way to send an Air Force aircraft overseas. I worked with some Martin performance engineers to determine if the aircraft could be flown to Japan. The major obstacle was the first leg from California to Hawaii – some 2300 nautical miles. Subsequent B-57B flights to Japan would have a 3000 lb ferry tank in the bomb bay, but our modified RB-57As had the bomb bay removed and skinned over to reduce weight. As a result – no 3000 lb ferry tank. But to my delight, the Martin engineers said I could make it with 2000 lb remaining under no wind conditions. So I took an aircraft and flew it 2300 nautical miles and sure enough I had 2000 lb of fuel when I landed.

The four RB-57s and their pilots arrived at Yokota on 4 September, 1955, having flown from Hamilton AFB via Hickham, Johnson Island, Kwajalein and Guam. MATS agreed to provide a lead aircraft as the Canberras had no navigation equipment except their radio compasses.

The European contingent flew to Rhein-Main AFB in West Germany and flew the northern route taking off from Robins AFB on the 18th August and flying via Goose Bay and Keflavik. They had no lead aircraft; navigating by dead reckoning. By way of reassurance two coastguard vessels were stationed *en route* to provide ADF positions. They landed at Rhein-Main on the 23rd August. They were assigned to the 7407th Support Squadron.

The German based RB-57s commenced their operations in September. The Far East pilots had had experience of flying the B-57, but all four had no experience of reconnaissance flying. For the first two months they had to learn the art of taking photographs with their aircraft.

An RB-57A, 52-1464. This aircraft was one of those assigned to the Heart Throb project. (USAF)

Two RB-57A Heart Throb aircraft flying a training mission over Japan in 1956. Joe Guthrie was flying 52-1432 which was stripped to ascertain which was harder to see. Black won! (Joe Guthrie)

The first Far East overflight took place on 26 November, 1955. Joe Guthrie was the pilot, backed up by Jim Bryant. The flight was to be staged from Chitose Air Base on the northern island of Hokkaido. The aircraft and maintenance support were flown up to Chitose on 24 November. Joe Guthrie:

> It was to be a complete radio silence mission. If radio silence was broken within the first 30 minutes the back-up aircraft would be launched. The mission profile was briefed to fly north from Chitose and along the eastern side of the island of Sakhalin far enough seaward and at an altitude of 100 ft to avoid radar detection. This profile was to continue to a point abreast the northern portion of the island where the tip tanks would be jettisoned and a climb initiated to the maximum obtainable altitude. Somewhere in the climb a 180 degree turn would be started in order to arrive over the northern tip of the island headed south at an altitude of about 55,000 ft. At this point a reconnaissance run would be flown down the entire length of the island with specific pinpoint targets and lines. The flight would then continue on to Hokkaido, break radio silence, and land at Chitose. The aircraft would be refuelled and the film left in place for an immediate return to Yokota. There, the film would be down loaded by the 548th Recce Tech Squadron for processing and photo interpretation.
>
> The day of the mission arrived and the weather was excellent. We gathered early for the briefing. We had a controlled take-off time, so it was imperative that I get dressed and get strapped in the aircraft in time to get airborne right on time. I went to the aircraft and completed the walk around inspection, then back inside to get suited up. "Suiting Up" was quite a task. I put on a pressure suit, an air vent suit, a padded suit, a water survival suit and a Mae West. Looking like the Pillsbury Dough Boy and moving with the dexterity of a robot made me wonder if I could still fly the aircraft. As a result of worrying about the controlled take-off time, I got dressed too early. It did not take long for me to get way too hot, so I went outside into the frigid Hokkaido weather to cool off. Finally, it was time to get aboard the aircraft. With all the equipment I was wearing it took a personnel equipment technician to stuff me into the pilot's seat. Then he spent some time getting my parachute buckled and everything hooked up before checking everything out thoroughly. At this point, for the first time in my life I really wished I were someplace else. The feeling did not last long…as soon as I got the engines started I was raring to go.
>
> We had a man in the control tower and as soon as he saw I was ready to taxi he told the tower operator to issue taxi instructions. Two minutes before take-off time, I was cleared on the runway and cleared for take-off.
>
> Exactly on time, I rolled down the runway, lifted off and took up my first heading. I passed over the northern part of Hokkaido and was soon over the ocean east of Sakhalin flying 100 ft above the water. However, it was not long before I ran into low clouds and I was completely IFR. I was flying at about 350

Wright Patterson AFB, 1955. Bill Gafford and Joe Guthrie dressed in full flight-gear wearing partial pressure suits, survival suits, mae wests and parachutes. Bill Gafford led the six Heart Throb aircraft to Europe and Joe Guthrie went to Japan. (Joe Guthrie)

knots indicated and this made for a sporty ride over the ocean. I decided I had better get a little altitude before I ended up in the drink, so I climbed to 200 ft and held that altitude the rest of the way north. I could not see anything. I went completely on dead reckoning. At the appropriate time on the flight card I punched off the tips, and initiated the climb. During the time I was in the clouds I was worried that the mission would be a washout because of the weather. But I was quickly on top of the clouds and as I gained altitude I could see that Sakhalin was completely clear the entire length of the island. I continued my climb a little north of the island and turned back south at a little over 55,000 ft. I had checked the cameras out previously so I was ready to start taking pictures. Everything looked just the way it had during mission preparation and I was going great until I saw that I was too far east to photograph an airfield. Not knowing any better, I made a 360 degree turn and picked it up. As a result I got every target assigned – but not without consequences later.

There were many airports and as best as I could see plenty of Migs on them. Also there was no doubt that they knew I was there. We had a warning device that told us when we were being tracked by radar. We could discriminate between airborne and ground radars by the tone of the oral warning – a high piercing tone meant airborne radar. I looked around a lot and changed headings when I could, but I never saw anything. When I changed headings I would lose the airborne tone, but then it would come back. There wasn't much I could do but head south. In frustration, I turned the warning device off and kept heading south.

It was good to see the island of Hokkaido slip under the nose and I broke radio silence and called Chitose for landing instructions. I made an uneventful landing and logged 4+40. After a quick turn around and a change into a normal flight suit we returned to Yokota, landing just before dark.

The next day we had a debriefing with Colonel Avery. The Colonel asked Joe Bitz how I did and Joe said I got it all but that I had made a 360. Colonel Avery turned to me and asked me if this was true. I said that it was. I then got a lecture about all the bad things that can happen if you make 360s and was told that it is 'one pass and haul ass,' period. So it was back to Recce school for a week.

Captain Joe Bitz was an officer in the 548th Reconnaissance Technical Squadron.

The operating procedures were different for the two Heart Throb detachments. The Far East missions were invariably undertaken with tip tanks, whereas in Europe this was never so. As we shall see this was to prove extremely problematic for Captain Jim Bryant during a later overflight. In Europe when contrailing was expected the flights took off with a wingman whose responsibility it was to look out for contrails. If contrails were evident then the mission was aborted. If this was not the case then, more often than not, the wing aircraft would return to base. Occasionally, however, if all other portents were good, both aircraft would proceed to separate targets. Gerry Cooke:

> I recall planning for four overflights. I believe I flew three missions, and aborted the fourth. I recall getting only one of my targets on one overflight due to cloud coverage. This was probably number three. I remember seeing Mig 17s on one overflight, in the vicinity of Budapest, probably flight two or three. I remember the first overflight included targets near Brno, Czechoslovakia and Brataslava, Hungary. The aborted mission would have been my fourth. At the point of penetration I was forming contrails. The engine exhaust under certain atmospheric conditions causes condensation to form at high altitudes. Such clear trails spinning out behind the aircraft would clearly expose both the aircraft and its direction. We always wanted to avoid contrails in the overflight areas. A second aircraft accompanying the mission aircraft would signal go / no-go depending on the presence or absence of contrails.

Contrails. Three of the European contingent of Heart Throb making contrails high above the skies of Germany. The presence of contrails at the outset of an overflight mission would cause the mission to be aborted. (Gerry Cooke)

My overflight missions were planned in a security area at HQUSAF. Colonel Holbury assigned the targets and oversaw the route planning, including turning points, entry points and times into the block country, altitudes, photo runs, camera operations, exit points and times, in short the complete and detailed flight plan. As I remember it each flight plan included approximately six targets, I don't remember it being more, and it seems that one flight plan included only four or five targets. I don't believe film supply limited target numbers. I seem to remember times when the cameras were left running to cover a target strip of some length.

Four mission plans were assigned to me throughout the Jan-August '56 time frame. Each mission was a complete flight and navigation plan and was referred to as a 'canned' Heart Throb mission. In this way it could be identified and called out in the clear. A mission could be executed by a reference to a code when all conditions were met.

The canned and coded flights plans were hand carried back from Wiesbaden to the squadron operations by the individual pilot, and were stored in the pilot's Top Secret safe. Each pilot had his own safe, which no one else shared. Each pilot's missions were completely compartmentalized. None of use knew anything specific about the other pilot's canned mission. This was the standard operating procedure.

It worked so well that to this day I don't know exactly when and where the other Heart Throb pilots flew an overflight mission. There were times when one could surmise. There was a higher level of intensity and concern throughout the squadron when an overflight sortie was underway. The operation activity was a little different when it was real and not a training flight. But at times we had that rise in concern for some sorties that turned out to be weather or contrail aborts, and even at times a misread of what was a training mission.

Pronto! Was the magic word. When the pilot used this code word the mission was real. When all the signs were right theatre and political intelligence and the weather in the mission area, the Heart Throb pilot would get the word from Colonel Holbury and given a time window for take off. The Squadron Commander and Operations Officer were alerted – a Heart Throb mission would now get underway.

Personal Equipment was made ready for pressure suit fitting and pre-breathing. Ground crew prepared the aircraft and cameras. The pilot did his pre-breathing of 100 per cent oxygen, a fellow pilot ran the aircraft preparation and checklist. The pilot boarded his aircraft, buckled and hooked up, started up, radios on – and announced to the control tower Pronto departure taxiing, south-west quadrant departure outbound. Pronto call sign signalled the tower to clear the taxiways, runways and air traffic control cleared the requested quadrant. This was the last radio transmission until descending for approach and landing. The mission was underway.

Project Heart Throb in Japan comprised four productive missions before the project was closed down. Missions were not always without incident. Captain Jim Bryant flew a deep penetration mission requiring the use of tip tanks. Lou Picciano:

> The tank spun and lodged against the fuel vent T mast. The other tank was in the Sea of Japan. He went into a spin and when he broke the spin he exceeded the red line, which pitched the airplane up into another stall and another pitch up. He finally decided to hold it in a spin until the stall speed and the red line had a wider envelope. All this time other aircraft were proceeding to his position. I guess they thought it was one hell of an evasive

A map illustrating the maximum mission radius of the Heart Throb RB-57As flying out of Rhein-Main. (Reproduced from the *Early Cold War Overflights Symposium Proceedings* papers by kind permission of Editor Cargill Hall)

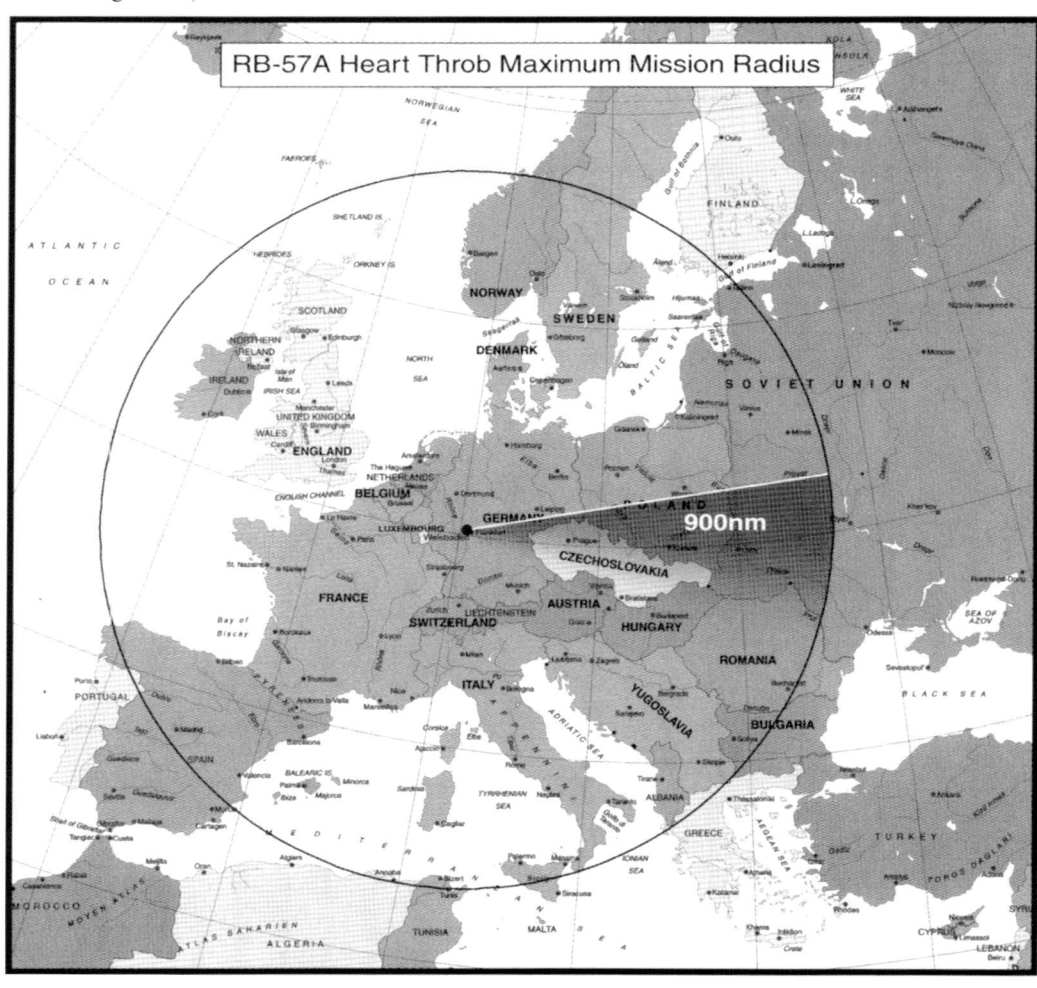

manoeuvre. He finally got the aircraft down to a lower altitude and started south-east towards home. The bird was vibrating badly. It was one of the engines so he shut it down. He didn't know at the time that the violent pitch-ups had caused some compressor blade to shear off and come through the nacelle. Then he noticed that his right armrest had bent outward 45 degrees. Fearing that he might inadvertently eject himself he tried to put the seat pin back in. No luck. The holes were not aligned meaning that as the firing pin travelled closer to the charge it could blow off the seat. Then he tried to cut the hose. Steel impregnated hose. Again no luck. He knew he had to make a smooth single-engine landing to preclude the seat from firing. There were never any radio transmissions on an ops mission. Another B-57 pilot would handle take-off and landing instructions from the tower with an Aldus lamp. On ops and training missions our fuel would be so low that the aft centre of gravity would not let the nose gear touch the ground making taxiing difficult. Someone would meet the aircraft and get in to add weight to the nose. On actual missions that would be the back-up pilot. In this case me. When I climbed into that bird I was in awe. Jim looked like he took a flight through hell.

An armourer was called to secure the ejector system before the aircraft was taxied to a hardstanding and Jim could safely get out. On the following morning he received a case of Scotch from the Martin company for a job well done.

Bob Hines recalls the occasion that he was over Vladivostok with a 'tail'

I lost count of the number of times my tail intelligence indicated a 'live one' was back there ready to lock on. I knew this enemy aircraft could not reach my altitude, but could successfully blow me out of the sky if he locked on long enough to set his guidance and release his ordnance. At that altitude my only defence could be very shallow turns.

Meanwhile this enemy Mig would make a near lock-on and I would be able to break it. This exercise continued for about 35 miles out over the Sea of Japan. Finally my hunter friend broke off his chase.

What effectively closed down the Heart Throb and RF-86 operations in the Far East theatre was the advent of a state-of-the-art Soviet fighter which did have the ability to overhaul and shoot down the RB-57A and the RF-86. This was the Mig 19.

The six aircraft and pilots in Europe undoubtedly flew many more missions than their Asian counterparts. It is impossible to be precise, but a best general estimate would be that between September, 1955 and August, 1956, between sixteen and twenty sorties were flown. These overflights covered most of the countries in the Soviet Bloc. Without exception they were shallow penetrations. Gerry Cooke:

My flight planning was in the middle area of the block countries: Czechoslovakia, Hungary and the northern provinces of the former Yugoslavia. I planned four missions in these areas around and on routes between these cities and airports: Brno, Bratislava, Budapest, Novi Sad, Belgrade, Zagreb and other targets on the route from Budapest east to the Romanian border.

To the best of my memory I flew two of these missions and a part of the third, possibly in January, March and August '56 (cumulus clouds covered some of the targets.) I can't be sure if this occurred on mission number two or three. I planned and attempted a fourth that was aborted due to contrails. I have a strong feeling that this fourth flight was in the summer before the Hungarian revolt. It was the last Heart Throb mission for me.

On this fourth mission Captain Thorne was flying wing to check the contrailing. If negative contrails, he was to return to base, and I would proceed. The entry point for this mission was a peninsula on the Yugoslavian [Croatian] coast of the Adriatic just south of Trieste. I remember this was also an exit point for an earlier mission. Contrail formation was very strong at the entry altitude and there was no reason to believe that it might subside.

The first mission planned for targets in and around the cities of Brataslava and Brno. Targets were usually very large airports and industrial complexes, sometimes just a quadrant of a city or a convergence of highway and railroads. I felt that we were trying to confirm or prove forward deployment of the USSR fighters and marshalling areas. The city targets that I remember most were near Budapest where I experienced the only aircraft sightings on these missions. While making a right turn off target, below my right wing and slightly to the rear and about 5000 ft below, were two Migs. They resembled F86s more than Mig 15s. I think in the debriefing we agreed they probably were Mig 17s. They did not appear to be in position for a 'zoom' manoeuvre. What kind of threat they might have been I didn't know, and don't know today either. I was not briefed on any likelihood of being intercepted. At our altitudes above 50,000 ft

Captain Gerry Cooke at Rhein-Main demonstrating the T-1 pressure suit. (Gerry Cooke)

Captain Gerry Cooke and Staff Sergeant Hendrus at Rhein-Main in 1956. (Gerry Cooke)

we were not concerned with a 'zoom' manoeuvre threat from block countries. Only the French based Canadian F86 demonstrated any ability to reach us at 50,000 ft. A few moments later two more appeared below and behind the first two. This raised the adrenalin a bit, but somehow I didn't feel threatened. I continued the flight plan and they fell away out of sight

The increase in international tension created by the Suez Crisis of June 1956 and the Hungarian uprising from August to November of that year heralded the end of Heart Throb operations in Europe. The RB-57 aircraft and their pilots continued to fly routine missions well into 1958 and the early months of 1959. The pilots and planes deployed to other bases and took a lot of photos all over Europe and elsewhere; from Spain to Norway to Turkey and from Morocco to Egypt. They continued to fly the Heart Throb flight profiles but over friendly airspace.

In Japan the end of the overflight operations meant the end of RB-57A operations out of Yokota. In 1957 Lou Picciano and Bob Hines went to Okinawa to train four Taiwanese pilots in the art of high altitude recce. They had with them two RB-57As. From Okinawa they moved to Taipei and Taoyuan Air Base. On the third mission over Red China one of the aircraft was shot down over the Shantung Peninsula and the project was abandoned. Lou and Bob returned to Shaw AFB.

In May, 1955, the 7407th Support Squadron of the 7499th Support Group formed Detachment 1

Badge of the 7407th Support Squadron. The red stylized aircraft is framed by turbine blades. Both the RB-57As and the Slick Chick RF-100s were a part of the 7407th. (via Gerry Cooke)

at Bitburg Air Base in Germany. The 7499th Support Group was based at Weisbaden. In addition to the 7407th the 7499th Support Group also included the 7405th, which flew a variety of transport in a covert role; The 7499th had been involved in clandestine work in Europe since the end of the Second World War when they had flown the B-17 in an ELINT role. Detachment 1 was a unit comprising three RF-100A reconnaissance fighters and their pilots and support personnel. Their mission was to fly recce missions over the Soviet Union and its allies.

Two years previously, in 1954, North American Aviation had received a contract to modify six F-100A aircraft to photo reconnaissance configuration aircraft under Project Slick Chick.

Project Slick Chick was to operate in two theatres: Europe and the Far East. Three aircraft, support teams and pilots would go to Yokota as part of the 6021st Reconnaissance Squadron and three to Bitburg AB in Germany. In the fall of 1954 the project officers for Slick Chick were selected. They were Captain Cecil H. Rigsby and Captain Ralph W. White. Both men had experience in reconnaissance work. Both had operated with the 15th TRS and had time on the RF-86A. During the latter months of 1954 and early 1955 they went through a programme of flight proficiency training at Edwards AFB which included qualifying on the F-86F and the F-100A. Meanwhile the remaining pilots were being selected for Slick Chick. Captain Rigsby would be accompanied to Europe by Captains Bert Dowdy and Ed Hill. Captains Boone and Moomaw would go with Captain White to Japan. Each of these four pilots put in time at George AFB flying the F-86; and then to Edwards for flying training on the F-100A.

Slick Chick RF-100 training operations were moved to Palmdale in the spring of 1955. Palmdale was a facility used by a number of aircraft manufacturing companies including North American. Cecil Rigsby:

> We flew aerial photography exercises with the RF-100A to check out the photographic system, with the film developed by North American. The firm would immediately correct any discrepancy. All the pilots were highly skilled in tactical reconnaissance, so we did not spend a lot of time on aerial reconnaissance. We concentrated our training time on maximizing the performance of the airplane. Many supersonic flights were made, some for extended periods. I worked out flight profiles with no external tanks, two external tanks, or four external tanks. The RF-100A did not respond well with four tanks. The airplane would yaw from left to right and the centre of gravity was such that the elevator control became very sensitive. When the fuel was expended from these tanks it helped, but the four external tank configuration was unpopular with the pilots.

In April 1955 the training at Palmdale came to an end and the respective teams made preparations to deploy to their operational bases in Germany and Japan.

The journey to Bitburg AB for the European contingent was a slow one. The

Major Rigsby and his ground crew at Bitburg in 1955. (Cecil Rigsby)

The European contingent Slick Chick pilots at Bitburg in company with 554. They are from left to right: Major Cecil Rigsby, Major Bert E. Dowdy, Captain Edgar H. Hill and CWO, W-2 Edward Brosche. (Cecil Rigsby)

Slick Chick RF-100s were not air-to-air refuellable The RF-100As were flown from Palmdale to Mobile, Alabama via Carswell, Texas where they refuelled. At Mobile the airplanes were cocooned for shipment to Belfast on board an aircraft carrier. At Belfast they were reassembled by Short Bros and from there flown to Bitburg. Bitburg had been chosen because it was destined to receive the F-100C within a short space of time. The presence of the three RF-100As would not attract as much notice there as elsewhere.

RF-100A Slick Chick penetration missions were high altitude, 50,000 ft, and short range and depended on the use of afterburner to maintain a speed of Mach 0.96. The aircraft was considered to be vulnerable to enemy interception if longer range missions using solely military power were attempted. One of the outcomes of the first flights over Europe was unexpected and produced some shock waves throughout the USAF. Major Roger K. Rhodarmer was assigned to the Sensitive Intelligence programme (SENSINT) and to HQUSAFE and had a particular interest in the Slick Chick project:

> And it was a flap when they first went in. It was not the photography that was such a shock. When they did that first penetration, wherever it was they went, they encountered ten times more radars than we ever thought existed. And they went in at 50,000 ft at Mach 1.0 and the Soviets still picked them up easily and tracked them easily every step of the way. The information came back to Washington and the joints Chiefs of Staff and everybody was shaken up to know that the Soviet radars were that good. That was the first time we had used a really high performance airplane to punch in over there. They realized that the air defence radar was good, really good.

Three RF-100As in flight. The 7407th lost one of its RF-100s, when, on a local flight, Captain Ed Hill had a flame-out and elected to bale-out. The cause of the flame-out was undetermined. (Cecil Rigsby)

A very rare colour photograph of 53-1554 at Bitburg. The modifications made to the aircraft can be clearly seen in spite of the covers. (Cecil Rigsby)

RF-100A 554 in flight over Germany. The mission profiles of the RF-100A required a lot of time in afterburner. Operating on only military power would make the aircraft more vulnerable to the Mig 17. (USAF via Cecil Rigsby)

RF-100A 53-1551 at Bitburg in 1955. Bitburg was the home of the 36th TFW which was scheduled to receive the F-100C. The RF-100s could retain a certain anonymity amongst the F-100Cs. (North American via Cecil Rigsby)

RF-100 53-1551 at Bitburg. RF-100s invariably took off with four external tanks and on afterburner. When all the tanks were dropped the aircraft could achieve a speed in level flight of Mach 1.22 at 35,000 ft. (USAF)

Between mid 1955 and mid 1956 it is likely that there were six RF-100A missions over the Soviet Bloc countries in Eastern Europe; two for each of the pilots assigned. Missions were flown out of Bitburg and Furstenfeldbruck. Because of the relatively short range of the RF-100 these were confined mainly to the close satellite countries of Hungary and what was then Czechoslovakia. Cecil Rigsby flew the first Slick Chick mission over Prague:

> I flew two overflight missions from Bitburg and was fortunate to have clear weather on both flights. The first flight was to Prague, Czeckoslovakia, and the surrounding area, where the primary targets were airfields. Following my take off from Bitburg, I cruised to an entry point a little south of Nurnberg. Afterburner was selected, and when I crossed the border my aircraft was at 50,000 ft moving at a speed of Mach 0.95 or 0.96 in full military power and afterburner. It was a perfect day and my visibility was unlimited, as the trimetrogen cameras began functioning. I observed no aircraft near the border area. As I approached my targets I could see through the viewfinder of my vertical cameras a number of fighters scrambling to get airborne at one of the airfields and other fighters circling over it. When I reversed direction to return to Germany after photographing all my targets I had a great deal of company. The Russian fighters were going all out to match my speed and reach my altitude, but they remained at a much lower level. If they had climbed they would have fallen much farther behind. One airplane managed to get in my eight o' clock position, but he was about 20,000 ft below me. I did not drop my external tanks because I never felt threatened. The fighters broke off when I reached the German border and I returned safely to Bitburg.

Captain Rigsby's second overflight was into East Germany. It was a successful mission which was again characterized by encounters with enemy fighter aircraft though not in such proximity as to cause any concern.

> I was less than 50 miles into East Germany when I saw something coming towards me at high speed. It was a flight of four Mig fighters in finger formation. They were only a few

RF-100A 53-1456. This RF-100A was assigned to the 6021st RS at Yokota AB in Japan. (Bob Gould)

> thousand feet below me and I passed directly over them. I was a little surprised that they were at such a high altitude. I hit the runaway switch for maximum photos on my trimetrogen cameras, hoping to get a picture.

At no point did Cecil consider aborting the mission. He covered all his targets and returned to Bitburg without encountering any more aircraft.

The advent of the U2 and the 'Black Knight' RB-57D placed the clandestine missions in the hands of others. Nevertheless the RF-100As and RB-57As were maintained at combat readiness in case they were needed. It is also of significance that the number of overflights flown by tac recce pilots with tac recce airplanes probably closely matched in total the number of U-2 flights.

A Heart Throb RB-57A is here in the company of one of the RB-57D long wing aircraft. The RB-57Ds operated overflights from Yokota under the auspices of SAC, until such time as they attempted a mass overflight with the aircraft and so aggravated the US Government that future overflights were banned. (USAF via Mike Hooks)

CHAPTER FOUR

USAFE

While the 67th TRW was engaging in the hot war in Korea, in the west the cold war was getting colder. The response of the United States Air Force was to begin a massive upgrading of it's strategic and tactical assets in Europe. Many of the initial units dispatched to join the United States Air Forces in Europe (USAFE) were National Guard wings and squadrons. One of these was the 117th Tactical Reconnaissance Wing which arrived in mainland Europe in January, 1952. It was the first USAF tactical reconnaissance unit in the theatre since the departure of the 10th Reconnaissance Group to the US in June 1947.

The 117th had been activated at Lawson AFB in Georgia. Three squadrons were assigned: the 157th and 160th TRS' (Photo Jet) both flying the RF-80A; and the 112th TRS (Night Photo) equipped with the RB-26. The two photo-jet squadrons had in May, 1950 been redesignated from Fighter Squadrons and had replaced their F-51 Mustangs with RF-80As. The 112th TRS had been assigned to the wing in October, 1950.

It had been planned that the 117th would deploy to the newly reconstructed base at Toul-Rosiere in France. In the event the base was not nearly ready and the squadrons were dispersed to bases in Germany; only the wing HQ being at Toul-Rosiere. The tactical group and 157th TRS went to Furstenfeldbruck, the 160th to Neubiberg, and the 112th to Weisbaden.

The aircraft of the 117th were flown by their pilots from Lawson AFB to RAF Burtonwood in England and thence to their German bases. They flew the Arctic route and their deployment was code named Fox Able 14 which took the RF-80s from Lawson to Dow AFB, Maine. The RB-26s went to Westover. From these two bases they went to Goose Bay, Labrador and thence to Blue

A publicity photo of an RF-80A of the 117th TRW photographed at Furstenfeldbruck in 1952. (USAF)

West One in Greenland. From Greenland they proceeded to Keflavik, Iceland. It was here that the only significant problem occurred. While the 160th flight was approaching the airfield; the squadron commander Lieutenant Colonel Maynard T. Swartz suffered the bends at 32,000 ft when an oxygen bubble lodged in his brain. He experienced a deterioration in eyesight and then faintness. He was led down by his wingman, Lieutenant Thomas H. Temple; and on finals was talked down by colleagues on the ground. The Air Force Flying Safety magazine of December, 1952 reported:

> Lieutenant Temple's action under unusual conditions is proof of his sense of leadership, excellent planning ability, and quick thinking, as well as superior flying technique.

From Iceland the squadrons flew to Prestwick in Scotland, then to Burtonwood, and then on to Germany.

The mission of the 117th TRW was to provide tactical, visual, photographic and electronic reconnaissance by both day and night as was required by the military forces within the European Command. Operational flying commenced on 3 March, 1952, when the 160th TRS began familiarization flights over their new homeland.

At the end of March the 157th began operations in earnest. On the 24th March their RF-80s were used to provide visual reconnaissance for an army manoeuvre. Photo missions for all the squadrons were delayed, due to a shortage of camera spares and inadequate processing facilities, until early April, when both the 157th and 160th TRS began photographing various tactical targets in the Western Defence Area. The supply problems and a lack of aircraft spares were to dog this unit and others in USAFE command for a long time ahead. On arrival in Europe the 112th TRS had only 15 days supplies which they had brought over from the States. This squadron's primary role of Night Photo was also held up for some time due to the lack of a suitable practise range for the use of flash bomb cartridges. Eventually SAC at RAF Lakenheath made their ranges available. As if to compound the problems encountered, in May and early June 1952 a refinery strike in the United States restricted the use of fuel. Flying was limited to 20 hours per pilot per month.

Exercise June Primer which took place towards the end of June 1952 involved all squadrons of the 117th in a variety of missions; a great many of which were accomplished with distinction in spite of the quite daunting problems referred to above. The exercise took place within an area bordered by a line drawn from Cherbourg to Geneva in the west and in the east by the Swiss, Austrian and Russian Occupation Zone borders. For the purposes of the exercise the 117th had to furnish ten RF-80 aircraft and four RB-26 aircraft.

Missions included vertical photography of the Birdenfeld area, vertical stereo coverage of the airfields of Jever, Fassburg, Celle. Sinsdorf and Gutersloh, night flash photos of the Sifgenburg range, vertical photography of prospective paratroop drop zones, oblique photography of the Danube and Rhine rivers and their bridges, and artillery adjustment for the 816th Field Artillery. These latter missions were facilitated by the use of wire recorders which had been installed in five of the 157th RF-80s in April.

Following the completion of June Primer the wing was tasked with the mosaic, oblique and vertical photography of airfields then under construction or reconstruction, notably Toul-Rosiere, Chaumont, Laon, Landstuhl, Bitburg, Hahn and Sembach; this on a monthly basis.

On 10 July, 1952, the 117th TRW was returned on paper to the United States. All equipment and personnel remained in place to be taken over by the newly activated 10th Tactical Reconnaissance Wing. After a period of five years this unit had returned to Europe. The Wing HQ remained at Toul-Rosiere and the group HQ at Furstenfeldbruck. The 157th TRS was redesignated the 32nd TRS and remained at Fursty. The 160th TRS was redesignated the 38th TRS and remained at Neubiberg. The 112th TRS was redesignated the 1st TRS and prepared to move from Weisbaden to join the Wing HQ at Toul-Rosiere. Just why this decision was made is not clear. By all accounts Toul-Rosiere was nowhere near ready. Much of the initial work of the

RB-26s of the 1st TRS on the flightline at Toul-Rosiere AB France in January 1953. Toul's facilities were rudimentary to say the least and the base had the nick name of 'Mud City'. (10th TRW Historical Office USAF)

squadron personnel involved erecting tents and temporary accommodation for all manner of uses from living quarters to operations and engineering facilities. However, by 23 July, 1952, the 1st TRS had made the move; all the equipment, personnel and all but two of their RB-26s. These aircraft had unfortunately been damaged in a violent storm at Weisbaden; a storm which had also initiated a flash flood which had severely damaged valuable photographic supplies, which were in very short supply.

If a shortage of spares of all types was a significant hindrance to operational efficiency, then the unpredictable and frequently inclement North European weather was equally so. During the latter part of 1952 the weather played havoc with the missions of the wing. A considerable backlog built up, as it did for all USAFE tactical units. One of the outcomes of this was to prompt USAFE command to look further afield, to sunnier climes, for suitable training and practise environments. As part of this process, Captain Moak and Major Ramsey of the 32nd TRS were dispatched to North Africa to photograph Sidi Slimane and Nousseur Air Bases in Morocco. In future years deployments to these two bases for all USAFE units was to be a very

An RB-26 of the 1st TRS refuelling at Toul-Rosiere in early 1953. Toul-Rosiere was a temporary base for the 1st until Spangdahlem was completed in July 1953. (10th TRW Historical Office USAF)

Four RF-80As of the 38th TRS. These aircraft are carrying the 165 US Gallon wing tip tanks. Later RF-80s were fitted with 230 gallon tanks that were the same as those fitted to the T-33. (Bill Shell)

regular occurrence. Operation Longstep took the 1st TRS to Italy to photograph the US 6th Fleet in the Mediterranean. On 5 November one of the aircraft of this detachment demonstrated the latest high-tech Hell Roarer magnesium illuminator system with split vertical night camera using the new A-18 magazine over the Bay of Naples. By all accounts this was a spectacular event and the tactical advantages demonstrated by the system were somewhat overshadowed by the mild panic that the demonstration created among the excitable Neapolitans, many of whom reported a sighting of a 'disco volante'. As if to further distract from the significance of the event, the demonstrating RB-26 was seen, in the light of day, to have a badly scorched vertical stabilizer!

Operation Blue Alliance teamed up the RF-80s of the 32nd and 38th TRS with the Meteor FR9s of 79 squadron RAF.

The supply problems did not diminish as 1952 drew to a close. In November there was a period

RF-80As of the 38th TRS, 10th TRW, 1953. The lightning flashes on the fuselage and tip tanks were blue and on the tail, red. (Bill Shell)

38th TRS RF-80As fly over Germany in 1953. 10th TRW aircraft had not been modified with the higher thrust J-33 engines and this, coupled with their smaller tanks, limited their range compared to the aircraft of the 66th TRW. (Bill Shell)

when only one of the 18 RF-80s of the 32nd TRS, was flyable, all the others needing flap actuators. Prior to this there had been a catalogue of accidents. Three RF-80s and one T-33 had been obliged to make emergency landings in fields, and three RF-80s had been damaged when one aircraft jumped its chocks and collided with two others. Fortunately, the aircraft that had made emergency landings were only slightly damaged, but for one. Captain Dixon of the 32nd

302nd RF-80 maintenance in the hangars at Sembach. (R. Schell via Dave Menard)

A 38th TRS RF-80A flies in formation with a 1st TRS RB-26. The 10th TRW comprised two jet photo squadrons, the 32nd and 38th, and one night photo squadron, the 1st. (Bob Webster)

TRS had experienced a flame out, and, using his undoubted skill, he had succeeded in putting his aircraft down carefully and relatively undamaged in a field near Augsburg. Unfortunately he had landed near a haystack and, on exiting his RF-80, he witnessed to his horror, a worried German farmer throw a heavy chain over the vertical stabiliser and drag the aircraft away with his tractor, causing considerable damage to the whole rear of the aircraft

In July, two significant events took place for the 10th TRW. The entire wing and tactical group became based at Spangdahlem in Germany on the 19th of the month. On the same day the 66th TRW came to Europe. The 66th had been activated at Shaw in January. The arrival of the new wing had considerable implications for the mission organization of the 10th TRW. The 66th TRW was similarly equipped to the 10th, and USAFE command decided, in December 1953, that, in order to avoid unnecessary confusion and mission duplication, the 10th TRW would confine itself to work in the Allied zones of Germany, and the 66th would work in the Allied zones of Austria. Order 287-53, for example, required the 1st TRS to map all the French and US zones of Germany.

The journey over the northern route to Sembach was accident free but occasionally fraught. Delays occurred at Goose bay and Keflavik due to bad weather. Frank Meyer flying with the 303rd TRS recalls:

Departure from Shaw was not a problem. The weather at Dow AFB, Maine was overcast

Russ Tansey of the 302nd TRS flies RF-80A 44-85244 in formation on a cross country run with Bob Sweet. (Bob Sweet)

RF-80A 45-8409 of the 302nd TRS over Germany 1954. This aircraft carries the 230 gallon Fletcher type tanks. (Roger Brunsvold)

with the ceiling below 5000 ft. When we took off from Dow we got into the clouds at a very low altitude. Arrival at Goose Bay was a nightmare, the weather just barely above minimums ... We were in solid clouds and never got on top.

The 30th TRS was the last in order of flight and at least at Keflavik they found better weather conditions but their survival clothing left much to be desired. Hal Grant was flying an RB-26 of the 30th TRS:

What a beautiful sight, flying through the fiords on the way to the airfield. The aircrews were outfitted with cold water survival gear which consisted of a rubber suit that fitted tightly round the neck. We had to fly with one hand and hold the rubber collar away from our necks with the other. It was a real sweat suit.

The RF-80A pilots of the 302nd and 303rd TRS were amongst the most experienced tac recce drivers in the USAF. For example, of the twenty pilots assigned to the 303rd TRS, twelve, possibly more, had seen action in Korea. The commander of the squadron, Major Jean Woodyard had been one of the three pilots who had flown the first ever combat air refuelling mission into

RF-80A 44-85330 belongs to the 32nd TRS. It is also one of those converted to recce configuration from the P-80A. These aircraft are recognisable by the distinctive hump in the nose contours. (Bill Shell)

An RF-80A of the 303rd TRS refuels at Sembach in 1954. The 303rd markings were blue. The fuselage flash was not always present as in this example. Ed Stoltz)

North Korea. Approximately eight of the pilots had flown the RF-80 in combat with the 8th/15th TRS out of K14. Two others had flown RF-51 Mustangs with the 45th TRS and two had flown the LT-6 with the Mosquitoes, the 6147th Tactical Control Group. Bob Sweet of the 302nd TRS had flown all three aircraft in Korea.

The 66th was ready to commence operations from Sembach virtually on arrival at the base. On the 22 July, just three days after arrival, the RF-80s of the 302nd TRS began involvement in an operation requiring continuous oblique coverage of the Rhine River, and a small mosaic of the Munich area. July, August and September were to be particularly successful in mission terms. Relatively fine weather allowed a significant number of missions to be flown. The 85 per cent success rate in Operation Coronet, which commenced on the 23rd July, was remarkable. The three squadrons of the 66th in this exercise flew a total of 327 sorties: 261 day and 66 night. However, the pilots found the north European weather difficult to contend with at times. On the 16 August 1953, an RF-80 of the 302nd TRS made a forced landing in a field near Augsburg. The pilot had been cleared into marginal weather; but had got lost and

RF-80s of the 38th TRS, 10th TRW. One aircraft jumped its chocks at full power and rammed two others at full speed. (Bill Shell)

The RB-26s of the 30th TRS arrived at Sembach AB with the 66th TRW in July 1953 from Shaw AFB. (Ron Lang)

had run out of fuel. This accident prompted a grounding of all the wing's aircraft while an intensive training programme was initiated updating all pilots on what to expect from the weather in northern Europe. This proved to be time well spent. For the remainder of the year only one major accident occurred in the 66th TRW: an RF-80 skidded off the runway at Landstuhl. In this accident, however, pilot error was deemed not to have been the cause. Frank Meyer:

> The runways at the air bases were camouflaged to make it difficult for any unfriendly force to find … The problem was the material used to camouflage the runways grew a moss that caused a lot of problems. The result was to clear the camouflage.

The RF-80s operated by the 117th and subsequently the 10th TRWs were the older models and were not modified with the higher thrust J-33 engine. They also carried the 165 gallon tip tanks as opposed to the later 230 gallon tanks. By comparison with the aircraft flown by the 302nd and 303rd TRS this limited their speed and range. The aircraft of the 66th were the 15 models and all were modified with the higher spec. engine and the larger tip-tanks. However, even in the 66th

Under glowering skies this 30th TRS RB-26 is undergoing an engine test at Sembach. (Ron Lang)

In the snow at Hahn AB in the winter of 1954 this RB-26 has been deployed for an exercise. (Frank Street via Dave Menard)

TRW itself there were differences between the aircraft of the two squadrons. The 302nd aircraft differed from the 303rd in the radios they carried. The 302nd had 15 channel VHF sets and the 303rd the later multi-channel UHF sets. The latter would normally have been the preferred option, but many areas in Europe did not have the UHF capability and the 303rd was limited in the operations it could undertake. This difference between the radios sometimes made for communication difficulties! Ed Stoltz:

> On one occasion an RF-80 pilot, returning late, opted to land without the services of a tower. He made a call in the clear announcing he was landing to the east on the Sembach runway. A second pilot, returning at the same time, elected to do the same and made a call in the clear that he was landing on the Sembach west runway. The two pilots became aware

Three RB-26s of the 30th TRS at Sembach in 1954. The terrain of the base was very undulating which was the cause of many problems throughout its use by the 66th TRW. (Ron Lang)

of each other as they were nearing the halfway point on the runway! Luckily, they each cleared to their right and passed untouched on the runway. As might be guessed, one aircraft was equipped with UHF and one with VHF thus neither heard the other make a call for landing.

One of the problems facing USAFE command, having two similarly equipped tactical wings at its disposal, was to avoid mission and operations duplication. To this end it was decided in September, 1953, that, in general operations, the 10th would confine itself to working the allied zones of Germany, whereas the 66th would work the Allied zones of Austria. On the 2 September the 30th TRS was tasked with the long term mission of mapping the British, French and American zones of Austria using mosaic photography. The 303rd was requested to undertake a mosaic mapping of the Austrian Alps. Ed Stoltz was involved in the latter operation:

Ed Stoltz with RF-80A, 45-8412, Sembach, 1955. In common with many 66th TRW pilots Ed had flown the RF-80 in combat in Korea and joined the 66th prior to deployment to Germany (Ed Stoltz)

> I seem to recall there was some urgency in completing the mapping of the Austrian Alps. It had to be completed before the agreement with the USSR that removed all occupation forces from Austria. That agreement dictated that combat aircraft would no longer overfly Austria. After that agreement became effective, flights to Italy, Greece and Africa were made through France and across the Mediterranean. It was interesting that we could not fly the unarmed RF-80 across Austria but we could overfly with a T-33 capable of carrying two 50 calibre machine guns.

Deployments during the summer of 1953 took the 1st TRS to Cognac, France to give the Armée de L'Air a demonstration of night photography; and the 30th to Leeuwarden in the Netherlands to an air show celebrating forty years of the Royal Netherlands Air Force.

Late autumn and winter of 1953 brought appalling weather conditions to northern Europe and a multitude of problems to the tactical units of USAFE. The 66th TRW in particular initiated further extensive flying safety programmes for the pilots, and the mission backlog over this period became acute for both the 66th and the 10th TRWs. The mosaic mapping undertaken by the 1st TRS in Germany and the 30th and 302nd TRS in Austria had to be shelved until early Spring, 1954. The exercises undertaken in conjunction with the 7th Army were severely compromised in air support terms because the aircraft simply could not get off the ground. In Exercise Harvest

On the 10th Anniversary of the Dutch Air Force the 30th TRS took two RB-26s to Leeuwarden for the air show. The 30th TRS crews wave as an RAF Meteor taxies by after doing his display. (Roger Brunsvold)

Trying to get the better of the weather, this 1st TRS RB-26 at Spangdahlem is undergoing maintenance in new English portable docks. (10th TRW Historical Office USAF)

Moon for example, commencing on the 13th October, the 30th TRS was to fly visual reconnaissance, photo confirmation and simulated atomic bombing missions. In the event there was very little participation in this or Exercise Power Play in November, when the squadron had a similar mission. The problems with the RB-26s were mainly concerned with severe icing and the entire cold weather operation of the aircraft was undertaken at this time.

In addition to problems with the aircraft there were other, no less pressing difficulties prompted by the weather. The 10th reported shortages of survival clothing for pilots, particularly gloves. Cameras, especially those of the RF-80s, were very badly affected by the damp so as to be unusable until dried out in a 'hot box' one day a week. However there was still much that could be done in spite of the weather. A heavy emphasis was placed on ground training. Captain Mouth of the 36th Fighter Bomber Wing, a Korean War veteran, briefed the pilots of the 10th on the fighting tactics of the Mig 15. It must be borne in mind that, although the operations of the reconnaissance units apparently kept them away from the sensitive borders with the Warsaw Pact up to this time, the reality of hostilities had been brought sharply home when, in March 1953, two F-84 Thunderjets of a German based USAFE Fighter Bomber Wing had been attacked by Mig 15s over West German territory, resulting in the loss of one aircraft. This increasing threat from the Warsaw Pact, and the dawning realization in the Air Force that much of their hardware was rapidly becoming obsolete, led to the decision to upgrade the equipment of the 10th and the 66th TRWs as soon as possible. The 1st and 30th TRS' were to convert to the Martin RB-57A Canberra and the photo-jet squadrons were to trade in their RF-80s for the Republic RF-84F Thunderflash. These conversions were to take place through 1954 and into 1955. As 1953 drew to a close pilots from the RB-26 squadrons were being checked-out on their respective Wings T-33 aircraft prior to checking on the RB-57. The prospect of converting from the Invader to the Canberra was greeted with mixed feelings. Hal Grant:

With the aid of a besom broom this 1st TRS RB-26 is getting a clean-up at Spang. (10th TRW Historical Office USAF)

The 42nd TRS joined the 10th TRW at Spangdahlem in March 1954. Its RB-26s carried a variety of aerials and sensors to enable it to carry out its ELINT mission. The tail markings were red with a white arrow. (Arthur Pearcy)

> I think maybe the biggest problem was morale, or fear. The B-57 was having one of the highest accident rates of any aircraft absorbed into the Air Force inventory. We discussed the accident reports in great detail in an attempt to prevent the same happening to us … an RB-57 was being flown into Sembach for familiarization of our crews. Unfortunately it crashed on final approach with all the 30th crews observing the accident. A short time later, the Air Force had Pat Tibbs, a test pilot with Martin, come to Sembach and put on an aerial demonstration and what a demonstration it was! He made the RB-57 do everything but talk. This helped morale tremendously.

On the 18th March, 1954, a new squadron joined the 10th Tactical Reconnaissance Wing at Spangdahlem. This was the 42nd TRS and its mission was 'to provide ground air and naval forces in areas of joint air-ground operations with information concerning the location and character of electronic emissions; and instrumented weather reconnaissance.' On activation the squadron had no aircraft assigned. The first RB-26 arrived on 18 June. The 42nd was divided into two flights: weather (Flight A) and electronic reconnaissance (Flight B). The unit had to wait awhile for their specially equipped electronic aircraft. It was not until December of 1954 that the first aircraft was assigned. A Flight had received its full complement of weather reconnaissance '26s much earlier. However on the 23 December a violent storm severely damaged a hangar roof at Spang' and two of the flight's RB-26s 44-34385 and 44-35858 were badly damaged. RB-26 44-35858 was later transferred to the 30th TRS at Sembach. Weather observers were checked out at the 53rd Weather

RF-80A, 44-85330 of the 38th TRS at Spangadahlem in 1954. (Capt. J. Smith via Dave Menard)

An RF-80A 45-8391 aircraft over the Rhine near Weisbaden in September 1955. Pilot is 1st Lieutenant Robert H. Clarke. The markings were the final scheme worn by 38th TRS RF-80s. (Dick Cathriner)

Reconnaissance Squadron at Burtonwood in the United Kingdom prior to their taking up active duty. The fact that the 42nd was equipping with the RB-26 when the 1st and 30th squadrons were relinquishing these aircraft in favour of he RB-57 may seem paradoxical. Realistically, the electronics mission of the 42nd's 'B' Flight required a platform of the type and size that only the RB-26 would fit. Indeed the aircraft continued with the squadron until the winter of 1956 when it was replaced by the Douglas RB-66C. The weather flight gave up their Invaders earlier, replacing them with WT-33s in 1955.

The replacement of both the 10th and 66th's aircraft was a priority throughout 1954. A general inspection of the 10th in May of that year acknowledged that the wing could not possibly perform it's mission satisfactorily in wartime because of obsolete and worn out aircraft, outdated camera equipment and poor depot support for spares. In March alone the accident rate for the RF-80s of the 32nd TRS bears testimony to the obviously acute problems with these aircraft. On the 5 March 45-8549 caught fire over Belgium. The pilot, Second Lieutenant Thomas J. Squire fortunately succeeded in parachuting to safety, avoiding the subsequent explosion which destroyed his aircraft. On the 12 March Lieutenant William T. Rodenbach barely succeeded in landing his RF-80 after losing an engine access door. On the 20th March 45-8465 crashed at Bitburg, killing the pilot.

The 66th fared better than the 10th in terms of accidents. In contrast to the bad luck of the 32nd, the 302nd was the only jet unit in USAFE to be accident free in the six months from December, 1953 to May, 1954. However, the jet photo squadrons of both wings looked forward to the transition to the RF-84F. Mobile Training Detachments (MTD) were set up at Spangdahlem for pilot and ground crew training on

What every RF-80 driver was wearing that year! 1st Lieutenant Howard Goldie mounts up at Sembach. (Frank Meyer)

A photo signed by 302nd TRS mascot 'Lesterbury'. His RF-80A has its own distinctive nose art. (Roger Brunsvold)

both the RF-84F and the RB-57. Pilots from both wings attended the courses at Spang' in addition to observers, mechanics, camera specialists and hydraulics specialists.

Operations during early 1954 were adversely affected by the weather but by spring the conditions had improved enough to allow a relatively high number of missions to be flown. By 30 June TRS had completed 65 per cent of it's Austrian mission. The 302nd TRS took part in Exercise Blue Danube which involved 28 sorties being flown. Four aircraft from the 302nd detached to Vaerlose in Denmark for a joint training exercise with the Danish Air Force. Also detached to Vaerlose at this time was the 1st TRS, which sent six RB-26 aircraft to commence the formidable task of photographing all of Denmark. This mission was to involve 206 hours of flying covering 22,242 miles of flight line. The 303rd TRS deployed to Geibelstadt on the 6 May for five days for what was effectively the first NATO tactical reconnaissance competition: the first Royal Flush. In addition to photographing some 21-army required targets and fifteen weather reconnaissance missions; the unit was given the task of taking oblique pin-point photographs of castles and other places of interest in Germany for publicity purposes. In August the 303rd detached to Gros Tenquin in France for Exercise falling Leaf. The

Lt Col Jack Graham and navigator prepare to climb aboard the first RB-57A assigned to the 1st TRS at Spangdahlem. Graham was the commander of the 1st TRS. (10th TRW Historical Office USAF)

weather was appalling during the period of the exercise and unfortunately claimed the life of First Lieutenant Jim Parmalee when his RF-80 collided with a hill.

On the 24th October, 1954 the first RB-57A arrived for the 1st TRS at Spangdahlem. Sadly on the same day an RB-26 of the squadron crashed. The aircraft took off and subsequently crashed at the end of the runway and burst into flames, killing all crew members instantly. Apparently, for no explicable reason, the pilot had attempted to abort take-off after he had become airborne with disastrous results. Bob Webster, a pilot with the 1st TRS witnessed the accident:

> This guy took off on 23 from mid-point and the tower said he actually got in the air a bit and called that he was aborting. He probably only had 1000 ft at most left. The 26 went off the overrun and there was a bit of a cliff then a downhill field. However, they had stacks of PSP piled up about 4 to 5 feet high and you don't push that stuff very far. The clerk and I were the only ones in our ops when we got the call and we beat the fire truck to the wreck. The front end stopped and the back end broke off and went a bit further. There wasn't much left of the cockpit. My navigator, Ted Miller, was in the nose.

This accident was ironic; not only that it occurred on the very day the new aircraft arrived at the base, but also, three months earlier, on 31 July, the squadron had received a commendation for having flown 15,000 hours without a minor or major accident.

The weather predictably played havoc with the mission success of the squadrons in November and December of 1954 and into the early months of 1955. Coupled with this, the serviceability of the RF-80s was becoming a problem. The 303rd TRS took part in Exercise West Wind with a primary mission of visual reconnaissance; in this instance, spotting the 280mm cannons used by both friendly and aggressor forces. In an unofficial competition Ed Stoltz was the winner:

> These (the 280mm cannons) were the first designed to fire an atomic shell. Twelve of the 280s were deployed to Europe and as I recall there were six on the friendly and six on the

A beautiful aerial shot of a 1st TRS RB-26 over the German countryside (Bob Webster)

aggressor side during Exercise West Wind. The 66th TRG C.O., Colonel Harvey Henderson, was flying my wing when the six aggressor weapons were located. What was not reported is that we also located four of the friendly weapons as well. The huge 280mm cannon was very heavy and very difficult for the army to manoeuvre and hide. Off road they left deep ruts and were easy to track across the fields. Although Colonel Henderson was impressed by the sightings I should point out that had there been AAA in the area locating the weapons would have been hazardous and far more difficult.

Lying prone, Charlie Smith is in the navigator's position in a 1st TRS RB-26. (Bob Webster)

The RB-26 squadrons were finding night missions and training difficult. Routine operations using photo flash bombs and cartridges were carried out on the Baumholder range, but the time allocated did not allow the crews to maintain efficiency. Other methods were adopted. Hal Grant:

> Although we were somewhat restricted on actual night photo missions, we did a lot of training in which we simulated night training. We were using Shoran as our means of navigation which meant flying an arc to the target. Crews were assigned targets and photographed them in the day using Shoran for navigation.

The 30th TRS deployed to North Africa for much of their training with flash bombs and cartridges. Kermit Helmke flew with the squadron and recalls the early days of deployment to Wheelus:

> One bit of real estate that was given consideration was some desert east of Wheelus AB near Tripoli, Libya. I drew the mission of flying the area cover as the front navigator. Our crew had the co-ordinates of the area. The only maps available were the 1:500,000 sectionals. Fortunately, there was a paved road running east and west along the northern

All RB-26 aircraft were transitioned out of USAFE via Manchester, England. Here Bob Helfrich is ferrying 889 to England en route back to the USA. (Bob Webster)

In October 1954 the 1st TRS deployed aircraft to La Var airport at Nice. Their mission was to search for a C-47 which had gone missing. An RB-26 from the 30th TRS was also deployed there. (Bob Webster)

> boundary. It was obvious that a photo one-way race track pattern was called for. We discovered that the palms on the south side of the highway were evenly spaced so we counted them to start successive runs. Not as precise as the GPS to-day, but it worked. When the photos were laid out, all the sand dunes lined up. The mission was complete.

Four RB-26s of the 1st TRS were detached to La Var airfield at Nice in the south of France for a period from the 25 October to the 1 November and were involved in the search for a missing C-47 out of Weisbaden. The aircraft was extremely difficult to find and two further RB-26s from the 30th TRS were drafted in. Eventually it was located 30 miles north of Nice where it had crashed on a mountain range. It had crashed on to a slope and slid down onto a shelf; which is why it had been so difficult to locate.

The beginning of 1955 saw the RB-57 and the RF-84F MTDs based at Sembach. This was useful because yet again the weather severely restricted flying, and the opportunity to become involved in ground training of all kinds was a welcome one. March produced uncharacteristically fine weather and all the reconnaissance units flew a high number of missions. The 38th, 302nd and 303rd TRS broke all previous records in terms of missions flown. At this time the 303rd was tasked with photographing and maintaining a portfolio of 'scenic' targets in Germany. Also during March six more RB-57s arrived for the 1st TRS; ferried in over the Northern route. Regrettably there were two unfortunate incidents involving the newly acquired RB-57s in early 1955. On the 9th February, an aircraft of the 30th TRS suffered considerable damage on taking off from Sembach when it slid to a long stop along the runway. The pilot had raised the gear before the aircraft had become completely airborne.

On the 1 March, 1955, one pilot from each of the photo-jet squadrons was detached to Shaw AFB in South Carolina for check-out on the RF-84F. Upon their return to their squadrons they would be Instructor Pilots (IPs) for their respective units. The pilots were First Lieutenants Bob Sweet, 302nd TRS; Ed Stoltz, 303rd TRS, Gustav Klatt, 38th TRS; and Lieutenant Conine of the 32nd TRS. The four were sent to join the 18th TRS. The pilots returned to their respective squadrons in early April feeling very well qualified on the new aircraft, but with some reservations. Bob Sweet:

> One bit of information that Ed Stoltz and I brought back which was not greeted with enthusiasm was we felt that in a close engagement with a Mig 17 we might come out second best.

The RF-84F was nicknamed the 'Super Hog' and was aptly named. It was underpowered and although it had an excellent range and cruise performance, the engines never came close to matching the airframe, which was robust in the tradition of all Republic aircraft. It is unfortunate that the J-65 engine of the RF-84F was chosen instead of another giving 9,000 lb of thrust. Allegedly politics played it's part in this decision.

The Armed Forces day on the 17th May at Sembach was marred when an RB-57 of the 1st TRS crashed preparatory to a display approach. Both crew members were killed: Captain Wallace

The 302nd TRS 'Bald Iggles' in a dive. The slot man, Lieutenant Russ Tansey often had to take the photos of his fellow Iggles because it was difficult to get someone else to hold formation. The other members of the team were Capt Bob Kilpatrick, Lieutenant Tom Whitworth and Capt Bob Sweet. (Bob Sweet)

Rodecker and First Lieutenant John P. Nodine. The event, though upset by this tragic accident, was marked by a display by the 302nd TRS display team, 'The Bald Iggles'. The 'Iggles' were Captain Bob Sweet, Lieutenant Russ Tansey, First Lieutenant Tim Whitworth and Captain Robert Kilpatrick. Formation flying in the RF-80 was not easy. It was for this reason that there are few photos of the full team in existence. Most extant photos of three of the team were taken by Lieutenant Tansey. They couldn't find anyone else to hold formation with them to take the four ship photos. Bob Sweet:

> Formation flying in the early '80s was a challenge ... During a climb a pilot would need to be throttling back in order to maintain a specific rpm and to prevent exceeding 100 per cent at high altitudes. Only a very limited throttle movement was available between idle and 100 per cent. Slow acceleration and limited thrust made formation flying, close or loose, hard work requiring considerable anticipation.

Regrettably, the 'Bald Iggles' was a short-lived aerobatic team and disbanded shortly after the Armed Forces day performance.

Exercise *Carte Blanche* in June 1955 was one of the largest exercises ever staged by the NATO alliance. It was designed to test the latest concepts in dispersal, tactical air control and execution of alert plans in the event of an atomic war. For the purposes of this exercise the 12th Air Force and the 4th Allied Tactical Air Force (ATAF) of NATO were pitted against the forces of the 2nd ATAF. The 10th TRW was not involved in this exercise, but the 66th was; providing reconnaissance for the 4th ATAF.

Carte Blanche commenced on the 20 June. The 303rd TRS deployed to Echterdingen near Stuttgart; while the 30th and 302nd remained at Sembach. In these initial days the function of all these units was picket duty. The RB-26s and RF-80s patrolled an arbitrary bomb line and reported all aircraft crossing that line. In the early morning of 23 June Condition Coco was declared. Hostilities had broken out at precisely 0450 hours! Within minutes the first reconnaissance missions were being flown. Throughout the exercise the squadrons of the 66th flew a total of 613 missions.

The benefits to the 66th of this exercise in terms of experience was considerable. One of the most significant of these underlined just how much needed was the eagerly awaited

The 'Iggles' at the top of a loop. They were a short lived aerobatic team; disbanding after one air show. (Bob Sweet)

Jim Tansey of the 302nd TRS 66th TRW poses beside his RF-80A and his Austin Healey at Sembach. (Bob Sweet)

RF-84 by the RF-80 squadrons. The RF-80s had flown alone and had proved very vulnerable to interception by the opposing fighters; pilots admitting that they would have lost some fourteen aircraft. Interceptions were invariably in pairs or fours. Very often, because they were working at maximum range, the only option the RF-80 had was to run for home, having no fuel reserves for evasive manoeuvring.

In the light of the exercise the 303rd TRS put together a number of recommendations on the tactical use of the RF-80A. The aircraft should have a total combat radius of no more than 400 miles. This would ensure that sufficient fuel reserves were available for some degree of evasive action. The reconnaissance missions should always be undertaken in pairs; the wingman being responsible for watching the skies for hostile aircraft. It was also concluded that some aggressive training in evasion tactics should be undertaken as a matter of urgency.

Significantly, in the event of a real war having been fought, the 303rd would have been in no position to make any recommendations. On the 24 June, enemy reconnaissance flew over Echterdingen and with their departure came the likelihood of an atomic strike. The squadron commander immediately dispatched a message to HQ, 66th TRW announcing his intention to move the entire squadron to an autobahn strip south of Stuttgart. In a simulated exercise the aircraft would fly along the autobahn until a suitable dispersal site was found; and the vehicles would follow by driving along the route until they found the aircraft. According to the timing the last RF-80 would have been airborne when the expected A Bomb struck. However, the umpires, while congratulating the ingenuity of the commander, declared the squadron annihilated!

The transition to the RF-84 took some time with the IPs having to maintain currency on the type by visiting RAF Bentwaters and flying the 81st FBW F-84Fs. The first two aircraft were collected from Marseille and flown to Sembach on the 5 August, 1955. In a cruel twist of fate, Ed Stoltz was sick at the time and so the 303rd aircraft, 51-19897, was flown by the squadron commander, Major James Shannon. It was his first flight in an RF-84F! Bob Sweet flew in the 302nd aircraft, 51-1841. The 32nd and 38th TRS had fared somewhat better. By the end of 1955 the 32nd had received seven and the 38th four of the aircraft.

The programme of conversion to the Thunderflash suffered a setback for the 302nd when one of their two aircraft, piloted by Major Aloysius P. McHugh suffered a loss of power at height. Major McHugh succeeded in recovering the aircraft and made a dead-stick landing at Landstuhl.

RF-84F 51-1841 was the first to be received by the 302nd TRS and was flown into Sembach by Bob Sweet. (Bob Sweet)

It was one of his first flights in the RF-84 and Bob Sweet was his chase pilot in an RF-80:

> … it was tough just keeping visual contact. However the traffic pattern and landing were the main events to monitor. At around 15,000 ft Mac called out that he had flamed out. I closed up and we went through three air start attempts with no response. Mac indicated he was going to eject. We were at a point which would be a high downwind leg for Landstuhl AB. I told him to turn base leg and Landstuhl tower, aware of the emergency, cleared him to land either direction but downwind was the only option left. I made sure the airspeed stayed up so the '84 wouldn't sink from under him. The gear came down on short final and he touched down just short of the runway barrier, going through it the wrong way. The '84 sliced through the tape and roll out was just great until the nose came down and the nose gear folded. It had not extended quite all the way.

The accident certainly confirmed the robustness of the airframe. The nose section was repaired and back in commission in a short time. The repair involved skinning over the lower camera port, but, as the initial training did not involve any photo work, this was acceptable.

Conversion to the RB-57 for the 1st and 30th TRS proceeded apace during 1955. The 30th TRS had completed to the type by the end of the year, possessing 17 RB-57As and one B-57C dual trainer. The 1st TRS did not complete conversion until mid 1956. It was a busy time for the aircrews. Hal Grant:

> The pilots were required to check out in the T-33 and accumulate about twenty hours of flying time in that aircraft before getting checked out in the RB-57. I remember one day flying the RB-26 in the morning, the T-33 in the afternoon and the RB-57 that night. Really

Another shot of 841 over Germany on one of its initial flights with the squadron. (Bob Sweet)

In addition to the RB-57As the USAFE Canberra units also had two B-57Cs each. 53-3850 'Nite Mare' belonged to the 1st TRS and was flown by Will Johnson. (Bob Webster)

enjoyed that, but it didn't last long. Due to lousy weather we sent several crews to Sidi Slimane for check-out in the '57s.

The RB-57s were ferried from the States by the squadron crews who had gone over to pick them up. For example: on 25 August five pairs of pilots and navigators of the 30th TRS travelled stateside to be followed by two more pairs on the 11 September. Three of these crews returned to Sembach on the 15 September with their aircraft; the remaining four crews returning shortly afterwards.

The first RB-57s of both the 1st and the 30th TRS did not have the rotating bomb bay fitted. The cameras were located in the rear of the standard bomb bay, thus leaving space for other ordnance to be carried, including photoflash bombs for night photography. It was intended for the RB-57 to have a dual role, it's primary function being tactical reconnaissance, but it's capability including weapons delivery.

The first five RB-26s to leave the 1st TRS line up at Manchester Airport in the UK. (Bob Webster)

The first RB-57 Canberra for the 30th TRS was 52-1426, seen here on the ramp at Sembach. (Ron Lang)

The B-57C differed considerably from the A in having the tandem seating and bubble canopy typical of all later models, and in spite of their 'non combatant' role they retained an offensive capability, carrying four 20mm guns and, like the RB-57A, four hard points on each wing for the carriage of ordnance. All models also had the rotating bomb bay.

1st TRS RB-26s were rotated back to the United States via Manchester airport, England.

The RB-57 proved troublesome from the start. On the 29 January, 1956, all the aircraft were grounded due to a faulty jack screw in the elevator trim control. This grounding lasted until the 20 February. The 30th TRS, on detachment to Wheelus at this time on Operation Sunflash, had to be relieved by the 303rd TRS who sent out four RF-80s to complete the mission, which involved the supporting the guided missile squadrons and reporting on weather, range clearance and photographing missile impact. Ninety-nine missions were flown between the 31 January and the 24 March. Later in the year, in May, the RB-57s were grounded again in common with all USAF

B-57C 53-3852 of the 30th TRS, 66th TRW. The C models were not equipped with cameras and were used as trainers and familiarisation aircraft. This aircraft carries the earlier chevron markings of the 66th TRW. The yellow fuselage bands are exercise markings. (Roger Brunsvold)

B-57s. This grounding lasted for two months and was caused by faulty actuators which had to be replaced.

Meanwhile, the 42nd TRS continued to develop its operational capability. During 1955 all weather flight RB-26s were exchanged for WT-33s. One of the first missions undertaken by these aircraft was the overflying of French airstrips in order to provide the relevant authorities with weather data. French Air Traffic Controllers were on strike!

The Electronics Flight soldiered on with its increasingly sophisticated RB-26s. Regular flights were flown by these aircraft; listening for electronic emissions, searching for radar and other

Wheels up immediately after rotating at Spangdahlem, this RB-57A does carry the squadron markings on the tail. (Bob Webster)

The old and the new. A 303rd TRS RF-80A flies in formation with two of the newly arrived RF-84Fs. (Frank Simons)

A 1st TRS RB-57A 52-1481 lands at Spangdahlem (Frank Street via Dave Menard)

sources. Echo route was the Mediterranean; Alpha, the North Sea; Bravo, from Spangdahlem to Marseilles; and Coco Special, the Bay of Biscay. During Exercise Beware for example, in which the squadron was a member of the aggressor team, they flew the Alpha route; probing the UK's electronic and radar air defence systems. In addition to involvement in exercises the duties of the 42nd were to respond to the demands of USAF operational orders where their particular expertise was needed. Order 331-5527, for example was to calibrate the Bitburg call sign. A detachment to Sidi Slimane in French Morocco was detailed to pinpoint all American radar sites in the area. This was essentially a fair weather exercise primarily for aircrew familiarization.

1956 began with the usual inclement north European weather severely restricting the missions of all the USAFE recce units. The jet-photo squadrons had a particular problem in that many operations had to be cancelled or curtailed due to the necessity of maintaining combat readiness in the RF-80 whilst transitioning to the RF-84. One such example of this was when a flight of four 66th RF-80s was detached to Bodo, Norway to photograph 183 isolated and widely dispersed targets. This mission had to be cancelled after only 25 per cent had been accomplished. The RF-80s were needed back at Sembach.

By mid 1956 both the 10th and the 66th TRWs had converted from the RF-80 to the RF-84. The introduction of the programme was not without its problems. The 303rd TRS reported in December, 1955, how the transition was being hampered by the usual adverse European weather.

51-1862 was the second of the RF-84Fs received by the 302nd TRS. The fuselage bands represent the colours of the 66th Squadron. (Bob Sweet)

An RF-84F of the 302nd TRS undergoing maintenance at Sembach in 1957. The 66th TRW adopted the new markings in that year. Both the 302nd and 303rd retained their red and blue colours. The 30th TRS colour was yellow. (USAF)

The 32nd reported shortages of spare parts and personal survival equipment. All aircraft experienced problems with the liquid oxygen system. Such were the problems for the 38th TRS that some of their aircraft awaiting repair were transferred to the 32nd TRS and temporarily replaced with RF-80s! For pilots who had for so long awaited the arrival of the Thunderflash, this was a bitter pill to swallow. It was not comforting for them to know that they were only 15 minutes from a

Captain Jack Coghlan flies RF-84F 51-17007 over Germany in 1956. Jack Coghlan was the Operations Officer for the 303rd TRS. (Ed Stoltz)

Another shot of 007 with Jack Coghlan at the controls. (Ed Stoltz)

The pilot makes some last minute cockpit checks on 862 before taking off for a mission. One of the squadrons RF-80s can be seen in the background. (Roger Brunsvold)

potential enemy when they flew the RF-80 on a regular basis. To have to return to it after experiencing the relative security of the RF-84 technology was a blow.

Regrettably there were a number of accidents in the early days of the Thunderflash. An RF-84F of the 32nd TRS, piloted by Captain Parnell, flamed out at 30,000 ft when on a routine instrument training flight over North Italy. Captain Parnell descended and succeeded in restarting his engine. He found a suitable field in which to land when his engine persisted in behaving erratically. He

Four 38th TRS RF-84s fl over a snow covere German landscape in th winter of 1956. Th notorious north Europea weather played havo with the transition trainin of all the RF-84 squadron in USAFE, (USAF vi Mort Cameron)

A formation of four 38th TRS RF-84Fs. There were many teething troubles for the RF-84s in the very early days, but in spite of these both the 10th and the 66th TRWs had fully converted to the aircraft by the middle of 1956. (USAF via Mort Cameron)

A lone RF-84F of the 38th TRS flies high over the German countryside. (USAF via Ron Colpron)

RF-84Fs of the 32nd and 38th TRS line up. The 32nd colours were red and yellow and the 38th, blue and red. (Frank Street via Dave Menard)

RF-84F 003 of the 38th TRS parked on the ramp at Pisa Air Base, Italy, in July 1956. This is the only RF-84F in the 38th Tac Recon Squadron that was equipped with two 230 gallon external fuel tanks (All of our other RF-84F's were equipped with two 450 gallon class II external tanks that were capable of withstanding speeds up to 1.175 Mach.) This airplane was assigned to 1/Lt John Falk, and has his name on the canopy rail. (Dick Cathriner)

Another view of 003 at Pisa. (Dick Cathriner)

The 38th TRS had access to the services of a very good cartoonist who immortalised their aircraft and their role in these two drawings. (Ron Colpron)

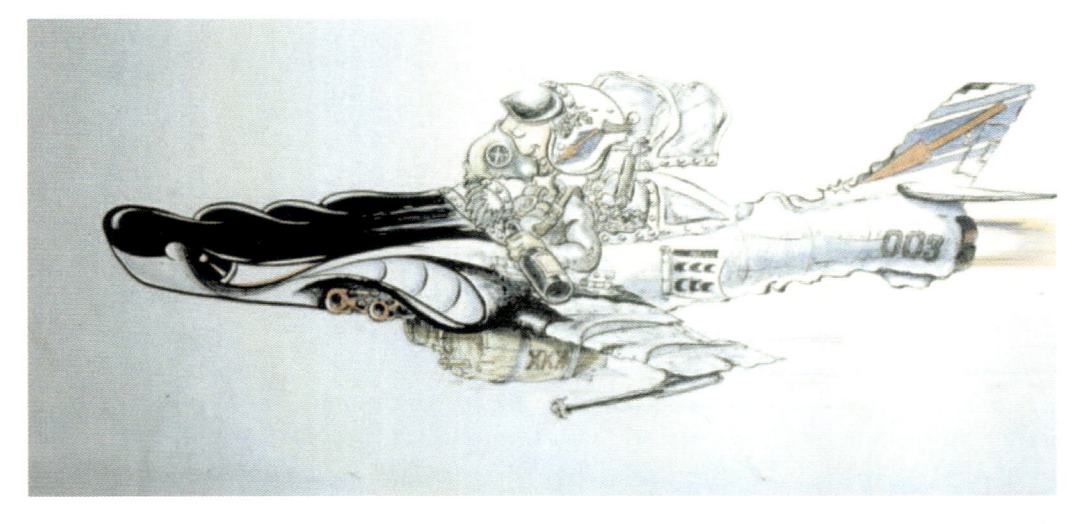

crash landed with relative ease and unscathed. However, when exiting from his stricken aircraft, his foot accidentally knocked the ejector mechanism and he was rushed to hospital suffering from a broken left leg and pelvic bone.

The 302nd TRS was stunned by the death of one of its best known pilots when, on the 26 June 1956, First Lieutenant James 'Russ' Tansey was killed when his aircraft went into a spin from which he could not recover some 26 miles from Sembach. The aircraft hit the ground and the pilot was killed. As a result of this accident all pilots were rebriefed on the spin characteristics of the RF-84F.

Pilots of both the 10th and 66th TRW RF-84s had to complete gunnery training. To those veterans of the RF-80, this was something very new. The RF-84F was unique in post-war jet-photo recce aircraft in that it was the last to be fitted with guns. These were four .5 calibre machine guns. Pilots had for some time argued for the inclusion of guns in the recce aircraft, including Clyde East:

This feature was built into the RF-84F at the insistence of several the Second World War recce pilots (including me) that found the guns of the RF-51 very useful for target designation and found the lack of such a system in the RF-80 to be a severe hindrance in Korea.

Paul Hodges, who flew the RF-84F with the 303rd TRS says of the later decision to abandon guns in recce aircraft:

> … later arguments in the air force went something like, if you put guns in a recce aircraft the pilot is going to look for something to shoot rather than take pictures, guns being more fun than cameras. (Quite true). In addition, it costs more, complicates training, increases aircraft weight, and recce aircraft are supposed to be light, fast and dedicated. So who needs guns?

The venue chosen for the gunnery training was Caseaux in France. The 66th first deployed there in November and December 1956. This was the first time that a tactical reconnaissance unit of USAFE flying jet-fighter type aircraft had ever been involved in aerial gunnery training operations. Basically the course entailed familiarization in low level strafing techniques against mesh nylon targets. The 32nd and 38th TRS of the 10th TRW deployed to Caseaux in January 1957. Regrettably bad weather played havoc with their schedule. High winds wiped out three days of the training.

In September, 1956, a major NATO exercise took place. Codenamed Whipsaw the purpose of the exercises to test, practise and evaluate current plans for the employment of nuclear weapons and the forces of Allied Europe. The exercise took place between the 25 and the 28 September. All the squadrons of both Wings took part. The principal missions were to fly pre-strike, post-strike and weather recce. Inevitably poor weather curtailed many of the missions, but, in spite of this, the 66th TRW notched up an impressive total of 118 sorties. The 30th TRS deployed to Echterdingden for the exercise which was, for them, a test of their mobility capabilities as much as their mission capabilities. Hal Grant:

> We equipped the squadron with quite a number of large trailers, the type you see being hauled on the highways. We put many of our maintenance shops into these trailers. When they blew the whistle to commence Exercise Whipsaw, the 30th TRS looked like Barnum and Bailey circus moving down the highway. All of the exercise was conducted under field conditions, tents etc. After our base was hit by a bomb we surprised the umpire by recovering aircraft on the autobahn. We had previously done reconnaissance of the area and found stretches of the autobahn long enough to accommodate RB-57 aircraft.

The 30th flew 33 bombing sorties against 54 targets all of which were successfully hit.

The 42nd TRS, 10th TRW flew only four missions during *Whipsaw*; the weather duly taking it's toll of the remainder. Their brief was to confirm existing target data on known radar sites, locate gun laying equipment, locate height finding equipment and early warning sites. This was to be the last full scale exercise involving the Invaders. Just prior to *Whipsaw*, on the 21st September, Spangdahlem had seen the installation of the Douglas RB-66 Destroyer simulator. Both the 1st and the 42nd TRS were to convert to the new aircraft. Nonetheless, in November, the 42nd began a regular deployment of two RB-26s to Pisa, Italy. The missions flown were along the Yugoslavian and Albanian borders searching for Dumbo, Knigerest and Token Soviet radars.

October, 1956, saw the annual NATO reconnaissance competition Royal Flush staged at Lahr in Germany from the 17th through to the 19th. USAFE was represented by the 30th and 303rd TRS supporting the 4th ATAF team. The competition involved both high and low photographic sorties. The 303rd RF-84F flown by First Lieutenant John Robertson won the low level competition, and First Lieutenant Ronald A. Krzan from the 30th TRS flew his RB-57 into second place in the high level competition. The 4th ATAF was the overall winner. John Robertson was a pilot of exceptional ability as Ed Stoltz recalls:

Camera bay maintenance on an RF-84F of the 38th TRS at Spangdahlem in 1957. (USAF)

During our RF-84F operation John, or 'Robbie' as all called him, had an engine failure on final approach to the Sembach runway. He was on a practice GCA approach at the time of the failure. Both the GCA operators and the control tower members estimated the RF-84 was at or below 600 ft when Robbie ejected. The RF-84 pilot ejection system was designed to permit survival at very low altitude but to be fully effective an 'automatic' parachute was required that connected to the seat firing mechanism. The squadron had not been issued with the new chutes, therefore we were flying with the older manual release chutes. We learned after the accident that Robbie flew without removing a safe pin installed in the ejection system handle. This safe pin was to be removed during cockpit pre-flight but

On the 9th October 1955 this RB-57A 52-1485 overshot and ended up in the ditch at Spang. (USAF via Bob Webster)

Smile please! As this 302nd TRS RF-84F breaks right it displays its camera windows to perfection. (Ed Stoltz)

Robbie elected not to do so as he had lost a friend by 'accidental' ejection from a parked airplane. When the engine failed Robbie said he pulled the flag attached to the safe pin, squeezed the ejection handle, pulled the ripcord and hit the trees all in quick succession. It appeared his parachute did not completely open and the shock of landing was absorbed by the chute canopy catching in tree limbs. Robbie landed in a French manoeuvre area and was immediately plucked from the tree and rushed to the hospital for treatment. Robbie probably was the only one in the 303rd quick enough in thought and action to have survived this low ejection under the conditions described.

RF-84F of the 38th TRS on the landing roll after touching down at about 155 Kts. The 38th participated in a "simulated forward air operation" in July 1956, at Hahn Air Base. The pilots lived in tents, and the squadron's mobile vans were brought along for aircraft support. The RF-84F's were dispersed on hard stands on the west side of the field, away from all permanent facilities. (Dick Cathriner)

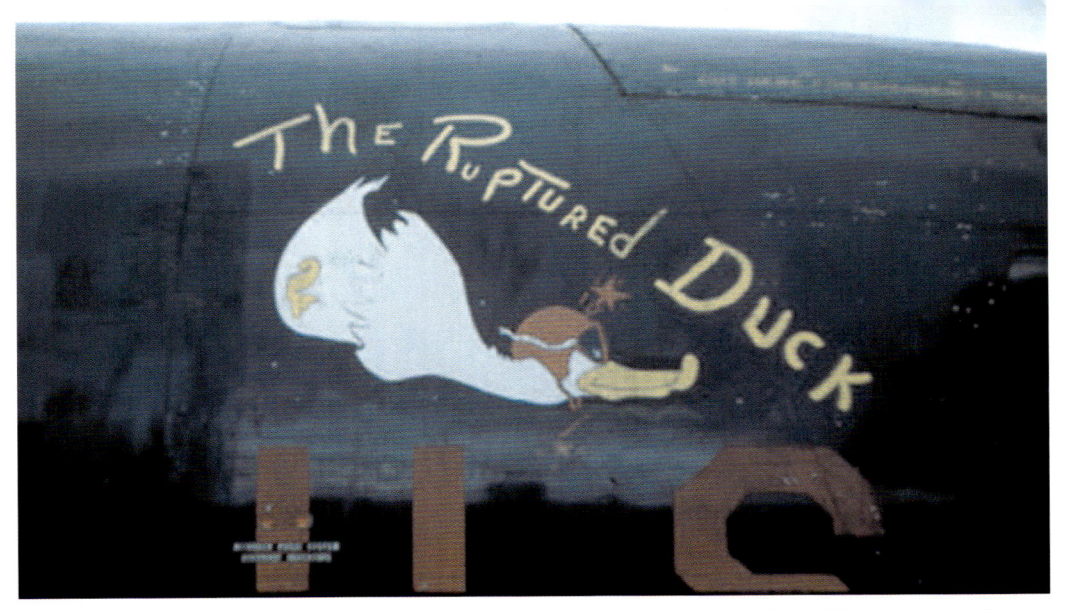

Appropriate nose art was applied to 52-1485 after its unfortunate accident. 'The Ruptured Duck'. (Bob Webster)

Sadly Robbie's luck did not hold out. Many years later he was flying an F-4C over Vietnam when he was shot down. He remains Missing in Action.

On the 28 November, 1956, the first RB-66 arrived at Spangdahlem. Originally it had been intended to equip the 1st TRS with the new aircraft first, but, in the event, the first Destroyer to arrive was a 'C' model and so went to the 42nd. The RB-66C differed from the RB-66B in having a pressurized compartment built into the bomb bay for four ECM operators and their specialized equipment comprising rapid scan receivers, panoramic receivers, pulse analysers, direction finders and a wire recorder. Under the wingtips the RB-66C also carried AN/APD-4 antenna pods. The RB-66s were ferried to Spangdahlem from Robins AFB by 47th BW crews stationed at RAF Sculthorpe in the United Kingdom. Paradoxically, on arrival at the German base they were immediately grounded. There were no fully trained crews to fly them!

The 19th TRS equipped with the RB-45C Tornado joined the 66th TRW in January, 1957. The squadron began converting to the RB-66 in February. In this photograph the RB-45C is in the company of one of the squadrons T-33s. (Ray Schrecengost)

RB-45C on the tarmac at RAF Sculthorpe where they were based with the 47th BW. When the squadron was assigned to the 66th TRW, it remained in the UK while it converted to the RB-66. (USAF)

RB-45C 8027. The Tornadoes of the 19th had originally belonged to SAC and had taken part in some of the clandestine overflights of Soviet Europe in the early 1950s. (USAF)

When the 19th converted to the RB-66 their RB-45s passed to the 84th BS of the 47th BW. 48-035 was photographed at Wethersfield Armed Forces Day in June 1957. (Mick Stroud)

Known as wad poling the polishing and cleaning of the RB-66s was not solely for appearance sake. Corrosion was found on several new arrivals to the 19th TRS when they arrived at Sculthorpe. (USAF)

This 66th TRW T-33 has gone the same way as RB-57A 'Ruptured Duck'. All wings had a contingent of T-33s for general purpose work. They were used extensively in the jet training given to pilots converting to jet aircraft with no previous jet time. (Frank Meyer)

The RB-57A was replaced by the RB-66B in the 1st TRS commencing in late 1956. Their RB-57s were put to extensive use at this time providing valuable multi jet time to the pilots of the 42nd TRS, who were replacing their aging RB-26s with RB-66Cs. (Thomas Cress via Dave Menard)

The end of 1956 saw the RB-66 simulator based at Sembach in preparation for the 30th TRS to convert to the type due in 1957. The RB-57As career in USAFE was to be short indeed. During December the 66th pilots were involved in some official 'happy snapping' for *Paris Match* who were doing a pictorial piece on aerial reconnaissance.

Although scheduled for replacement the RB-57 squadrons were kept as busy as ever in the final months of 1956. One operation which is of particular interest in that it accentuated the dual role of the RB-57 was Twelfth Air Force Operations Order 607-56 which required a series of low oblique photographs to be made of training targets for the low altitude bombing system (LABS); more commonly known as 'toss bombing.' The recce runs were made at 1,000 and 10,000 ft and resulted in a picture portrayal of the actual bomb run to be made with the terrain features clearly defined. This enabled B-57 crew briefing to be made much more effectively and clearly. Regrettably Exercise Sabre Knot, which took place from the 2 to the 9 November, 1956, clearly demonstrated the shortcomings of the aircraft. This exercise, in support of the 7th Army, required an operating ceiling of below 3000 ft. The restrictions placed on the RB-57s following the groundings early in the year prohibited them from taking part. It was one of several factors that led to the decision to replace them.

On the 1 January, 1957, another squadron joined the 66th TRW. Flying the North American RB-45C Tornado, the 19th TRS was resident at RAF Sculthorpe in the United Kingdom; where it was attached to the 47th Bombardment Wing. The squadron did not move to Sembach and remained based at Sculthorpe. This fact in itself presented numerous problems to the parent wing, not least of which was communications. Direct radio contact was invariably impaired by static and weak signals. This certainly hampered 66th operations for some time.

The flight line at Spangdahlem in mid 1957. RB-66s are much in evidence and are accompanied on the taxiway by a 1st TRS RB-57A; whilst a lone RF-84F stands idle on its hardstanding. (Ron Colpron)

RB-66B 54-421 of the 19th TRS, 66th TRW at Wethersfield in May, 1957. The 19th RB-66s served with the 66th for a brief period before becoming part of the 10th TRW in December, 1957. (Mike Hooks)

The 19th TRS had been in the United Kingdom since 1954. At the time of its attachment to the 66th, the 19th TRS had twelve RB-45 aircraft assigned. On the 1 February three RB-66Bs arrived. By the 31 March twelve of the new aircraft had been received and the squadron had transferred five of its Tornadoes to the 84th Bomb Squadron at Sculthorpe. Unfortunately, disaster struck the 19th early on in the career of the RB-66, when aircraft 54-420 aborted take-off, left the runway, and sheered the nose wheel. Extensive damage was caused to the entire nose section of the aircraft and it had to spend some time with the 47th Field Maintenance Squadron for repairs. Corrosion was found on several of the new RB-66s and an extensive wad poling (cleaning and polishing) programme was instigated. Conversion for the 1st and the 42nd TRS was well under way at the beginning of 1957. Training the pilots of the RB-26s with no previous jet experience was carefully planned. From T-33 single jet experience the pilots were sent to Laon, to the 38th BW for check-out on their B-57s. On return to Spangdahlem time was taken on the RB-57s of the 1st

Detail of 54-421 at Wethersfield in '57. The 19th badge was carried on the port fuselage side just forward of the wing. The wing badge was carried on the starboard side. The distinctive star markings of the 66th TRW are wrapped around the engine nacelles. (Mike Hooks)

Ms. Jackie Collins paid a visit to Sculthorpe in the summer of 1957 and had a 19th TRS RB-66 named after her. (USAF)

TRS. Then to the RB-66 simulator before actual flying. Pilots were obliged to have 50 hours multi-jet time and a total of 100 hours jet time before check-out on the Destroyer.

The 30th TRS also began transition to the RB-66 at this time. Prospective pilots had to complete 15 hours on the Sembach simulator in preparation for the aircraft which were due to arrive in the summer. The first RB-66 to land at Sembach was, in fact, a 19th TRS machine on the 26 February, 1957. The purpose of this flight was to check out the runway at Sembach for RB-66 operations. There was an element of doubt as the whether or not its 8000 feet was long enough. In the event the 30th was sent to Landstuhl later in the year because of the longer runways and overruns. An additional factor, if one were needed, was that Sembach's runway was buckled by the heat wave experienced in the summer of '57; and not only the 30th, but also the 302nd and 303rd TRS had to deploy elsewhere: the 303rd to Landstuhl and the 302nd to Caseaux in France.

Meanwhile the RB-57As of he 30th were detached to Wheelus on the 16 January to take part in Operation Sunrise in support of the 11 Tactical Missile Squadron; which was doing some target

Pictured at RAF Wethersfield Open Day in 1957 this highly polished 30th TRS RB-57A is resplendent in its yellow markings. (Major S. Sloan via Dave Menard)

practice. The job of the RB-57 pilots was to find the missiles in the desert after they had landed and to photograph them to aid assessments of accuracy. The target was a large 'T' in the desert. Up to the time of Sunrise the 30th had the best safety record of all the B-57 units in the air force. This record was to be broken. Hal Grant:

> A frontal system was moving in off the sea, but the weather people didn't catch this and failed to mention anything about it at the dawn briefing. When Captain Ranger Cevelin and his navigator Captain Moeller returned to Wheelus AFB it was socked in. They did not have sufficient fuel to fly to an alternate so flew locally, hoping the weather would break. It didn't and Captain Cevelin elected to try an emergency in the desert rather than bale out. The desert can look smooth from altitude, but when down low, the terrain turns into many sand dunes. When ranger landed he hit one sand dune and then bounced and crashed into another. The fuel tank slid forward, killing the navigator. Miraculously, Captain Cevelin survived the crash although seriously wounded ... I was airborne at the time, having relieved Cevelin in the target area. When I returned to Wheelus the field was still clobbered in. I made a GCA approach, went down to minimum altitude and still did not break out. I poured on the full power for a go around, but due to the power lag, the aircraft sank just enough to break out below cloud level. I immediately retracted power and landed. By this time I was pretty far down the runway and wound up using most of the overrun. However, I was mighty happy to be on the ground

In June, 1957, Operations Order 80-57 ordered the 32nd and 38th TRS to Phalsbourg in France. This was a considerable operation, not only in logistical terms, but also because there was an international border to cross, which made for a mound of paper work. All transportation was by road, using ninety vehicles, apart from three 322nd Air Division C-123s. The 32nd commenced movement on the 20 June and the 38th on the 27 June. By 31 July all equipment had been transferred with the exception of some bins and lockers.

Just prior to this, in May, the last RB-26 left the 42nd TRS at Spangdahlem and on 25 June the last RB-66C arrived. At the end of June the squadron had eleven RB-66s and nine WT-33s assigned. However the transition for both the 42nd and the 1st TRS was not without it's problems: in mid year the 10th TRW had four very different aircraft to maintain and this heavy workload tended to compromise operational efficiency. In addition there were other problems: non-availability of flash bomb cartridges for night photo missions, the lack of a gunnery trainer, the necessity to operate out of dispersed operating bases while Spangdahlem's runway was being repaired and only twenty-one out a required thirty-six ECM operators were assigned.

An RF-84F of the 38th TRS, 66th TRW 1958. After the 32nd and 38th joined the 66th TRW in December 1957 the squadrons adopted the 66th markings scheme. The 38th colours were green and the 32nd yellow. (Don Watt)

A close up of the forward fuselage of 52-1486 at Wethersfield shows that this is the aircraft of the commander of the 66th TRW, Colonel Robert R. Gideon. The badge of the 30th TRS is clearly evident. (Mike Hooks)

However, the work of the squadrons did go on of course. One of the regular missions flown by the 42nd Weather Flight at this time and hereafter was known as Wild Goose. The WT-33 and later the WB-66 would fly a reverse route to that planned by tactical units on deployment to report on the weather. Examples of Wild Goose in 1957 were from Erding to Adana, Turkey in support of the 490th FIS; from Soesterberg in the Netherlands to Wheelus in support of the 32nd FDS; and from Bitburg and Landstuhl to Wheelus in support of the 23rd FDS and the 86th FIW respectively. The first WB-66 arrived at Spangdahlem for the 42nd in October, '57 and by 31 December, seven of these aircraft had been received.

Royal Flush in 1957 took place at RAF Laarbruch in Germany. This time no prizes were taken by the USAFE units represented by RF-84s and RB-57s for the 4th ATAF. The Swift FR.5s of 2 Squadron, RAF helping to secure the Greunther Trophy for the 2nd ATAF.

Operation Open Skies took place in June 1957. It was an Open Day held at Sembach for the French and German press. The visiting newsmen chose a target from a number available for both a day and night photo reconnaissance. The day mission was to photograph the Mannheim bridge. 'Robbie' Robertson took off in his RF-84 and returned with his pictures which were distributed to the waiting newsmen within three hours. The mission was the shortest of those suggested because of the prevailing weather at the time. One of the significant reject targets was the house of German Chancellor, Conrad Adenauer, at Rehondorf.

During November, tragedy struck the 302nd TRS when, on the 13th of that month, whilst flying formation over RAF Manston in Kent, two RF-84Fs collided. Unfortunately both First Lieutenant Orville O. Buck Jr. and First Lieutenant James R. Bulgar were declared missing, presumed dead, when no trace of their bodies was ever found. Incidences of near misses in formation flying had occurred in the 303rd TRS and for both squadrons a rigorous formation flying training programme was initiated in the 66th TRW. Selected pilots were required to fly a satisfactory flight in a T-33 before returning to their respective units as instructors. Each squadron pilot had to complete six formation flights before requirements were satisfied, in addition to attending numerous lectures on flight safety.

On 6 December, 1957, HQ USAFE issued General Order 88 which assigned the 32nd and 38th TRS, both resident at Phalsbourg, to the 66th TRW. The 19th and 30th TRS were assigned to the 10th TRW; the 30th moving to Spangdahlem while the 19th remained, for the time being, at Sculthorpe. The 66th now became an all RF-84 wing and the 10th an all RB-66 wing. The problems for both wings of maintaining different aircraft types was thus solved.

For the 66th TRW more changes were imminent. It was announced in January, 1958, that the 32nd and 38th squadrons were to convert to the McDonnell RF-101C Voodoo. The 66th HQ and the 302nd and 303rd TRS were to move to the French base of Laon, displacing the 38th Bombardment Wing. This move to take place in July.

If 1958 was a year for much change and the prospect of change, it also marked the most successful period for the Thunderflash in Europe. The decision to utilize Nouasseur in Morocco as a training base for the 66th TRW all the year round had much to do with this successful 'swan song' for the aircraft. For some time the northern European weather had taken its toll of mission effectiveness. Operation Follow the Sun put an end to much of this. All four squadrons detached to Nouasseur for extended periods throughout 1958. They achieved an incredible peak of combat effectiveness during these detachments. The 32nd TRS detached in January for seven weeks and again in April and May; and reported an average of 700 hours flying time per month for the period January to June. At this time they were also preparing for transition to the RF-101C. The 303rd TRS, during 33 days at Nouasseur flew seventy sorties, accomplished 140 briefings, and 200 rolls of film were interpreted and scored. The 302nd detached in January and again in April and May. All airfields and seaplane stations and ports in Morocco, and some in Spain were photographed. Other training for all units included low level navigation, all aspects of photography, instrument flying, formation aerobatics and evasion tactics and night flying. Pilot proficiency in the RF-84F was developed to an extent never before realized. All new pilots were transitioned at the Moroccan base. There were some difficulties. Although the squadrons were able to accomplish a very efficient mission rate; the North European weather did not entirely relinquish its influence over events. Bad weather at Sembach, Laon and Phalsbourg often interfered with the inspection cycle when the RF-84s were routinely returned to the parent bases. Bad weather regularly prevented the aircraft from gaining access to the bases, and, furthermore, often delayed the return to Nouasseur. When the

The Wing Commander of the 66th TRW flying a 303rd TRS aircraft leads the squadron commanders in formation. The front three are from top to bottom: the 32nd TRS, the wing commander and the 302nd TRS. In the slot is the 38th TRS squadron aircraft. (USAF via Hank Sharringa)

303rd returned to Sembach from one detachment in April, they were prevented from making a grand entrance by a very heavy fall of snow at the German base. They diverted to Phalsbourg. The pilots left the aircraft there and were 'smuggled' into Sembach to celebrate their return over the weekend, retrieving their Thunderflashes on the Monday. Deployments to Nouasseur from Laon and Phalsbourg refuelled at Zaragoza in Spain, and those from Sembach paused at Chateauroux in France.

The 42nd TRS was assigned the task, under its Wild Goose mission, to provide weather reconnaissance for all aircraft movements to North Africa. In January and March the 81st Fighter Bomber Wing and the 20th Fighter Bomber Wing took advantage of this service, which required a permanent detachment of WB-66Ds at the Moroccan base. Unfortunately, an aircraft was lost at Nouasseur. On the 31 January 55-403 bounced on landing and porpoised. The 1st TRS also detached to Morocco in the first quarter of 1958. Approximately 683 mission hours were flown! The 19th TRS from Sculthorpe, had three aircraft on rotational deployment during the year.

This 38th TRS RF-84F is flying over the Atlas mountains. (USAF via Paul Hodges)

The 42nd TRS maintained the regularity of its routine electronic missions, one of which caused headaches for USAFE command. In the early part of the year an RB-66C had inadvertently violated the East German Air Defence Zone (ADIZ). Fortunately for all concerned, the aircraft was not intercepted by air defence fighters and returned to its proper course. Subsequent investigation of the incident revealed that the navigational radar was inoperative and other aids were unreliable. This prompted 10th HQ to issue a directive forbidding any of its squadrons to fly east of the Rhine River if the navigation radar was in any way suspect. This curtailed the squadron's activities for some time and was compounded by a problem discovered in the RB-66C with the ECM observer's ejector seat. For over a month, from 5 January to 11 February ECM observers were banned from flights. Regular Space Cadet missions were defined for the WB-66s at this time, also requiring them to fly close to hostile borders in the ADIZ for the purposes of obtaining weather information for the use of USAFE tactical units.

There were many problems with the RB-66s in these early days. These were primarily concerned with maintenance and the shortage of manpower to perform both the routine and unscheduled tasks required. Problem areas included fuel vent checks and centre of gravity malfunctions, de-ice and anti-ice systems, APN-82 radar navigation system, APD-4 radar receiver and pressurization and heating systems, to name only a few. A high proportion of missions were aborted due to malfunctions in these areas. It is a matter of conjecture whether or not the maintenance difficulties were a factor in the accident rate at this time. There were certainly a number of major incidences during the first part of 1958. In addition to the accident at Nouasseur there were four crashes. On the 14 April a 10th TRS machine 54-422 crashed on approach to Sculthorpe. On two consecutive days, the 3 and 4 July, aircraft 54-437 and 54-433, both of the 19th TRS crashed in the UK. On the 8th July a 1st TRS aircraft 54-444, crashed at Spangdahlem some 7,200 ft from the end of the runway, killing all three crew members.

In March, 1958, the RF-101C MTD was set up at Phalsbourg for the training of the 32nd and 38th TRS personnel on the Voodoo. When, in July, the 66th HQ moved to Laon, the 32nd and 38th remained at Phalsbourg. The 32nd TRS was the first to convert to the Voodoo, and had completed this conversion by the end of the year. The RF-101s were in fact delivered to Nouasseur in Morocco and all transition training took place there, where there was also a resident McDonnell technical team. The programme proceeded with marked success for the 32nd and 38th TRS with no accidents, but some delays. 'Scotty' Schoolfield flew with the 32nd TRS. He was in the initial batch of pilots to go to Nouasseur. He had previously transitioned to the RF-101A at Shaw in 1957 from the RF-84F, and on being posted to the 32nd in the spring of 1958 had become re-acquainted with the Super Hog, as the RF-84F was not so affectionately known. He was one of those who anxiously waited at the Moroccan base for the 'one o' wonders' to arrive.

> We anxiously waited some more, and more. Finally we were advised that delays would prevent delivery for several more weeks but not to fear, headquarters would borrow some RF-84s for us to fly. Joy! Joy! We received several aircraft from the 302nd at Laon. We demonstrated a great lack of appreciation for their generosity by scratching three machines in a short period of time. All losses, as I recall, were due to engine failure.

At the very time that the 66th was moving house and changing its aircraft there occurred an incident that was to have considerable implications for the units of USAFE. On the 15th July 1958, President Eisenhower alerted the United States Armed Forces when the Republic of the Lebanon requested assistance from the USA because of a political crisis. The 10th and 66th TRWs went into sustained alert status. USAFE Operations Plan 100-58 was put into effect. Operation Post Card as it was known put the units on standby to deploy to the Lebanon and remain there until relieved by units from the United States. In fact this never occurred as hostilities lessened and the physical move was never necessary. The 42nd TRS flew a number of weather missions in support of surface and air movements of the US Task Force into the area, and the electronics flight flew a round the clock operation during the entire episode monitoring hostile electronic activity.

From the 24 August to the 12 September, Spangdahlem hosted the Royal Flush event. Both the 10th and the 66th TRWs were represented; both flying for the 4th ATAF and using the RF-84F and the RB-66. The French, Belgians and the Dutch also flew the RF-84F. The Royal Air Force

An RF-101C of the 32nd TRS *en route* to Nouasseur flying over Gibraltar in 1960. (via George Cowgill)

This 1st TRS RB-66B has just landed at Spangdahlem and is about to jettison its drag chute. The 10th wing badge is just forward of the wing root. (Bob Ganci)

flew the Swift and the Canberra. The latter aircraft took the high-level trophy and the French RF-84F the low level.

The RF-101 conversion programme was based primarily at Nouasseur, and by the end of 1958 the 32nd TRS had completed conversion to the aircraft and the 38th was well under way. Neither squadron experienced an accident during the transition. The Voodoos were delivered directly to Morocco, where a technical team from McDonnell were among the personnel waiting to receive them.

The 302nd and 303rd TRS were destined never to receive the Voodoo. It was decided to deactivate both these units and bring two RF-101 squadrons over from Shaw: the 17th and 18th

In company with a Gooney Bird this 10th TRW RB-66B was photographed at Lakenheath in 1960. In this year the wing removed all individual squadron colours from the engine nacelles of the aircraft. (Via Bob Green)

As the formation banks to the left the wing tip ECM pods on the 42nd aircraft can clearly be seen. (Bob Ganci)

TRS. In May 1959 these two squadrons arrived at Laon after what was for two of the 18th TRS pilots an eventful Atlantic crossing. Paul Carrodus was one of those pilots:

> I was on Lee's left wing about 4000 out and checking out my lunch of yesterday's candy bar and a soft drink. I removed my oxygen mask to eat and drink and the next thing I saw was the rear end of the biggest jet exhaust with my aircraft tucked under the right side of his fuselage. Speculation is I may have momentarily passed out. The nose of my aircraft contacted his right wing and folded back towards my canopy. I ejected at 35,000 ft and my parachute opened since the low altitude bale-out lanyard had not been disconnected. I was unconscious after the ejection and regained consciousness in a cold white mist with a loud ringing noise in my ears.

Paul landed safely in the water and was picked up eventually by the Coastguard cutter *Mendota*. Lee Skinner also baled out from his tailless RF-101.

An RB-66B of the 19th TRS, 10th TRW keeps company with three RB-66Cs of the 42nd TRS in 1958. Two of the aircraft have been modified with the ECM tail cone while two retain the tail-gun barbette. (Bob Ganci)

The tail of my old bird was broken off and I started a backward tumble. Sitting forward of the centre of rotation I was held firmly in my seat, and during the tumbling I saw the other bird break in half and explode in a violent ball of orange fire.

Skinner ejected at 14,000 ft:

The next thing I knew I was hanging peacefully in the harness of the prettiest parachute in NATO. The ejection seat had broken free and was already out of sight below me. I began looking around and saw both our aircraft crash into the ocean. Even in my peculiarly perilous position there was an unexplainable sadness about the death of the airplane. With his airplane goes the pilot's most precious contact with reality.

It was nothing short of miraculous that both men survived this ordeal. Some of their survival gear proved highly suspect and some of it did not work at all. All RF-101 survival equipment was subsequently checked, including the aptly named Jayne Mansfield water wings!

All the other RF-101s of the 18th TFS made the trip to Laon non-stop. The 17th were not so fortunate in that one flight of eight aircraft was prevented from making a refuelling rendezvous because of a thunderstorm and had to divert to Bermuda. The Shaw AFB *RECON Recorder* of the 22 May, 1959, tells of the landing of the 17th Commander's Voodoo in Bermuda:

As the 17th Squadron commander landed in Bermuda to refuel, his drag chute popped out with a long streamer bearing the inscription '18th Tac Leads the Pack.' Still adding fuel to the incident, the lead plane of the 17th TAC's second flight to Laon bore the same words on its nose wheel faring and external fuel tanks.

The friendly rivalry between the two veteran recce squadrons was further perpetuated by this incident!

In early 1959 a programme was begun to fit all RB-66s with refuelling probes. However, on June 20th, 1959 the 302nd and 303rd TRS were deactivated.

Operation Taxi Cab introduced and developed the pathfinder role for the RB-66, which was to be used with some success in south-east Asia. Taxi Cab was initially conceived as an experiment to ascertain whether or not the RB-66 could be used to lead in F-100 fighter bombers to a target in bad weather or at night, ie, when IFR (Instrument Flight Rules) were required. For the purposes of the evaluation exercise RB-66s of the 1st TRS and F-100Ds of the 49th TFW deployed to

An RF-101C 56-019 of the 38th TRS at the Paris Air Show in 1959. The initial markings worn by the 66th Voodoos were the same as those worn by the RF-84Fs. (Mick Stroud)

Nouasseur. When the details had been worked out and practised the 1st TRS aircraft returned to Europe to manoeuvre with the F-100Cs of the 36th Tactical Fighter Wing. Essentially the form of Taxi Cab was that the F-100s were led to the target area by the RB-66. At a specified distance from the target the fighter bombers broke away and, at a signal from the navigator of the Destroyer, performed their target run. After a successful bombing run had been accomplished, the RB-66 would fly over the target and photograph the damage. The 'Pathfinder' concept was tried and successful and was to become part of USAFE's operations systems from July 1959; when two WB-66Ds of the 42nd TRS formed the alert force at Bitburg with four F-100Cs.

In July 1959, General de Gaulle ordered all foreign nuclear forces from French soil. This necessitated a major move for many of USAFE's assets in Europe. The 49th TFW moved with their F-100Ds from Etain Rouvres to Spangdahlem, displacing the 10th TRW which moved to three bases in the United Kingdom: Alconbury, Chelveston and Bruntingthorpe. The 66th TRW remained at Laon; now being the only USAF recce unit on mainland Europe. A 66th TRW RF-101C was represented at the Paris Air Show in 1959.

The RF-101C pilots of the 66th TRW developed their own particular brand of low level, high speed photographic reconnaissance. The wing received the accolade of the 7th Army for its commitment to Exercise Fair Play from 2nd to 7th February, 1959, when sixteen day reconnaissance missions were flown every day under very adverse weather conditions. Don Karges:

> All training in Europe was based on high-speed, low-level tactics. The reasons were simple – we had only a day capability with no ECM or radar warning devices. We did not believe we could survive a heavy SAM environment (above 1000ft) and the prevailing weather in Europe would force us to photograph targets at low altitude. A typical mission was 2 hours and 10 minutes and consisted of a high-low-high profile. We would climb to 30,000ft and cruise in a straight line for about 40 minutes, let down below the clouds and fly our planned low level mission at 420kts at 500ft for about 30–40 minutes – usually with two–three pinpoint targets like com sites, bridges etc. and one route reconnaissance of a highway or railroad. These practise missions had both photo and visual requirements since the wartime missions required us to give visual reports on the way home (in case we were shot down and to give the intel folks some advance information). After the low-level portion we climbed back to altitude (around 35,000), made our visual report back to squadron intel and returned home ... Missions near the border were very strictly controlled – positive radar contact at all times – and were in support of army exercises.

Royal Flush 1V took place at Eindhoven. The race is on to download and process the film. The 66th TRW enjoyed some success in the competition but took no prizes.

A prime example of the low-level high speed mission was in response to a request from CINCUSAFE for photo coverage of the Suippes gunnery range. The first photos had to be taken 10 miles from the target at a height of 1,500 ft. At intervals of a mile thereafter and with ever decreasing altitude the RF-101s had to take further pictures. Within 2 miles of the

In the summer of 1960 RF-101C 56-0216 comes in to land at Laon, France; the home of the 66th TRW. (George Cowgill)

target the aircraft were down to 500 ft. The purpose of this mission was to aid in orientation training of tactical combat aircrews using the range.

The move of the 10th TRW to the UK went smoothly enough but was to have a considerable effect on the missions of the squadrons. Taxi Cab, barely started, was cancelled. The component parts of the Alert Force were based too far apart to make the it viable. The 19th TRS, having just moved from Scultthorpe to Spangdahlem, was obliged to move yet again, to RAF Bruntingthorpe. The 1st and 30th TRS went to Alconbury and the 42nd to RAF Chelveston. It became necessary for the squadron to plan new ECM routes. The increased distance to the borders of the Soviet zone of Germany and Czechoslovakia, coupled with the air traffic control procedures of the UK, considerably restricted 'watch time' over target. From 15 October, daily KB-50 refuelling exercises were introduced for the RB-66s in an attempt to overcome this problem, and as a result watch time was increased to 2 hours 20 minutes. However, poor weather took its toll of some missions and it was estimated that ECM missions were cut by as much as 50 per cent after the move to the UK.

On 22 December, 1959, the 42nd undertook a covert operation against two Soviet radar complexes in East Germany located near the towns of Zerbet and Morseburg. The two radars, codenamed Barlock and Stonecake were unknown quantities and the object of the exercise was to ascertain whether they were synchronized one with the other. In this mission the 42nd was aided by F-102s of the 86th Fighter Interceptor Wing. These aircraft made supersonic incursions into East German airspace to encourage the Soviets to turn their radars on so that they could be checked out by the 42nd ECM crews. The mission was successful.

High above the clouds an RB-66 of the 19th TRS takes on fuel from a KB-50 tanker. (Bob Ganci)

Royal Flush IV took place at Eindhoven in the Netherlands from 2 to 4 June, 1959. The 10th TRW entered RB-66s for the high level competition and the 66th entered an RF-101C for the low level part of the competition for the first time. Both the 32nd and 38th TRS' were involved and enjoyed marked success in the event. Dick Vaughters flew in the competition for the 32nd TRS:

> I was lucky enough to participate in that one. We at least scared everyone and didn't score too badly. A little known fact about the competition was that those airplanes weren't exactly 'stock'. The Pratt and Whitney J-57-P13 ran at 92–93 per cent RPM (That was all the power the Air Force had paid for and that was all they got). Our birds were tuned to run at 102 per cent RPM and 715 Degrees. My Voodoo would indicate an honest 645 knots on the deck. Naturally fuel consumption was sky-high and we would arrive back at Eindhoven with little but fumes left.

One of the most significant events for USAFE tactical reconnaissance began in January, 1960, when the Green Dragon mission was assigned to the 10th TRW. To implement Green Dragon the 10th TRW was assigned twelve specially modified B-66Bs. These were taken from the 47th BW and each was fitted with a special pallet in the bomb bay in which was installed a suite of

Nick Pishvanov flies RF-101C to Wheelus in 1964. Aircraft 56-0055 carries the Royal Flush VIII emblem on the nose. (Nick Pishvanov)

Nick Pishvanov with RF-101C at Wheelus in 1964. Nick flew with the 18th TRS until he went to south-east Asia in 1967 with the 20th TRS at Udorn. (Nick Pishvanov)

Royal Flush V in 1960 took place at Bremgarten. The medium range team for the 17th TRS were First Lieutenant Billie Williams, First Lieutenant John Wood and Captain Paul Hodges. (Paul Hodges)

electronic countermeasures equipment including the AN/ALE-1 chaff dispenser, AN/APS-54 radar warning set, and an array of jamming equipment. An ECM tail cone was to be fitted as standard, though not all aircraft had them at the commencement of the programme. The K-5 bomb navigation system was also installed. The job of modifying the aircraft was a considerable one and fell to the Roma Air Material Area (ROAMA) who completed the job in just four weeks. After modification the Brown Cradle B-66Bs were assigned to the 42nd TRS which phased out its WB-66Ds during the first half of 1960. Echo Alert went into operation at RAF Alconbury on 1 May. Toul-Rosiere was chosen as the forward operating location for the Echo Alert force. The 10th, or part of it at least, was going home!

Back in the United Kingdom, at Chelveston, the 42nd TRS played host to personnel from the 9th TRS based at Shaw AFB. Deployments of these crews and aircraft continued throughout the

Eight RF-101Cs of the 66th TRW *en route* to North Africa. The 'sun bases' provided much needed intensive training for all the units of USAFE. (via George Cowgill)

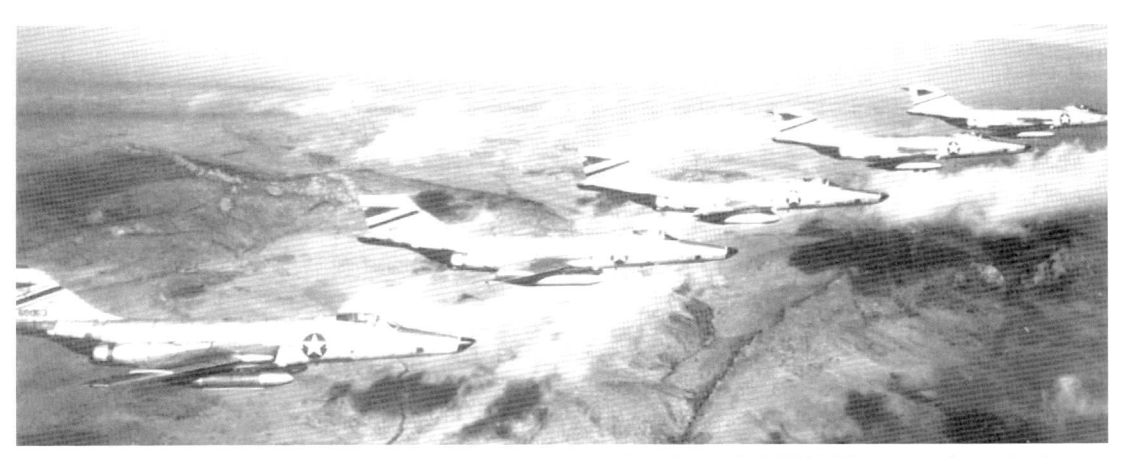

These five RF-101Cs are over Spain on the way to Morocco in the winter of 1960/61. They carry the revised markings worn by all 66th Voodoos. There was no longer any differentiation between the squadrons. (via George Cowgill)

year codenamed Swamp Fox for sixty day periods. The object being for the Shaw based crews to be integrated with the 42nd TRS and fly ECM missions.

Toul-Rosiere was a busy base at this time. In April the 17th and 18th had detached there for four months while the runway at Laon was being repaired, and in October the 32nd and 38th TRS moved there from Phalsbourg under Operation Young Gal. The two squadrons were at this time operating as one unit. Maintenance, Intelligence and Photo Lab became an integrated unit, though the squadrons did retain their separate identities and commanders.

During their sojourn at Toul-Rosiere the 18th TRS lost two pilots when RF-101Cs 56-0076 and 56-0077 collided during a night formation take-off. Paul Hodges:

> That was a bad scene since the wing was tasked for mass night-intruder missions to test the air defences of the UK, I think, and were all on the runway awaiting take-off when the accident happened in front of them all.

Both Captain Park Baker and First Lieutenant Jimmy Duren died in the accident when their aircraft crashed and burned.

A good deal of desert work was scheduled for both wings during 1960. When the Agadir earthquake devastated Morocco, aircraft of the 18th TRS were dispatched to take photos. Many of the photos that they took were used in the fund raising for financial and medical aid for the stricken area, and many found their way onto the front pages of national newspapers in the US and Europe.

In February the 42nd was ordered to detach and maintain on station two WB-66Ds at Wheelus. They were to launch one sortie a day in order to ascertain high-altitude wind direction for a minimum period of three weeks. The operation, code named Golf Ball was ordered as a direct result of the French nuclear tests in the Algeria. It was necessary for the USAF to have data relating to the high-altitude air currents in order for the B-57 and WB-50 aircraft efficiently to collect fallout samples from the tests. Thirty-one missions were flown over uncharted areas of desert.

On the 6 April the 18th TRS was again involved in desert operations when four aircraft were detached to Wheelus to photograph and map approximately 8000 miles of the Libyan desert. The search had been instigated for the ill fated survivors of the Second World War B-24 'Lady B. Good' which had crashed in that area of desert. This difficult and sensitive mission was completed on the 28 April, 1960.

Royal Flush IV in 1960 took place at Bremgarten. Paul Hodges flew the RF-101C for the 66th TRW and recalls the event:

> The French team was flying the RF-84, we were in the Voodoo, Brits in a little airplane whose name I can't remember, Italians in the '84. The competition was replete with sometimes scandalous behaviour by teams in an effort to win, and this excluded no one. For example, one mission flown by a French '84 was at low altitude, got all the targets and made the route in a time that our team captain calculated had to be Mach 1.2, not easily done in an aircraft that was supersonic only going straight down at high altitude … As I remember the French won.

Detachments to North Africa were regular for all units of USAFE, not least the tac recce squadrons. Not all flights on these detachments were routine. Clyde East commanded the 18th TRS:

> We almost created an international incident … prior to take-off we were called into the Nouasseur base Commander's Office and asked if we would photograph Boulhaut Air base, as they had info reporting Soviet Migs recently arriving there and currently in the process of being assembled. He made no reference to the fact that the Moroccans might object to such a thing! I agreed without a second thought and almost immediately after take-off at 5/6000 ft, made two passes down the runway with Bob on my wing (Bob Archibald), cameras clicking. We continued our flight back to Laon, had the film developed and sent the prints to the Commander, Nouasseur.
>
> Apparently, the Moroccans observed us, identified the type of aircraft, and deduced our purpose. They obviously lodged a stiff complaint through political channels. I could have flown at a much higher altitude and avoided detection, but I had no idea they would be so sensitive about our spying on their new aircraft!

Bob Archibald recalls the incident as well:

> We dropped down to low level and blasted across the field with cameras on, no radio contact. Sure enough there was a Mig 17, the first I saw. When we developed the film we found on the same oblique frame a row of large boxes just beyond the Mig, the first box opened. Those were the shipping containers for the Migs. We got the first one out of the box and the full squadron lined up still in their boxes.

Both Clyde and Bob had a good deal of explaining to do before the matter was laid to rest. Paul Carrodus remembers later trips to Nouasseur:

The 38th TRS, 66th TRW at Ramstein, Germany. In 1962 the 38th TRS deployed to Ramstein where it remained until conversion to the RF-4 in 1966. RF-101s operating with the 38th out of Ramstein had a dual role of recce and nuclear weapons delivery. (M. Marrant)

This detail of 56-0072 at Ramstein in 1962 reveals the forward and side oblique cameras of the Voodoo. (M. Marrant)

> We would occasionally fly to Nouasseur and be told to pull up abruptly after take-off and not to overfly the Russian detachment on the end of the runway. Needless to say, we took off with the forward and side oblique cameras on.

The Berlin Crisis of 1961 had implications for all the NATO air forces, USAFE no less than all the rest. The 66th detached eight RF-101s to Spangdahlem at this time and these aircraft flew single ship sorties to Berlin. They flew in one corridor, turned over West Berlin and came out via another corridor. On many of these missions Migs joined up and flew formation with the single RF-101.

Three Voodoos of the 38th TRS refuel from a KC-135 over Germany in 1964. (Fred Muesegaes)

In 1963 the colours of the Voodoo squadrons of the 6th TRW were changed yet again. From a star on the tail radiated the four squadron colours. Aircraft 56-0058 is photographed over France in the autumn of 1962. (via George Cowgill)

They tried to push them out of the corridor into East German airspace. It was also at this time that the wing began to take up a nuclear commitment. The RF-101C Voodoo had always been nuclear capable like the F-101A and C Fighter Bombers flown by the 81st Tactical Fighter Wing. Up to this time the pilots had not been involved in any specific training in special weapons delivery.

The 38th TRS deployed to Ramstein in Germany; the French prohibiting any foreign nuclear forces from their soil. Aircraft had to be modified with the fail-safe code devices and an intensive training programme was initiated. Don Karges was with the squadron at this time:

> The RF-101 had a very rudimentary delivery system based on high-speed low-level tactics which we were very good at. We had the capability of lay-down delivery or low-altitude

Aircraft RF-101C 56-0180 over Laon in 1964. (USAF)

Some of the 10th TRW aircraft retained their tail-gun barbettes for some time. (Bob Ganci)

drogue delivery. Two different weapons but both had a parachute retarding device for arming and (hopefully) to allow the aircrew to escape before bomb detonation. The Mk 43 was designed for lay-down delivery and the Mk 28 for a LADD. These were visual deliveries with approach to the target at 100 ft and 480–600 kts. Since these were visual only – no radar – we could be very accurate.

The Cuban Missile Crisis placed all of USAFE and NATO on alert. Fighter Bomber crews sat in their aircraft ready to go at literally a moments notice and deliver their special weapons. The tac recce units too had their targets and the pilots sat alert on first light to last light readiness. Fortunately, the Soviets backed down and the world was pulled back from the brink. USAFE was, however, prompted to maintain the nuclear delivery role of the 38th TRS for some time.

During the Cuban Crisis and in its aftermath regular reconnaissance flights were scheduled along the border. Johnnie Reeder flew with the 66th at this time:

> Anyway, the 66th was tasked to fly in the ADIZ at 15,000 ft or so and use large camera side obliques and photo all that we could of what the East Germans / Russians were doing as far as the camera could reach. I flew couple of these missions with Dick Newberry as you had to have flights of two to keep out of trouble. We were under constant radar control by our side and of course the other side as well. Dick Bultman and his wingman were doing their thing when our radar guys informed Bultman that he had unfriendlies, four of them, approaching from the east on a potential 90 degree intercept. Bultman was a sharpie and asked if it looked like a good intercept and the radar controller advised that it looked like the bogies were going to undershoot and Bultman asked if the controller was uncertain of the undershoot and he replied affirmative. Bultman and wingman continued taking photo and watched as the Mig 19s flew behind him and crossed into West Germany in doing so. Ramstein in the meantime launched several flights of F-100s to take on the

Migs. Bultman watched as the Migs did a quick 180 and high tailed it back across the border.

Exercise Cold Turkey in 1961 involved the 42nd 'Brown Cradle' B-66Bs. These aircraft did not often turn off their jamming devices except over the UK and the open ocean. Cold Turkey marked the first time since the Second World War that the USAF had conducted active ECM over the continent of Europe. At this time Brad Mosher flew with the 30th TRS out of Alconbury:

> We had very specific targets located inside East Germany. They were RR marshalling yards, RR bridges, major highways, tunnels, troop movement, any SAM sites we happened upon, and airfields not already identified. After many years it dawned on me that we only learned ONE target, they must not have planned on many successful missions. All our practice missions were similar to the actual target site, these we flew in France and Germany. I have no idea as to declassification of targets, or equipment that was installed on the RB-66Bs. I do know that if we turned all the ECM gear on at one time while at cruise altitude we could blank out most of Western Europe.

The RB-66Bs of the 10th TRW were fitted with tailcones which enabled them to undertake jamming operations in addition to their photo reconnaissance mission.

In the summer of 1961 the 10th TRW was tasked to provide ECCM (Electronic Counter Counter Measures) training for the NATO air defence units using the tailcone equipped RB-66Bs. Willi Bruenner was the EW (Electronic Warfare) officer responsible for the programme:

> This was the start of the Dancing Girl programme, which eventually included the Dutch, Belgians, Danes, French, UK, Italians, Greeks, Turks, our 6th Fleet, and the German Navy. To get final approval, I had also to brief the BFS (the German FAA) in Frankfurt because we were going to use jammers and chaff in a very crowded air traffic environment. We usually flew three missions per week, using one or two RB-66s. Both the RB-66 aircrews and the NATO air defenders enjoyed these sorties, because they provided more realism than the canned training provided by the ground radar computers. The RB-66s were the only in-theatre capability NATO had for this type of training at the time, except for a few RAF Coastal Command Second World War four engine bombers. Major problem arose when the

This formation of four 10th TRW RB-66Bs over Germany in 1958 carry no unit markings to determine the squadron they were assigned to. (Bob Ganci)

navs did not calculate the chaff drop winds aloft correctly and chaff drifted over neutral Switzerland in bad weather obstructing Zurich radar which did not have any ECCM features. For me, the major by product was that the Soviets, who could observe these exercises, were constantly reminded of the West's technical superiority in electronics. The exercises lasted till the RB-66s had to be deployed to south-east Asia in 1965.

In July, 1961, an RB-66 of the 42nd TRS crashed at Chelveston. Of the seven crew members on board only three survived. Both engines had flamed out over the runway. The EWO compartment had ejected downwards as it was designed to do. The aircraft was too low and the three were killed instantly. The gunner was also killed.

The 66th used the Suippes range in France as well as North African bases for special weapons delivery training. These missions were usually flown in four-ship formations; each aircraft carrying a small pod housing six bomblets. This enabled six bomb runs to be made. However, there were occasions when more realism was required. Don Karges recalls:

> Occasionally we dropped a 2000 lb concrete shape which had a drogue chute similar to the real weapon. This was much more realistic, but caused a few laughs and scary moments. If we were doing a LADD delivery, the shape would release while we were in a steep climb, the chute would deploy immediately and fall behind and below the aircraft. Our escape manoeuvre to avoid the blast was to roll inverted, pull 4gs towards the ground and escape straight at high speed/low level. But, once in a while the chute would not deploy and when we rolled inverted to pull toward the ground the 2000 lb concrete shape was right opposite the canopy as if it were flying formation! Obviously the shape goes into a ballistic curve and lands who knows where.

Nick Pishvanov while flying with the 18th TRS out of Laon and later Upper Heyford remembers Suippes for a very different reason:

> I ejected at the Suippes bomb range in France. I landed on solid ground. It was immediately after a lay-down practice drop at 500 (or less) and 500kts. Hydraulic line ruptured and pumped fluid into the 16th stage regulator in the engine. It vaporized and pumped smoke in the cockpit. I was beginning a pull up and was blinded, so I blew off the canopy. Still blinded, I couldn't tell if I was upright or inverted, so my next step was to pull the seat handle for an ejection. Helmet still stank of burned hydraulic fluid long after the chopper brought me home.

Nick was further reminded of his mortality when, in October, 1967, while flying with the 20th TRS from Udorn, he was shot down over Laos. Thankfully he was rescued.

In March, 1962 the 10th TRW took control of Toul-Rosieres in France and moved the 19th and the 42nd TRS there. Both RAF Chelveston and Bruntingthorpe were closed down for military operations.

The William Tell Fighter Weapons meet at Nellis AFB in Nevada included, for the first time in 1962, a reconnaissance competition. Teams from USAFE, PACAF and TAC took part in this competition which was won by a team from the 66th TRW led by Major Ray Schrecengost. Each team had to fly ten missions: five photo recce and five visual recce with photographic confirmation.

The Royal Flush competitions continued year on year. Unfortunately, in 1963 the event was marred by the death of one of the 66th pilots in training for the operation. On the 28 April, whilst flying under very low cloud Captain Wes Brooks flew into a blind canyon in the French Alps. On realizing his predicament he lit the burners and went into a maximum climb. He hit the vertical cliff only 60 ft from the top.

On 10 March, 1964, an RB-66B of the 19th TRS took off from Toul-Rosiere on a routine navigational training mission. The aircraft was commanded by Major David Holland. On board were also Captain Melvin Kessler and Second Lieutenant Harold Welch. It was Welch's combat qualification check ride. The flight plan was for the Destroyer to fly a high-low-high mission to undertake a low-level photo run of bridges and rivers near Osnabruck in West Germany. At approximately 3 pm the aircraft crossed into East German airspace in the vicinity of the Berlin corridor. It was some 120 miles off course. It's flight plan should never have taken it within 70 miles of the border! The crew were unaware of this and as they began what they thought was their descent to the target area, they were attacked by Mig 19s, four of which had been scrambled to intercept them. The aircraft was critically damaged and when it descended through 15,000 ft the order was given to bale out. The RB-66 crashed in flames. The crew were picked up and taken into custody.

The Soviets claimed that the aircraft had been on a recce mission to test their air defences and had been caught and destroyed in the act. The USAF stuck by their story that the plane had wandered off course due to a navigational error. The crew were returned a few weeks after the shoot down. At a subsequent Flying Evaluation Board held at Toul-Rosiere it was established that malfunction had occurred in the N1 compass system and this had caused the RB-66 to go off course.

Don Karges climbs down from the cockpit of RF-101C 56-0229. Don flew with the 38th TRS out of Ramstein before going to south-east Asia where he flew with the 20th TRS out of Udorn. He returned to USAFE after the war to command the 1st TRS at Alconbury flying RF-4Cs. (Don Karges)

The war in south-east Asia was becoming hotter in 1965 and the need for experienced Voodoo pilots to serve with the squadrons flying out of South Vietnam and, later, Thailand was becoming acute. Many of the 66th pilots went on to serve with the 20th and 45th TRS, including Don Karges, Nick Pishvanov, Jack Nelson and Jim Young, who was also shot down and became a prisoner of war. There is no doubt that the European experience paid dividends for the pilots who went on to serve in south-east Asia. Don Karges:

> For most of us a European tour was where we really learned how to fly and navigate. The lack of airspace restrictions, bad weather, constantly being intercepted by our own friendly forces (UK, French, Canadian, German, US etc) and the soberness of sitting alert with a nuclear weapon only 30 minutes or so from enemy airspace made confident, proficient pilots of us all. The training and experience did, in fact, lead to a high level of proficiency in south-east Asia. All of us who had tours in Europe were able to fly combat missions immediately on arrival in south-east Asia. There was no time for checkout flights etc. You arrived in south-east Asia as a combat qualified crew member and were expected to perform immediately.

In the mid '60s much occurred which was to anticipate the departure of the Voodoo from Europe. The two most significant events were the imminent entry into service of the F-4 Phantom and the decision by France to remove all foreign armed forces from the country.

One incident which occurred in April, 1965, could have had a part to play in the French decision to go it alone. On 16 April an RF-101C of the 66th inadvertently photographed a French nuclear plant at Pierrelatte. This provoked a very strong reaction from the French and resulted in a blanket restriction being placed on any USAFE aircraft flying reconnaissance training missions over France. This placed the 66th TRW in the intolerable position of being based in a country where they were not allowed to train. Captain Joe Smith was the pilot of that Voodoo and Don Karges was the duty officer at Ramstein on that day:

> Every pilot had certain training requirements every semi-annual period. I looked at the board and saw that Joe needed an area to cover for that period and decided to make it hard for him. I picked an area in the French Alps by simple random selection – far from home and not many checkpoints – just to make him work. He was probably one of the best recce pilots ever. He noticed the plant was not on his map when he was taking pictures but had no idea what it was…..I was still minding the store as duty officer when all the high ranking USAF and French officers from 4ATAF began pouring in the door.

Captain Joe Smith tells the story:

> At that period of time the RF-101 was receiving brand new cameras. The previous cameras had been the KA-2 system that basically had been lifted out of the RF-84 and they were very reliable cameras, but were not equipped with image motion compensation which means at high speed, low level, when you took a picture, the airplane moving across the ground at such a speed caused the film to be slightly blurred. So, they developed a new system for the oncoming RF-4 and decided to upgrade the RF-101 with those cameras. Prior to this flight at Pierlatte and in the preceding six months, our wing had gone through an ORI (Operational Readiness Inspection) and we had used those new cameras. And we flunked the ORI primarily because of a high incidence of camera failure. Those first cameras had a number of plastic parts in them and they simply could not take the heat and the stress from continuous high-speed operation. So, the technical people were racking their brains trying to come up with solutions to the problem and upgrading the cameras as we went along. In the meantime, the entire wing, the three squadrons over at Laon and the one squadron at Ramstein, the 38th TRS, were continuously tasked to go out and fly area cover or mosaic photo missions because that was the specific mission that caused us to flunk the ORI. Mainly, because the cameras failed in the middle of a multi-run effort to make photomaps of a particular area.
>
> On this particular day, it was in April, of course, 1965, the weather was cloudy, low overcast all over Germany, all of northern France, up into Belgium. Most of the training we did was either in southern Germany or in France and so I was tasked to go out and fly this area cover mission. So, trying to find a place to go take pictures, I walked into the weather shop and I said, "Where can I find some weather decent enough to fly a low level area cover, just a small one, four lines, perhaps forty square miles and make this photo map." So they went there and looked at their weather charts and they said, "OK, well it looks like the only place you can really go is along the Rhone River south of Lyon, France." And I said, "Fine." And I went back to Intel and I said, "This is the general area where I need to go. Pick out a spot, draw a four-line mosaic for me and let's have at it. So they did. They took their grid, and because the weather was forecast to be approximately 5000 ft overcast, we decided to fly the mosaic at very, very low altitude for that type of photography. In other words, 2000 ft above ground using a 6-in camera would give us a scale of 1:4000.
>
> So anyway they picked this one area out down along the Rhone River, and on our maps, all the way from our sectional charts, 1:500,000 to our low-level flying charts, 1:250,000, the area depicted nothing but a river and agricultural property: no towns, no villages, certainly no cities, and no build-up of any kind. So we just, by happenstance, picked this

one area. Our Intel types laid down the grid and I traced this four-line mosaic on the map. I went in, filed my flight plan. I was flying French Operational Radar Control which means that we would depart Ramstein IFR to VFR on top, cross into France, contact French Military Radar and I had filed for, picked the coordinates for the centre of this mosaic area, and I filed for 30 minutes within 20 miles of this area. No restricted areas. No city buildup. No town buildup. No nothing. It was just a very very simple little device.

So I proceeded to go out to the airplane, took off, crossed into France, contacted French Military Radar and they gave me flight following. I got to the point where it was time to start down, and I cancelled out and I said I would see them on the way back out. I let down and there were scattered clouds around and a few broken layers which I got through OK and I finally broke out into bright sunshine. Here was the river and, by golly, there was the spot I was supposed to take the pictures.

So, here's what we do when we make a mosaic. First of all we have our map, 1:250,000-scale map and we have the grid lines laid out. The camera is set up for the speed and altitude at which we're flying to give a 60 per cent forward overlap and a 40 per cent sidelap so that when you lay the prints down side by side and shove them all together, it makes a level map.

The first thing you do is to pick out your starting point and your ending point for the first line and this was four lines being flown side-by-side from a course from east to west. The first time I picked out the starting point, and lined up, turned around and went out and got on about an 8 mile final, set the airplane up on autopilot, 2000 ft AGL on the altitude hold function and got into the viewfinder. Now the 101 had an optical viewfinder that the pilot could look through and look at a point directly underneath the airplane called the nadir point. And there was a grid superimposed on this glass scope that you could electrically rotate left and right. The way we solved for wind drift correction was to pick our starting point up, find it in the viewfinder, make sure we were on the exact heading we were supposed to be by the map, overfly directly the starting point on the heading that we were supposed to fly, and observe the terrain passing through the viewfinder. If it diverged or converged to this superimposed straight line, it meant that we were drifting left or right. This was called a drift correction pass. I did this at 360 kts. I made my first pass without taking any photos, and thought that I had the wind drift correction killed. I rotated the grid, and was tracking it parallel, so I said, " Ok this is good." I turned around, went back out about an 8 mile final turned back again, lined up on the starting point, came in. The starting point is coming down my viewfinder and, before I actually got there, I activated my cameras and they were automatically clicking away taking this beautiful black and white, 12 in by 12 in format, photography of a beautifully highlighted area that was lit by sunlight. Very bright but it was going to make great photographs.

I got about half way down this line and noticed that I was beginning to drift off and I said, "Aw, doggone it. I did not get the wind drift correction factor correct the first time, so I'm going to have to cancel this run, go back out, and re-establish myself, and check the wind drift correction again.

Now, the 101 was typical of early century series airplanes. Lots and lots of power, but also lots and lots of weight and not much wing. So, as you know, the airplane had a pitch up tendency. If you got too many gs on the airplane and too high a weight, the airplane could lose control. So we had to be very careful about that. I was still very, very heavy. I still had fuel in my drop tanks. After all, I was only 40 minutes south of Ramstein and not only still had fuel in my drop tanks, but of course I still had full internal fuel which made me very heavy. So, I'm going along the ground and I said, "Rats! I'm going to have to start this thing over." So I clicked off the autopilot, rolled up into about a 45-50 degree left bank, and, because the airplane is heavy and sluggish, I needed to get rid of the fuel anyway, get rid of the weight I lit the afterburners to help me get around the corner and as I'm accelerating and turning this corner, I looked down and I could see my shadow racing across the ground, and, all of a sudden, I noticed there was another shadow racing across the ground right behind mine. I turned around and looked up to the right and here was an old French twin engine interceptor called a Vautour with two fellows in it sitting in tandem. They were staring over their oxygen masks at me, flying formation in this 45 degree left (right, sic) bank. Of course, I'm accelerating because I'm in afterburner now. I waved to them. Being intercepted in France or Germany or Belgium or Holland when you flew in Europe in those days, was a daily common occurrence. Airplanes all over the place and if you saw another countryman's airplane or one of your buddies, the natural thing to do was jump him. You'd zip over there, go "ha, ha, ha, I got you", waggle your wings at him, and go about your business. And I thought that's what was going on.

I continued my turn around to the downwind leg, rolled out, came out of afterburner, and that Vauteur was gone. He had departed. Left the area.

So I sailed up there again about 8 miles north of my starting point, turned around, came back, got lined up on it, made a little more drift correction, 2000 ft, altitude hold on, and I proceeded to take my photos. And I completed this four-line mosaic, and I noticed of course that right in the middle of my area was a plant or factory of some kind. It looked to me from the air like it was a cement factory because there was a lot of white construction dust around and all over the place. It didn't mean anything to me. It was not on the map, there was no restricted area. I just thought, "Oh, well, France is coming along, too. After all this is 1965 and they have built some kind of plant down here. No big deal."

I completed my mission. I turned north and headed back towards Ramstein. I re-contacted French Military Radar and they gave me flight following to the border. I then contacted Ramstein approach and made an IFR penetration through the clouds and broke out and landed at Ramstein. Now it is late afternoon at this time.

As I was taxiing back to our parking revetment, I passed our squadron operations building, and as I passed, I looked over there and I noticed that the squadron commander, Lieutenant Colonel Whity Hurlburt had come running out the front door and went running over to this bread truck we called it, this van that serviced the flight line. And I thought, "Well, no big deal. I don't know what that is." So I taxied up to our revetment and stopped. One of the grading points for the reconnaissance effort is how rapidly we can get film downloaded from the airplane, processed and on the viewing table. So, every time we flew a training mission, when we parked, even before the engines were shut down, the camera guys were downloading the film, they had the forward hatches open, pulling the magazines out, into the bread truck, off to the automatic processing laboratory. So this had taken place. I shut down and wrote up the airplane. About this time Whity Hurlburt comes driving up in the blue van. He got out of the van, and I'm deplaning about this time, and I step down, and he looks at me kind of funny and says, "Joe, come with me. There's been some claim that you have been overflying a restricted area." I said, "What! Me!? Not me. I didn't overfly a restricted area."

So he didn't know. We drive back to the squadron ops building and I walk in there, and, of course my heart is in my throat now, because I didn't intentionally do anything wrong. And I thought, "My goodness. Maybe I made a mistake," and I was scared. I walked in there and the only officer I saw other than our own people was Brigadier General Gordon Blood. He was a 17th AF up in staff somewhere. He'd obviously been given the task to find out what was going down with those recce pukes down there. Go find out what's going on.

So he comes walking in and he looks at me and he says, "Captain," he says, "the French claim you flew over this such and such restricted area." And the one he mentioned was way off in south-west France. Well I knew I hadn't been there. I hadn't been within 200 nautical miles of that area.

Gordon Blood said that the French are demanding this film. We don't even want to look at it. We want to put it up in the film canisters and I have a T-33 set up to fly that film directly to French Military Headquarters and we are not even going to look at it.

What he didn't know was, that because of our pride in getting the film developed, the film of course isn't printed but it is in a roll of negatives, and the photo interpretation people learn to look at negatives. Obviously the dark is white and the white is dark, and it is in a reverse image, but they are very very good at doing their photo intelligence work before the stuff has even been printed.

And this roll of film was on the viewing table. Already there. So our Intelligence Officer says, "General, I'm sorry. The film, we didn't know, has already been processed and it is on the viewing table. And the General in somewhat of a panic, says, "Well take it off, take it off. Put it in the canister. We don't want to look at it. Send it to the French."

And I said, "Just a moment sir, excuse me. If you do that, I will not be able to prove to you that I did not overfly this restricted area that you are claiming or the French are claiming that I overflew. So we must look at it at least to confirm that I was where I said I was going." He looked at me and said, "Ok. We'll look at it."

So sure enough, we put it on the table. I got my map out. We rolled the film through and here was the Rhone River, and here were the hooks and curves and here was the starting point of my reconnaissance mission, my photo mosaic. And it was beautiful photography, was bright sunlight and it came out wonderfully well and of course, right in the middle of it was this plant. I had no idea what that was, the general didn't, the Intel guy didn't, no one knew what that was. So, after, the squadron commander is standing there, Gen. Blood is standing there, the ops officer is standing there, Don Karges is standing there, and I'm standing there, and our Intel guy is there. After we ascertained, that I had, in fact, gone and taken pictures of what I had planned to do of the area that I was fragged to go take pictures of, we all said, "Ok, we don't know what the French are talking about." We rolled that thing up, we put it into a canister, taped it shut, took it out to base operations, gave it to a T-33 crew, and they flew it to France.

Well, things got very interesting for me after that, obviously. Because everybody thought that I had violated a French restricted area. Our Director of Operations from the wing came over and talked to me about what do you think they were going to do to you, with all the way up to court martial.

It was a very, very bad thing. Telephones calls constantly up to 17th HQ, the general's mad, everybody's mad, there are cables coming from the White House staff to USAF HQ to USAFE HQ to find out what the hell is going on, what have you guys been doing, why have you screwed up. I remember one time, I was called up to 17th AF HQ there on the base, and I went into this colonel's office. I don't remember his name and I don't remember his job, but, he was talking to me and he said, "I've received a telephone call from the Air Staff in the Pentagon and they want to interview you. You sit here until that phone rings and when I get them on, I want you to answer the phone, and I am going to be monitoring this other phone over here, and he said you look to me because I don't want you saying anything I don't want you to say". So, I said, "Ok."

So this voice comes on and he says, "Capt Smith, this is Col So and So from the Air Staff in Washington and I have one question for you. Did you, or did you not overfly a French military or restricted area?"

And, by this time, I knew that we had. Let me back up a moment. We found out that the French had, in fact, published this area for their own Air Force in an obscure French 1:250000 tactical map and it was on there as a restricted area. But that information was never passed to USAFE, that information was never passed to our chart and graph people who are responsible for printing the maps and printing our operating procedures and our restricted areas. We had no idea that it was a restricted area. We found that out, sort of

The 22nd TRS stayed but briefly in USAFE with the 26th TRW at Toul-Rosiere before returning to the USA, to the 67th TRW at Mountain Home AFB. (USAF)

under the table by a 4th Allied Tactical Air Force French Liaison officer who found this map and went to our people and who said, "Look, there really is a restricted area here, but we didn't tell you about it." So I knew that we had overflown a restricted area, but it was our position that we didn't because we didn't know it was a restricted area. We did not intentionally violate a French restricted area. We had no way of knowing it was a restricted area. We had no way of knowing, did not know, that there was an atomic energy plant down there.

So, I'm sitting there talking to this colonel from Washington and he asks me this very direct question because obviously he's been tasked to find out what the hell went on.

Now you can imagine if I said to him, " Colonel, yes, we did. We overflew this French military plant." What kind of ramifications that would have. So I'm looking up at this other colonel sitting in his office at Ramstein and he's shaking his head violently from side to side. In other words, say no. Do not admit we overflew a restricted area because we did not as far as we were concerned. So I had to tell a white lie to this guy and say, "No sir, we did not overfly a restricted area."

OK, it went on from there, and I've got copies of cables that went from the White House Staff to USAFE HQ. Eventually, USAFE learned what the deal was. They learned that, yes, there was a restricted area down there. Yes, we did overfly it. Yes we did photograph it. But no, we did not know it was a restricted area. It was one in a million shot that it happened to be right in this place that I wanted to go exercise the cameras. We had no way of knowing what it was when we saw it. So as far as we were concerned, we were totally innocent.

So, the French military, of course, had been ranting and raving, and Charlie DeGaulle wanted us out of France. So eventually when USAFE found out what the deal was, the USAFE Commander General Gabriel P. Dissasway, a really nice man, said to his French contemporaries, let's get bi-country, your country and my country, we'll get our air forces

In 1966 the 38th TRS at Ramstein received the RF-4C. The first aircraft delivered were in the gull grey and white paint scheme. (Fred Muesegaes)

together and we will do a formal investigation of this matter to see, in fact, what happened and if any blame is to be placed. And the French responded because, they, by that time, realized, that yes we had overflown this area but we had no idea of what the area was and no way of knowing it because they didn't tell us. So they responded to USAFE by saying, "We consider the incident closed."

General Dissasway wanted it wiped off the books, however, so he formed an official USAFE investigation. He sent an investigating team out to establish all the details about how this mission happened and what we did. There were some twenty-eight allegations the French had initially said. I did not file to the correct area, I did not fly my flight plan, I tried to avoid their airplane by using afterburner. I violated the low-level flying over a built- up. I did all manner of things.

The USAFE guys came down and poured through every map, every regulation, every pamphlet that we had trying to determine if in fact I had done anything wrong and they came out and totally exonerated me. And that was the end result. But for about 10 days there, it was a very uncomfortable period of time for this young captain.

This event undeniably provided one of the excuses for De Gaulle to dismiss all USAF units from French soil. This had far reaching implications for the NATO alliance.

This RF-101C was with the 17th TRS at Upper Heyford after the move. Here it is visiting RAF Bentwaters for an Open Day in the summer of 1967. (Alan Johnson)

The 10th TRW at Alconbury received its first RF-4s in May of 1965. The 1st TRS was the first of the squadrons in the wing to become combat ready on the Phantom. (Kirk Ransom)

The mid 1960s were the period when there was much reshuffling of USAFE's tactical reconnaissance assets. In July 1965 a new Tactical Reconnaissance Wing joined USAFE. Based at Toul-Rosiere the 26th TRW took over the 32nd and 38th TRS from the 66th TRW. The 32nd had been resident at the French base for a time and remained there. It was joined by a newly activated RF-4C squadron, the 22nd TRS on 1 December, 1965. The 38th remained at Ramstein and was joined there by the Wing HQ in September, 1966. Both squadrons converted to the McDonnell Douglas RF-4C Phantom. The 32nd TRS was assigned to the 10th TRW at Alconbury in 1966, although at this time it had no aircraft or aircrew assigned, these having been assigned to the 12th TRS at Mountain Home prior to deployment to south-east Asia. The 22nd TRS ceased to be part of the 26th TRW in September, 1966, also joining the 67th TRW at Mountain Home AFB in Idaho. The Squadron did maintain a commitment to USAFE however.

In 1966 on a deployment to Moron Spain the RF-4Cs of the 1st TRS shared the ramps with four B-58s from Indiana. Kirk Ransom's RF-4C is here receiving an engine change. (Kirk Ransom)

Film download at Upper Heyford during Royal Flush XII. An 18th TRS pilot, Major Ed Satterfield was the victim of a very sick joke at the time. But he went on to take the individual trophy. (USAF)

On the 1 July, 1965, the 25th TRGp was activated at Chambley, France and took control of the 42nd TRS. It was the first USAF group or wing to be formed whose sole mission was Electronic Warfare. The move from Toul-Rosiere to Chambley was not a welcome one for the pilots and crews of the RB-66s. Not only were facilities poor and very basic, but it soon became evident that the runway was not what it should be. Ned Colburn:

> At Chambley, we made the startling discovery that the French had only poured 50 per cent of the concrete that the engineering plans called for. This fact wasn't evident during the time that lighter-weight fighter aircraft operated from Chambley, but the weight of the B-66 caused the thin concrete in the taxiways and ramps to break-up – and the runway to break and sink into the ground from the heavier landing weight of the B-66.

The 25th TRW was activated on 1 October, 1965 and the 19th TRS joined the wing at Chambley. The escalation of the conflict in south-east Asia prompted the establishment of Detachment 1 of the 42nd TRS at Takhli Air base in Thailand. This detachment took five of the 'Brown Cradle' aircraft to Thailand. In early 1966 these aircraft were designated EB-66Bs. So successful were the aircraft in south-east Asia that in May, 1966, all the squadron's EB-66s were moved to Takhli and the 42nd was deactivated. In Takhli the EB-66 detachment formed the 6460th Tactical Electronic Warfare Squadron (TEWS).

The French decision to expel all foreign air forces from France initiated a move for the 66th TRW to the United Kingdom, to RAF Upper Heyford. On 11 September, 1966, the remaining two squadrons of the 66th Tactical Reconnaissance Wing landed on United Kingdom soil. The first of 36 Voodoos landed at RAF Upper Heyford at 4.30pm.

The wing soon settled into RAF Upper Heyford. However, 1967 was a year of change and achievement. The 18th TRS won the medium range daylight category in the annual NATO *Royal Flush* reconnaissance competition; beating, amongst others, 17 Squadron RAF and 439 Squadron, RCAF. The Royal Flush XII team of the 18th TRS consisted of twelve pilots led by Major Edward Satterfield. The NATO reconnaissance competition had been staged annually since 1956 when the 66th had fielded the RF-84F and won the low level part of the competition. Every year subsequently the wing had taken part in the competition with varying degrees of success and failure. In 1966 Nick Pishvanov had picked up the trophy for the 18th TRS. He also remembers a cruel trick played on Ed Satterfield the following year:

On 8 April, 1966, Jim Payson flew this RF-4C into Ramstein for the 38th TRS. (Jim Payson)

Ed was leading on points and had picked up on some very good, difficult targets. He was looking like a winner and sweating his last mission. It turned out good. Weather was excellent and he hit his targets dead-on. He taxied in right on the time, within seconds of his assigned chock-time. This was very important to keep the photo lab from getting overloaded by getting a group of undisciplined and untimely arrivals. It is probably

Four recently camouflaged RF-4Cs of the 38th TRS fly over Germany in 1967. Two of the aircraft retain the white radome of the original paint scheme. (USAF)

something that had penalized our competitors. We had the approach time from the English Channel and touchdown plus and taxi time nailed to the second. Nevertheless, the boys in the photo lab cooked up a great (but cruel) practical joke. They rushed up to the aircraft and had the camera doors open as the engines wound down; had the film canisters out of the nose and were rushing them to the photo truck. Ed was smiling like a possum eating something strange. He knew he had nailed all targets and had perfect photos. His in-flight report was dead-on, also. At that point, one of the camera crew clumsily dropped a canister and 50 ft of film came streaming out across the ramp. Poor man almost had a combination coronary and neurocirculatory collapse. You could hear Ed howl clear back to the officers' club on the other side of the field. Unbeknown to him, the real film was already being processed. Poor Ed! He just couldn't understand why we were so mean to him. What a day that was! Everybody did well.

The RF-4Cs of the 10th TRW did not feature in the success of the 1967 Royal Flush, a fact which led to a flight of four Voodoos indulging in an impromptu flypast over RAF Alconbury with their refuelling probes raised in the classic single digit salute! In fact the Phantoms of the 10th were not very photo capable for a while. Larry Garrison:

> … the photo systems were quite a ways behind the airplane and the RF-4 at Alconbury was unable to take much photo for the period 65 to about 67. They essentially had a great flying club for a while.

During 1968 the inevitable tide of progress caught up with one of the two remaining squadrons of the 66th TRW. The 17th TRS was to convert to the RF-4C Phantom in 1969. The 18th TRS would remain with the RF-101 and would assume a purely daylight role and the RF-4Cs would perform their greatly enhanced mission by day and night in all weathers.

On 26 September, 1969, it was announced that the 20th Tactical Fighter Wing was to move into Upper Heyford and displace the 66th TRW. In the early part of 1970 the 17th TRS moved to Zweibrucken in Germany to join the 86th Tactical Fighter Wing which had also been reactivated at Zweibrucken. The 18th TRS moved it's Voodoos to Shaw AFB to rejoin the 363rd TRW. This unit equipped with RF-4Cs almost immediately and it's RF-101s were transferred to the Air National Guard.

On arrival at Zweibrucken the 17th TRS did not find all to the their liking. The base had been inoperative for some time and the facilities were either damaged or non-existent. The first six Phantoms arrived at the German base on 7 January, 1969. Leading the first flight was the commander of the 17th TRS: Lieutenant Colonel Arthur R. Gould. Bob Gould was a very experienced recce pilot, having flown RF-80s and RF-86s with PACAF both during and after the Korean War. In the mid 1950s he flew the RB-45C and the T-33 with the 6021st RS out of Japan. In the mid to late 1950s he had flown the RF-84F and the RF-101. He had been with one of the first recce units in south-east Asia with the Pipe Stem detachment at Tan Son Nhut. More recently he had been with the 17th flying RF-101s and then the RF-4C when the squadron had converted to the type.

Operating from Zweibrucken brought its own set of problems. The base was very close to the French border and under no circumstances were the aircraft to overfly France. During bad weather all traffic patterns were conducted over the German side of the airfield. Zweibrucken was also very close to Ramstein and during IFR the GCA pattern took the aircraft too close to that of Ramstein so a shortcut had to be defined.

In spite of the shortcomings of the base and its facilities there was a mission to be performed. Throughout the move from the United Kingdom to Germany, the squadron was required to have six aircraft on an alert status at all times; ready to get airborne within an hour. In the early stages of the move this alert was maintained at Upper Heyford. Later it transferred to Zweibrucken. The wartime mission of the 17th was to do post strike photography of targets flown by the fighter bomber units in the Eastern Bloc countries. Bob Gould:

Typically, the fighter-bombers had one or two targets depending on how many weapons they carried. These missions were planned well in advance and if the time came, they reviewed the planned mission and they were ready to go.

The recce force didn't have preplanned targets. We know what the targets were, but we didn't have advance knowledge of which targets would be hit. It wasn't until after the whistle blew, that we were given targets to photograph. Of course, we would have several targets to photograph so some last minute flight planning was required.

We had mapped the strike targets and sorted them into sectors. There might be half-dozen or more targets in each sector. Aircrews were assigned to each sector, which they studied to the point where they had all the landmarks memorized. When we were given the targets to photograph, Intel pulled the appropriate maps, marked the targets, usually three to four per aircrew depending where they were located, and gave the maps to the appropriate aircrew for flight planning. As the nav plotted the courses, measured the mileage and marked minute tick marks on the maps, the pilot completed the flight logs. The course to the sector had been planned previously.

Of course, time was critical. We had a limited amount of time to get airborne after the targets were assigned, usually an hour or less. The upper echelon troops could not fathom that we could do the necessary flight planning (it seemed to them that we started from scratch) and get airborne in the time allotted. We had learned from a lot of practice, that if we cooperated, we could graduate.

Not every crewmember was required to fly at the same time, so they, along with other operations personnel, were assigned duties to perform that accelerated the procedure. When a crew was ready to go the aircraft, PE had their helmet and chute harness ready to go. When they got to the aircraft, it had already been pre-flighted, power was on and the electronics were warmed up. All they had to do was strap in, start engines and they were ready to go. We repeatedly had to prove that this procedure worked. We proved it to the wing several times, to 17th Air Force, to 4ATAF, to USAFE and even to the vice chief of staff of the Air Force.

The EB-66 returned to USAFE in 1969 with the 39th TEWS based initially at Bitburg AB. (MAP)

The 17th had their fair share of inspections in those early days at Zweibrucken. They were the new kids on the block! There were Wing ORIs, 17th AF ORIs, USAFE ORIs and 4th ATAF Tactical Evaluations. The squadron came through all with flying colours.

As the 17th was settling into Zweibrucken, in June 1969, the 39th TEWS was activated at Bitburg as part of the 36th TFW. The 39th brought with it sixteen EB-66s. For too long had the NATO allies been deprived of an ECM component and ever since the departure of the last of its RB-66s in 1966 the lobbyists had been working hard for their return. The mission of the 39th TEWS was to provide electronic warfare support, an electronic order of battle for Eastern Europe and to provide ECM and ECCM training for NATO defence forces. The 39th TEWS brought with it to Europe a great deal of experience in Electronic Warfare. Many of the crews attached to the squadron had seen service in south-east Asia. Unfortunately, because that war was still in full swing at the time; aircraft and crews would be lost to the south-east Asia squadrons over the ensuing months and years.

One of the missions revised by the 39th TEWS was the Dancing Girl air defence mission. Renamed Creek Girl these mission were similar to those originally flown by the 19th TRS. The main difference was that the exercises were, if anything, more realistic as a result of the experiences of the south-east Asia war. There was a huge demand for the squadrons expertise from USAFE and the NATO allies.

In December 1971 the 39th TEWS moved to Spangdahlem AB.

In mid April, 1970, a Phantom of the 17th TRS took off from Zweibrucken on a routine mission. The weather was not good. It was wet and miserable and storms were close. Shortly after take-off the nose of the aircraft was struck by lightning. The pilot was Captain Robin M Lake. GIB First Lieutenant Benny Watkins takes up the story:

> The strike rendered the navigation system between Robin and myself inoperative. We immediately actuated the standby attitude system and emergency generator and continued the climb in order to get out of the clouds.
>
> About this time, another RF-4C of the squadron joined us to look for damage. Only a slight discolouration was seen on our radome. Even so we aborted the mission and requested an immediate recovery at Zweibrucken AB.

Zweibrucken AB in 1970. When the 17th TRS arrived from Upper Heyford they found base facilities in a poor state of repair. (USAF via Bob Gould)

This 17th TRS RF-4C was hit twice by lightning, but succeeding in making it back to Zweibrucken. This photo was taken with the KA-56 low-pan camera in the RF-4C by Sam Miyamasu as he and pilot Dave Dargitz dropped Robin Lake and Benny Watkins off on finals. (USAF via Sam Miyamasu)

On our approach a second and more violent strike occurred which caused the aircraft to go into a 90 degree bank. We were able to right the plane and begin a climb by using the afterburner and the standby attitude system. If I hadn't had a great deal of confidence in Robin's ability I think I would have left the plane at that point.

On surveying the damage inside the cockpit, we noted that the airspeed indicator and angle of attack system were both out. The altimeter and vertical velocity indicators were fluctuating wildly and were useless.

Upon reaching VFR conditions above the clouds we made a mayday call and were again joined by the other 17th TRS aircraft. At that point we were told that part of the nose and the top of the tail were missing.

The 86th TFW Command Post advised us to recover at Ramstein since the weather was better there. Ramstein was then called and told to prepare for a barrier engagement. We were going to make a 'no flap' approach at a pretty high airspeed since a lot of buffeting and shaking were felt at normal landing speeds. We flew this approach on the wing of the other aircraft that had joined us earlier.

In the event, due to the skill of the crew, the aircraft was landed safely and lived to fly another day. The routine was not always so routine!

The 39th TEWS with its EB-66s was finding it difficult to fulfil its mission and its responsibilities to the combat units of USAFE. The demands of the war in south-east Asia for aircraft, equipment and personnel placed enormous strain upon the resources of the squadron. In addition the air defence systems of the Warsaw Pact nations had grown in sophistication in recent years; a development fuelled no doubt by experiences in the south-east Asia war. The EB-66 fleet was stretched to breaking point and the squadrons in Thailand, involved in the hot war, had

Captain Robin Lake and First Lieutenant Benny Watkins stand beside the shattered radome of their RF-4C at Zweibrucken. (USAF via Sam Miyamasu)

146 Tactical Reconnaissance in the Cold War

An RF-4C of the 1st TRS 10th TRW flies over East Anglia in mid 1970. (USAF)

An RF-4C of the 10th TRW on finals for Alconbury in 1975. The squadron is identified by the colour on the top of the vertical stabilizer, in this case blue for the 1st TRS. (USAF)

When tail codes were introduced for all USAFE aircraft in 1970, AS was assigned to the 30th TRS, 10th TRW at RAF Alconbury. (Alan Johnson)

USAFE 147

Aircraft RF-4C 64-1069 belonged to the 32nd TRS at Alconbury. (MAP)

Aircraft RF-4C 64-1026 was one of the 1st TRS aircraft at Alconbury, here seen at Upper Heyford in 1970. When the codes were standardized for the wing rather then the squadrons, the 10th TRW adopted AR. (MAP)

An RF-4C of the 38th TRS at Jever Tactical Air Meet, 1982. Note the shark mouth on the nose. (MAP)

Aircraft RF-4C 65-901 of the 38th TRS, 26th TRW based at Ramstein in 1971. The 26th TRW had two squadrons assigned: the 17th TRS and the 38th TRS. The 17th was at Zweibrucken and the 38th at Ramstein until 1973 when the whole wing became based at Zweibrucken. (USAF)

A 38th TRS RF-4C refuels from a KC-135 over Germany in 1970. (Fred Muesegaes)

In 1971 the 39th TEWS moved to Spangdahlem and became attached to the 52nd TFW. However, the demands of south-east Asia for aircrew and aircraft and the ever growing sophistication of the Warsawa Pact defence network hastened the deactivation of the 39th. The EB-66s returned to Shaw. (MAP)

RF-4C 64-1077 served with the 32nd TRS at Alconbury. Ramp Rat must have spent a lot of time in maintenance! (Via Dave Menard)

This RF-4C with the tail code ZR is with the 17th TRS out of Zweibrucken. (USAF)

An RF-4C of the 17th TRS in bicentennial scheme, 1976. (Authors Collection)

priority in terms of support. TAC deactivated the 39th TEWS in 1972, and the EB-66s were returned stateside.

Throughout the remainder of the 1970s and the 1980s the 10th TRW and the 26th TRW were the only units dedicated to tactical reconnaissance in USAFE. The 30th and 32nd Tactical Reconnaissance Squadrons of the 10th Tactical Reconnaissance Wing were deactivated in 1976, leaving the 1st TRS as the sole tactical reconnaissance squadron with the wing. The 10th acquired the 527th Tactical Fighter Training Aggressor Squadron (TFTAS) in 1976 and in 1987 was redesignated a Tactical Fighter Wing. At this point the 1st TRS was deactivated.

The 17th TRS remained part of the 86th Tactical Fighter Wing until January 1973 when it became part of the 26th TRW which had moved into Zweibrucken from Ramstein, taking with it the 38th TRS. The 86th TFW moved into Ramstein. The 17th TRS was deactivated in 1976 and the 38th TRS became the only dedicated tactical reconnaissance unit in mainland Europe.

During the course of the late 1970s and 1980s the RF-4Cs of both the 1st and 38th TRS were given many upgrades. Following the deactivation of the 1st TRS in 1987 the 38th at Zweibrucken with only approximately twenty aircraft became the only recce unit in USAFE. It was necessary to supplement this force with deployed units from the USA in times of tension and, to this end exercises were set up and regular deployments put in place. The 16th TRS from Shaw and units of the 67th TRW at Bergstrom paid regular visits to Europe in exercises such as Salty Bee and Coronet Hoop. Battlefield Eye was an exercise which brought the RF-4C ANG units to the European theatre, notably the 106th TRS from Montgomery, Alabama.

Not all exercises were straightforward as Mike Ross can testify! Mike flew with the 12th TRS at Bergstrom and later with the 38th TRS in USAFE:

> I was flying in Exercise Display Determination and was flying a TEREC bird. Our job was to find the fleet by using our TEREC capability. When we went out to the area we had to refuel first. While refuelling a USN F-14 rejoined to the observation position of the tanker we were refuelling from. When we were finished refuelling we turned toward the exercise area, the F-14 rolled in behind us and followed us for 15–20 minutes as we worked our way toward the Carrier Group. Our TEREC failed so we happened to have the Carriers TACAN frequency so we locked them up and started in towards them. When we got a visual on the carrier we started down to do a flyover like we had the previous Friday. The F-14 was still behind us camped at approx 3000 ft'. As we continued down and were passing through 10,000 ft' we lost sight of the F-14. We couldn't see him so the ROE was to remain predictable and to continue doing what we were doing prior to the loss of sight. So we continued our 'S' turn descent towards the carrier. Going through 6500-7000' we had a big bang on the aircraft and then everything on the airplane went haywire. Got the two fire lights and tried to regain control of the airplane which was shaking pretty terribly. I then commanded the bale out. At the time of the ejection we were doing 550 kts and $2^1/_2$ Gs. Randy, my pitter, went out upside down. I went out then next 1/2 turn later. I followed Randy down and landed in the water 70 yds away from him. It took 45 minutes for them to pick us up and take us back to the *Saratoga*, the Carrier that the F-14 was from.

An EF-111A of the 42nd ECS, 66th ECW 'Cherry Bomb' at Mildenhall 1987. (Author's Collection)

We spent the night and flew back to Aviano the next day. The accident board found that the Lieutenant was grossly over indoctrinated and grossly under trained. That being said he was grounded from further flying and, I'm told, left the Navy'

Realistic training!

The 38th TRS entered the Reconnaissance Air Meet at Bergstrom in 1988 (RAM 88) and won the competition in the face of opposition from four active duty USAF teams, four active duty navy and marine teams, five ANG units and units from Germany and Australia. In the competition aircrews were judged on five night missions, seven low level, high speed day missions and visual reconnaissance of Allied and Soviet equipment. The Top Team trophy was taken home to Zweibrucken.

The 38th played a significant part in Operation Desert Storm in early 1991. Six RF-4Cs and support personnel were detached to Incirlik, Turkey where the 38th TRS came under the operational control of the 7440th Combat Wing. Initially the mission of the 38th in the campaign was BDA. As time in theatre passed this changed, and pre-strike target designation and development missions made up approximately 50 per cent of the workload.

The 26th TRW and the 38th TRS were deactivated in mid 1991.

Meanwhile, in 1985, the 66th Wing had returned to USAFE in the new guise of the 66th Electronic Combat Wing. Two squadrons were assigned: the 42nd and 43rd Electronic Combat Squadrons (ECS). The 42nd ECS operated out of RAF Upper Heyford flying the EF-111A Raven electronic countermeasures aircraft. Logistical support for this aircraft was provided by the 20th TFW which flew the F-111.

The 43rd ECS operated the EC-130H Compass Call variant of the Hercules.

The 42nd ECS EF-111s had been at Upper Heyford since 1983 when they were assigned directly to the 20th TFW. They were the first aircraft deployed to USAFE with a specific electronic countermeasures since the departure of the 39th TEWS EB-66s in 1972. The EF-111Es were used effectively in the attack on Tripoli Airport in 1986 by 48th TFW F-111s: Operation El Dorado Canyon. Three aircraft provided stand off jamming support while the fighter bombers carried out their attack. Aircraft of the 66th ECW also operated in the Gulf war.

Aircraft EC-130H 73-1585 of the 43rd ECS 66th ECW at Fairford, 1987. (Authors Collection)

CHAPTER FIVE

Back Home

Every *Recce Puke* who saw service overseas throughout the Cold and Hot Wars of the three decades following the Second World War received his training at one of two main bases dedicated to the training and retraining of tactical reconnaissance crews. These were initially Langley AFB in Hampton, Virginia, and latterly, Shaw AFB in South Carolina. It was at these bases that the RF-51, RF-80 and RB-26 crews were prepared for combat in Korea and travelled to Europe to face the communists across the Iron Curtain. Crews from Shaw were amongst the first to deploy to the Middle East at the time of the Lebanon Crisis in the late 1950s, and it was from Shaw that the majority of the RF-101, RF-4C and R/EB-66 crews went to south-east Asia. These home-based crews had to react fast when the Cold War came to the very door of the USA at the time of the Cuban Missile Crisis. It was tac recce crews who, in fact, bore the brunt of operations over the Cuban mainland at this time.

The post-war mission of the 363rd TRW at Langley was 'to train and maintain proficiency of combat reconnaissance crews.' In January, 1948, the 363rd had three squadrons assigned: the 160th, 161st and 162nd Tactical Reconnaissance Squadrons. Eighteen FP-80s were assigned to each of the 160th and 161st squadrons and the 162nd crews flew the A-26 of which twenty were assigned including two dual control models.

These were the early days of flying jets operationally. The learning curve for pilots and ground crews of the two jet photo squadrons flying the FP-80 was quite steep. Also it was a time when these pilots and their aircraft were in great demand. In addition to routine exercises and missions there were many air shows where the public wanted to see new jet aircraft. The FP-80 had a radio compass and was regularly flown in poor weather conditions to destinations where the F-80 fighter could not go, having no instrument navigation system. Major Jean K. Woodyard was with the 160th TRS:

Aircraft FP-80A-5-LO, 45-8314 of the 161st at Langley in 1948. The 161st was a component of the 363rd TRW. The squadron received its first FP-80As in 1946. (USAF)

Aircraft FP-80A 44-85491 of the 161st TRS takes off on a routine mission. There were many demands on the squadron's time in the early days of jet flying, particularly participation in Air Shows. (USAF)

> One of the most interesting air show demonstrations was at Randolph Air Base, TX, for the School of Aviation Medicine in mid 1948. Two RF-80s were to pass in opposite directions head-on in front of the viewers at speeds to demonstrate 1,000 mph rate of closure. I had separated six aircraft in flights of three which flew in two spread out string formations. The flights passed each other head-on flying on the deck using the main runway as a separation line. Timing to get two of the six aircraft to pass the reviewing stand at the same time was tricky. On the second fly-by attempt two passed head-on at 475 mph each for the 950 mph rate of closure in front of the reviewing stand.

Amongst a multitude of events there was also an aerial demonstration by 12 RB-26s and 24 RF-80s at the dedication of Idlewilde Airport on the 31 July 1948. Woodyard was less than enthusiastic about this particular air show:

> President Truman was there and the news columns read that the F-80 aircraft performed intricate manoeuvres over the grandstands. The weather was lousy and a variety of aircraft were operating uncontrolled under a 1000 ft ceiling. It was aerial mess without a catastrophe!

The FP-80s were grounded on two occasions in 1948. The first occasion began on the 10 May following a fire in aircraft 45-8424 and involved checking the fuel systems. A month later, on 10 June, the FP-80s were grounded again following the inspection of air lines following the crash landing of 44-85477. In June also, the 162nd TRS FA-26s were also grounded for inspection of the nose gear assembly after cracks were found in struts.

Routine recce missions at this time included 9th Air Force Mission 966 which demanded the vertical and oblique photography of all the National Cemeteries, sadly much expanded by the casualties of the war; and an Operational Readiness Test (ORT) in June in which 171 missions were flown successfully in spite of adverse weather conditions and low ceilings.

In July 1948 Langley played host to six Vampire 111s, two Avro Yorks and a Mosquito from the RAF's 54 Squadron based at Odiham. On Air Force Day the Vampires gave a twenty minute aerobatic display.

In April of 1949 the 160th TRS was deactivated and with it the 363rd TRW. The 161st TRS moved to Shaw AFB in September 1949 and became attached to the 20th Fighter Wing. The 162nd remained at Langley.

In 1949 the 161st moved to Shaw and became part of the 20th TFW. One of its newly designated RF-80As is seen here on the ramp at Shaw. (Ed Stoltz)

On the 1st September, 1950, the 363rd was reactivated at Langley,; and along with it the 160th TRS. The 162nd had meanwhile been assigned to 5th Air Force in the Far East at Itazuke in Japan in August. On the 10th October, 1950 the 160th was redesignated the 16th Tactical Reconnaissance Squadron (Night Photographic). Also attached to the 363rd at this time were the 84th and 85th Bombardment Squadrons flying the B-45 Tornado and the 4400th Combat Crew Training Squadron responsible for all B-26 training. Only the 16th TRS had a reconnaissance role with the RB-26.

Training requirements for FP-80 pilots were demanding. Altogether 350 hours were divided between: Ground Training, fifty hours, including pre-flight of aircraft and proper use of flying equipment; twenty hours on communications, GC systems, Loran and Shoran; twenty hours on radar. 50 hours on the principles of photography, use of aerial cameras, photo interpretation; fifty hours each on visual recce and photo recce; twenty hours on navigation; twenty hours on weather recce and twenty hours on artillery adjustment. Training on photo recce was divided between

One of the primary responsibilities of the 161st at Shaw was the training of replacement crews for the 15th and 45th TRS in Korea. These two RF-80s of the squadron, 45-8310 and 45-8419, were photographed over Carolina in 1950. They also carry their buzz numbers in different places.(Ed Stoltz)

oblique and vertical photography. This training was clearly defined even down to the number of missions which must be satisfactorily flown in order to meet the individual requirements. For example, in oblique photography two missions must be flown at low altitude with the camera angle at 30 degrees. These missions to include two pinpoint targets and one straight line strip 15 miles long. Two low-altitude missions were also required with the camera angle at 45 degrees. Four high-altitude missions were also required; two with the camera at 30 degrees and two at 45 degrees. Two forward oblique missions with the camera angle at 30 degrees had to include a strip of river or coastline approximately 20 miles in length, a moderately irregular strip and one pinpoint. Demonstrating proficiency in vertical photography required many more missions; the emphasis being on overlap, minimum roll and pitch of aircraft, a straight flight line and use of the F2 computer in vertical pinpoint and strips, mosaic, and trimetrogen.

Visual reconnaissance required the pilots to demonstrate proficiency in the techniques of visual recce at altitudes of 3000 and 5000 ft in good and bad visibility. Missions included area searches over a maximum area of 2500 square miles which placed emphasis on photographing targets of opportunity such as shipping, airfields, factories, troop manoeuvres and marshalling yards. Route reconnaissance required the visual reconnaissance of a route of a minimum of 250 miles and was to include large cities, small towns, wooded areas and targets of opportunity. Weather reconnaissance missions included reporting on the type of cloud, temperatures at different altitudes and visibility.

Ed Stoltz received his training on the RF-80A with the 161st TRS at Shaw commencing in August, 1950:

> I was introduced to the RF-80A on assignment to the 161st TRS (Photo Jet) at Shaw AFB in August 1950. After the obligatory T-33A local area flight I moved on to the RF-80A with the first flight being on 10 August. The reconnaissance training was completed by the end of October with some 107 hours logged in the RF-80A. The training was a great learning experience for new pilots as the trainee completed his own flight planning, conducted the

In October the 161st was redesignated the 18th TRS. After modification to –15 specs this aircraft joined the 303rd TRS and later transferred to Sembach, Germany. (Ed Stoltz)

An RF-80A 45-8419 of the 18th TRS. (Mort Cameron)

> training flights solo and was, in effect, his own boss. The proof of success or failure of each training mission was in the photography and visual sighting reported. Trainees also received artillery adjustment experience with the Army at Fort Sill, Oklahoma.

On 11 October, 1950, the 161st TRS at Shaw became the 18th TRS. It was the sole squadron responsible for training replacement crews for Korea.

On the 8 March 1951 the 363rd TRW received orders to move to Shaw AFB. The wing headquarters and the 16th TRS commenced operations from Shaw on the 15th April, 1951. Assigned at this time was the 18th TRS. The 17th TRS, also flying the RF-80, was activated and assigned on the 2 April, 1951. The 363rd was also responsible for checking out the RF-80 pilots assigned to the 117th Tactical Reconnaissance Group at Lawson; a unit destined to depart for USAFE in early January, 1952. Ed Stoltz returned to Shaw to the 18th TRS after a tour in Korea. The 18th was a training squadron:

> Student pilots performed their own mission planning and in most cases were unaccompanied as they flew training missions in the RF-80. Photo training included using the various camera set-ups of the RF-80. This included vertical photography using the 6, 12, 24 and 36 in focal length camera installations; the 12 inch left oblique camera; the tri-met set up using 6 in focal length, and the forward pointing 12 or 24 in 'dicing' camera. The vertical camera training also included area coverage, or mapping, using the mosaic method. The adjoining strip photography required for the mosaic was somewhat difficult as the RF-80 lacked an onboard method for vertical vision. Training also included visual reporting on communications lines with emphasis on 'quick' estimates of vehicles on the road or engine and cars on railroad tracks. Instructors reviewed and critiqued the missions flown by the students. In most cases the proof of success or failure of the training flight was in photos taken by the student.
>
> The final phase of the recon training included artillery adjustment with Army. In 1950 we received artillery adjustment training from the back seat of army liaison aircraft. This was not exactly 'high-speed' artillery adjustment but did offer the basics and the experience of adjusting with an Army unit. After Korea commenced the program changed and RF-80s were used for truly 'high-speed' artillery adjustment. This training was conducted with the Artillery School at Fort Sill, Oklahoma and included classroom instruction on Army procedures and nomenclature. We staged the RF-80s from Tinker AFB, Oklahoma to the gunnery range at Fort Sill.

An RF-80A 44-85489 flown by Wes Brothers of the 18th TRS 1952. (Bob Sweet)

This way up! 18th TRS RF-80A 45-8425 goes over the top of the loop. (Bob Sweet)

Night-photo training at Shaw was initially the responsibility of the 16th TRS. Here RB-26, 44-35663 waits on the ramp for its next mission. (Colonel R. Uppstrom via Dave Menard)

Hostilities in the Far East had a considerable impact on training, missions and exercises, and in some cases drew attention to the inadequacy of equipment and aircraft. Exercise ASWET (Air Support Weapons Effectiveness Test) was instigated in July 1951; the purpose being to test equipment for possible use in tactical fighter reconnaissance. As part of the test recce units were required to direct and lead bomber units into enemy targets and photograph concealed or camouflaged sites. One of the more significant outcomes of this exercise was the problem faced by the 16th TRS. The aircraft had no A2 cartridge ejector equipment and the M46 flash bombs were delivered without any fuses. They also had no K-19 cameras. The 117th TRG came to the rescue and loaned the 16th some of its equipment, but it was an unsatisfactory state of affairs.

At this time all squadrons complained of a shortage of aircraft. The 16th TRS had only two RB-26s assigned out of an assigned strength of eighteen. The 17th TRS had only nine out of eighteen RF-80s. The 18th TRS did not fare so badly, having sixteen out of eighteen RF-80s on strength. A spate of accidents did nothing to help the situation. Two RF-80s crashed in the period

Another view of RB-26, 44-35663. The red and white chequered tail markings were carried for some time by 363rd aircraft. (Colonel R. Uppstrom via Dave Menard)

In January, 1953, the 118th TRW became the 66th TRW and its two squadrons of RF-80s were destined for USAFE. Here three aircraft of the 303rd TRS are getting ready for departure. (Ed Stoltz)

Aircraft of the 303rd and 302nd TRS at Shaw preparatory to departure for Europe. First stop for the RF-80s was Dow AFB in Maine. (Ed Stoltz)

When travelling long distances the camera bay of an RF-80 was spacious enough for most of the wardrobe! (Ed Stoltz)

July to September, 1951, fortunately without loss of life. This situation was not to be rectified until May, 1952, when the squadrons were brought up to strength.

October 1951 saw the assignment of the 4426th RCTS (Reconnaissance Crew Training Squadron) to the 363rd. The responsibility of this unit was to train night-photo crews for FEAF (Far East Air Force). The lack of a suitable range for these RB-26 crews to hone their skills was a handicap for the new squadron from the start. It was not until January 1952 that the bombing range at Fort Jackson was made available for flash bombing missions, this between the hours of 2200 and 0300 hours. Certain restrictions were imposed on the use of this range. Aircraft were to fly at 7000 ft. No more than four aircraft were to be in the pattern at any one time. No more than three flash bombs were to be used on each run, and after each final bombing run an aircraft was to fly over and look out for fires. If any were detected Fort Jackson was to be notified at once.

Exercise Snowfall was conducted in the early months of 1952 at Pine Camp in the New York area. Detachments from the 16th and 17th TRS took part in an exercise designed to train both army and air force units in operating in conditions of snow and extreme cold, such as could be experienced in Korea. Lessons learnt on this exercise were particularly pertinent to the RF-80 crews in relation to the role of visual reconnaissance. Target identification in daylight snow conditions was simplified and successful. What was more difficult was visual recce in conditions of partial snow and earth. In this instance target identification was extremely difficult. Included in Snowfall was a test of the ability of the RF-80A to act in the role of the 'Mosquito' aircraft; currently being filled by the T-6. This role was basically as a spotter for the army. The trial yielded mixed results. Although the RF-80 had the speed and manoeuvrability to avoid enemy aircraft and ground fire, time over the area was restricted by fuel. If the RF-80 were to replace the T-6, operations would require more detailed planning. The pilot would have to be able to pinpoint his position at any time.

In March 1952 Operation Longhorn took the 17th TRS and its RF-80s to Mathis Field, San Angelo, Texas. This was a joint Army/Air Force exercise and was the first occasion that an entire infantry division was airlifted; in this case from Fort Jackson, S. Carolina to Fort Hood, Texas. Two other units taking part in Longhorn were the 155th and 185th TRS. These were also based at Shaw as part of the 118th TRW which was an activated Air National Guard unit. Both were converting from the RF-51 to the RF-80.

On the 7 May, 1952, the mission of the 363rd became Combat Crew Training. This change of mission required an increase in the aircraft attached to each squadron. The 16th TRS was assigned twenty-three RB-26s and two dual control TB-26s. The 17th had eighteen RF-80 and two T-33s and the 18th, twenty RF-80s and two T-33s. As a direct result of the change in mission of the wing, the 4426th RCTS was deactivated on the 1 June, 1952.

In April, 1951, the 17th TRS was activated at Shaw. These four RF-80As belong to the squadron. (Mort Cameron)

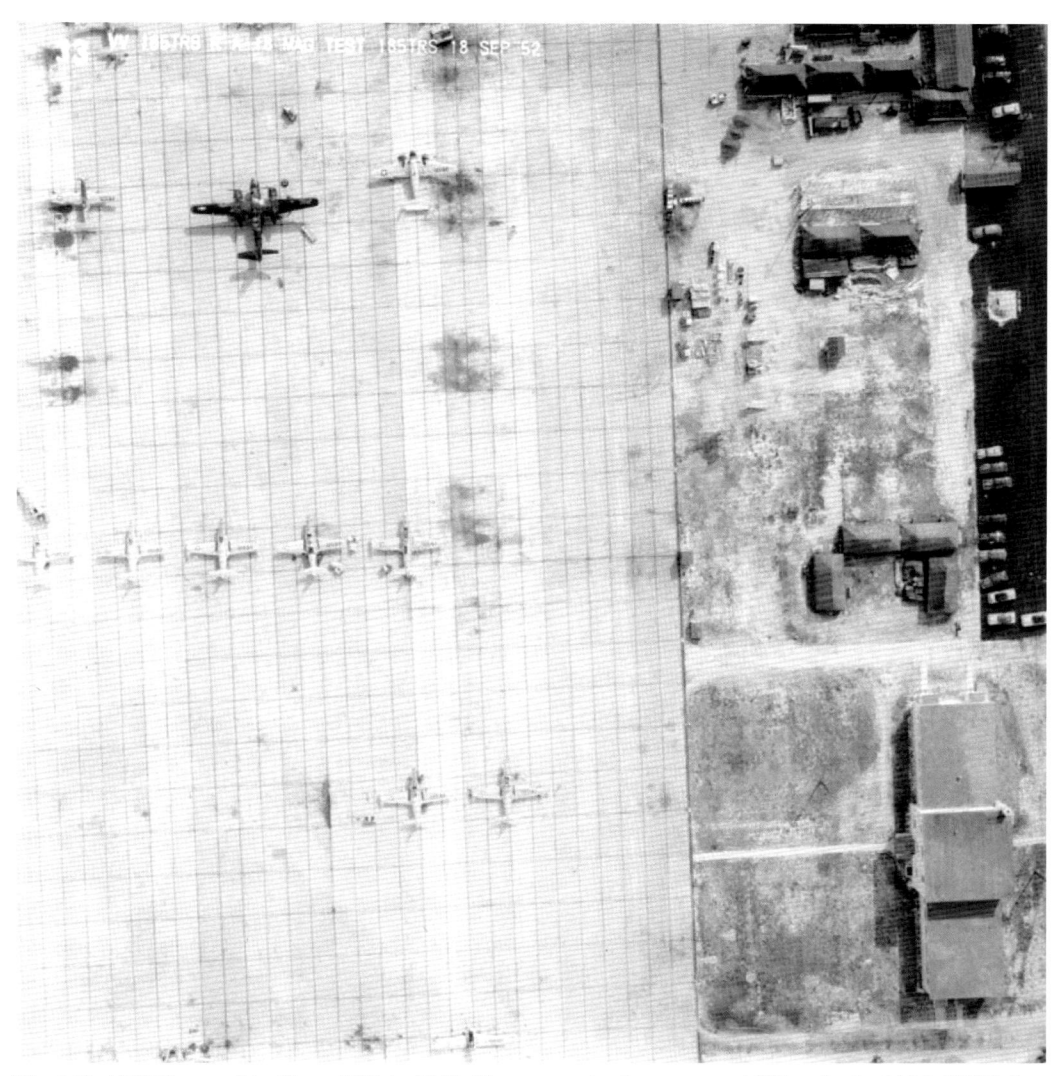

The 363rd TRW moved to Shaw AFB in 1951. Shaw was also home to an ANG unit, the 118th TRW. One of the squadrons of the 118th was the 155th TRS. In 1952 the 155th converted from RF-51s to RF-80s. In this aerial view of the 118th ramp some of the 155th RF-80s can be seen along with a lone RF-51 and a night photo squadron RB-26. (Via Roger Brunsvold)

In October, 1952 the 16th TRS acquired two TB-25J aircraft and their crews from the 507th Tactical Control Group at Pope AFB. The TB-25s had been configured for electronic reconnaissance. The modifications consisted of radar receivers, pulse analyzers, electronic jammers and chaff dispensers. The 16th TRS did not have facilities to support the Mitchells or their particular equipment. Nevertheless the experiences of Korea were emphasizing the need for the development of an electronic warfare capability in Tactical Air Command and so the number of personnel assigned to this particular duty in the 16th TRS increased over the ensuing months. In November, 1953, the 363rd reactivated the 9th TRS (Electronics and Weather). All personnel associated with the electronic warfare mission of the 16th TRS were assigned to this squadron. Initially the TB-25s went to the 9th but eventually the squadron received and flew RB-26 aircraft. Within the year the 9th TRS received WT-33s for weather reconnaissance.

Four RF-84s of the 17th TRS in formation over Carolina in 1956. The 17th TRS commander Captain Barnard, put together an impromptu aerobatic team to develop formation flying skills in the squadron. Flying here are Barnard, Captain Bob Sweet, Lieutenant Severtson and Lieutenant Nunis. (Bob Sweet)

The experience of Korea had an effect on the training of the reconnaissance pilots. In early 1953 Larry Garrison entered his recce training at Shaw:

> Our training there consisted of photo missions in and around the south-east for about 80 hours. We did not fly low level missions but many at 3000 to 4000 ft, and some maximum range missions when we returned with minimum fuel. We were told not to use our navigation aids and I did not. It was some of the best training we got. Each photo mission was graded but no one failed the course. There were two training aquadrons at Shaw at that time, with about ten pilots in training in several classes on the base. One pilot from each aquadron in each class was selected to stop by Nellis AFB for a check-out in the F-86 prior to Korea.

On the 1st January, 1953, the 118th TRW became the 66th TRW and its three squadrons became the 30th, 302nd and 303rd TRS. Preparations were put in hand for the newly activated 66th TRW to deploy to Europe, to Sembach AB in Germany.

In March, 1954, the 432nd Tactical Reconnaissance Group was assigned to the 363rd and had three squadrons assigned: the 41st TRS flying the RB-26, 43rd converting to the RB-57A Canberra and the 20th and 29th TRS, shortly to acquire for a short time, the RF-80A, prior to conversion to the RF-84F in 1955. This brought the total number of squadrons assigned to Shaw AFB, in the reconnaissance training role, to seven.

A 17th TRS RF-84F at Shaw in 1956. The chequers are natural metal and red, unlike the RB-26s which used red and white. (Bob Sweet)

The mid 1950s witnessed a period of change for all recce units in the USAF. In USAFE, PACAF and in the Continental USA (CONUS) the transition to new aircraft became a priority. The 16th and 43rd acquired their RB-57As in 1954. The RF-80 squadrons at Shaw converted to the Republic RF-84F Thunderflash in 1955. The 9th and 41st continued to operate the RB-26 until 1956 when they converted to the RB-66.

The 43rd TRS Canberras in common with all other units RB-57s spent a lot of time grounded because of recurring problems. There was, however, some affection for the aircraft and its mission. Ed Gorman flew with the 43rd:

> We had fun, during the late 50s, photographing SAC bases from over 40,000 ft, at night, just for practice! For illumination we dropped 250 lb magnesium flash bombs which lit up the sky so bright you had to shut your eyes when they went off. The resulting pictures, however, came out just like they were taken in broad daylight. Ancient technology by today's standards but it was pretty cool, then.

This 20th TRS RF-84F is over Shaw AFB in 1956. The 20th was activated at Shaw in 1954 and for a brief period flew the RF-80 before converting to the RF-84F in 1955. (Ed DeBoom)

In 1954 the 432nd TRGp was assigned to the 363rd TRW. The 43rd TRS was assigned and received the RB-57A Canberra. One of their aircraft is here seen in the company of some of the 20th TRS RF-84s. The 20th was also assigned to the 432nd. (Ed Gorman)

> We thought it appropriate, since the aircraft were painted all black and we frequently tooled around at night, to adopt a mischievous looking bat as our squadron insignia.

The 16th and 43rd retained their troublesome RB-57As for a brief period only before they began to check out on the RB-66. The 16th was the first squadron to convert to the RB-66B; having sixteen assigned by June 1956. The 9th TRS received its first RB-66C on the 11th May, 1956. This was an historical event recalled with enthusiasm by CMSGT John Madrishin:

> One day I was called by the Wing CO, who told me to pack a bag as I would be going with him and a Navigator to the Douglas Aircraft Co to pick up the very first RB-66C. We flew out to California and after spending one day touring the aircraft company, where we were presented with chrome plated models of the RB-66. When I told the company rep that I had a model by Revell a long time back, he could not believe it. How the model company ever got the plans to build the model was a mystery. Prior to departing California, the Wing CO had a large decal installed on the nose of the aircraft. It said 'The City Of Sumter South Carolina.' Now Shaw AFB is located on the outskirts of the city of Sumter. When we landed the C-model at Shaw, after landing and refuelling in Texas, we were greeted by the Mayor and many of the citizens from Sumter. The three of us were each presented with a large gold key to the city of Sumter. It has the outline of the state of South Carolina and inscribed MAY 11 1956. On the reverse side is printed CREW-CITY OF SUMTER RB-66C. The aircraft was assigned to the 9th Tactical Recon Squadron. Today that key hangs on the wall in my den. I would like to visit Sumter once again and see if the key will get me a free cup of coffee from the present Mayor.

One of the major problems in transitioning to the RB-66 was the shortage of in-commission RB-57As. It was necessary for the pilots with no multi-jet experience to check out on this aircraft prior to RB-66 training. For this purpose the 43rd deployed to North Field for a thirty day period on the 1 May 1956. A series of accidents to the RB-57s caused a curtailment of this programme on the 24 May. The acquisition of two B-57Cs for the wing did something to alleviate the situation, but it was still problematic.

North Field was often used as a venue for the conversion to new aircraft at Shaw. There were no facilities there; only a 10,000 ft runway. Even the control tower had to be brought in! Ed Stoltz converted to the RF-84F in 1955 with the 18th TRS.

> We were immediately put to work flying the T-33 while the 18th TRS made a move to North Field, South Carolina for a category field exercise of the RF-84F. I flew my first

A 20th TRS RF-84F at North Field in 1955. North Field was often used as a venue for new type conversion at Shaw. (Howard Peckham)

flight in the RF-84F from North Field on 4 March, 1955. The 18th TRS was required to furnish only 10 hours flying time for the RF-84 checkout but the squadron commander, short of pilots, invited us to remain for the entire month. This was arranged and during twenty-four days in March I flew over 57 hours; 46 hours of this time in the RF-84F. We flew all photo phases, mid-air refuelling from the KB-29 and marked targets with the 50 calibre guns. There were no distractions, as this was a bare base operation. We lived in tents and our sole job was to fly, fly, fly.

Ed was one of four pilots from USAFE, two from the 10th TRW and two from the 66th TRW. The four were transitioned onto the RF-84 and subsequently returned to their units as Instructor Pilots.

On 5 January, 1956, Operation Red Berry was instigated. This was to become a regular operation for units of the 432nd TRG and involved a deployment to Eielson AFB in Alaska. Initial deployment date for the operation was 1 January, but this had to be deferred to March because of

The 20th TRS RF-84F is at North Field undergoing maintenance. There were no facilities at the base so all equipment had to be brought in including the control tower. (Howard Peckham)

An RB-66B, 53-429 of the 16th TRS at Shaw in 1959. The 16th was the first squadron to convert from the RB-57A to the Destroyer. (Authors Collection)

the problems encountered with the cold weather operations of the J-65 engines of the 29th TRS RF-84s.

Both the RF-84s and the RB-66s had their fair share of problems during this period. All 9th TRS RB-66Cs were grounded for a period when Centre of Gravity problems were encountered. This was attributed to fuelling problems in the forward fuel tank. The manufacturers had to be called in to fit a fuel booster pump and the squadron borrowed two RB-66Bs from the 16th TRS. The 16th also suffered a grounding of its aircraft when rapid deterioration of the windshield glass on some aircraft became evident. It was ascertained that this was due to the unguarded nature of the de-icing control switch which was being accidentally turned on and causing excessive heat to be applied to the glass.

RF-84s were grounded from the 18th to the 24th March, 1956, when two aircraft experienced flame outs. The cause was determined to be the external tank configuration. The low pressure fuel filter was icing up on the 450 gallon tanks to a critical point. The increased surface area of the larger tanks would cause excessive condensation which was absorbed by the fuel. At high altitude the moisture would freeze on the filter and restrict the passage of fuel thus causing a flame out. The low pressure filter was removed and a bypass filter fitted. Throughout CONUS there were many bases without pressure air starting units. The pilots were also experiencing difficulties fulfilling Mosaic requirements. The aircraft were difficult to fly precisely enough to meet the exacting demands of the requesting authorities. This problem was further compounded by a shortage of scale maps.

The 9th TRS flew a variety of successful ECM missions in its RB-66Cs in spite of the intermittent

An RF-84F 51-1853 of the 17th TRS in flight over South Carolina. (Jim Payson)

An RF-84F of the 363rd TRW refuelling from a KB-50 tanker 1956. (USAF)

Three RF-84Fs of the 18th TRS, 363rd TRW. (Via Bob Sweet)

problems. Operation Winter End in February of 1956 involved the unit's aircraft in an operation to evaluate Continental Air Defence Commands radar system. Twelve successful missions were flown. In July the RB-66Cs flew an active ECM mission against units of the 3rd Army AAA at Fort Stuart in Georgia. At this time the 9th was flying three types of aircraft: the RB-66 for Electronic reconnaissance, the T-33 for weather recce and the TB-25 for jamming. The first WB-66s did not arrive for the squadron until early 1957.

Transition to the RF-101A Voodoo for the 17th TRS began in March, 1957, when three pilots went to Bergstrom AFB Texas for simulator training and thence to the McDonnell factory at St Louis for check out on a YF-101. The three pilots were Captains Martin J. Barnard, Robert Smith and Robert Sweet:

> Going from the RF-84 with its slow acceleration and long take-off roll to the '101 was one great experience ... Barnard, the 17 ops officer, brought the first RF-101A into Shaw

An RF-84F 52-7431 of the 17th TRS at Shaw's Open House in the Spring of 1958. The wrenches painted on the side of the fuselage contain the names of the ground crew. (Bill Talley)

on 6 May, 1957. Shortly afterwards he took a flight of four out to Clovis, NM for the dedication of Cannon AFB. During the briefing conducted by the F-100 flight commander, he indicated how the aircraft would line up depending on the wind. He asked Barney how much of a tail wind the '101s would take and was informed anything up to 40kts. That produced the desired effect on the fighter jocks in whose dust we had trailed for so long!

In June, 1957, the 363rd and 432nd Groups had, between them: thirteen RF-101s, fifty-four RB-66Bs, seven RB-66Cs, one WB-66D and forty-five RF-84Fs. The 17th had twelve Voodoos on strength and the 18th, had one.

In 1957 Tactical Air Command strove to develop the Composite Air Strike Force (CASF) concept. This entailed creating an autonomous strike force of aircraft able to move overseas at short notice to respond to any situation that arose which, in the opinion of the USAF government, merited a military response. The precise composition of the CASF would depend on the nature of the emergency being responded to. One of the initial consequences of this was the need for intensive in-flight refuelling training. The 429th Air Refuelling Squadron from Langley was primarily responsible for providing this training to both RF-101 and RB-66 crews using the KB-50 by the probe and drogue method. One of the initial requirements of TAC in relation to the CASF was a photographic one. Therefore, 363rd aircraft were photographed in flight in company with F-100s, KB-50 Tankers and C-130 aircraft.

The 9th TRS received its first RB-66C in May 1956. This aircraft is being refuelled by a KB-50 tanker. With the growing worldwide commitment of the CONUS based forces through the CASF, concept regular training in AAR was essential. (Bob Webster)

The 17th TRS received its first RF-101As in March 1957. A series of publicity photos was taken at this time. Here 54-1503 is seen in clean configuration. (USAF via Bob Sweet)

Another shot of 503 over Shaw AFB in March 1957. (USAF via Bob Sweet)

An RF-101A 54-1516 of the 18th TRS over South Carolina in 1957. The 18th began equipping with the Voodoo in June 1957. (USAF via George Cowgill)

RF-101A 54-1521 of the 18th TRS at Shaw in 1958. Roland 'Mr Voodoo' Richardson stands in front. Rich ended up with the most RF-101 hours of any pilot. (USAF via George Cowgill)

The 9th TRS flew both RB-66Cs and WB-66Ds for weather recce. Both types were heavily involved in the Cuban Missile Crisis. This WB-66D 55-393 was photographed at Shaw in February 1962. (John Bevette via Dave Menard)

This line up of RB-66Bs in July, 1962, belong to the 16th TRS. (MSgt Merle Olmsted via Dave Menard)

RF-101C 56-165 Sun Run 3. This aircraft was flown in the Sun Run by First Lieutenant Gus Klatt who established a new Los Angeles to New York speed record of 3 hours, 7 minutes and 43.63 seconds. (USAF via George Cowgill)

The first CASF deployment was in November, 1957, to the Far East and was called Mobile Zebra. Major Barnard led the first deployment of RF-101s outside the USA when he took five aircraft from the 17th TRS to Japan as part of this deployment. Mobile Zebra also involved the 9th TRS which sent WB-66Ds to Japan. Refuelling *en route* was provided by KB-50s.

In October, 1957, six aircraft from the 18th TRS had deployed to George AFB to practise for Operation Sun Run. Three pilots from each of the Voodoo squadrons were involved in the project. The Voodoo was the aircraft chosen to attempt to establish three official speed records. TAC Headquarters Operations Plan No. 15-57 stated:

> Headquarters USAF has directed Tactical Air Command to establish four F/RF-101 international speed records between 2 November and 31 December 1957. Four RF-101C aircraft will participate in a speed run from west coast (Los Angeles, California) to east coast (New York) with two of the aircraft returning to the west coast in an attempt to set east to west record in addition to west to east and round trip record attempts. All aircraft will be refuelled with KC-135 tankers.

The name Sun Run was conceived because the planners wanted the RF-101s to match the sun's time from Los Angeles to New York.

The pilots were Lieutenant Gus Klatt 18th TRS, and Captains Don Hawkins 17th TRS, Bob Kilpatrick 17th TRS, Bob Burkhart 18th TRS, Bob Sweet 17th TRS and Ray Schrecengost 18th TRS. The 18th TRS commanding officer Major Stan Sebring was the Sun Run operations officer.

While at George AFB practise runs were organized. As a result of poor organization there was a grand mix up. Some of the tankers weren't on station where they were supposed to be. Gus Klatt had to land at Gallup, New Mexico, a high altitude airfield with a short runway. Fuel and a starting unit were brought in from Kirtland AFB and, by the time Klatt took off, a large crowd had gathered to watch. Ray Schrecengost had to land at Kirtland. Bob Sweet was next in line and the tanker was on station. However, he had to return to George because his next tanker failed to show. These events did not bode well for the record attempt.

Sun Run was scheduled for Wednesday 27 November, 1957, and the pilots and aircraft were moved from George to Ontario International Airport. The six RF-101Cs serial numbers 56-163 through to 56-168 were painted in three separate paint schemes and three different colours. Two yellow aircraft with two different designs, two red and two blue. This was to make the individual aircraft instantly recognisable to those monitoring the record attempts. At seven o' clock on the morning of the 27th Ray Schrecengost took off from Ontario in 56-161 which he had named 'Cin Min' after his daughters Cindy and Mindy. He was followed by Kilpatrick, Sweet and Klatt. The spares, Hawkins and Burkhart were not needed and did not participate in the record attempt.

Captain Bob Sweet, flying 56-163 established a new Los Angeles to New York to Los Angeles non-stop round trip speed record of 6 hours, 46 minutes 36.21 seconds; and a new New York to Los Angeles speed record of 3 hours 36 minutes 32.33 seconds. He also broke the existing Los Angeles to New York speed record. First Lieutenant Gus Klatt established a new Los Angeles to New York record of 3 hours, 7 minutes 43.63 seconds. Captains Kilpatrick and Schrecengost broke existing speed records but did not establish any new ones. Captain Sweet:

This photo was one of several taken by the Air Force to publicize the CASF concept. KB-50s from the 429th ARS at Langley were responsible for the training of pilots in the probe and drogue method of in-flight refuelling. Here a 363rd RF-101 is seen in company with two C-130s, an F-100 and an RB-66B of the 16th TRS. (USAF)

> One of the first things we found out was not to let the Ground Controller turn the KC-135 too soon; a tail chase on a '135 was a losing cause if you were not fat on fuel, and we never were during the real operation. It was much better to maintain a high closure rate until you were right on the tanker. There were four AARs each way; eight for the round trip which meant a considerable time hooked to the '135. The one ways had the advantage because they didn't completely have to top off at the last refuelling. It was a 80 or 100 mile refuelling track when you had to stay hooked on the tanker and you would drop off and it was programmed so you'd have enough fuel to make the next one. Well, if you're going to land at Maguire, once you took on enough fuel you could unhook and finish, whereas if you were going round trip you had to go to the end of the track and by that time it was kinda late to accelerate. I enjoyed it but the night before we left there was a lot of talking about it. There's a lot of ifs in this stuff, I think everyone would have felt a lot more comfortable if the first they heard about it was when somebody lands. You feel pushed. I think if you'd asked any of us before that started if everybody would complete the trip without somebody having to peel off into Scott Field or some alternate someplace I think that probably most of us would have thought that somebody's going to have to hang it up early. I think it turned out pretty darn well.

Sun Run. as well as providing well earned publicity to the recce community and the Voodoo, also brought operational benefits. In particular, the pilots themselves acquired considerable experience on boom refuelling with the KC-135s. This experience was to benefit all Voodoo pilots and was also a lift for TAC which was often regarded as the poor relation of SAC.

Sun Run 3 takes on fuel from a SAC KC-135. (USAF via George Cowgill)

Sun Run 5, 56-167 was one of the spares flown by Captain Don Hawkins of the 17th TRS. The colour scheme was blue. (USAF via George Cowgill)

Sun Run 6 had an orange scheme and was another spare flown by Bob Burkhart. Neither of the spares were used in the event. (USAF via George Cowgill)

Captain Robert M Sweet stands in front of RF-101C 56-163 with the crew chief Staff Sergeant Carter. Bob Sweet established a new Los Angeles to New York round trip record of 6 hours, 46 minutes and 36.21 seconds. (Bob Sweet)

In February 1958, the 363rd and 432nd groups were redesignated as wings. Both remained at Shaw AFB. The 363rd controlled the 9th, 16th, 41st and 43rd Tactical Reconnaissance Squadrons and the 432nd: the 17th, 18th, 20th and 29th Tactical Reconnaissance Squadrons. Effectively the 363rd had become an all RB-66 wing and the 432nd an all RF-101 wing.

Operation Red Berry IV to Eielson which departed Shaw on 28th March, 1958, became involved in Army Mapping Project No. 51 which required photography of 2301 nautical miles of

RF-101C 56-163 returned to its 18th TRS, 432nd TRGp colours after Sun Run, but retained the logo for a while. (Authors Collection)

the Alaskan peninsula from Beckoraf Lake in the North to Bechevin Lake in the south and the area south from Anjak to the sea. Specs for the project were very stringent; nigh impossible to fulfil. There was to be minimum snow cover, no clouds, minimum sun angle of 30 degrees and flight altitude from 20,000 to 21,000 ft. The available weather meant that the project was doomed from the outset. In addition to this, the distance from Eielson to the south of the Alaskan peninsula was long and time was limited at low altitude for the photo runs.

In June, 1958, the 4414th Combat Crew training Squadron was assigned to the 432nd TRW and became responsible for the training of replacement RF-101C pilots.

In July, 1958, Double Trouble took a CASF to the Lebanon in response to the crisis there. Eight RB-66Bs, three WB-66Ds and eight RF-101s formed the task force, including the spares. On 15 July, at 2200 hours six RF-101s took off from Shaw for Incirlik, Turkey, planning to refuel NE of Bermuda, the Azores, Chaumont and Wheelus. One aircraft aborted due to a hydraulic problem. The remaining five eventually made it to Turkey. Four WB-66Ds and six RB-66Bs departed Shaw on the 16th July, flying via the Azores, Chateauroux and Wheelus. One RB-66B was lost over the Atlantic. Failure of the N1 compass being the likely reason. Of the deployed aircraft, five RF-101s, Five RB-66Bs and three WB-66Ds made it to Incirlik. By the 19th July the task force was in place. RB-66Cs did not make the crossing to the Middle East. It was proposed that ELINT and ECM would be carried out by the 42nd TRS resident in Europe at Spangdahlem.

The task force remained in Lebanon until October, 1958. supporting the US Marine peace-keeping force.

In the autumn of 1958 the 363rd was involved in another CASF deployment; this time in response to the Taiwan Straits Crisis. The Communist Chinese were threatening the islands of Quemoy and Matsu in the Formosa straits and their belligerence extended to threatening US shipping. The USA had a commitment to defend the Republic of China and dispatched a force to the islands which included a large naval contingent in the Straits. The journey for the 17th TRS Voodoos was eventful and they arrived at Clark AB on the 7th September, 1958, after penetrating a typhoon. Operations began the next day. Bob Sweet was with the 17th RF-101s.

> We started out flying to the north end of Taiwan and return, sometimes in flights of two and sometimes single ship, and I guess the idea was to put out some radar returns for the Chinese Communists to look at. Usually we put a flight out in the morning and one in the afternoon. The afternoon flight caused the most sweat because of the chance of bad weather. There was no in-flight refuelling so no one was fat on fuel. The squadron also picked up some photo missions throughout. The operation turned sour when a '101 and pilot were lost as a result of a mid-air collision while returning from Taiwan.
>
> The squadron sent two '101s along with a flight of F-100s to join up with a couple of KB-50s making a low level flyby of the main street of Saigon; a show of force to impress the natives. While I was down with the flight Bill Kirk was photographing a list of targets we were provided with. Some of us thought we would be back before too many years went by.

The CASF left the Far East on the 8th December, 1958, to return to Shaw. Bob Sweet had to spend a few days on Wake Island while one of the J-57s on his Voodoo was being repaired. He eventually arrived back at Shaw just in time for Christmas.

At the end of 1958 the programme of fitting all the RB-66s with ECM tail cones began. Aircraft 53-424 of the 16th TRS had the distinction of being the first of twenty-eight aircraft scheduled for this upgrade.

In May of 1959 the 17th and 18th TRS departed for Laon in France and became part of the 66th TRW. With their departure the operations aspect of the 432nd TRW ceased to exist. The 41st and 43rd TRS were inactivated. The 20th and 29th TRS rejoined the 363rd TRW. Thus the 363rd became a four squadron wing with the 9th, 16th, 20th and 29th TRS assigned, the former two squadrons flying the RB-66 and the latter two the RF-101. In June the 432nd TRW was inactivated. The 4411th CCTG was activated and two squadrons were assigned: the 4414th CCTS responsible for RF-101C training and the 4415th CCTS.

Generally routine missions were in support of the army in a variety of roles. Exercise Day Hills from the 19th to the 23rd May, 1959, was in support of the 4th Infantry Division. Six RF-101s deployed to Lawson AFB in this simulated nuclear warfare scenario. Fifty-four recce missions were flown in response to army requests. The wing provided airborne ECM in support of the Army Defense School at Fort Bliss, Texas. Three ECM tail-cone-equipped RB-66s were based at Biggs AFB for the duration of this exercise. On the 18th June, 1959, what was to become a regular ECM exercise was initiated against the air defence systems of the south-east United States. Five RB-66 aircraft equipped with the AN/ALT-6B electronic jammer and the AN/AST-1 chaff dispenser flew five high-altitude penetration routes, extending from Jacksonville, Florida to Norfolk, Virginia, commencing at a common H Hour control line 200 miles off the Atlantic coast. This regular exercise was mutually beneficial. The 32nd Air Division would get good practice and experience at interception, and the ECM crews would get realistic training.

One of the regular European commitments for the 9th TRS were the Swamp Fox deployments. Swamp Fox 1 took place in April, 1960. Two aircraft and two crews were involved and prior to departure from Shaw they posed for this photo. From left to right they are: Rear: Captain Ed Malone, Raven 4; Captain Jerry Welkom, Raven 3; Lieutenant Buck Wade, Raven 2; Lieutenant John Knoeppel, Raven 1; Lieutenant Ed Breck, ELINT shop; Unknown; Lieutenant Dave Smiley, Raven 1; Lieutenant Roy Fair, Raven 2; Captain Tom Sterling, Raven 3 and Captain Paul Duplessis, Raven 4. Front: Captain Jim Ely navigator; Captain Earl Johns, Pilot; SSgt Joe Melton, Gunner; Unknown; Unknown; Unknown; Lieutenant Mike Barbolla, Navigator; Lieutenant Bob Stamm, Pilot; and Staff Sergeant Charles Floyd, Gunner. (Bob Stamm)

Sadly there were three accidents to RB-66s mid year. On the 7 May aircraft 418 was taking an air-to-air photo of a formation of RB-66B aircraft over Sumter on their return from Anderson AFB where they had performed a fly by. Aircraft 473 collided with the photo aircraft and crashed 6 miles north of Sumter. Aircraft 418 made it back to Shaw, landing safely. At about the same time WB-66D 55-400 experienced hydraulic problems following a weather recce mission. This aircraft did succeed in landing at Lajes.

Regular exercises with Air Defense Command (ADC) and the army provided the ECM crews with valuable training. Kermit Helmke flew with the 9th TRS in the late 1950s and early 60s:

> There were five or six ECM training routes which we used to fly out of Shaw AFB for ferret proficiency in the late 50s and early 60s. All were over land. One went south to Jacksonville Florida, then west to the New Orleans area and back up across Alabama and Georgia to Shaw AFB. On this particular day our weather front-end crew was flying with the squadron lead ECM crew. As I walked out to the aircraft with the squadron ECM officer, he complained about another boring mission, nothing to cut but commercial broadcasting stations, VOR's etc. He had been over this particular route many times. All was routine until we were maybe 90 miles east of New Orleans on the west bound leg. Then ECM called wanting to know whether I knew our exact location. All navigation systems were working so I reassured lead ECM and asked what was going on. He gave me a quick "Tell you later" and went back to work.
>
> What had happened? We had picked up a radar signal out of Cuba which was known to support nuclear weapons. This was a rarity as recce missions by the 66 over Cuba generally yielded a shut down of everything of military importance.
>
> Did our routine mission have any bearing on events which were to subsequently transpire? We may never know.

Aircraft RF-101C 56-187 of the 363rd TRW at Shaw in 1959. The two Voodoo squadrons, the 20th and 29th TRS rejoined the 363rd in May 1959. (Via George Cowgill)

Aircraft RF-101C 54-1515 as flown by Brigadier General Stephen B. Mack who commanded both the 432nd TRGp and the 363rd TRW at Shaw at one time. (via George Cowgill)

However, this training fell short in a number of specific areas. The radar systems in the Continental US that the EWOs were ranged against were not the Soviet systems that they would encounter in a real war. Neither were they mobile. It was expected that enemy systems would be regularly moved. In order to provide regular training of a more realistic nature Exercise Swamp Fox was born. Under Swamp Fox, RB-66C aircraft and crews would regularly deploy to the United Kingdom, basing at RAF Chelveston with the 42nd TRS. From here they would fly missions along the East German and Czech borders finding, identifying and analysing Soviet radars. Swamp Fox deployments began on 14 April, 1960. Two RB-66Cs flew, first to Lajes in the Azores and thence to Chelveston, arriving there on the 15th. Practise missions were flown regularly over the UK both prior and during the periods when missions were flown along the Warsaw Pact borders. Approximately four Swamp Fox deployments took place every year.

In addition to Swamp Fox there was a marked increase in overseas deployments in the early 1960s. Operation Long Pass in February, 1961, took eight RF-101 aircraft of the 29th TRS to the Philippines for a joint army air force manoeuvre. Broadway Bill took six RF-101s and four RB-66Bs to the United Kingdom over the Northern route. Departing on the 12th June the RF-101s flew first to RAF Bentwaters and then to Moron, Lajes and back to Shaw. The RB-66s flew to RAF Bruntingthorpe and from there followed the same route home as the Voodoos. In September, 1961, Exercise Checkmate 2 involved three RB-66Cs of the 9th TRS, three RB-66Bs of the 16th TRS and six RF-101s of the 20th TRS deploying to Incirlik, Turkey.

On 14 October, 1961, Sky Shield 2 involved elements of both the 16th TRS and the 29th TRS in an exercise designed to test the ability of NORAD to defend the North American continent and for SAC to launch missions while under attack. Four RB-66Bs and four RF-101s were assigned to the force attacking the US. The RB-66s were attacking Charleston SC, Macon, Savannah and Atlanta GA, Jacksonville FL, and Hunter and Patrick AFBs. The RF-101 targets were Baltimore MA, Washington DC, and Richmond and Norfolk VA. One RB-66B was deemed lost after hitting its target at Savannah but only after suffering 14 continuous intercepts by F-101B aircraft. The aircrew had exhausted their supply of chaff, having broken the lock-on of the fighter twenty-four times. Two RF-101s were lost: one before the target and one on weapon release.

In October, 1961, in response to the closing of the border between East and West Berlin; Operation Stair Step heavily involved the 9th TRS. Ten ANG squadrons were deployed to Europe to reinforce USAFE and provide a timely reminder to the Soviet Union and its Allies that any escalation they may have in mind would be inadvisable. On the 25 October, the 9th TRS sent five RB-66Cs from Shaw to Lajes via Newfoundland, Goose bay, Keflavik and Greenland to provide electronic reconnaissance along the deployment routes. Two aircraft on Swamp Fox VII at Chelveston joined the task force.

In early 1962 there were two significant exercises which involved the 363rd. Exercise Great Bear took four RF-101s to Elmendorf. This exercise drew attention to several issues relating to the cold weather operations. F-100s at Elmendorf melted the snow on the runways on take-off. This then froze to slick ice which caused problems for following aircraft. In addition de-icing fluid caused slush underneath the aircraft which made for a ground safety hazard and when carried on the pilots feet made rudder and brake controls difficult.

In April RB-66s and RF-101s deployed to Eglin AFB to take part in a firepower demonstration for the President. The RF-101s were to take oblique photos of the reviewing stand and provide an air-to-air refuelling demonstration with a KB-50. The RB-66Bs were also to take part in the refuelling demo and provide a twenty-one gun salute by firing off twenty-one M-123 photoflash cartridges during a formation fly-by. There was also a static display. Eight RF-101s took part in the deployment and seven RB-66Bs. The Destroyers mission was successful but the Voodoos oblique photography was barely satisfactory.

The 20th TRS was involved in trials of the KA-52 camera in March, 1962. The KA-52 was designed by Fairchild to provide low-altitude high-speed horizon-to-horizon panoramic photography. Aircraft 56-190 was used in the tests and the camera was mounted in the rear vertical station. It was necessary to replace the standard camera window in this station with a new window which protruded 2.3 in below the aircraft. The first test took place on the 20 March. The programme of testing was deemed a great success and very good photography was obtained. The KA-52 would meet a lot of recce and surveillance requirements.

In October, 1962, what has become known as the Cuban Missile Crisis began and the 363rd TRW took the centre stage. During the initial phases of the crisis the 363rd was on alert and the recce crews began preparing target folders and planning missions. On 21 October, the wing deployed to MacDill AFB as part of the TAC build up. Lieutenant Colonel Joe O' Grady led the first RF-101 contingent of the 29th TRS out of Shaw at 1700 hours. By 2240 all Voodoos were in place. That same day the 9th TRS deployed five RB-66Cs. On the 22nd the 16th TRS launched eleven RB-66Bs. On arrival all of these aircraft were put on one hour alert status to carry out photo missions against assigned targets. All aircraft were in place by 22 October and ready to carry out any reconnaissance missions requested; some of the RF-101 pilots standing cockpit alert. On the 24th and 25th flights were directed to check out dispersal airfields in Florida.

At 1030 hours on Friday, 26 October, the first full flight of two RF-101s was airborne and on the way to photograph targets in Cuba. This was followed by two more flights of two. These initial missions were designed to confirm the presence of the missiles on Cuba. After Krushchev's climb down on the 29 October recce missions were to confirm the dismantling and removal of the missiles. However, an RF-101 mission flown on the 29th October by Lieutenant Colonel Joe O' Grady and Captain Jack Bowland met with bursts of anti-aircraft fire. Operation Blue Moon was, for the RB-66Bs, a surveillance programme designed to obtain pre-strike intelligence on selected Cuban targets by night whilst the RF-101s did the job by day, though it must be stressed that the US Navy flew regular successful reconnaissance by day also. The aircrews of the 9th TRS RB-66Cs spent many hours in cockpit alert between the 22 October and the 30 November. Both they and the 16th TRS had the secondary role of delivering crucial film at high speed to where it was needed.

The RF-101s cameras proved to be inferior at low level to those used by the Navy RF-8s. At altitudes of 500 ft or less at relatively high speeds image motion was causing blurring of the images. Part of the solution was found in the rediscovery of the K-18 Strip camera. Originally designed by the then Colonel George W. Goddard in the Second World War. The strip worked on the principle of moving a strip of unexposed film past an open slit at a speed consistent with the apparent movement of the subject of the photograph. The continuous strip photo produced had a clarity rarely obtainable by a shutter camera at a corresponding altitude and speed. Following consultation with Brigadier General Goddard several K-18As were taken out of storage at Wright Patterson and installed in some of the Voodoos. Regular flights were also undertaken by the RF-101s from MacDill to a Naval Air Station for modifications to the camera suite.

Routine RF-101 missions over Cuba were flown until the 15 November. Fred Muesegaes:

> All profiles were high-low-high with the low portion beginning approximately 100 nautical miles from the island. The ones that had targets in the western end of the island or around Havana were flown without refuelling I believe. I didn't fly any in this area, so I'm not sure. The typical mission to the mid and eastern part of the island required one refuelling which occurred on the outbound high leg of the profile and was near San Andros Island in the Bahamas. Usually after leaving the tankers (KC-135s) we would get oriented over one of the islands as an IP and descend to low level to try to get under the radar coverage but usually we would be alerted (by the nose radar-warning system) that search radar was sweeping us as we approached the island. When this occurred we turned on the wire recorder for the ELINT that could be gained from the radar signals – type, search or lock- ons, duration, etc. Navigation was dead reckoning and pilotage only, so it was a real challenge when the first target was on the coastline when you had been flying at 500 ft or less over the water for the last 100 nautical miles or more. Assigned targets were SAM sites, airfields, barracks areas, military facilities, communications, port facilities including ships, and, of course, nuclear missile assembly and deployment areas or sites.
>
> Threats were AAA, SAMs and MIG-17s and MIG-21s. I saw a lot of each on the ground, but only one MIG-17 airborne over one of the airfield targets. Fortunately there was no way he could catch us even if he wanted to. I don't believe any active firing AAA was observed after the first couple of days, but it was always disconcerting to fly over a targeted SAM site that was active, but at our altitude and speed they really weren't a threat to us, just to the U-2s.
>
> The last mission I flew was the longest and possibly the longest of any flown. We (we flew in flights of two aircraft) criss-crossed the island from just east of Havana to practically the east end for approximately 1:15 hours over the island. I believe some missions were probably as short as 15 minutes over the island. One thing that I'll never forget is as we approached Guantanamo Bay on the east end of the island I saw dozens of troops running for their AAA emplacements and thought here it comes. But as we flew by them they were all waving, so I rocked the wings back. So not all the Cubans were hostile. On this mission we required two refuellings over the Bahamas outbound and inbound due to the length of the low-level portion.

Many of the eager pilots of the RF-101s in particular were frustrated by the number of missions which they flew over Cuba. There were never enough to go round and playing the waiting game did not sit well with the fervent desire to fly the missions. Little did many of these eager men realize that within a couple of years they would be flying intensive, dangerous and unrelenting missions over the countryside of Laos and Vietnam.

The successes of the Cuban Missile crisis for the US are well documented in terms of the political and international outcomes. In terms of outcomes from the tactical reconnaissance missions much was learnt. The numbers and location of IL-28 aircraft bases and assembly points was discovered. Soviet AA-2 air-to-air missiles which were intended for use by Mig 21s in the air intercept role were identified. SAM sites were the subject of regular low level, high speed RF-101 recce sorties. Much was learned about the number, type, and location of all these sites. During flights aircraft were the subject of regular lock-ons from enemy radar sites, often when flying as low as 200 ft. Much information was gained about the capabilities of the SA-2 systems operations. Information that was to be invaluable in south-east Asia.

Missions over Cuba also pointed out some grave inadequacies in the recce equipment and the training of the aircrew. Increased training in low-level techniques was instituted for the RF-101 pilots and it was felt necessary to upgrade completely the recce suite of the aircraft. To satisfy the latter requirement Modification 1181 was instigated.

Modification 1181 included a complete revision of the Voodoos recce suite and included an attempt to give the aircraft a night capability. The Hycon KS-72A framing camera, being developed for the RF-4C was included in the upgrade, which did, however, retain the KA-1 36 in focal length camera with a 9 × 18 in plate which gave superb coverage at high altitude and which was to prove so successful in south-east Asia.

The RB-66B modifications at this time included the installation of strobe lights and infra red sensors to optimise night-photo capabilities

Following the Cuban Crisis the Aunt Mary programme was set up. This required six pilots and six RF-101 aircraft to be on call at Shaw should any recce missions over Cuba be required. In addition to this these same pilots would be required to perform regular recce missions over the US simulating missions over Cuba. Every week at least the Aunt Mary crews would be fragged with targets by TAC. Fred Muesegaes:

> The planning was conducted just like we would for an actual mission and we would fly a low level mission to the assigned targets, which were in the south eastern US (not Cuba – of course). Upon returning from the flight the film downloading, processing, and interpreting were done on a priority basis with the pilots flying the missions going to Recce Tech to assist the PI. The film and the results were sent to TAC Hq for review. I am unaware of any future missions being flown over Cuba after the Aunt Mary programme was commenced.

A standard Aunt Mary mission lasted 4 hours 30 minutes. Four aircraft, each with four cameras, would be required to photograph eight pin-point targets. Some 400 feet of film was to be taken and processed. Photo processing was to produce one duplicate positive and one duplicate negative of each original negative. RB-66Bs of the 16th TRS also had an Aunt Mary, commitment. Both RB-66 and RF-101 aircrews had to complete two missions each quarter. An example of a typical Aunt Mary mission took a force of three RB-66Bs and six RF-101s in March 1963 to Larson AFB

Aircraft RF-101A 54-1512 was one of the aircraft which received an experimental camouflage scheme before camouflage became the norm. The Cuban Missile Crisis mission pilots were the first to suggest that camouflaging the aircraft may make them less susceptible to attack. (George Cowgill)

The 16th TRS received the first RF-4Cs at Shaw in January 1965. These aircraft were delivered in their gull-grey and white 'navy' scheme. (Kirk Ransom)

to photograph the entire manoeuvre area of the forthcoming Exercise Coulee Crest. Both types of aircraft performed low level photo missions.

While the RB-66Bs and the RF-101s were involved in Aunt Mary, the RB-66Cs of the 9th TRS were engaged in regular peripheral electronic reconnaissance of Cuba in Operation Cold Cream.

The year 1964 was characterized by the planning for the arrival of the RF-4C and the phasing out of the WB-66D and the subsequent reorganization of the squadrons that this entailed. The 16th TRS relinquished its RB-66Bs to the 9th TRS, which retired its WB-66Ds to storage at Davis Monthan. The original plan had been to commence equipping the 16th TRS with the RF-4C in the third quarter of 1965. However, the conflict in south-east Asia had emphasised the need to accelerate the introduction of the aircraft and, in the event, the first of the Phantoms was received by the 16th TRS on the 28th January, 1965.

Meanwhile, routine exercises intensified to provide the training necessary for all crews. One Shot on the 9 September, 1964, involved six RF-101s and two RB-66Cs of the 20th and 9th TRS

Aircraft RF-4C 64-016 hangs everything on its approach to Shaw in 1965. (Kirk Ransom)

The 16th TRS began deployment to south-east Asia on the 27 October, 1965, when nine aircraft and two spares left Shaw, flying to TSN via Hawaii and Guam. (Kirk Ransom)

respectively flying out of Shaw. Units provided recce support for Air Assault 3 in the Carolinas on the 21 September. Coulee Cross on the 5 October took three RF-101s of the 29th TRS from Shaw to Fairchild AFB to provide recce support to the 4th Infantry Division. On this day also six RF-101s were deployed to Kadena for Operation One Buck-4.

Cold Fire 1 on the 26th October, took a large recce force to NAS Memphis and McConnell AFB. Seven RB-66Bs, four RB-66Cs, two WB-66Ds and ten RF-101s took part in this joint

Aircraft 54-046 taxies out to take off for Saigon, while family and friends say goodbye. (Kirk Ransom)

service exercise. Whilst on deployment these aircraft were assigned to the 4487th Composite Reconnaissance Squadron. The squadron also included six F-100s for print delivery and two C-47s. Four of the RB-66Bs were strobe equipped and one also had a T-11 mapping camera.

On 1 December the 20th TRS sent six RF-101s to Ayacucho, Peru for joint manoeuvres.

In December, 1964, nine RB-66Cs of the 9th TRS received Modification 1199 designed to enhance their ECM performance ability. This included the addition of two active ECM systems in each aircraft and adequate three phase power to all ECM stations.

The intensity of training exercises continued into 1965. From the 4th to the 7th January three RF-101s were deployed to Fort Hood for participation in Exercise Cactus Burner in support of the US Army 11th Corps. From the 4 to the 18 February Operation Polar Strike took a Composite Reconnaissance Squadron to Elmendorf. Three RB-66Bs, Six RF-101s and three T-33s were involved. On 22 March Exercise Quick Kick was a joint amphibious and airborne assault on the island of the Vieques in Puerto Rico. Four RF-101s and four RB-66s took part.

Concurrent with the introduction of the RF-4C was the upgrading of 9th TRS RB-66Cs under the Big Sail 1 and 2 programme of modifications. Big Sail provided an increase of three jamming systems and the installation of eight ECM systems including QRC-49/95, QRC-114 and AN/ALT-15. There was also the addition of a fourth AN/ALA direction finding antenna.

Two Big Sail modified RB-66Cs were deployed to south-east Asia in April, 1965, following three Strobe and IR equipped RB-66Bs which had deployed in March to Tan Son Nhut. When these aircraft moved to Takhli in May, two further 9th TRS RB-66Cs went out to join them.

The RF-4Cs suffered from several deficiencies in the early days. Of significance, bearing in mind the aircraft's imminent deployment to south-east Asia, were the flight control and directional control problems encountered when taking off from wet runways.

On the 1 October, 1965, the 41st TRS was activated at Shaw attached to the 363rd TRW. This unit had one airman assigned. The squadron effectively moved to south-east Asia and took over the assets of the 9th TRS at Takhli in November. Commensurate with this the 20th TRS moved to Tan Son Knut (TSN) and took over the RF-101 Able Mable mission from the 15th TRS using the aircraft resident there. The 20th received considerable support from the 29th TRS which unit furnished eighteen combat crews and made ten deliveries of aircraft from the US.

The deployment of the RF-4Cs necessitated the compression of much of the training, particularly on the newly installed APQ-99 Forward Looking Radar (FLR). Aircrew were required to fly an additional twenty-two sorties. There was a notable lack of confidence on the reliability of the hardware, and there was an element of doubt as to the RF-4s readiness for night and all weather recce. Also, many of the pilots were ex RB-66 pilots and not experienced fighter pilots. One notable problem was pilot fatigue on long-haul flights. A lumber pad was sorely needed!

However, regardless of the difficulties and shortcomings of the pilots and the aircraft the first deployment of nine aircraft and two spares took off from Shaw on the 27 October, 1965, flying to TSN via Hawaii and Guam. The second increment of eleven aircraft departed Shaw on the 28 December. During November a series of tests on the RF-4C systems took place both at Shaw and in south-east Asia. Altogether 468 sorties were flown in order to test the following: the KS-72 framing Camera, the KA-56 low-altitude panoramic camera, the KA-55 high-altitude panoramic camera, the AAS-18 infra-red (IR) detecting kit, the APQ-102 Side Looking Radar (SLR) and the APQ-99 FLR.

In early 1966 the 9th TRS relinquished its RB-66s and converted to the RF-4C. The squadron was declared combat ready on the new aircraft on the15th June. Prior to this, in May, the 363rd had subjected the squadron to an Operational Readiness Test (ORT) to determine the units readiness to deploy to south-east Asia. The test was generally considered satisfactory. However, equipment failures in the IR and KS-72 camera systems contributed to a low night-mission achievement of only 66 per cent. A further ORT in June still produced mixed results. Daylight-photo missions enjoyed an 85 per cent success rate; while night time missions were still below par. In spite of this, Detachment 1 of the 9th TRS was activated and ordered to deploy to Udorn to be in place by 31 July, 1966.

In the event the 9th TRS did not deploy RF-4Cs to Udorn. This fell to another tac recce squadron, the 12th TRS, activated at Mountain Home AFB on the 1 July, 1966. The 9th TRS was deactivated on the 1 July, 1966. The 12th TRS was activated as part of the 67th TRW on the 1 July, 1966. The 67th TRW had been reactivated at Mountain Home on the 1st January, 1966. The 12th and the 67th had been together before, of course, in the Far East under PACAF. The mission of the 67th TRW included aerial, optical, electronic, thermal and radar reconnaissance, and RF-4C replacement training primarily for the south-east Asia squadrons. In addition to the 12th Tactical Reconnaissance Squadron, the 67th in 1966 also comprised the 10th and 11th TRS.

Although the 67th had been activated in January, it did not receive its first aircraft until 6 April when the first RF-4C arrived. The first training sortie was flown by the 10th TRS on the 11th April. The 10th was designated a Replacement Training Unit (RTU) in May. A further aircraft arrived on the 3 May; and on 21 May at an Armed Forces day, an RF-4C was dedicated to the State of Idaho. Both the Wing's aircraft were involved in the search for a missing child in Southern Nevada on 3 June.

By the end of June a total twelve RF-4Cs had been received. The 10th TRS/RTU training schedule placed great emphasis on Combat Profile training: to train aircrews in navigation and target acquisition during day and night operations. As a part of this training the aircrews were given in-flight target assignments and had to do their planning whilst *en route* to the target.

On 28 August aircraft from the 32nd TRS arrived at Mountain Home from Toul-Rosiere. Fifteen RF-4Cs were ferried over from France by crews from the 22nd TRS. These RF-4Cs were assigned to the 12th TRS which, up to this time, had no aircraft. The 12th also received five aircraft and crews from the 22nd TRS and one aircraft and aircrew from the 11th TRS. On the 2nd September the 12th deployed to Tan Son Nhut in south-east Asia with twenty-nine RF-4Cs.

Although some aircraft and aircrews had deployed to Mountain Home previously, the 22nd TRS officially arrived at the Idaho base from Toul-Rosiere on 19th September. The 22nd TRS was in reality a dual based squadron, maintaining a commitment to USAFE while based at Mountain Home. As part of its commitment it would, in times of international tension, deploy to Ramstein where it would come under the control of the 26th TRW.

The 11th TRS sent twenty-two crews to RAF Alconbury in September, 1966, to join the 32nd TRS. On the 25th October the squadron departed to Udorn, Thailand.

Following the departure of the 11th TRS the 22nd became the only operation-ready tactical reconnaissance unit based in the continental United States. It was continually called upon to perform photography all over the country. This was often difficult because of the high turnover in aircrews: those departing for south-east Asia and those returning. It was anticipated that eventually the squadron would be manned solely by south-east Asia returnees.

Back at Shaw in September of 1966 the 19th TRS joined the 363rd TRW and was redesignated the 19th TEWS flying the EB-66B. It joined the 4416th Test Squadron (TS) which had been activated in July 1966 and was specifically responsible for testing of electronic sensor and reconnaissance equipment for the EB-66. This was a development born of the growing need to support the war effort in south-east Asia. The 4417th CCTS had also been activated at this time to fulfil the increasing need to train aircrew and ECM crews for USAFE and south-east Asia. It had fourteen aircraft. In July, 1967, the 4416th was also designated a CCTS. There was a growing problem at Shaw in keeping pace with the progress of the war. The adequate training of EWOs was becoming particularly problematic. There were simply not enough available EB-66Cs to do the job. Whereas flight crews could be trained in other variants of the aircraft, EWOs could not. There was also, at this time, no Flight Simulator for EWO training. This meant that a

An RF-4C of the 9th TRS flies over Elmandorf in August, 1970. (Kirk Ransom)

An EB-66 of the 39th TEWTS, 363rd TRW, at Shaw post-camouflage. (K. Buchanan via Dave Menard)

An EB-66E of the 39th TEWTS, 363rd TRW, in 1971. As its name implies the 39th TEWTS was a training squadron from 1969 through to 1974. (Authors Collection)

RF-101C 56-044 in the final 'Vietnam' camouflage scheme of two greens and tan. This aircraft was at Shaw. Towards the end of the south-east Asia war only the 29th TRS and the 31st TRTS flew the RF-101 in CONUS. Both units were primarily concerned with training pilots for the 45th TRS at Tan Son Nhut. (Authors Collection)

In August, 1970, RF-4Cs of the 9th TRS, 75th TRW, deployed to Alaska for cold weather exercises. (Kirk Ransom)

Aircraft RF-4C, 64-1056 of the 75th TRW out of Bergstrom in 1967. The 75th TRW was primarily involved in the early days of reactivation with the training of replacement crews for the south-east Asia squadrons. (Kirk Ransom)

great deal of the training had to be done in the field. This in turn had implications for mission effectiveness in the combat zone.

Meanwhile at Bergstrom AFB, on the 17th May, 1966, the 75th TRW had been activated. Initially, the unit had no squadrons or aircraft assigned and existed in name only. In November, 1966 the 4th TRS was reactivated and joined the wing. The 75th was essentially an RTU for RF-4C crews. In July, 1967, the 4th TRS was joined by the 91st TRS. This squadron became operational in September 1967. In April, 1967, the 14th TRS was activated before its departure for Udorn, Thailand in November. In September, 1969, the 9th TRS was reactivated as part of the 75th TRW.

In 1969 the 39th TEWTS was activated at Shaw flying the EB-66B in an effort to meet the increasing demands to train crews for south-east Asia.

In January, 1968, a detachment from the 363rd TRW took four EB-66Es and two EB-66Cs to Osan in Korea as part of the US response to the USS *Pueblo* incident. On 24 January the North Koreans had seized the vessel and its crew, claiming that it had violated their twelve-mile limit, had fired on their patrol boats and had been spying. The detachment came under the control of the 18th TFW which had been deployed there from Kadena, Okinawa. The aircraft moved to Itazuke in February. In December the 19th TEWS moved from Shaw to Itazuke and came under the direct control of the 18th TFW, and, as a consequence, took the four EB-66Es of the 363rd Detachment; the EB-66Cs having returned to Shaw in February. This state of affairs did nothing to alleviate the serious manpower and equipment problems experienced by the training units at Shaw.

In August, 1970, the 19th TEWS was deactivated and the EB-66s returned to Shaw.

In October, 1969, the 4414th CCTS at Shaw was inactivated and the 31st TRTS was activated with responsibility for RF-101 training. At this time there were only two Voodoo units at Shaw with the 363rd. The 29th TRS was the last remaining operational squadron and became responsible for putting the finishing touches to the pilots trained by the 4414th and subsequently, 31st before they were sent to the 45th TRS at TSN. With the return of the 45th Voodoos to the United States and the Air National Guard in November, 1970, the two Shaw units briefly became responsible for the training of ANG pilots. When, in early 1971, the Voodoos of the 29th were delivered to the Michigan ANG at Selfridge, both the 29th TRS and the 31st TRTS were inactivated. The 33rd TRTS was activated at Shaw in October, 1969, at the same time as the 31st TRTS and was responsible for RF-4C training.

In January, 1970, the 18th TRS returned to Shaw from USAFE and brought with it from Upper Heyford its RF-101Cs, which were immediately transferred to the ANG. The 18th TRS converted to the RF-4C.

Pilots coming to RF-4 training were required to have at least 1,000 hours of AC (Aircraft Commander) and/or first pilot time. Charles Munroe entered the RTU at Shaw in 1971:

> Like a number of my RTU classmates, I arrived from the Air Training Command (ATC), where I had recently accrued about 1200 hours, mostly as IP (instructor pilot) in the T-38. A few years later, the 1,000 requirement was dropped for the RF-4C, and some students who graduated from the top of their UPT (undergraduate pilot training) class came directly to the RF-4C RTU. By that time the Vietnam War had essentially ended and there was not as much concern for the experience and skill-level of pilots just entering RF-4C training.
>
> That original concern for pilot skills was due mainly to the fact that the RF-4C, like its RF-101 predecessor, generally flew missions alone, whereas armed fighters generally flew in formations with inexperienced pilots relegated to flying 'wing.' In the RF-4C, even newly qualified aircraft commanders usually flew either as solo 'lead' or on the wing of another RF-4C. If armed escort was provided for a particular mission, the RF-4C pilot was 'lead.'. Many missions required a lot of good judgment as they were planned, and excellent navigation and piloting skills when flown.

After returning to CONUS from south-east Asia Munroe returned to the RTU at Shaw as an Instructor Pilot.

RF-4C training missions could sometimes be fraught with danger as Phil Rowe recalls:

> One daytime, low-altitude mission will not be soon forgotten. It was a routine flight, south and east of Austin, to photograph a target on the western shores of the Sam Rayburn Reservoir. The terrain is flat and heavily wooded, with only a few open pastures and farms.
>
> We were back on the ground, debriefing our mission with the instructor, when we first heard about our close call. Our crew chief, the mechanic who cared for our plane like it was his personal baby, stormed into the squadron operations area in a real tiff. He was really upset and demanded to know why we damaged his pride and joy.
>
> "What in the heck are you talking about, sergeant?" my pilot asked in total puzzlement. "We didn't do anything to your bird."
>
> "Well, sirs," the irate crew chief exploded, "you better come out and see. There's a bullet hole in my plane, and it wasn't there this morning."
>
> We followed the sergeant back out onto the flight line, and by now had a small entourage in tow. The squadron operations officer and several others followed along. This was something very much out of the ordinary.
>
> Sure enough. There on the right side, just aft of the engine inlet, was a 6 in long gash in the skin of the airplane. It could not have been caused by our flying into a bird or other object, because the gash was nearly vertical. And there was the tell-tale copper-colored mark of a jacketed rifle bullet. We had indeed been hit. But when? and where?
>
> The Office of Special Investigations (OSI) soon got involved. This was a reportable incident, a potentially lethal one that could have gotten someone killed. That someone was this writer, because the impact of the bullet was just two feet to the right of my seat. Boy, war is hell. The OSI demanded that I re-plot my navigation charts with minute by minute details of our two-hour training flight. They wanted to know exactly where we were, how high and at what speeds all along the route.
>
> It happened, by dumb luck, that the photography from the flight included one frame that captured the shooter. There in the picture, with the aid of a photo interpreter's magnifying lens, we could see someone pointing a rifle at us. With that picture and the detailed re-plot of the flight, authorities were able to track down and arrest the guilty farmer.

On the 15 July, 1971, the 75th TRW was inactivated at Bergstrom and the 67th TRW moved to the base and took over its assets: the 4th TRS, the 9th TRS and the 91st TRS. The 4th and the 9th TRS were inactivated in October and August, 1971, respectively. The 67th had brought with it to Bergstrom the 22nd TRS and this, too, was inactivated in October. In August, 1971, the 12th TRS was assigned on its return from south-east Asia, taking over the assets of the 9th TRS. The 45th TRS was assigned in October, 1971, taking over the assets of the 4th TRS. The 45th was inactivated in October 1975. At the end of the decade the 67th TRW had two squadrons assigned: the 12th and the 91st TRS.

In February, 1971, the 363rd at Shaw had been joined by the 16th TRS after returning from a brief sojourn with the 475th TFW at Misawa; whence it had gone from the 460th TRW at Tan Son Nhut. In October, 1971, the 62nd TRS was activated as a component of the wing.

At the end of the decade the reconnaissance assets in CONUS consisted of six squadrons. The 12th and 91st at Bergstrom and the 16th, 18th, 33rd and 62nd at Shaw. All were flying the RF-4C. In 1981 the 363rd was redesignated a TFW and retained only the 16th TRS in addition to its fighter squadrons. The 67th TRW was redesignated the 67th Intelligence Wing in 1993 with no aircraft assigned.

Shaw AFB in 1972. Doug Sontag took this photo from an RF-4C (Doug Sontag)

RF-4C at Shaw in the summer of 1972 at an Open House. (Doug Sontag)

Aircraft RF-4C 67-0467 of the 16th TRS 363rd TFW. The 16th TRS had a commitment to USAFE as well as to CONUS. This aircraft is in the Lizard or European 1 camouflage. (MAP)

A fine study of two RF-4Cs of the 363rd TRW in flight in 1972 (Doug Sontag)

In Egypt 1 camouflage this RF-4C belongs to the 91st TRS of the 67th TRW out of Bergstrom. (MAP)

CHAPTER SIX

PACAF Between the Wars

The Korean War was, officially, never over. A peace treaty was never signed. The armistice was a temporary device for keeping the warring factions apart and was not intended to be a lasting peace agreement but a cessation of hostilities while the details of a lasting peace were worked out. They never were.

The establishment of the Demilitarised Zone (DMZ) kept the antagonists at arms length. In order to ensure that the terms of the armistice were adhered to , it was necessary for the DMZ to be monitored on a daily basis. The United Nations forces needed to know details of the enemy's strength, disposition and movements. The task of monitoring fell to the 12th TRS which had in fact taken up the mission with its RB-26 aircraft immediately after the signing of the armistice. While the 12th was resident at K-14 the regular flights along the DMZ, although fraught with danger and difficulties, were relatively easy to maintain in logistical terms. The aircraft were based within easy reach of their target. The squadron could also maintain its other photo recce commitments in Korea with relative ease.

In March of 1954 the 15th Tactical Reconnaissance Squadron moved from K-14 to a new base at Komaki in Japan. The 45th , 11th and the 12th TRS' remained at Kimpo at this time. The 11th and 12th moved to Itami, Japan in December and November 1954 respectively. The 45th was destined to remain at K-14 until March of 1955 when the squadron moved to Misawa.

When the 12th TRS moved to Japan regular DMZ monitoring missions were flown from Itami. This proved impractical to maintain and in early 1955 the squadron set up a detachment at Kimpo. Two RB-26s were based there with support facilities and Project Hawkeye was born. Initially Detachment 1 of the 67th TRW also included three RF-80s of the 15th TRS. The mission of the RB-26s was to provide day photographic reconnaissance of the DMZ upon request of the Korean Joint Operations Center (KJOC) and to maintain a Photo Processing Center (PPC) capability in Korea. In addition, the detachment had to fulfil other missions which had historically been undertaken by the 12th TRS when it had been resident in Korea: photo mapping, mosaic photography, and pinpoint and strip photography of other targets. Clearly the unit was overstretched with very limited resources.

One RB-26 was always available to take off on a mission within one hour of the request coming through. The aircraft flew two types of mission in relation to the DMZ: oblique photography of the DMZ looking north; and oblique and vertical photography of areas south of the DMZ. The oblique photo missions were ordinarily flown at altitudes of 14,000 feet to 16,000 feet and in good weather these missions provided very good intelligence on enemy dispositions and movements to a depth of 15,000 metres from the front line. To obtain such good results entailed flying as close to the DMZ as possible commensurate with safety. Navigation was difficult at the best of times. The navigator guided the pilot through the twists and turns of the demarcation line over the interphone. The photos could only be taken in level flight. The oblique camera, installed in the space originally intended for the rear gunner was fixed in position. The pilot was forced to cross control the aircraft or retard power on the inside engine in order to negotiate the DMZ in level flight. In effect he needed to skid the aircraft around the bends. In winter time the problems of navigation were much worse when the ground was covered in snow, and the winds aloft often reached 60 to 80 knots, and the navigator had to sit cramped in his position in the nose of the aircraft in the freezing cold!

Bearing in mind the difficulties associated with reconnaissance of the DMZ it is a wonder that regular violations of the zone by the RB-26s did not occur. There were occasional overflights of North Korean territory and when these occurred they were met with severe reprimand by the 5th AF personnel and, of course, various ordnance from the North Koreans!

One such violation occurred on the 7th January, 1957. An RB-26 inadvertently breached the zone much to the delight of the North Koreans who fired on it. Fortunately no hits were taken and the aircraft returned to base. Unfortunately on that very day the 67th TRW Commander just happened to be visiting the Hawkeye detachment!

Following the Korean War the 67th TRW remained the sole wing with a responsibility for tactical reconnaissance in the Pacific Theater. At the beginning of 1955 it comprised four squadrons: the 11th, 12th, 15th and 45th TRS'. The 11th and 12th were based at Itami, the 15th at Komaki and the 45th at K-14, Korea. The 11th and 12th flew the RB-26 Invader, the 15th the RF-86 and the 45th, the RF-80.

Also in the theater, but responsible for more strategic reconnaissance missions was the 6021st Reconnaissance Squadron (Composite). This squadron was designated in December 1954 from the 6091st RS, which in its turn, had been part of the 6161st Air Base Wing. The 6021st flew a variety of aircraft over time including RF-86s, RF-100s, RB-57As and RB-45C Tornadoes.

The crews of the RB-45s had been attached originally to the 6091st which came directly under the operational control of FEAF. They came from a variety of backgrounds, including Tac Recce. The new RB-45 Aircraft Commanders had all previously flown the B-45 at Lockbourne AFB. The co-pilots were RF-80 pilots from Korea. The Navigators, except for Major William Meikle, who had been with SAC, came from RB-26s in Korea. All the co-pilots got one flight from the front seat; but they were frustrating times for the RF-80 pilots in particular, who, almost to a man, wanted to fly single engine jets. The Commanding Officer of the squadron, and an RB-45C AC himself, Leonard Kaufmann, recognised the frustration of the co-pilots; and made special

The 15th TRS at Komaki operated RF-80As alongside its RF-86F Sabres for several years, eventually giving them up when converting to the RF-84F in 1956. This aircraft is carrying the larger T-33 Fletcher type wing-tip tanks. (Bob MacDonald)

A flight of four 15th TRS RF-86F sabres fly over Japan. The 15th TRS operated both Ashtray and Haymaker type RF-86s until replacing them with RF-84s. (Bob MacDonald)

arrangements for them to be checked out on the squadrons RF-86s. Bob Gould had flown RF-80s in Korea and was a co-pilot in the RB-45C commanded by Kaufmann and flew many missions along the shores of Russia and China:

> On many of our missions we carried a fifth crewmember. He would be an Air Force NCO from the USAF Security Service who carried a lot of radio gear. They sat in the aisle next to the entrance door. They would never tell us what they were doing or that they spoke Russian, but over time, we figured it out. A case in point: Our crew was on a night flight, orbiting about 20 miles off the coast of Russia, near Vladivostok. The mission was routine and boring. We could see the lights from this famous city. Suddenly, the "Listener" called to the AC and said, "I suggest we leave, NOW." Col Kaufmann in his gravelly Swiss accent said, "just as soon as I finish this orbit." In a matter of seconds, we saw a flash of light, much like a shooting star go overhead from left to right, descend and explode. Then we heard the roar directly above us and could see the glow from the engine of a jet aircraft. Needless to say, we hastened for home.
>
> At the debriefing at FEAF headquarters in Tokyo the next day, the debriefers accepted, with reluctance, our belief that a night fighter fired a rocket at us that missed and that he almost rammed us in the process. We were totally blacked out in a black aircraft, so he probably never saw us. On future missions of this type, we moved out to 25 miles, as if the extra five miles would make a difference. But we never had another incident of this type that I know of.

In March, 1955 the 45th TRS moved to Misawa, Japan, and began transition to the RF-84F Thunderflash. The first of these new aircraft arrived on the 21st May. During this month seven RF-84s were received. Exercises with the new aircraft were routine air defence exercises and artillery adjustment for the army. The range for the artillery adjustment was in the Mount Fuji area and very often the weather in this area severely limited operations.

The 15th TRS, though involved heavily in the clandestine overflight programme, still had their routine work as a front line tac recce unit. This included the usual TDYs, training missions and exercises. The squadron had retained some of the RF-86F Ashtrays and flew missions with these as well as the Haymakers. There were routine photo recce and weather missions in support of exercises; for example Operation Crossfire which was the FEAF main air defence exercise.

One of the regular TDYs for the 15th TRS was to Taiwan. One such deployment took place in September of 1955. The squadron took part in a joint manoeuvre with the US Navy's 7th Fleet and Fighter units of the 5th and 13th Air Forces; together with units of the Chinese Nationalist Army and Air Force. Five RF-86s took part in this exercise which was designed to test the mobility readiness of the squadron. The deployment was a success with an aircraft in-commission rate of 96%. Forty eight photo recce sorties were flown and ninety four visual recce sorties. 1st Lieutenant Bill Goldfein took part in this TDY:

> We flew local sorties taking pictures of locally generated targets over Taiwan. We never flew over the islands and did not participate in any of the real combat missions that the Chinese RF-86 recce wing flew. We deployed with our portable photo lab to demonstrate our ability to set up and handle our mission from a bare base. We were hot debriefed by the Intell guys while we sat in the cockpit right after engine shutdown and our camera

The 45th TRS of the 67th TRW began conversion to the RF-84F from the RF-80 in March, 1955, after the move to Misawa AB in Japan. (via Dewey Hemphill)

Mount Fuji was often used as the backdrop for publicity photographs of FEAF aircraft; this 45th TRS RF-84F being no exception. (Dewey Hemphill)

repair guys quickly downloaded and ran the film magazines into the photo lab to process the film. By the time we were in the mobile photo lab, the film was on the viewing table and we identified for the Intell debriefers our exact location and the corroborating "evidence" of our visual sightings. The report was hand-written as we spoke and then was run out to be "transmitted" while the photo lab made prints of the film frames that were to be forwarded with the visual recce report. We also "played" war games with the Navy during the same deployment. They were embarked in a small fleet off the northeast coast of Taiwan. 2nd Lieutenant Bill Kirk and I were on alert one morning and were scrambled and vectored on a bearing of 045 degrees out over the water. Our task was to find the fleet and report on our sightings. After nearly 30 minutes of search, we spotted the three-ship "fleet". The carrier was the *Hancock*, the last of our straight deck carriers. We had plenty of fuel so we took abundant pictures of the ships to corroborate our sightings. The carrier was involved in flight operations and Bill and I took pictures with our different camera configurations. I was flying a "Haymaker" and took both 6" and 40" split vertical camera pictures of the deck of the carrier from relatively low altitude and Bill, in his "Ashtray", took dicing strip shots of the carrier from several angles with his 36" forward oblique camera. As we approached "bingo fuel", we departed the area to return to base. On his egress from the fleet, Bill picked up a a pair of F-9F Panthers with whom he practiced some air-to-air combat training. When our pictures were developed, it took three frames end-to-end to complete the full view of the carrier deck. You could make out expressions on the faces of the deck crews and the waving arms as I passed by. The dicing shots were equally as vivid and the last photo covered only a small part of the ship, like the windshield of the Bridge where the helmsman and the captain pulled their duty. Some of our training missions did allow for some fun. This was one of them.

Following the move to Yokota in August of 1955 the 15th TRS prepared for conversion to the RF-84F Thunderflash. The 45th TRS at Misawa was also expecting the aircraft.

The 11th TRS at Itami received 5 new ECM RB-26 aircraft in October, 1955 and flew a record number of ECM missions. Morale was high. There were more ECM officers assigned and more aircraft in commission than had been the case for a long while. On October 14th, 1955 an RB-26 flew a special jamming mission against radar controlled anti aircraft weapons systems at Komaki Air Base as part of a demonstration for a 5th AF Electronics Conference. Routine missions for the 11th at this time included *Delta* and *White Owl* missions over the Yellow Sea between Itami and K-14 in Korea. Bob Stamm flew these missions in the WB-26:

> We flew daily recce missions at 1500 feet across the Yellow Sea to just off the China coast, then a long run to the south before coasting in abeam Chejudo Island. The WB-26s carried external tanks to get the required range for the 5-6 hour missions. The weather observer in the nose had a good hand-held camera for taking photos of any shipping that we encountered. This required that we leave our route, get down on the deck and take photos that ID'd the vessel. Most shipping seemed to be headed to or from Port Arthur. This, of course, was an exciting portion of our rather routine weather mission, and I always kept a lookout for ships. That and the coast of China. The navigator had a big job on those flights keeping us out of trouble. We relied on DR and pilotage, becoming very adept at reading waves to get a notion of the wind.

Both the 11th and 12th TRS experienced problems operating with the RB-26 in the mid 1950s. Conversion to a new type was long overdue. Waiting in the wings was the Douglas RB-66. Early in 1956 it was decided to convert the 12th TRS to this new aircraft followed by the 11th TRS. In addition to the frustration with obsolete aircraft was the regular interference with training schedules caused by exercises where the 67th squadrons were obliged to operate as intruder, penetration or diversionary aircraft and not for reconnaissance. Of all the exercises in early 1956 only the 11th TRS was involved in flying ferret and weather recce missions in Operation Redcheck.

By mid 1956 the 15th TRS had completed transition to the RF-84F. In August of that year it was all change for the squadrons and their bases. The 67th TRW HQ moved to Yokota from Itami taking with it the 12th TRS. For the time being the 11th remained at Itami, flying the RB-26. The RB-66 was imminently expected by the 12th and the runway at Itami was not suitable for the twin jet. The 15th TRS moved to Kadena with 16 RF-84s and a T-33. The 45th remained at Misawa.

Two RF-86Fs of the 15th TRS take off from Komaki: in the rear an Ashtray aircraft and in the front a Haymaker. (Bob MacDonald)

RB-26 of the 11th TRS Itami 1957. The RB-26 was replaced by the RB-66 in the 11th TRS in 1957, following the conversion of the 12th TRS type. (David Cooper)

In September of 1956 eleven Reconnaissance Task Forces (RTF) were set up. Each task force consisted of six aircraft each using RF-86, RF-84 and RB-66B. The purpose of the RTFs was to provide for day and night photo coverage of some 200 assigned targets. The creation of the RTFs was due in no small part to the increase in international tension prompted by the Czech crisis in

WB-26C *Vicki* belongs to the 11th TRS. at Itami in 1955. The 11th TRS flew both RB-26 in the ECM role and WB-26s for weather recce. (Bob Stamm)

particular. At this time as well the 5th Air Force published a revised list of Emergency War Plans designating post atomic strike photo recce targets. These targets were assigned to the RTFs.

While the 12th TRS was converting to the RB-66B they dispatched their RB-26s to the 11th at Itami. At this time, while the 12th was shut down, the 11th was responsible for all the photographic and Electronic reconnaissance in the Far East; and it was fulfilling this responsibility with the RB-26.

In late 1956 Project Hawkeye had become the responsibility of the 11th TRS. In early 1957 FEAF recognised the need to replace the RB-26 in Hawkeye and, furthermore, give the operation a more permanent establishment at K-14. The difficulty facing the 67th TRW, which was given the responsibility for coming up with an alternative, was what aircraft to use. One of the terms of the armistice was that new aircraft could not be brought into the theatre. The wing looked at the RB-50, helicopters and, rather half-heartedly, balloons. The final choice was the C-47, the 'Gooney Bird.' The aircraft was plentiful and supplies were easy to come by. They were easy to maintain. They were reliable; and they could perform a dual mission if required. On the 19th February, 1957 the RC-47 proposal was put to FEAF with the stipulation that the aircraft could only carry oblique cameras and would not perform a vertical mission. The proposal was accepted and two C-47s were assigned for modification and to commence operations in July, 1957. In fact operations did not begin until September as the two aircraft would not be ready before then.

The basic modification for the RC-47D was the installation of a K-38, 36 inch oblique camera at the rearmost window just forward of the main service door. The framework to hold the camera was easily removed so as to allow the aircraft to return to its transport function. An adjustable screw also enabled a camera angle of between 23.5 and 32 degrees to be selected. The cockpit contained the switches for the camera power and the intervalometer. The aircraft was fitted with a driftmeter which was installed on the left of the aircraft as the photo flights were made from west to east.

Initial tests of the RC-47 were carried out in the mountains around Itami Air base. This area resembled the topography of the DMZ. The tests were successful and the first photo run over the zone was made on 30 August, 1957. Two navigators were always carried on the aircraft to ensure, as far as possible, that no violation of the DMZ occurred.

RB-66s for the 12th TRS had begun arriving with the squadron towards the end of 1956. In January 1957 there were four aircraft at Yokota. 53-486, 54-418, 54-419 and 54-424. By the end

The 15th TRS received its RF-84Fs in 1956 and in August of that year moved to Kadena AB. (Lieutenant Colonel B. Matthews via Dave Menard)

Three RF-84Fs of the 15th TRS over the Pacific. With the 15th TRS the RF-84F proved to be a reliable aircraft. For 27 months to December, 1957, the squadron had been accident free. (Jim Payson)

RF-86F Ashtray 52-4529, 15th TRS. Alongside the RF-80s of the squadron, the Ashtray aircraft were flown in the routine missions and exercises. (Charles Witmer)

of May '57 the number of aircraft had increased to 17; including two for the 11th TRS. The aircraft were flown to Japan from McLellen AFB under Operation Flying Fish. As the RB-66s arrived so the RB-26s were ferried out to Clarke where they were stored pending auction or salvage.

In January, 1957 the 67th at Itami was involved in the making of the Warner Bros Marlon Brando film *Sayonara*. The base was used extensively for the ramp shots of Brando and his F-86; and wing personnel were used as extras.

In July, 1957 the 12th TRS received the last of 20 RB-66Bs. As was the experience with USAFE the transition to the RB-66 in the Far East theatre was occasionally fraught. There was a low in-commission rate due primarily to maintenance requirements. There was a slippage in delivery schedules due to the lack of experienced ferry crews; and the shortage of T-33s meant that training schedules also slipped back. There was a requirement for all crews to undergo T-33 jet training. A classic example of the problems is exemplified by the experience of Major Shinn, 1st Lieutenant Harvey and 1st Lieutenant Harrington who took off on a routine training flight in May 1957. The early phase of the flight was normal apart from some fluctuation in the readings of the N1 compass. Then the N1 began to give readings some 40 degrees different from the standby compass. The pilot used the standby. At this point the radio decided to cease functioning. The pilot tried to use the liaison set and that too was out of commission. The navigator tried the radar equipment but that too was on strike!

The pilot elected to fly a right hand triangular pattern, put his parrot on emergency squawk and began climbing. Deciding that if he could get high enough it would trigger a GCI. In the meantime he turned for home. In the climb the N1 compass disagreed with the standby by 80 degrees and the altitude gave up at 20,000 feet in the clouds. The climb continued and the aircraft broke out into the clear at 40,000 feet. A radio range was obtained.

About twenty miles from home the clouds dissipated and a let down was made to 24,000 feet above the lower clouds which broke sufficiently to give a pilotage fix and a letdown was made. Later it transpired that the emergency squawk had been received and some fighters had been scrambled just in case.

The 12th TRS also experienced problems in fulfilling its night photo mission. The equipment for the mission was not installed in all aircraft and there was no photo flash bombing range.

In November the 11th TRS commenced its classified missions. The first such mission was led by Captain James Furneaux on the 15th November. This was followed on the 22nd and 27th November by two further missions. By December, eight such missions had been flown with no problems experienced. These missions were generally involved in listening for emissions from North Korea, China or the Soviet Union and were flown along the coasts of those countries. The arrival of the RB-66C saw these missions taking place, for the first time, by day as well as night. Invariably they

RF-84F, 51-1932 of the 45th TRS over Japan 1957. (Panetta)

The RB-66C replaced the RB-26 in the ECM role in the 11th TRS. The 11th operated the RB-66 from Yokota as the runway at Itami was too short. This aircraft was photographed en route to Guam in January, 1959 (Dave Cooper)

involved refuelling by KB-50J tanker aircraft. Missions were flown out of Kadena, Misawa and Yokota and were not without mishap. Neither were they all routine. David W. Cooper flew several such missions:

> Probably one of the most interesting situations we got into occurred on one of our missions out of Misawa. As I recall, the Russian navy was having an exercise and we were placed on alert at Misawa. On this particular morning we were scrambled and as would usually happen, after becoming airborne we were turned over to a GCI site. We were vectored and directed to climb to a particular flight altitude (probably around 28,00 feet). Shortly after reaching that altitude, we were told by a rather excited controller to reverse our course and begin an immediate descent to some 10,000 feet to make an identification of an unknown target tracking a certain direction. We responded. Ben Maloney used the speed brakes and we went into a port turn. While in the turn and descending rapidly, I looked out of the little side window at my navigator station and saw two Migs go screaming by us. Apparently the Migs had approached us visually and neither the GCI site nor we had made electronic contact with them. That was the last time we saw those particular Migs. Continuing our descent and while reversing course we made contact with the 'unknown' aircraft which we were directed to identify. The unknown aircraft was an RB-50; most probably from the 6091st Recon Squadron at Yokota and on a similar mission to ours. I am most grateful that the balance of our missions was never that spontaneous and uncoordinated.

The 12th TRS continued to experience quite serious problems with its RB-66Bs; so much so that at times the in-commission rate of squadron aircraft dropped down to one; and was seldom more than three in the latter part of 1957. In September a succession of accidents broke the squadron's safety record of 45 months without a major accident. RB-66B 54-428 took off on a round robin navigation flight. Take off and climb were normal. About thirty minutes out the pilot, Captain GH Slever, heard two loud rumbles and the tachometer on the left engine dropped to zero. The three crew members ejected at 25,000 feet and landed safely apart from Captain Slever who sustained broken ribs when he landed in a tree. On the 6th September instrument trouble caused aircraft 54-417, piloted by Captain W.D. Brown, to return prematurely to base during a routine mission. The aircraft landed in a very nose high attitude and the aft fuselage struck the runway causing major damage. On the 16th September 53-439 was on a radar scope photo mission when the weather deteriorated and the pilot, Lieutenant B.J. Wassell, contacted Yokota and requested an instrument let down. The aircraft landed short of the runway and skidded 2000 feet. The gear collapsed.

Approaching the tanker. An RB-66C of the 11th TRS comes up on the KB-50 to take on fuel. (Dave Cooper)

Routine exercises continued to occupy the squadrons time and effort. There was some degree of frustration with these exercises when for a great deal of the time the recce squadrons were obliged to participate as attackers or defenders rather than in practicing their reconnaissance skills. For example in Flash House the 45th used their RF-84s flying enemy attack missions against targets in Japan

One of the most significant events in 1957 was Mobile Zebra. Units from the United States deployed to the Far East as part of a rapid deployment exercise and were hosted by 67th TRW

In late 1957 the RF-84s began to be replaced by the RF-101 Voodoo, seen here waiting in the wings by this 15th TRS Thunderflash. (Lieutenant Colonel B. Matthews via Dave Menard)

units during their sojourn. The 12th provided base facilities for the 9TRS detachment and the 15th TRS hosted Five RF-101 Voodoos from the 17th TRS. Both units were from the 363rd TRW at Shaw AFB.

In October, 1957 the 67th TRW gained control of the 6091st Reconnaissance Squadron based at Yokota.

Exercise Helpmate took elements of both the 15th and the 45th TRS with their RF-84s to K.55 at Osan in Korea. This deployment was in response to a 8th US Army request for photo reconnaissance and was to be an ongoing commitment.

The RF-84s of the jet photo squadrons had proved reliable and relatively stable aircraft since their introduction in 1955. Indeed the 15th TRS had been accident free for 27 months up to December 2nd 1957 when 2nd Lieutenant Donald D. Snyder baled out of his RF-84 over the sea. The aircraft had lost all hydraulics.

By the end of 1957 the RF-84s had reached the end of their useful lives. Furthermore, Mobile Zebra had brought the Voodoo to Japan and the pilots of the 15th and 45th TRS' were eagerly awaiting conversion to this aircraft. In spite of showing very definite signs of its advancing years the RF-84s maintained a mission readiness. One such regular mission was ship surveillance. Lieutenant Frank Dunn flew the aircraft with the 45th TRS in 1957:

> April 17th, another shot at getting some shots of Russian shipping. Today they've assigned me to an RF-84K. The K model looks very much like the F model except that the horizontal stabilizer droops downwards … Preflight and take off went well. I climbed out to 25,000 and headed for the straits. Got some photos of several ships that I know were just fishing vessels, but let the photo interpreters make sure. Then I spotted one with wires hanging everywhere. There were more antennae on this little fishing vessel than on a well equipped radar picket ship. I rolled into a dive, thinking I'd got a nose oblique shot of her, a dicing shot. As I got closer I noticed an anti aircraft gun mounted amidships. I kicked the left rudder, skidding the plane to the left. The barrel moved with me. I kicked the right rudder and again the gun tracked my skid. 'Well….' I thought. 'A vertical shot of this ship would be just as good.' So I broke off, climbed to 5000 feet and took a nice safe vertical. Better a good vertical photo than a picture of flak coming at me, or worse."

In 1957 the 45th acquired four RF-84Ks, all ex SAC machines, originally modified to be carried by a B-36 bomber. These were 52-7260, 52 7262, 52-7265 and 52-7275.

The 11th TRS continued its clandestine operations against Chinese and Russian targets. Often Russian aircraft would transition through Japanese airfields. When this occurred an RB-66C would be launched to photograph the aircraft. On May 21st 1958 one such mission was launched to photograph two TU-104s at Tokyo International Airport. Designated Project Orange Crate this mission involved the interception of data from the two aircraft on the ground at Tokyo and on landing and take off. The operation was deemed successful.

The 12th TRS achieved successful night photography using the K-45 camera configuration in the RB-66B. The K-38 configuration had proved problematic because crews had great difficulty getting through the camera compartment to access some of the emergency systems.

At this time also the 67th Wing HQ put in a request to retain an RB-57 aircraft and install a K-30 and *Sharpcut* camera in it. The K-30 could not be installed in the RB-66 without making a number of structural changes.

The 11th TRS continued to fly its ELINT missions along the borders of the Soviet Union over the Sea of Japan. As the missions progressed so did the techniques for gathering information and Soviet response! Soviet interceptors came within 50 feet of the RB-66s. The visual interception technique employed by the Soviets was to place at least one aircraft on the side of the RB-66 closest to Japan. This aircraft would position slightly higher than the RB-66 at about 1000 feet from it. One or more aircraft would then slide up on the other side of the RB-

Devoid of all unit markings this RF-101C, 56-0041, has been newly delivered to the 15th TRS at Kadena. (Jim Payson)

66C and to within 50 feet. Both the Soviet pilots and the '66 crews would take the opportunity to photograph one another. In the period January to June 1958 eighty two classified missions were flown.

In June, 1958 the 12th TRS deployed two RB-66B aircraft on a goodwill mission to Bangkok, overflying Vietnam and skirting the Cambodian border. The crews of these aircraft could not have foreseen that, within a relatively short time their aircraft would be returning to the area in anything but a goodwill role.

During 1958 the 11th TRS received some WB-66Ds.

During the first half of 1958 the 15th and the 45th TRS' completed conversion to the Voodoo. As each squadron went through the process the other, together with the 12th TRS, would pick up the target folders of the converting unit. A Reconnaissance Task Force (RTF) was also physically present at the base of the converting squadron; thus ensuring that the interference with the wartime commitment of the wing was kept to a minimum. Operations Plan Zips Idea was an evaluation of the comparative qualities of the RF-84 and RF-101C necessary to fulfilling the mission. The conclusions of this evaluation were: The increased speed of the RF-101 enhanced the recovery of more intelligence information. With the RF-101 there was more latitude in changing profiles in flight, thus lowering the incidences of photography with cloud coverage. Camera stations in the RF-101 gave a greater choice in the selection of the type of photographic intelligence needed.

Nevertheless the RF-84F was warmly remembered by some pilots. Frank Dunn was one of the those who flew the last two Thunderflashes out to Kisarazu in Japan prior to their moth balling

Frank Dunn flew both the RF-84F and the RF-101C with the 45th TRS. He unfortunately had a serious crash in aircraft 56-0059 which put him in hospital for quite some time. (Frank Dunn)

An RB-66C, 54-474 of the 11th TRS approaches the Guam ADIZ on a mission in January 1959. (Dave Cooper)

and return to the USA. Kisarazu was a small field with a short 5000 feet runway. The RF-84F had a fondness for long runways!

> We arrived over Kisarazu with empty external tanks and Reggie went in first. I watched him land, deploy his drag chute almost on touch down and roll off the runway onto a taxiway at a pretty good clip. There was no 50 knot wind this day. Well, I had put two of these planes into this field with no trouble so today should be a piece of cake. I touched down within 3 to 4 feet of the start of the runway, with power off, doing about 120 knots, normal touch down speed is about 135 knots. Holding the nose as high as I could to increase drag, I pulled the drag chute release, but nothing happened. The drag chute door had opened but the chute did not deploy. I continued to hold the nose up and applied as much brake as I could, since there wasn't enough runway left to get off the ground. With no wind conditions the runway was just too short. Finally I had to call the tower and tell them I would be taking their barrier. I engaged the barrier at a speed barely too fast to turn off the runway. The barrier did its job. The nose wheel tripped a cable that caught the main gear and started to pull a big anchor chain that was laid along the border of the 500 foot overrun. I came to a stop about 60 feet past the end of the runway, having dragged two or three of the links of that big chain out of place.

Frank and Reggie got a helicopter to Tachikawa and travelled back to Misawa courtesy of Japan Airlines. Frank Dunn never saw another working RF-84 again; but he did fly the RF-101C with the 45th; unfortunately crashing in the aircraft.

Prior to the arrival of the RF-101 in the theatre, a survey of TACAN facilities within the area of the the 5th Air Force was undertaken. The Voodoo depended on TACAN as a navigational aid.

These WB-66Ds were photographed on their way to the 11th TRS at Yokota in January 1958. (Dave Cooper)

An RF-101C of the 45th TRS out of Misawa AB. The Voodoo was welcomed by 15th and 45th squadrons because of its greatly increased capability as a recce platform compared to the RF-84F. (Ray Tiffault)

During the latter part of 1958 the 11th TRS gained an additional number of EWOs when the 6091st phased out its RB-50s. In October the squadron conducted three jamming missions against the control tower at Iwo Jima. The purpose of this mission was to test the ALT-7 jammer. During the course of the tests it was concluded that the antennae furnished with the AN/ALT-7 were unsatisfactory. All these jamming transmitters were removed and scheduled for replacement by the Douglas Corporation. Such testing and analysis missions were part of the routine mission of the 11th TRS. In January, 1959 two RB-66Cs flew a mission to ascertain the effectiveness of the

In Operation Square Deal the 45th TRS Voodoos visited Australia and New Zealand on a goodwill visit. This aircraft 56-0084 has received a zap in the form of a jumping kangaroo on the forward fuselage. (Duane Seymour)

Two 45th TRS Polka Dot RF-101Cs in flight over Japan in 1959. (Duane Seymour)

jamming of the E-4 Fire Control System on the F-86D. As only one mission was flown the results could not be considered conclusive. However, it was discovered that the ALT-6B 'X' band jammer could cause some interference to the E-4 and, when used together with chaff, could break the lock.

In 1959 it was decided to deactivate the 67th TRW in early 1960; and for the latter part of the year much of the work of the wing was directed towards this. However, the squadrons were also

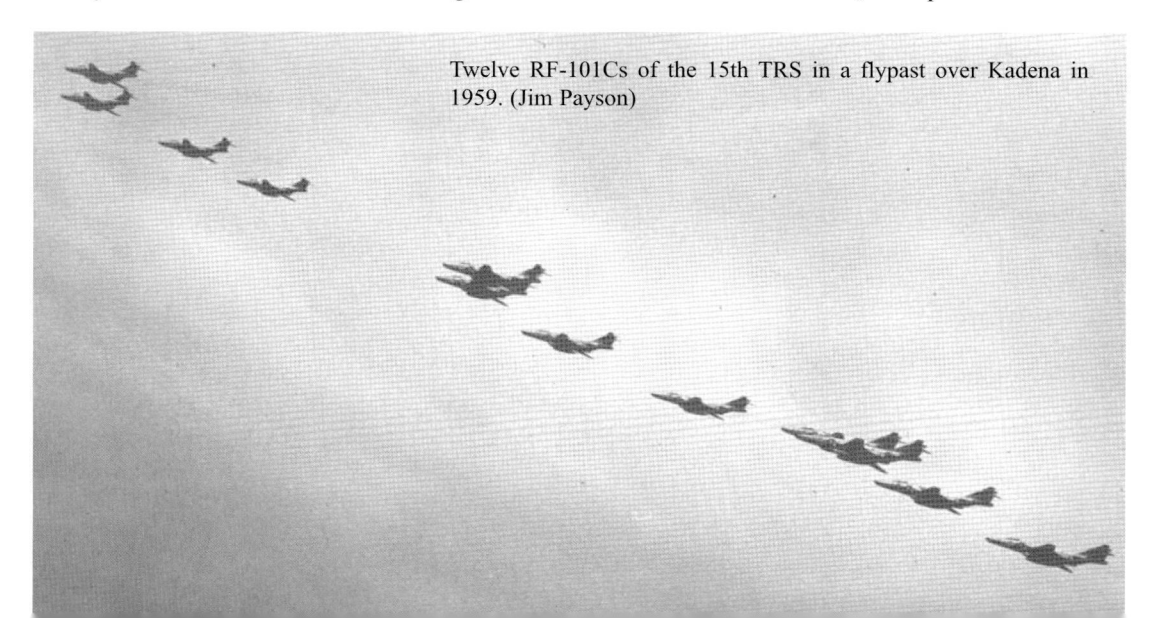

Twelve RF-101Cs of the 15th TRS in a flypast over Kadena in 1959. (Jim Payson)

The 45th TRS overflies Misawa during a 4th July flypast in 1959. (Duane Seymour)

obliged to be combat ready and practice their mission. In February, 1959 an RB-66 task Force was deployed to Misawa for a ten day period on a priority classified mission.

Operation Square Deal took elements of the wing to Australia and New Zealand on a goodwill mission. Slide Rule involved the training of Chinese Nationalist pilots on the RF-101C. Operation Yogi Bear was an assessment exercise which took an RTF to Taiwan; to Tao Yuan in July and Kung Kuan in December. Rough Road involved five RB-66s and eight RF-101s flying high altitude tracking through 39th AD air space for the purposes of evaluating the air defence systems.

In July, August and September Show of Force missions were flown over South Korea by all the squadrons. These were low altitude over-flights of selected towns in the Republic of Korea.

Operation Flying Fish was in the planning stage at the end of 1959 and commencing in January, 1960 this involved the ferrying of all RB-66 aircraft back to the Continental USA; as the 11th and 12th TRS' were deactivated. The last RB-66 departed on the 29th January.

The 6091st took their RB-57As to Clark AB in May for Operation Full House. During this operation a total of nineteen classified missions were flown.

Another photograph of the flypast at Misawa in July 1959. (Duane Seymour)

This RF-101C 56-0066, the squadron commanders aircraft, still bears the kangaroo zap at Misawa in 1960.(Fred Muesegaes)

Three RF-101s of the 45th TRS in perfect formation over Japan in 1960. (Ray Tiffault)

The RF-101C was replaced by the RF-4C in the 15th TRS in 1967. This example is seen flying over Mount Fuji. (Doug Sontag)

At an Open House at Misawa in the summer of 1960 this Voodoo shows its forward oblique camera station. (Duane Seymour)

At the Open House at Misawa in 1960 this RF-101C is paying host to some of the many visitors. (Duane Seymour)

In April, 1960, the 45th TRS became attached to the 39th AD at Misawa following the inactivation of the 67th TRW. Here a KB-50 tanker refuels an RF-101 of the 45th and an F-100 of the 531st TFW also attached to the 39th AD. (Duane Seymour)

RF-101C 56-0204 of the 45th TRS over Mount Fuji. (Fred Muesegaes)

This RF-101C 54-1512 of the 15th TRS, 18th TFW at Kadena is sporting one of the several experimental camouflage schemes worn by a few Voodoos before the Vietnam scheme of green and tan was finally decided upon. (USAF)

In March, 1960 the 15th TRS became attached to the 18th Tactical Fighter Wing at Kadena as part of the 313th Air Division. The 45th TRS became attached to the 39th AD at Misawa in April, 1960. The 67th TRW was deactivated in December, 1960.

Post Script
Following the end of the war in SE Asia and the return of USAF deployment to a semblance of normality; the tactical reconnaissance assets in place with PACAF in the mid 1970s consisted of three squadrons. The 432nd TRW remained at Udorn until 1975 when it was inactivated, having, in November 1974 been redesignated a TFW. The 432nd TRW's reconnaissance units consisted of the 4th TRS which had been activated in October 1972, and the 14th TRS. Both these squadrons flew the RF-4C. Assigned to the 18th TFW at Okinawa was the 15th TRS with RF-4Cs. At the end of the decade the 15th TRS was the only recce unit attached to PACAF.
In 1989 the 460th TRGp was reactivated at Taegu in Korea and took over the 15th TRS. Both the 460th and the 15th were deactivated in 1990.

An RF-101C 56-0075 of the 45th TRS. (Duane Seymour)

An RF-101C 56-0080 also belongs to the 45th TRS. (Duane Seymour)

CHAPTER SEVEN

South-east Asia

In 1961 both the 15th and 45th TRS at Kadena and Misawa were approached to find pilots who would be willing to volunteer for a very particular TDY codenamed Project Field Goal. This was a recce assignment using not the state of the art recce aircraft the pilots were used to flying, but a single aircraft, which, at that time, was not even in the USAF inventory. The object of Field Goal was to support the government of Laos in it's fight against communist aggression from the North Vietnamese and Pathet Lao forces. Fred Muesegaes of the 45th was approached by the squadron commander:

> I believe he came to me first after receiving the priority commitment for the 45th TRS to provide a recce pilot who was RF-101 and T-33 qualified. The 45th had four pilots who were so qualified. The other three were married and since I was the only single one, I believe Osborne approached me first to see if I was interested in volunteering for this TDY. As best as I can recall, he was uncertain of exactly what it was all about, but because of the highly classified nature of the request and what it may have inferred he knew that 13th AF, at Clark AB was just the intermediate point in the TDY. But he must have had other info and/or just intuition that made him believe that it might involve flying recce missions in south-east Asia in an other than a friendly environment

The operation was to utilize the Lockheed RT-33 aircraft. One had been obtained from the Philippine Air Force in exchange for a T-33. Udorn Royal Thai Air Base was chosen for the operations because it was the nearest to Laos.

The Field Goal team was put together at Clark AB in the Philippines and comprised eight people: two pilots, Fred Muesegaes of the 45th and Bob Caudry, who came from the 15th TRS and five enlisted men for support: a crew chief, engine specialist, communication specialist, camera specialist and one other, possibly a structures specialist. A Major Vermillion was given command of the operation. Time at Clark was spent in intelligence briefings on the political and military situation in Laos. Bob Caudry:

> Two things stand out in my mind about those intel briefings. First they were considering 'sanitizing' us: taking the markings off the aircraft and making us civilians – I assume we would have become part of Air America, the Central Intelligence Agency's air arm. Both Fred and I said we didn't want to consider that option (they never mentioned the money we would be paid). The second thing was a missionary who briefed us. He had been in the back country for some time but was pulled out when the Pathet Lao, with Viet Minh support, overran his position. We were told how to approach villages and the people, an idea of the terrain and some opinions of what was important in the minds of the natives. I remember a photo of a typical village had a Coca-Cola sign nailed to a tree, which seemed incongruous.

The issue of whether or not to sanitize the RT-33 and the mission was brought up again while the unit was at Udorn. It met with the same highly negative response from Muesegaes and Caudry then as well!

The RT-33, 53-5347 at Don Muang in October 1961. Operation Field Goal moved to Don Muang from Udorn in June 1961. The F-102s belong to the 16th FIS. (John Linihan)

The RT-33 was generally in a good state of repair with the exception of the cameras which were conspicuous by their absence. These were delivered in boxes and had suffered from corrosion. The expertise of the camera specialist in the team eventually successfully installed the suite. The configuration was a 12 in nose oblique, 6 in Left Oblique, 6 in Right oblique and a 6 in vertical. The rear-seat space carried additional fuel in the form of a 172 gallon tank. The aircraft was test flown on the 14th April and again on the 17th and 18th. On the 20th April Bob Caudry flew the RT-33 from Clark to Udorn RTAFB via Da Nang. The rest of the detachment travelled by C-130. On arrival at Udorn Caudry had to make a pass down the runway to chase off the water buffalo and people who frequently used it as a walkway in preference to the marshy ground around.

Udorn was to become one of the busiest of the bases used by USAF personnel during the conflict to come, but at the time of Field Goal it consisted of the main 7500 ft concrete runway, which was

'Hoss' Linscomb prepares to take off on a Field Goal mission in October 1961. The RT-33 ramp was adjacent to the civilian facility at the airport. (John Linihan)

First Lieutenant Fred Muesegaes of the 45th TRS with his RF-101C. Muesegaes flew both with Operation Field Goal out of Udorn and the Able Mable Task Force out of Don Muang. (Fred Muesegaes)

raised above the surrounding terrain, a crossing runway of laterite, a large shed roof house and a tent city occupied by a Marine Air Base Battalion. It had originally been designed as an emergency recovery strip by the Navy. The RT-33 was parked on the laterite south of the main runway and on the north side Air America parked their H-34s. The main runway had no overruns, no runway distance markers and no arresting gear. In the event that any aircraft left the end of the runway in an emergency it would be a write off as there was a

An RT-33 target photo of Vang Vieng. It was here that Bob Caudry first encountered AAA fire from Dodge trucks. The fire was not accurate enough to cause Bob any inconvenience! (USAF via Fred Muesegaes)

10 ft deep, 20 ft wide ditch at the end. The fuel dump was on the south side of the airfield and consisted of expeditionary fuel bladders, filters and pumps. The marines were responsible for the fuel. Living conditions could best be described as adequate! The team was, however, reasonably well supported by the USAF. Bob Caudry:

> When we got to Udorn we were billeted in squad tents. There were no floors, just dirt with a consistency of face powder. There were no coolers to protect our film canisters from the extreme heat and we did not have a tug to toe the aircraft. We contacted 13th AF at Clark requesting those items and the NEXT day a C-124 landed, didn't even shut down, the clam shell doors opened up and a truck rolled out carrying two-by-fours, sheets of plywood and two gas-operated refrigerators. By that evening our airmen had floors in our two tents, the coolers were humming away and we had a truck to serve as tow.

It was however not just the accommodation which proved problematic for the Field Goal team! Fred Muesegaes:

> A Navy Flight Surgeon had a dispensary (large tent) where he had a collection of snakes in large jars of formaldahyde. These were all snakes that had been killed in the camp area – I believe all were poisonous, most neurotoxic, I don't believe any snakes in that area were non-poisonous. I hate snakes! When it would rain, and it did often, the snakes would sometimes come into the tents (at night when there was no activity). After we heard of a 'snuffy' who had put on his combat boots one morning only to find a small pit viper had crawled in one during the night. After that our ritual in the morning was to pull up the mosquito netting (we slept on cots with air mattresses and mosquito netting), look under the cot then beat the heels together with our boots upside down so we wouldn't have the same misfortune.

The first flight out of Udorn was flown by Fred Muesegaes:

> We decided it would be best to fly a local flight on the day after we arrived before we got a mission assigned for a couple of reasons. Needless to say there was no published jet penetration procedure or GCA available. We learned that there was a 25 watt (I believe) radio beacon just off the east end of the runway, so Caudry and I drew up our own teardrop jet penetration from 20,000 ft and established our own minimum altitude for the approach. Also we got into the performance section of the Aircraft Flight Handbook to compute the take-off roll. Since we didn't have any runway markers there was no sense in computing go-no-go and abort speeds. I don't recall how we determined the runway temperature – we probably found a thermometer somewhere – and we couldn't compute the density altitude, but what the hell, we knew the field elevation so we used that. As I recall temperatures usually ran around 100 or more, so our computation was that 7,500 ft of runway was slightly more than needed for take-off. Since it was my turn to fly I got to find out whether our computations were 'close enough for government work'. We towed the aircraft onto the east end of the runway – at the very end of the pavement of course – and started the engine (we made all departures and arrivals to the west and always towed the aircraft onto and off the runway with engine shutdown to prevent FOD). Major Vermillion decided to watch and stood with Caudry and the five troops beside the runway for the first launch out of Udorn. I would have felt more comfortable if I had some abort data and there wasn't the big ditch at the west end of the runway, but our computations said it would fly (if the engine was providing it's proper thrust) so we would soon see. Knowing that I didn't want to go off the end of the runway into the ditch, I decided that I'd rotate before that happened even if the airspeed was a little low. Fortunately, before I got to the end I had enough speed to fly, so as soon as I broke ground I pulled the gear up and levelled to accelerate. Caudry related to me afterwards that from their perspective

they couldn't tell whether I had gotten airborne and the jet wash created such a dust cloud when I reached the end of the runway and over the dirt that they completely lost sight of the aircraft. He said that Vermillion thought he had lost his whole Air Force on the first flight out of Udorn, which we afterwards thought was quite amusing. I made a flight check on our jet penetration procedure and it worked out pretty well (subsequently Caudry checked it too and agreed with me), so we now were an all-weather operation, such as it was. This was pretty important as we would not have any airborne communications with anyone and we were in the monsoon season. At least we could penetrate the weather. Eventually a tactical control unit came in with a somewhat archaic GCA unit (a TPSQ-1 or TPS-1Q I think they called it), so we practised GCAs with them whenever we could, and this improved our low weather capability – at least it was more accurate than a non-precision approach.

Missions flown from Udorn by the RT-33 were assigned from Vientiane by MAAG (Military Assistance Advisory Group), Laos. Muesegaes, Caudry and Vermillion were briefed on the political situation once again and exchanged information on their capabilities and limitations and received information on their mission. They would be assigned missions as and when the need arose. Fred Muesegaes recalls a typical mission profile:

On a typical mission all cameras would be loaded (after the previous mission's film was processed at MAAG Laos they would reload the magazine with film and we would bring the magazine back to Udorn with us) and the aircraft would have a full load of fuel. Because the RT had a fuel tank replacing the rear seat, this would give us 172 gallons more than the T-33 for a total of 978 gallons of JP-4. So the range and endurance was much better than the T-33, however the take-off gross weight was a bit more than the T-33. Our crew chief would tow us out onto the runway for engine start. No tower, of course, which really didn't matter as there wasn't much traffic, so we pretty much did what we wanted. The mission was flown navigating by Dead Reckoning. Cloud cover was usually a problem, especially on a high-low-high profile into northern or southern Laos, because when letting down in the target area it was necessary to find holes in layers of clouds or just descend on instruments in the clouds and then hoping to get oriented when the ground was in sight. The maps proved to be the greatest shortcoming in situations like this. After returning to Udorn we used our radio beacon, which had about a 25 nautical miles range with thunderstorms around, to home in on and then fly our jet penetration and later on with a GCA final approach. After landing (to the west) we would back taxi down the runway and shutdown on the runway, and then tow to our parking place on the laterite. The camera magazines would be downloaded and placed on a waiting (usually) H-34 and off we'd go to Vientiane.

Bob Caudry flew his first mission out of Udorn on the 24th April:

I went north to Dien Bien Phu at high altitude and at 20,000 ft over the Plain of Jars shooting verticals, then ran down highway 13 from the intersection with highway 7 to the river crossing at Ban Hin Heup taking nose obliques at about 200 ft. It was on this run that I observed my first AAA (at Vang Vieng) being fired from quad-50 calibre mounted on the back of Dodge trucks. The field had fallen two days before and the 50s were captured. They were lousy shots, apparently not using an inch of lead. That evening we went to Vientiane to plot our targets and help with photo interpreting (PI). Our usual procedure was for Fred and I to fly one mission each then go up to Vientiane to do the PI work. Generally there was an H-34 to take us and the film up, but coming back the next day we had to more or less hitch-hike. After all, it was the film that was important, we were not. I remember one time an H-34 landed and Fred and I went running up to it to return to Udorn but the pilot waved us away and proceeded to shut down. When he started climbing out of the cockpit we could understand why – he had been shot in the leg by small arms fire and was bleeding. He had fashioned a tourniquet for himself. As he hobbled by, he apologized for not being able to give us a ride but 'thought' he should get his leg looked at! Tough guys, these Marines. There were missions that had specific pinpoint targets such as Xaignabouli, Paksane, Thakhek, Savannakhet, Salavan and the southern-most target I can remember, Pakse. Most of the targets were roads, particularly roads from China and North Vietnam. Roads leading from Kunming and Jinghang in China into Laos with entries at Muang Sing, Ban Xongta and Ban Neua were very difficult because the charts were so ill defined. Often there were areas, particularly over higher terrain where the chart was blank with a notation saying that there was no information available.

More than once we targeted highway 7 from Muong Xen in North Vietnam running to Ban Ban (we learned to call it Bang Bang because of all the AAA present) through the Plain of Jars all the way to Highway 13. Other entries from North Vietnam covered were Highway 12 from Na Phao to Gnommalat and highway 9 from Lao Bao to Savannakhet. On one of our Highway 7 runs, an army guy operating close to the Plain of Jars reported that about 5 minutes after we left the target area he saw a swept wing orbiting that looked to him to be a Mig. At one point we were restricted from flying over Laos for a few days, then were permitted to go in again and, finally restricted again. It was then I went home. When we were restricted, we would fly along the Mekong River shooting obliques into Laos.

Field Goal operations out of Udorn ended in May, 1961, although, there is some confusion about precisely when the last mission was flown. Official histories state that the operation was closed down on the 10th May. However, Muesegaes recalls flying his last mission over Laos on the 17th of the month and his flight log confirms this. Furthermore, he was replaced on the operation by First Lieutenant Jack Weatherby of the 45th TRS. The RT-33 was flown to Don Muang base in Thailand in late June and did not return to Udorn. Flights over Laos continued until 7 November, 1961.

Whether or not *Field Goal* can be deemed to have been a success is debatable. Certainly valuable intelligence was obtained for the Laotian government; and when the ICC (International Control Commission) ordered a halt to the flights in May it was considered imperative to get them going again. The operation was certainly not without hazard to the pilots. The threat from ground fire and AAA was very real. There were no encounters with Migs, but some suggestion that on at least one occasion enemy aircraft were launched to intercept the RT-33.

Don Muang provided better facilities for maintenance and supply of the RT-33. It was also arguably the better equipped of the Thai bases; doubling as a civil airport. In October, 1961, a decision was made by the US Government to request the Thais to allow the establishment of a more permanent reconnaissance presence in Thailand to overfly Laos and South Vietnam. Both PACAF recce units, the 15th and 45th TRS were equipped with the RF-101C Voodoo and it was proposed to base four of these aircraft from the 45th TRS at Don Muang as Task Force Able Mable.

The RF-101C Voodoo was no stranger to the region. The Chinese nationalists had been flying the aircraft for some time over China, and the US Government had for some time sent detachments flying the aircraft there. The 17th TRS deployed to Japan during Exercise Mobile Zebra in November, 1957. In September, 1958, the 17th deployed to Clark AFB in the Phillipines during the Formosa Straits Crisis as part of the US response to Chinese aggression against the islands of Quemoy and Matsu.

In 1960 the four RF-101s flew to Don Muang to photograph objectives for the Thai government; and in early 1961 three aircraft, two F-102s and an RF-101 from the 15th TRS at Kadena, took part in another air show at Tan Son Nhut air base in South Vietnam. In October,

Pipe Stem personnel November 1961 at Tan Son Nhut. In the rear row left to right: Bob Gould, pilot; Jerry Miller, pilot; the remainder unknown. In the front row: Stan Menese, pilot; Al Strout, Pilot; Lieutenant Colonel Earl Butts, Squadron CO; Mark Stevensen, pilot. Remainder unknown. Mark Stevenson was killed in action flying an RF-4C in 1967. (Jerry Miller)

1961, another request for air show participation at Tan Son Nhut was accepted by the 15th TRS and four Voodoos duly arrived on the 18th of the month only to discover that the air show had been cancelled. This detachment was nicknamed Pipe Stem and as all support facilities were in place the detachment was invited by the South Vietnamese Government to assist in the assessment of flood damage caused when the Mekong River had burst its banks. It was an opportunity not to be missed. The US Government had a legitimate reason to base '101s in the area.

Pipe Stem November, 1961. Jerry Miller returns from a mission photographing flood damage. Four RF-101s arrived at Tan Son Nhut on 18 October, 1961, for an Air Show and remained there for several weeks assessing flood damage and secretly photographing targets in Laos which could have tactical significance! (Jerry Miller)

The Able Mable ramp at Don Muang. (Leland Olsen)

In addition to photographing the flood damage the aircraft also photographed other targets in Laos, including the Plain of Jars and the Ho Chi Minh Trail. Photos of the flood areas were taken with the forward oblique cameras. The military photos were taken with 36 in split verticals. These latter cameras were downloaded at night away from the prying eyes of the ICC. On the 23rd October, Pipe Stem pilots were ordered to photograph the airfield at Tchepone. They flew four sorties and brought back much needed evidence that the Soviet Union was parachuting supplies to the Pathet Lao and North Vietnamese. Marv Reed actually photographed Il.28s dropping supplies. However, the mission and subsequent ones were not without hazard. The Voodoos encountered anti-aircraft-fire on more than one occasion. Again under pressure from the ICC when it became evident that the flood waters had subsided, the four Pipe Stem RF-101s returned to Kadena on 21 November, 1961. They had flown sixty-seven reconnaissance missions mostly over Laos.

On the 29 October, 1961, while the 15th TRS was flying Pipe Stem missions out of South Vietnam; the 45th TRS was ordered to detach four RF-101s to Don Muang as Task Force Able Mable. The move to Thailand was completed on 7 November. Missions began to be flown the following day.

The four pilots were Major Harbst, the detachment commander, Captain Ralph DeLucia, First Lieutenant Jack Weatherby and First Lieutenant Fred Muesegaes. The two resident Field Goal pilots:

The initial Able Mable detachment photographed at Don Muang Thailand December 1961. Rear: Captain Ralph De Lucia, Captain Bill Whitten and First Lieutenant John Linihan. Front: First Lieutenant Fred Muesegaes, Major Ken Harbst and First Lieutenant Jack Weatherby. The Voodoo was the aircraft flown by Fred Muesegaes named 'Mary Ann Burns'. (Fred Muesegaes)

First Lieutenant John Linihan and Captain Bill Whitten joined the Able Mable team when the RT-33 flying operations as a courier were taken over by other 5th or 13th AF pilots. All the necessary facilities were in place: photo processing and interpretation, aircraft maintenance and support, and the Task Force had its own Intelligence Officer.

The first three missions out of Don Muang took place on 8 November, 1961. There was little to alarm and interfere with the missions over Laos, save for AAA and some small arms fire encountered mainly in the region of Tchepone airfield and the Plain of Jars. Fred Muesegaes was hit by 23mm AAA over Tchepone in January, 1962.

> On 9 Jan '62 (I know the date because it is on a plaque Ben Welsh made up with the armor piercing projectile on it) I got hit by a 23mm armour piercing round approaching Tchepone, Laos from the west at approx 500 ft and 500 kts in a right bank. The round just missed the cockpit and hit between the splitter vane and the fuselage and continued approx 10 ft between the intake duct and the fuel tanks untill entering the No. 2 fuel (feed tank) cell but did not penetrate the fuel bladder. There was a small entry hole (approx. 3 in diameter) but in passing through the aircraft it damaged quite a bit of electical wiring, which resulted in the loss of the right generator and all four fuel transfer pumps. Although this occurred on the first target it did not prevent me from continuing on to the other targets and the completion of the mission. Damage was beyond permanent repair at Don Muang, so a beer can patch was riveted over the entry hole and the electrical wiring was temporarily repaired for a flight back to Misawa on the next rotation. The aircraft was not flown on any more missions. Once the aircraft returned to Misawa it took approx six weeks in Field Maintenance to remove skin etc. and to find the final resting place of the armour piercing projectile – the case hardened steel had only a small scratch on the nose of it.

There was much to frustrate the pilots, however. Navigation was difficult, often being dependent on out of date and unreliable maps The weather was always problematic. It was possible to get accurate forecasts from Thai weather experts at Bangkok for Thailand, the Laos panhandle and Southern North Vietnam. Elsewhere, in Laos and North North Vietnam the forecasting was non existent and some missions were aborted because bad weather intervened. In addition to this, the almost permanently low cloud base caused problems with any high level photography.

An RB-57E 55-4237 at Tan Son Nhut in 1964. Eventually all Canberras in the theatre were painted black. (R.C. Mikesh via Dave Menard)

An RB-57E 55-4245 in all black finish at Tan Son Nhut. This aircraft was one of the two initial Canberras in south-east Asia which commenced Patricia Lynn operations in 1963. (R.C. Mikesh via Dave Menard)

Because of a prohibition placed on overflights of the Plain of Jars in Laos, the first Able Mable missions were over the Ho Chi Minh trail. Shortly after the arrival of the Voodoos the restrictions on the Plain of Jars missions was removed. This enabled the intelligence on the military positions in that area to be updated on a regular basis. The Able Mable missions were the subject of innumerable restrictions imposed upon them from time to time, not by PACAF or CINCPAC, but by politicians fearful of the political consequences for the US if an aircraft were shot down over Laos in particular.

On the 18 November, the Pipe Stem support facilities at Tan Son Nhut were designated Operations Location No 2 for the Able Mable Task Force. Voodoo missions over South Vietnam had often required the aircraft to refuel at the base, and it seemed logical to remove the film for processing at this point and replace it so that the aircraft could fly another sortie on the way back to Don Muang.

Able Mable had originally been detached for a period of thirty days. So vital did its mission become that it settled down for an indefinite stay. Aircraft and pilots were rotated from the 45th TRS every six weeks. From May, 1962, the 15th TRS provided aircraft and pilots. The 45th and the 15th subsequently rotated the detachment every six months. The RF-101Cs were tasked to complete many and varied missions using a variety of recce suites. There was even a suggestion that the aircraft should undertake mapping duties using the T-11 precision mapping camera in place of the KA-2 cameras in the second camera bay. This did not happen; there being tactical and practical considerations mitigating against its potential for success. A proposal to install the K-18 strip camera also fell by the wayside. For some missions the oblique cameras in the second camera bay were replaced by 24 or 36 in focal length cameras.

The night capability, Toy Tiger programme, took two RF-101s and two pilots, Marv Reed and Hoot Gibson from Kadena to Hill AFB in May 1962. The modification consisted of modifying the right drop tank to fire M-123 photo flash cartridges, a Doppler navigator system, the APN-102/ASN-7, two high-speed focal plane shutter cameras, KA-47s, in the rear vertical position and four 4.5×4.5 in KA-45s in the forward positions. After testing the aircraft were flown back to south-east Asia. They were not used effectively in the theatre at this time because they were returned to the US to perform recce over Cuba during the crisis.

The south-east Asia environment altered many of the standard recce mission tactics. Pre-strike photography of targets in dense jungle areas proved difficult and the pinpoint photography of such targets virtually impossible. The RF-101Cs spent a great deal of time in flying area covers in order to enable the Photo Interpreters to locate elusive targets. This was not only time consuming, but also dangerous. Post-strike photo recce was difficult for the same reasons, the difference being that the enemy would invariably be waiting for the Voodoos to return after a strike and the small arms fire would intensify.

On the 14 August, 1962, an RF-101C was hit by small arms fire over Laos. The pilot, Captain Tom O' Meara, was uninjured and succeeded in nursing his stricken aircraft back to Don Muang. Jerry Miller was flying out of Don Muang at the time:

> The aircraft took a hard hit in the nosewheel area which blew the right-forward. maintenance access-panel off the aircraft. It was recovered and publicized by the Pathet Lao. The nose gear would not extend and the landing closed Don Muang International Airport for about 2 hours while the Thais got the aircraft off the runway. I was flying that day and had to recover at Korat.

This was the first serious damage to the Voodoos and initially caused a brief cessation of flights over Laos. This prohibition was lifted but further restrictions imposed on operating ceiling and route did not enable any useful photo recce over Laos to take place. The benefit of being able to overfly saved a lot of time for the Voodoos, but that was about all. Overflights were again denied from the 14 September when the presence of a radar capable of tracking the aircraft was detected at Vinh in North Vietnam.

One result of the denial of Laotian airspace to the Voodoos was that the move of the Able Mable task force to Tan Son Nhut air base became highly desirable. By the 14 December, 1962, the four RF-101s became stationed at the Saigon base. Sorties from Tan Son Nhut were shorter in to South Vietnam than those from Thailand, but demands were high and realistically beyond the capability of the four aircraft to fulfil. In March, 1963, the 45th TRS detached two further RF-101s to Tan Son Nhut bringing the Able Mable strength up to six.

On the 8 July, 1963, the Able Mable Task Force was assigned to the 33rd Tactical Group at Tan Son Nhut. The unit became Detachment 1 which controlled all assigned reconnaissance aircraft. The RF-101Cs were completing some four to five sorties daily at this time, with one aircraft standing alert throughout the daylight hours to fulfil unplanned and urgent recce requirements.

On 6 May, 1963, two Martin RB-57E aircraft landed at Tan Son Nhut and joined the RF-101s as part of Detachment 1 of the 33rd Tactical Group. These were specially modified B-57E aircraft which had previously been used for target towing. The modifications had been completed by General Dynamics and comprised a redesigned nose to contain a 36 in KA-1 forward oblique

John Linihan flies his RF-101C over Udorn *en route* to photograph targets in Laos. (John Linihan)

camera and a KA-56 Panoramic camera. The bomb bay was also redesigned to accommodate a KA-1 vertical camera and a K-477 day and night camera, an infra-red scanner and a KA-1 left oblique camera. There was a viewer in the rear cockpit where the back seater could see in real time what the IR scanner could see. The RB-57s commenced operations immediately on arrival at the Saigon base. On the 7 May, the aircraft performed day and night photo reconnaissance against a variety of Viet Cong targets. The Canberras operated in both North and South Vietnam in the early days although this changed later. The results were successful and very soon the two aircraft were flying regular recce sorties under the code name, Patricia Lynn. The RB-57s gave to the US forces in south-east Asia an efficient night reconnaissance capability for the first time; albeit a small one.

Beginning in August, 1963, the RF-101s undertook a limited night reconnaissance role using the suite originally installed in the Toy Tiger aircraft. Although the limitations of the system over jungle areas had not changed, the Voodoos could undertake acceptable night photo reconnaissance of explicit targets such as coastal shipping and villages. Clearly, however, there was a pressing need to increase and improve the night photo recce capability in the theatre. This was not going to be done efficiently by the RF-101 Toy Tiger modification. The US Forces increasingly looked to the RB-57 detachment to fulfil the night recce requirements. It would be some time before the RF-4C Phantom would be available.

The Vietcong were receiving much of their supplies through Cambodia. The USAF had been extremely careful about not overflying that country and violating it's professed neutrality. Nonetheless, it became necessary to attempt to obtain some intelligence about the potential enemy's movements inside Cambodia. The RF-101s flew along the border in specific areas using very long focal length cameras. By the end of the year they had succeeded in photographing 85 per cent of the border some considerable distance inside Cambodia.

On the 17 May, 1964, the Laotian neutralist forces were attacked in the Plain of Jars by Pathet Lao forces and forced back towards the Royalist lines. This was the turn of events that the US Forces had been waiting for. It had been some time since overflights over Laos had been prohibited and frequent requests for them to be reinstated had been turned down by the State Department. However, on the 19 May four Voodoos crossed the border at low altitude to photograph targets in the panhandle. They returned to Tan Son Nhut without incident. On the 21 May RF-8 Crusaders from the US Navy Carrier *Kitty Hawk* joined the Voodoos and flew into Laos to photograph the infiltration routes from North Vietnam. From that moment the flights became regular and the programme of Laotian recce flights was given the nickname of Yankee Team. Flights under Yankee Team concentrated on the infiltration routes by the North Vietnamese to gain access to South Vietnam. They also served to provide intelligence to the friendly Laotian forces. The pilots were given specific details about how the missions were to be flown. On more than one occasion, however, it was necessary to modify the detailed route in order to obtain the best results. As might be expected the pilots knew better than the planners the capabilities of their aircraft and its systems. For the first time in the theatre the RF-101s used air-to-air refuelling; initially from Navy A-3 Skywarriors and later from USAF KC-97s. As a result of the increase in workload produced by the Yankee Team programme, the Able Mable Task Force strength was increased to ten aircraft. Three of these aircraft were modified to carry KA-45 cameras in place of the KA-2s. Producing a 4.5 × 4.5 in negative, these cameras were not popular with the photo interpreters. Nonetheless the modified aircraft were used regularly for daylight low-altitude high speed missions with considerable success.

On the 6 June, 1964, a US Navy RF-8A Crusader was shot down by hostile anti-aircraft fire over the Plain of Jars in Laos. On the 7 June an escorting F-8 was also brought down. A brief cessation to missions over Laos followed. Two days later a force of F-100s attacked the AAA positions in the region of Xieng Khouang. The mission was only a partial success as an RF-101C photo post-strike mission confirmed. However, when regular reconnaissance missions resumed on the 14th June, 1964, the two Voodoos were escorted by four F-100Ds. Subsequent missions

RB-57E 55-4245 photographed during a stopover at Danang in May 1965. (Dave Menard).

RF-101C 'Deuce' of the 45th TRS waits in the revetments at Tan Son Nhut for its next mission. (George Cowgill).

The 45th TRS revetments at TSN in 1966. One of the Voodoos still has to receive its coat of camouflage paint. (George Cowgill)

Three uncamouflaged 45th RF-101Cs at TSN in 1966. In the early days the duties at TSN were shared between the 15th and the 45th TRS. (George Cowgill)

found that the anti-aircraft threat to USAF operations over Laos to be increased. During July alone, in excess of twelve new 57mm guns were discovered and photographed. On the 31 July an RF-101C was hit by anti-aircraft fire over Nhommarath. The escorting F-100s attacked and destroyed the gun emplacement.

In August, 1964, the Able Mable Task Force was increased to twelve aircraft. This amounted to a large proportion of available aircraft. On the 2 and 4 August, when North Vietnamese torpedo boats attacked US navy Destroyers in the Gulf of Tonkin, the action prompted the further augmentation of the force by another six aircraft. This left the 15th TRS at Kadena drastically short of RF-101s and required the ferrying of eight aircraft from the US, six of which were a part of the 20th TRS from the 363rd TRW at Shaw AB which went to Okinawa.

On the 7th August, a reconnaissance sortie photographed the North Vietnamese air base of Phuc Yen. The photos revealed a number of Mig 15s and Mig 17s parked in revetments. These posed a new and more potent threat to the unarmed RF-101s and to a change in ordnance carried by the escorting F-100s to include air-to-air armaments. US Forces were authorized to attack any aircraft that threatened them and to conduct hot pursuit of those aircraft.

In Northern Laos near the North Vietnamese border was the area designated Barrel Roll. When the area drew the attention of the F-100s and F-105s in regular bombing missions; the Voodoos

Aircraft RB-57E 55-4249 at Elmandorf, Alaska, en route to Saigon. This aircraft commenced operations in December, 1964. (via Dave Menard)

RF-101C 56-088 returning from a mission in April, 1966. The pilot George Cowgill baled out of the same aircraft in June 1966. (George Cowgill)

became involved in regular pre- and post-strike missions. On the 18 November an F-100D on a reconnaissance escort mission was shot down whilst attacking an anti-aircraft artillery position at Ban Phan Nop. The loss of this aircraft triggered a full scale hunt for the missing pilot. He was found dead on 20 November. On 21 November, Captain Burton Waltz of the 15th TRS was flying RF-101C 56-0230 over the same area photographing the gun position that had downed the Super Sabre when his aircraft was hit by ground fire. It burst into flames and Waltz ejected. On landing he sustained injuries, but, thankfully, he was picked up by an Air America helicopter and flown to Korat for medical treatment.

Burt Waltz was the first RF-101C casualty in the south-east Asia war. Sadly he was not to be the last and many that followed him were not rescued and many died. In fact he should not have been at Tan Son Nhut at all, but the 45th TRS had been unable to replace the 15th on schedule because their RF-101s were undergoing Modification 1181. This expensive modification involved the installation of the KS-72 and panoramic KA-56A cameras in place of all but the KA-1 split verticals. It also involved the installation of the KS-72A framing camera that was being developed for the RF-4C Phantom. The modernization programme was designed to give the RF-101C improved low altitude capability and an increase in sensor reliability through the use of automatic exposure control and improved camera control systems.

The Voodoos continued throughout late 1964 to concentrate on the infiltration routes the North Vietnamese were using to move men and materials in to the south. The Ho Chi Minh trail was used extensively whenever the weather permitted and the Voodoos succeeded in photographing a great deal of this activity, albeit from a minimum height of 10,000 ft. The F-100 and F-105 escorts frequently went in fast and low to deal with any hostile AAA batteries. If the '101s had been allowed to fly at the same height as their escorts, the amount of intelligence about the enemy's movements would have been considerably enhanced. As it was, much was missed; hidden under the jungle canopy.

The Patricia Lynn RB-57s continued to fly their day and night missions throughout 1964 and in December, Detachment 1 received two further aircraft. Regular upgrades to the reconnaissance systems required return to the USA for all of the aircraft at one time or another.

An RF-101C of the 20th TRS out of Udorn flies low and fast over the jungle terrain. (via Don Karges)

Jim Young of the 20th TRS taxies his RF-101C to the ramp at Udorn after a successful mission. Shortly after this mission Jim was shot down and became a POW. (via George Cowgill)

An RF-101C Voodoo at Udorn December, 1965 having just completed a mission. (George Cowgill)

In early 1965 the RB-57s began regular night BDA missions into Laos. For these Steel Tiger missions the RB-57s were teamed with B-57 bombers out of Bien Hoa and a C-130 flare ship. The aircraft, two B-57s, a C-130 and an RB-57, would approach the target area. The C-130 would drop flares and the B-57s would attack any exposed targets such as trucks and structures such as bridges and boats on rivers. The RB-57E would subsequently do a BDA run over the target area. These night missions were extended into North Vietnam in March of 1965.

The commencement of 1965 saw a further growth in the tactical reconnaissance deployed in south-east Asia. The 45th TRS took over the Able Mable Task Force at Tan Son Nhut completely. All the squadrons RF-101s had undergone Modification 1181 and their recce capability had been improved. There were plans laid at this time to deploy six RF-101s of the 15th TRS to Udorn in Thailand to take over the Yankee Team work over Laos and North Vietnam. The 45th at Tan Son Nhut would be known as Able Mable Alpha and the Udorn detachment as Able Mable Bravo. However, Udorn would need much work before it was a suitable base for the Voodoos. It had changed little since the Field Goal days. At a minimum the runway would need to be lengthened, an arresting barrier installed and appropriate photo processing facilities set up.

The beginning of 1965 saw an escalation in the attacks on US Forces by the North Vietnamese. This inevitably led to an increase in the number of retaliatory strikes. The Tan Son Nhut RF-101s undertook weather reconnaissance missions in the target areas of US strikes and pre- and post-strike photo recce. The aircraft spent a lot of time loitering in the area following their role as pathfinders to the initial flak suppression strikes. As a consequence of this the post-strike photographs were often worthless, being taken too soon after the attack when the target was obscured by dust and smoke. It was therefore necessary to have these photos taken by a different pair of Voodoos. The typical mission in support of Rolling Thunder strike missions would commence with a pre-strike mission against the target the day before the planned strike. Generally the strike missions were flown against fixed targets such as bridges. If the pre-strike mission was successful, the photos would be picked up by an F-105 and flown back to Korat or Takhli to enable the strike pilots to have sufficient time to plan effectively. On the day of the strike a pair of RF-101s would photograph the target some 20 minutes before the strike force was due to attack. Post-strike photos would be taken by another pair of RF-101s 20 minutes after the strike when the smoke and dust had had the chance to settle. There were of course problems associated with this 'routine' once it had become established, not least being that, on the day of the strike, the unarmed RF-101s would always be expected. This was more critical for the post-strike aircraft!

A pre camouflage RB-66C over South Vietnam in 1966. (Kirk Ransom)

In March, 1965, regular recce missions were flown over North Vietnam to carry out weather, visual, photographic, infra-red radar and other sensor missions. Initially these missions were still confined to a minimum height of 10,000 ft. By the end of the month these restrictions had been lifted and low altitude missions permitted. On 29 April pilots from Tan Son Nhut flew the first tactical ECM mission over North Vietnam. Carrying four QRC-160 ECM pods each, the RF-101s flew a mission in support of Rolling Thunder strikes, jamming enemy radar.

The Udorn RF-101C force had become active on the 31 March, 1965, and was nicknamed Green Python. The Tan Son Nhut detachment reverted to the name of simply Able Mable. Udorn was not completely ready for the Voodoos. The runway had been lengthened to 10,000 ft; but was

Aircraft RF-4C 64-1045 of the 16th TRS receives fuel from a KC-135 *en route* to south-east Asia from Shaw in 1965. (Kirk Ransom)

still very narrow at 150 ft. The arresting barrier had not yet been installed. Eventually arresting gear was installed at both ends of the runway and in the centre.

The need for an effective electronic reconnaissance force had for some time been acknowledged by those responsible for planning the air war in south-east Asia. The only aircraft in the USAF inventory capable of performing the ELINT mission was the RB-66 Destroyer. In March, 1965 three RB-66B photographic reconnaissance aircraft arrived at Tan Son Nhut. Part of the 9th TRS from Shaw AFB, the specific mission these aircraft was to fly photo recce in support of allied operations in south-east Asia. The aircraft were equipped with an IR system which was operated by the gunner. The RB-66Bs flew two missions a day, both photo and night IR. They did not have an electronic role. IR missions were generally flown at heights of between 300 and 500 ft. At night the aircraft were primarily concerned with locating enemy bivouac areas and campfires. Their effectiveness rating was 91.2 per cent and in the period from March to July they carried out 647 missions covering 900 photo targets. An RB-66B is also unofficially credited with the destruction of a Viet Cong machine gun nest. An aircraft piloted by Bill Puckett was fired upon by the guns when it was outbound on a mission. They were unable to acquire their target due to poor weather conditions and on returning they were fired upon by the same gun position. They dumped their entire load of photo flash cartridges on the site and destroyed it!

On 19 April these four B models were joined at the Saigon base by two RB-66Cs. The RB-66C did have an ELINT role and their arrival was fortuitous in that it coincided with the increase in development of the North Vietnamese SAM defences and their associated radar systems.

On 25 May the RB-66Cs moved to Takhli Air Base in Thailand where they were joined by two further aircraft deployed from Shaw. From their Thai base the Destroyers engaged in their ELINT work, gathering data on the number, location and variety of the enemy's radars. As the number of SAM missile sites and their threat to strike aircraft increased the RB-66Cs became more involved in missions in direct support of the bomber and fighter bomber strikes, providing jamming of the North Vietnamese AAA and SA-2 fire control radars. Missions were usually conducted in pairs. Two aircraft would take off from Takhli and after rendezvousing with the strike force they would proceed to the target area. The RB-66Cs would maintain an elliptical orbit out of the reach of AAA guns. They were principally searching for 'Fire Can' radar emissions from the AAA batteries which the EWOs would jam. Commensurate with this they would also be listening for the Fan Song SA-2 missile radars. If these were identified the strike force would be informed and the EWOs would jam these radars also.

Aircraft RB-66B 53-415 at Takhli in 1965. The RB-66Bs were used mainly for photographic and infra red reconnaissance over South Vietnam. (George Cowgill)

The capacity of the RB-66 to survive in a Mig and SAM dominated environment was limited. By August 1965 the threat to its operations was so great that all the aircraft adopted a role as Stand Off jammers operating in support of the strike aircraft but outside the area of severest threat. The RB-66C aircraft's electronic systems had been state of the art when the aircraft had first deployed to PACAF and USAFE in the mid 1950s. It quickly became apparent in south-east Asia that the aircraft had only a limited use against the threat posed by the ever growing and sophisticated defensive systems being installed by the North Vietnamese.

On the 1 April, 1965, Green Python became operational when an RF-101C recce mission took off from Udorn. By the end of the first week the force was averaging four sorties a day. A month after becoming operational the force was augmented by six 363rd TRW Voodoos. This increase in capability was fortuitous because, commensurate with the cessation of the bombing campaign from the 12 May, the workload of the RF-101s increased dramatically. In three days from the 13 to the 15 May the USAF and the US Navy flew a total of 184 reconnaissance missions. Even when the bombing recommenced on the 18 May the recce commitment continued at a high level.

The period from May to July, 1965, was characterized by two things: the continued intense reconnaissance workload and the increase in the threat posed to those missions by newly constituted and operational SAM missile sites, and an increase in the number of Migs based in the north. One of the consequences of the latter was the directive requiring daily photo recce of all jet capable airfields in North Vietnam above 20 degrees north. The US Navy and the Green Python Task Force shared the workload on these missions. Following the shoot down of the first USAF aircraft, an F-4 Phantom, by a missile on the 24 July, 1965, the hunt for SAM sites occupied much of the mission time for the Voodoo pilots.

However, the biggest threat to the Voodoos continued to be anti-aircraft fire and it began to exact its toll of aircraft and pilots. On the 29 April, 1965, Captain Charlie Shelton's aircraft was hit by automatic fire in Laos. Shelton ejected safely but was captured. On the 29th July Captain Jack Weatherby and Major Jerry Lents had been tasked with a recce mission against a SAM missile site north-west of Hanoi. Weatherby had taken the lead and was flying at 600 kts at an altitude of 200 ft. His RF-101 was hit by a shell which passed through the fuselage without exploding, but punctured the fuel tanks and started a fire. He continued his photo run ignoring Lents' pleas to bale out. Shortly after leaving the target his aircraft exploded and crashed. Weatherby was awarded the Air Force Cross posthumously in November 1965.

Fifteen days after Weatherby's death, on the 13 August, Captain Fred Mellor's aircraft was hit while on a lo-altitude high-speed photo run between Phu Tho and Viet Tri. On the 5th October a Voodoo piloted by Captain Robert Pitt ran into heavy anti-aircraft fire approximately 8 miles from

An RB-66C of the 41st TRS deploys its drag chute on landing at Takhli in 1966. (Lous Herry)

A 16th TRS RF-4C, 64-1037 returns from a mission in 1965. (Kirk Ransom)

the target at Long Met. The mission was to obtain BDA photography of the ammunition dump and a nearby bridge. Pitt had no option but to abandon his photo run and he made for the Gulf of Tonkin. His wingman flew on and completed his photo run in spite of his aircraft having being damaged, though not as badly as Pitt's. Captain Pitt eventually succeeded in nursing his aircraft to Da Nang in spite of damaged hydraulics and fuel cells and no rudder controls.

For the purposes of mission planning the operational areas of the north of Vietnam were divided into zones called Route Packages (RP). RPI was south of the 18th parallel and RPs II, III, and IV above it. The most dangerous areas were RPs V and VI. RP VI was centred on Hanoi and Haiphong and RP V to the west bordering on Laos.

One way in which the RF-101s sought to avoid damage from anti-aircraft fire was a tactic devised by Major Harry Runge of the 15th TRS. Major Runge's background had not been exclusively in tac recce. In Europe he had flown the F-86D with the 86th TFW. He was not hide bound by the notion that jet photo recce meant going in low and fast; the mission profile that had prevailed in Europe as practised by the RF-101 pilots of the 66th TRW; many of whom were now in south-east Asia. One of the major problems with many of the pre-strike and post-strike missions was, as we have seen, that the RF-101s were invariably expected by the North Vietnamese. They also knew only too well how the Voodoos would be coming. It was all too predictable. The pop-up manoeuvre entailed a low level, high speed run to a point approximately 5 miles from the target. The pilot would then engage afterburner and climb to about 15,000 ft with cameras on. The target would be crossed in level flight still in afterburner and then the Voodoo

Some 16th TRS Phantoms in their revetments at TSN. The RF-4s routinely flew eighteen missions out of Tan Son Nhut every day, of which twelve were night reconnaissance missions. (Kirk Ransom)

The RF-4Cs shared revetments with 45th RF-101Cs at the Saigon base. The role of the RF-101 was primarily day recce, so the two types, together with the Patricia Lynn RB-57s, certainly had all potential targets covered round the clock. (George Cowgill)

would make a rapid descent to low level and high tail it for home. Undoubtedly the tactic dramatically reduced the incidence of anti-aircraft hits and restored flagging morale.

The predictably of the timing of the missions was as much a problem for the RB-57 pilots as it was for the RF-101s. The route target missions: rivers, roads and trails were generally flown at altitudes of between 3000 to 8000 ft. Habitually the missions would often be flown day after day or night after night at the same time. No wonder that the bad guys would often set up traps to shoot down the aircraft. Night area cover missions were flown along lines side by side. These missions were often when the aircrews experienced a significant level of small arms fire. On 5 August, 1965, the first loss occurred in the Patricia Lynn RB-57E detachment. Aircraft 55-4243 was hit by small arms fire while on a low level night recce mission. The crew were close to home and ejected near to their home base at Tan Son Nhut. Both men landed safely, the aircraft was destroyed. In November, 1965, a further RB-57E arrived at Tan Son Nhut, bringing the total of aircraft to four.

The RB-66B detachment at Tan Son Nhut also suffered a loss on the 22 October, 1965, when aircraft 53-452 crashed on a mountain top with the loss of all three crew members: Captain Robert

George Cowgill with his RF-101C shortly after landing from a high-altitude mission to Dien Bien Phu using split vertical cameras. (George Cowgill)

Mann, First Lieutenant James McEwen and First Lieutenant John Weger. The cause of the crash was never known and the bodies of the crew members were never recovered.

In October, 1965, the reconnaissance force in south-east Asia underwent a considerable reorganization. Nine RF-4C Phantoms arrived at Ton San Nhut with the 16th TRS. The 45th TRS returned to Misawa and the 20th TRS moved into the Saigon base to take over the Able Mable mission using twelve RF-101s of the 15th TRS. The 15th TRS retained it's Green Python at Udorn with six RF-101s. The 363rd aircraft moved back to Kadena.

The RF-4Cs were equipped with the AN/AAS-18 infra-red system which enabled them to undertake night reconnaissance missions immediately. Routinely the aircraft would fly night missions in support of the ground troops and identifying Viet Cong targets. One of the early missions involved the aircraft looking for campfires in a similar mission to that flown by the RB-66Bs. The crews flew sometimes twice a night for six days a week. The night-photo runs were set up by the GIB (Guy in the Back) and for illumination the RF-4C was equipped with four banks of photoflash ejector cartridges mounted in pairs on compartments either side of the upper rear fuselage. The use of these photoflashes proved problematic initially. It was common practice in training for the crew to fire off all their cartridges in a photo run; a flash exploding every second. In the hostile environment of North Vietnam however this was most unwise. After the first few flashes the enemy had got his bearings on the RF-4 and all the system was doing was illuminating his target for him. It became routine for the crews to fire no more than four cartridges and make these count. Apart from the dangers associated with the use of the photoflashes, night missions were generally considered safer than day missions; the risk from small arms fire being minimal. Col. Don Nash was with the 16th TRS at Tan Son Nhut:

> For a night mission, the crew would show at the Squadron 2.5 hours before take-off to get the assigned targets, intelligence briefing and plot the course on the charts. We went to the aircraft about 11 pm for a take-off at 12 am. The RF-4C had a radar so the GIB was primarily responsible for navigating to the target area, finding the target on radar and making the target run. The 'Area cover' was flown back and forth along parallel flight paths. At the end of each pass we did a 'woofer manoeuvre.' This involved full throttle, pulling the nose up abruptly, then doing one-half of a figure 8, descending back to the altitude for the next run. The only sensor used at night on these runs was the infra-red camera to detect the heat differentials. The total flight time was about one hour and 50 minutes. If we were on a mission with air-to-air refuelling, then the flights were 3 hours and 15 minutes.

The missions flown by the RF-4s complemented those of the RF-101s and the RB-57s. They were, however, faster and more manoeuvrable than both these aircraft and in high risk areas their superior speed would often get them out of tight spots which might prove fatal to the '101s or '57s. They also routinely carried ECM pods which greatly enhanced their survival chances.

The RF-4Cs of the 16th TRS were flying eighteen sorties a day out of Tan Son Nhut. Of these six were daytime missions, primarily for crew familiarization, and twelve were at night. Of these eighteen missions approximately six were flown over the north, usually into Route packages I, II and III. The pilots of the 16th were obliged to complete a tour of a year; but for every twenty missions flown into the north they could reduce that by a month. Bearing in mind the distance from the north and the squadrons's primary mission, which was to support the ground troops in the south, not many pilots succeeded in going home early!

Night infra-red area covers were only flown by the RF-4C in South Vietnam. Photo flash missions were reserved for the north with great care, as were missions using the APQ-102 Side Looking Radar (SLR).

Five B-66B Brown Cradle aircraft arrived at Takhli in October, 1965. These aircraft had been flown over from Europe and were established as Detachment 1 of the 25th TRW. Their departure from USAFE and NATO had left that area without any form of Electronic Warfare aircraft. Bearing in mind the development of the Warsaw Pact forces at this time this was considered by many a foolhardy act. The Brown Cradle Destroyers were not primarily Electronic Reconnaissance aircraft. Their specific role was as Electronic Countermeasures (ECM) vehicles, capable of jamming all the radars in the North Vietnamese inventory. The aircraft's weakness was that, when operating as a jamming aircraft, its radar warning system was rendered ineffective. In order to overcome this difficulty the B-66B and the RB-66C worked in unison. The B-66B flew with the strike force as a jamming aircraft while the RB-66C operated in a stand-off role providing warning of SAM launches and monitoring the coverage of the B-66Bs' systems. For some time the North Vietnamese maintained an advantage with their GCI radars; directing their fighters against USAF fighters and fighter bombers with some success. They were also integrating their defensive systems to such an extent that the job of jamming all the frequencies at any one time was well nigh impossible even for the Brown Cradle aircraft.

Meanwhile, the RB-66Cs of the 9th TRS at Takhli were assigned to the newly activated 41st TRS. The 9th TRS personnel were given the choice of either transferring to the 41st or returning to Shaw. Those who remained at Takhli would be expected to remain in Thailand for twelve months minus the time already done, or until they had completed their 100 missions. Most of those who had completed over 50 per cent of their assigned missions elected to remain with the 41st TRS. There were those however who chose to go home, even though they knew that the chance of them returning at some point in the future was very likely. It was becoming evident that the New Year was going to bring with it some significant personnel shortages, in particular in Electronic Warfare Officers (EWO). EWOs were flying as many as two and often three missions a day. It would not take long to complete 100.

The advent of the Mig into the equation naturally concerned all the recce crews and not least the RF-101 pilots, in spite of the reassurance given by headquarters, 2nd Air Division to CINCPAC that the Voodoos were highly manoeuvrable and could evade the Mig 17 with ease! It was, in the event, the superior speed of the RF-101 which got the aircraft out of many a tight spot. The RF-101 was many good things but it was never a dogfighter! On the 15th November, 1965, two Voodoos were jumped by two Migs in the area of Yen Bay. Whilst the lead aircraft concentrated on his photo run the wingman attempted to distract the Migs and in the process found himself being out manoeuvred to the extent that he was being forced in the wrong direction. It was only when the pilot put the aircraft down on the deck and engaged afterburner that he shook off the enemy aircraft. Similarly, on the 26th November, two RF-101Cs were attacked by four Mig 17s. The Voodoos broke to the left and down to 200 ft at high speed. The Migs did not follow.

Many of the missions fragged for the pilots involved photographing several targets. George Cowgill flew out of Udorn on 14 February, 1966, in RF-101 56-120 on such a mission:

> Targets were all in the Thanh Hoa area. Specifically the bridge that we called 'The Dragon's Jaw', a nearby SAM site, an airfield under construction at Bai Thoung and a barracks area in the mountains. Really bad wx [weather] due to the monsoon season. I flew lead with Jimmy Wylie as 2. Dead reckoned via time distance from Udorn to Vinh, letdown still dead reckoning over the gulf until we were down to 100 ft on the radar altimeter, at this time I had Jimmy stack slightly above me in case I hit bottom. Went into the target run-in at extremely low altitude, below 50 ft. Left rooster tails going across the rice paddies. Over land the ceiling picked up to around a 1000 feet due to ground heating. We covered the first three targets while accelerating from 480 kts to something well above 600 kts at varying altitudes from near zero up to 800 ft. Escaped up a valley till we got out of the target area. Then climbed to 25,000 or 30,000 ft to go home. Missed the last target due to wx. Jimmy said at times he could barely make out my aircraft due to the intense ground fire coming up at us. I couldn't tell you as I was concentrating on getting the target coverage.

'The Iron Eyeball' in the maintenance hangar at TSN showing detail of the nose art on the port side of the nose. (George Cowgill)

On the starboard side of the nose the legend reads: 'The eyeball has come, has seen, has conquered' (George Cowgill)

Jerry Miller celebrates his 100 RF-101 missions in less dignified style at Urdon. Jerry was among the first recce pilots into SE Asia when he flew into Saigon with the PipeStem deployment in 1961. (Don Karges)

Replacement RF-101s were ferried from the USA via Hill AFB throughout the war in SE Asia. This one is being refuelled by a KC-135 over the Pacific. (George Cowgill)

Don Karges of the 20th TRS at Udorn parks his RF-101C after completion of his 100th Mission. (Don Karges)

Don Karges shares a bottle of champagne with the CO of the 20th TRS at Udorn: John Bull Stirling. Don completed his 100 missions in the RF-101C in five months and returned to Shaw AFB in January 1967; from where he went on to command the 1st TRS flying RF-4Cs at RAF Alconbury. He retired from the USAF as a full Colonel in 1983. (Don Karges)

In February, 1966, the 460th TRW was activated at Tan Son Nhut to take control of all USAF tactical reconnaissance assets in south-east Asia.

In April, 1966, the 20th TRS moved its twelve RF-101s from Tan Son Nhut to Udorn to take over Green Python. The 15th TRS returned to Kadena. The 45th TRS sent twelve aircraft to Tan Son Nhut to take over Able Mable. In May the 20th increased its complement of RF-101s to sixteen; taking four from the 15th TRS at Kadena. Four aircraft and their pilots joined the 20th from USAFE in July and the 15th sent its four Voodoos to Tan Son Nhut to augment the 45th TRS. On the 23rd July the 45th moved all its aircraft and personnel to Tan Son Nhut. The 15th TRS, destined to receive the RF-4C Phantom, maintained its Voodoos as replacement for those lost in Vietnam. When an aircraft was destroyed the 15th would ferry another aircraft to Udorn or Tan Son Nhut; a duty it was to perform until the end of 1966 when the last of its RF-101s was delivered.

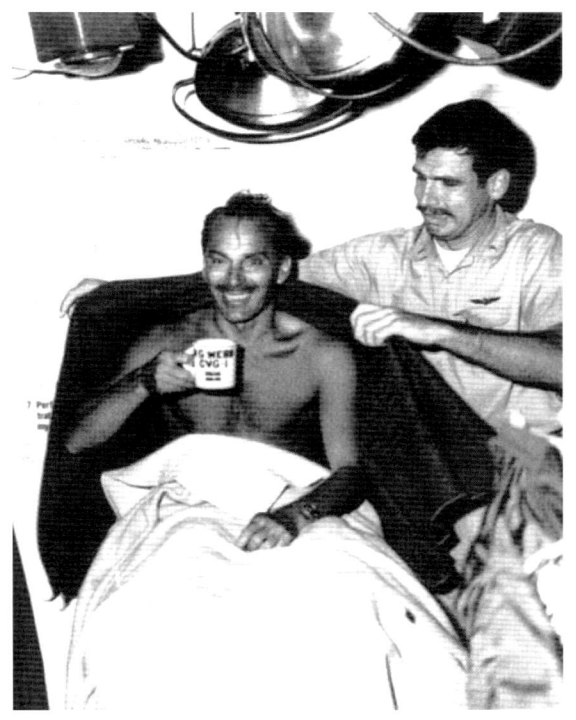

Bob Walker was the pilot of the ill fated EB-66C, 54-457, which was brought down by a SAM near Vinh south of Hanoi. The crew baled out over the Gulf of Tonkin and were picked up by the USS *Ranger*. (Bob Walker)

Not all RF-101 missions over North Vietnam were in pairs. There were many times when a single ship mission was the only practical option. Indeed from mid June 1966 most missions were single ship. There were not enough aircraft to cover the scheduled missions. Pilots of the 20th at Udorn bore the brunt of the single ship sorties into the heavily defended areas of Route Packages V and VI. On the 31st July, 1966, Don Karges joined the 20th at Udorn. Don had been in the 38th TRS at Ramstein in Germany and was an experienced RF-101 pilot. On the 1st August he flew his first mission into RP I. In common with many of his fellow pilots Don flew virtually every day, sometimes twice a day. He recalls one of these missions to photograph a railroad and marshalling yards in the north-east of North Vietnam, in RP VI:

> Decided to take the long way around – north until well past Thud Ridge, turn east way north of the alley, long low level over the karst. Didn't think anyone could see me and thought it was uninhabited area. Wrong – every time I crossed a road I received volumes of small arms fire. Never hit but could see the muzzle flashes as I crossed the roads. Had planned to approach the railroad at a 90 degree angle and make a turning pop to the north-east to get the marshalling yard and about 3-4 miles on each side of the yard. All was quiet until I began the pop at 600kts. Immediately the RHAW gear went wild and the AAA was everywhere. I pulled over 6 gs in the turning pop and was using 80–90 degrees of bank so lost all that lift and topped out at 8000 instead of 15,000 ft. Took a short strip with all cameras running and then made a hard descending left turn back to the west. I thought I was dead meat. Kept it at 600 kts on my escape heading and down in the dust. After a few minutes I checked my map and nothing matched! Don't know how long I kept looking for something I recognized but eventually checked the mag compass and realized I had pulled so many gs the DG (directional gyro) had precessed about 45 degrees. By my best

Two RF-4Cs of the 12th TRS, 460th TRW out of Tan Son Nhut photographed over South Vietnam in 1968. Very often on return from their missions the RF-4s would join up in informal formations for landing at TSN. (Phil Rowe)

estimates on my 1mm scale world chart, I was probably in China – never debriefed that little fact! But I now faced a bigger problem. I was in China, much further from Udorn than I had planned and below Bingo fuel. Had not planned to climb until back near Laos but now I had to start climbing deep in NVN [North Vietnam] near Chinese border. Naturally there is no one airborne, no SAR, tankers, fighters, etc. Did a cruise climb to over 45,000 ft and for the first time in my career got real serious about the cruise charts in the back of my checklist. Anyway it was uneventful – I was a sitting duck if a MIG came up. Finally shut one engine down, pulled the other to idle and did a long slow descent to Udorn where I started up the other engine on a long straight-in and shut down with fumes. I have low pan prints that show the radar guided bursts directly on my centreline while in my 80 degree bank turning pop. If I had not turned so hard I would be buried on the NE railroad and would not have had the free tour of southern China.

An RF-4C of the 12th TRS in the revetments at TSN in 1968. (Phil Rowe)

These two RF-4Cs have joined up for their return to TSN after completing their missions. (Phil Rowe)

On the day that Karges had arrived at Udorn the 20th had lost an aircraft and a pilot on a solo mission into RP V. Major William D. Burroughs disappeared without trace while on a mission north-west of Hanoi. He was declared MIA and it was not until his repatriation in 1973 that it was learned that his Voodoo had been downed by AAA.

Larry Garrison flew with the 20th out of Udorn, frequently into Route Package VI. One such mission was two ship with two targets:

> My mission was an afternoon flight with a TOT 5 minutes after two Fighter Strikes. We were not happy about it but had no choice but to go after them. The targets were the Thai Nguyen Rail yard to be struck by F-105s and the Doumer Bridge to be struck by F-4s.
>
> My wingman was a very experienced pilot that I had flown numerous times with, so that was not a problem.
>
> We took off on schedule and proceeded north at about 15,000 ft and at a relatively slow speed. We crossed the Red River and used 'Thud Ridge' as a mask against any SAMs that might head our way. There had been some discussion of cameras and the quality of the

Patricia Lynn RB-57E 55-4245 at Tan Son Nhut undergoing routine maintenance. (John Harris)

An EB-66E 'Chitty Chitty Bang Bang' of the 41st TEWS at Takhli in 1967 weathering the monsoon. (via Ned Colburn)

photo so I determined to use the 36 in split verticals over the target and pop up to get the imagery. I increased speed to full military at this time and the wingman was holding position very well. I could hear [on strike frequency] the 105s hitting the rail yard and knew we were OK on timing. I could not hear the F-4 flight but that was not the time to worry about that. We went straight for the target and popped up to about 12,000 ft over the

An EB-66C of the 42nd TEWS formates with another EB-66 prior to a mission over the north in 1967. (via Ned Colburn)

rail yard to get the photo. Actual BDA on these types of missions was hard to get because of the smoke and dust from the bombing.

So I was then left to decide about the second target and though I had not heard the F-4s. I felt, though not likely, they might have been early to get the target. In fact, they were late and it seemed to me that the whole of North Vietnam was waiting for them and took it out on us. So off we went jinking between 3000 and 8000 ft to the bridge. The ground looked like a bunch of arc welders as guns were being fired. I am not certain any more if that was true but I seemed to me that was the case. We continued the 50 miles or so to the bridge and began to pull up for the photo. I looked at the wingman and he was literally surrounded by Triple A fire and I thought to myself, they are shooting the devil out of him, not thinking of course it was the same for me. We popped for the target again to about 12,000 ft and exposed the film. All was well at this time and again the wingman was doing very well. We planned our escape with a left diving turn after the target back to the north. As we popped, the wingman who had been on the left changed to the right side.

About this time I noticed a SAM tracking us and to me it seemed very big and very lethal. I could quickly see the missile was going to miss me. I saw the wingman bank sharply to the right and the missile explode at what I thought was just below his aircraft. I was sure it got him. I could do nothing for him and continued the dive away from the target at about red line speed of 600 kts. Very shortly here came the wingman and shot by me though he was slowing down and we joined in formation again. He had been doing a good bit better than 600.

At this time via hand signals he told me he had only 1500 lb of fuel left which was 1500 lb below bingo. I initiated a climb regardless of the Mig threat and levelled at 42,000 ft. I began calling for a Tanker to come north to meet us but could not make contact. Fortunately, the Triple Nickel F-4s heard us and relayed our call. After some discussion as to the type of tanker we needed, probe and drogue or boom, we got the point across we could take either. So here came the tanker. We rendezvoused about 70 or 80 miles south of Hanoi and I led the wing man down to about 20,000 ft for refuelling and felt like things were going to be OK. By the way, the wingman had lost his radio and nav aids. I was concerned about losing my TACAN as well.

As we approached the Tanker, (it was probe and drogue) the wingman attempted to raise the probe on his aircraft but it only came up half way and he could not hook up. By this time I was certain he would not make Udorn but perhaps we could get over Thailand before he ran out of fuel. We again climbed to about 42,000 ft and got radar vectors to the base. Things were going to be close but as the minutes went by I began to think we might just have a chance to make it. The best descent to save fuel on the 101 was to start about 30 miles or so out and pull the engines to idle and begin the descent. This is what we did and we made a big circling 270 turn to the active and he landed with about 200 lb of fuel remaining.

In 1966 the USAF redesignated all its electronic warfare Destroyer aircraft. The RB-66C became the EB-66C and the B-66B Brown Cradle became the EB-66B. The RB-66B retained its R prefix as it was primarily engaged in photographic reconnaissance.

By careful planning and constant vigilance the EB-66s were able to operate with relative freedom in support of the strike aircraft. Their effectiveness was compromised by the need for them to operate in safe environment; orbiting some distance from the targets area. These orbits were over the Gulf of Tonkin, and inland, above the mountains to the north-west of the Red River delta.

On 25 February, 1966, an EB-66C was shot down by an SA-2 missile near Vinh south of Hanoi. The crew ejected and all but one were fortunate to be picked up in the Gulf of Tonkin by the US Navy. Bob Walker was the pilot of EB-66C 54-457:

EC-47s of the 360th TEWS at Tan Son Nhut. The 'Gooney Birds were constantly being upgraded, the better to fulfil their ARDF role. (Phil Rowe)

Because of bad weather RB-66 was the only Air Force plane out that afternoon. It was the first day after President Johnson's bombing pause of North Vietnam had been called off. Our Mission: attempt to determine whether or not the Chinese had supplied a newly discovered missile site with surface-to-air missiles during the bombing pause period. This new site had been discovered electronically. At that time no SAM activity had been detected. The only way to determine whether or not the site had been supplied with any birds was to act as a decoy target. We flew the race track pattern above the site at 27,000 ft, 'asking' them to launch a missile against us. Then we would know, and be able to pass this warning to all concerned. We had the capability to jam guidance radar when it was activated, and believed that we could blind any SAM that might be launched against us. Probably, because of help from the Russians or Chinese, the enemy had learned a new method of launching their SAMS before the guidance radar was activated. Our first bird was on the way before John (Captain John B Causey, Chief EWO) detected the radar signature. The plane's radios were knocked out of commission when the first SAM exploded next to the plane causing severe damage. Fortunately for us, Captain Causey had detected the guidance radar and immediately alerted me. His warning surely saved all our lives, because it gave me an instant to take immediate and violent evasive action, which probably prevented complete destruction of plane and crew. We could hear a second missile explode, but it caused no further damage. The plane's battery power lasted just long enough to warn the crew over the intercom that we were going to have to bale out. My attempted mayday call was, of course, unanswered.

Bob elected not to order a bale out over land but rather to chance making the sea over the Gulf of Tonkin where a Navy task force 'Yankee Station One' was on station. Not only would the crew have a better chance of survival but the valuable and secret equipment that the aircraft carried would not fall into enemy hands. The crew were all rested and became grateful guests of the US Navy on the carrier USS *Ranger*.

The extension of North Vietnamese SAM defences was problematic for all USAF aircraft, not least for the EB-66s which, because of their vulnerability, were forced to change their orbit patterns in order to keep them as far out of the reach of the missiles as was possible.

Bill Reeder and Hank Holden with RB-57E 55-4245 at Tan Son Nhut in 1966. Hank Holden has written a book about his experiences with the Patricia Lynn team in south-east Asia entitled *Moonglow* which was the call sign for all RB-57E missions. (Hank Holden)

In May, 1966, USAFE reluctantly gave up the last of its ECM aircraft when the 42nd TRS was deactivated at Toul-Rosiere and the remaining eight Brown Cradle EB-66Bs were sent to Takhli. Together with the five aircraft already in Thailand they formed the newly activated 6460th TRS.

The role of Pathfinder came to the EB-66Bs in 1966. USAFE had pioneered the use of the Destroyer as a Pathfinder in 1958 and 1959 when Operation Taxi Cab had teamed the WB-66s of the 42nd TRS with the F-100s of the 49th TFW. In south-east Asia the EB-66Bs flew with the F-105s, F-4Cs and B-57s. Use of the Pathfinder was prompted by the onset of seasonal bad weather over North Vietnam. The missions flown were more sophisticated than those rehearsed by the Taxi Cab crews eight years earlier. The EB-66B would fly as many as four bombing runs on any one sortie with perhaps three different aircraft. The Brown Cradle aircraft were unique in that they were fitted with the K-5 radar navigation and bombing system, a legacy of their ancestry as bombers. The K-5 would identify the target, direct the EB-66 to it, followed by the strike aircraft, and indicate the optimum moment for bomb release by a tone which would be transmitted to the strike aircraft. In areas defended by SAMs and Migs the Pathfinder role was not used.

Early in May, 1966, Patricia Lynn RB-57E 55-4249 returned to General Dynamics at Fort Worth for an update of its recce suite. This was to became a regular occurrence for all the Detachment's aircraft over the forthcoming months and years. This first upgrade was to improve the aircraft's infra-red system with a remodelling of the Texas Instruments RS-10. In addition to this a KA-2 split vertical camera configuration was installed, a 2000 ft Terrain Following Radar (TFR) fitted and in addition, a TV viewfinder, a 5000 ft radar altimeter and a magnetic recorder for the infra-red system.

One of the RF-101 reconnaissance operations begun in mid 1966 was an intensive programme to survey and record all Petroleum, Oil and Lubricants (POL) storage depots in North Vietnam. The name given to this operation was Blue Tree. It increased the work load of the '101s quite dramatically. Unfortunately, this led to a backlog of BDA photography. In order to be effective this must be done as soon as possible after a strike in order to ascertain whether or not further strikes are necessary. The Voodoo squadrons were stretched as far as they would go. On the 29 August it was decreed that the Tan Son Nhut squadrons operate in South Vietnam, the southern tip of Laos and the south of North Vietnam, and that the Udorn units cover only Northern Laos and North Vietnam.

On the 9 September, 1966, the 12th TRS flying RF-4Cs arrived at Tan Son Nhut as part of the 460th TRW. The 432nd TRW was activated at Udorn and in October the 11th TRS arrived with their RF-4Cs.

Fitting the RF-4Cs for the day and night mission when so many missions, were being flown, was problematic. For night missions a KS-72 6 in focal length camera was favoured. For day missions the KA-55 12 in panoramic camera was used. About half of the 11th TRS RF-4Cs were fitted with split verticals and half with pans. Since radar was a prime requisite for night missions an aircraft had to be scheduled which had a good radar and an appropriate camera configuration. It was not always an easy matter to configure every aircraft correctly on the flight line in a combat zone.

Also in September the 42nd TRS was reborn at Takhli as the 42nd Tactical Electronic Warfare Squadron (TEWS) taking over all the assets of the 6460th TRS which was deactivated. The 41st TRS became the 41st TEWS. The 41st flew the EB-66C and the 42nd, the EB-66B.

On the 5 November a flight of four F-4C Phantoms (call sign Opal) from the 480th TFS, 366th TFW were escorting an EB-66C when the formation was attacked by a pair of Mig 21s. The Migs were undoubtedly trying to down the EB-66C. The 'C had originally been part of a two ship team with an EB-66E, which unfortunately had to abort early in the mission, which was in support of a strike north of Hanoi. Arthur 'Kibby' Taylor was the pilot of the Destroyer:

> We started jamming low frequency, long range radar, to degrade enemy tracking of the inbound strike force. Entering North Vietnam airspace we changed radio frequency to monitor strike forces, Opal Lead and 2 took defensive positions behind us on each side, Opal 3 and 4 held high but maintained visual contact with our flight. As we proceeded to our orbit we could tell by radio calls that strike aircraft should be close to planned TOT. The orbit area was called 'The Pocket' because it was an area about 50 miles long west to east and 20 miles south to north, on the north was a buffer zone at the Chinese border, the rest was circled by active SAM sites except for a narrow 5 mile wide entry corridor. On entering The Pocket at the Red River I revised orbit tactics to adjust for the aborted EB-66E. Airspeed was increased to 0.78 MAC (300 kts indicated) to permit a faster rate of turn and therefore allow more wing-level jamming time and give the F-4Cs a speed more suited to their performance envelope. We also began jamming to cover the strike force while they were approaching the target area. The situation was tense in orbit at 30,000 ft in The Pocket but with clear skies and the normal thick haze below restricting our visibility of the target areas.
>
> About five minutes before TOT, Red Crown, a friendly radar warning station, issued a Mig warning to the force indicating that hostile fighters were within 50 miles west of us on our outbound route. We were west bound at the eastern end of the orbit when my EWOs advised that they were receiving enemy fighter radar at 12 o'Clock and I advised Opal Flight. After overcoming poor radio reception we determined that the last strike aircraft was off target about 2 minutes after TOT. Just after I told the F-4Cs that we were cleared to egress Red Crown called 'Newark', our call sign, with a Mig warning. Within less than a minute my EWOs advised me that the enemy fighter radar signal was a 6 o'clock and I passed this news to the F-4Cs. Then things happened fast.
>
> From a position to my right rear Opal Lead's GIB (Guy in the Back) called "Mig" and Opal 2 also saw the Mig coming between the two F-4Cs headed for the B-66 at a high rate of overtake. From our EWO tape it sounds like his radar was locked-on to us and ready to

The 20th TRS at Udorn photographed on 1 November 1966. From left to right. Rear: Bob Butt, Bob Archibald, Frank Donald, Don Karges, Tex Carey, Bob Sipes, Sandy Sisco, Bob Pettijean, Mike Williams, Jim Parker, Art Warren (KIA), Don Oyer. Front: Jim Phillips, Jim Carpenter, Kent White, Jim Yeager (KIA), Mike Moore, Jack Langille, Chuck O' Connell, Walt Smethwyke. Sitting in the front of the group is John 'Bull' Stirling. (USAF)

fire. The Mig fired a missile at the B-66 as it passed between Opal Lead and Opal 2. Opal Lead called "Break Right 66"; a call that I did not hear but is on the tape. When I did not respond to the break call he repeated it twice with a shout. As they jettisoned their external fuel tanks to clean up their aircraft for a fight, the second Mig came in between them. I heard the second "Break Right" and in one motion, I went full power, hard right-bank, lots of right rudder to start the nose down followed by a hard pull into the turn. About that time my navigator repeated, "Break right and all the way down". I could not see the threat and for the next 60 seconds I was totally dependent on Opal Lead for guidance about evasive actions. Fortunately, the missile missed to my left. I was descending rapidly in a tight right spiral at above 0.92 MAC, redline speed, on the edge of a buffet pulling all the Gs I could get. The first Mig followed me into the spiral and Opal Lead was in afterburner going after him. I heard Opal 2 say "Lead you've got a Mig on your tail" and Lead respond simply "How are you doing on him?" This confirmed that we had five aircraft following in trail down a steep spiral. We were in front with the EB-66C, the first Mig-21 on our tail, Opal Lead (an F-4C) on him, a second Mig-21 on his tail and Opal 2 (an F-4C) on the second Mig. Opal Lead told me later that and he flew his aircraft very close to the Mig to try to drive the Mig off the B-66 and that we were pulling too many Gs for he or the Mig to get off a missile (which was my intention). The Mig did pull off and swing out to the left for a position to come in at a better angle and get off another missile. Opal Lead called for me to reverse my turn to the left. When I reversed the spiral to the left, we cut back under the

Mig to deny him a shot at us. By this time we were below 15,000 feet. I saw a small cloud, in an otherwise clear sky, to our right. I turned back hard right and headed for the cloud. As we entered the cloud I pulled back hard to level flight at 10,000 ft and continued the turn. I could not sustain the high turn rate and rapidly lost airspeed at full power so I had to ease off the turn and look for a new solution.

The '66 returned to altitude and home to Takhli. The aircraft had exceeded operating limits reaching a speed of Mach 0.92 in the evasive manoeuvres and pulling over 4 Gs! 'Kibby' Taylor was to fly another 95 missions, most of them over North Vietnam before rotating back to the States in July 1967.

The standard evasion tactic for the '66 when attacked by either SAMs or Migs was high G turns in a rapid descent to maintain airspeed. Not only did this place a great deal of stress on the airframe, but it also brought the aircraft down to a low altitude where it was at the mercy of Anti-Aircraft fire. For this reason the EB-66s were not scheduled to fly in areas where there was a significant SAM or Mig threat.

In 1966 the 460th TRW at Tan Son Nhut acquired a new role and two new squadrons. The 360th and 361st Reconnaissance Squadrons were activated flying the venerable RC-47. Their role was to conduct daily day and night all weather Airborne Radio Direction Finding (ARDF) missions against enemy operated transmitters in the Republic of Vietnam and permitted areas of Laos. The programme was named Phyliss Ann. The RC-47s carried very sophisticated equipment for the detection, plotting and recording of enemy transmitters including an array of aerials carried under the wings and fuselage. It was possible to locate the transmitters to within a few metres. The 360th was based at Tan Son Nhut and commenced operations on the 8 April, 1966. and the 361st Reconnaissance Squadron arrived at Nha Trang in October, 1966.

The two day truce called by Lyndon Johnson in Christmas 1966 provided the tac recce pilots with a lot of additional work. Such truces were invariably used by the North Vietnamese as an opportunity to move troops, equipment and supplies. The roads and waterways became extremely busy with traffic in the night and daylight hours. A great deal of the success of the previous months in reducing the enemy's capacity to wage a guerrilla war was undone in those two days.

On 12 August 1967, an RF-4C flown by Captain Ed Atterberry with GIB Captain Tom Parrott was shot down by a SAM missile. These extraordinary photographs were taken by the cameras of the No. 2 aircraft. In the first picture the SAM is seen shortly after launch at the very bottom of the picture and the RF-4C at the top. In the second photograph the Phantom has been hit. Both Atterberry and Parrott ejected from the aircraft. Sadly Atterberry was killed by the North Vietnamese when a PoW. Parrot died in 1998. (USAF via Bob Sweet)

A similar truce over the New Year produced the same results. All this activity was photographed, but as far as strikes were concerned it was out of bounds. With the resumption of the bombing the BDA reconnaissance missions out of Udorn increased in intensity. Often the RF-101s would refuel in the air after leaving North Vietnam and fly directly to Tan Son Nhut for the photos to be processed and acted upon. During the Tet celebration in 1967 President Johnson ordered a five day truce and this produced the largest resupply effort of the North Vietnamese so far. Voodoo sorties alone recorded 2799 trucks and 3112 water craft in the southern third of North Vietnam. Amphibious craft were photographed at Quang Khe and a Russian Mi-6 helicopter on the Dien Bien Phu airfield. Best estimates were that, during the truce, the North Vietnamese army divisions in the South and in Laos had received enough supplies to last them in excess of a year!

The majority, though not all, of reconnaissance missions for the Tan Son Nhut squadrons was centred around the area to the north and west of Saigon throughout the latter part of 1966 and into 1967. The re-equipment of the Viet Cong and regular North Vietnamese army units during the truce ensured this. The requirement for infra-red night missions also ensured that the heaviest workload in this area fell to the RF-4C and RB-57E units.

An EB-66E and EB-66C of the 42nd TEWS out of Takhli. The EB-66E had 130 external antennas that radiated electronic jamming signals throughout the Full Radio & Radar Spectrum. The big white antenna mounted on the belly of the aircraft was for Communications Jamming. The EB-66E performed Electronic Jamming, and carried three crew members in the cockpit: Pilot, Navigator & Electronic Warfare Officer. The EB-66C performed Electronic Reconnaissance and Jamming and carried six to seven crew members: Pilot, Navigator and four Electronic Warfare Officers in downward ejection seats in the bomb bay. After the tail guns were removed and replaced with the Tail Cone that housed jammers and chaff, the Gunner's Seat in the C-Model cockpit was used by Instructor pilots and Instructor navigators while checking out other Pilots and Navigators in the B-66. (via Ned Colburn)

On the 1 February, 1967, a further squadron joined the Phyliss Ann programme. The 362nd Reconnaissance Squadron was activated at Pleiku. In March all three squadrons were renamed Tactical Electronic Warfare Squadrons (TEWS) and their RC-47s became EC-47s the following May. One of the most serious threats to the mission of the EC-47s was from ground fire. On the 10 March, 1967, ground fire was thought to be the reason behind the crash of an aircraft in South Vietnam with the loss of all seven crew members. One of the means by which the squadrons sought to reduce the threat from ground fire was to introduce a minimum operating height of 2000 ft above ground level.

The night missions flown by the pilots of the Patricia Lynn RB-57Es moved into the north in the early months of 1967. Bill Reeder was assigned a number of special missions which often took him and his GIB as far north as Route Pack 3. Bill flew thirty-six missions over the north during this time. But night missions for the Canberras were as fraught with danger as they were for the RF-4Cs. Bill Reeder:

> The night missions had some built-in problems. Most were IR missions and due to a resolution of about 1/4 MR, we had to fly them at 2000 ft or lower. In most of our target areas there were mountains much higher than that. The only thing we had to navigate with was visual and often that was under a low cloud deck. When doing IR at night I would turn my cockpit lights nearly off so I could see the ground. This was much tougher for the backseater because he had his eyes in the IR scope and he was blind when he looked outside … One night I flew with a back seater who had never flown with me and had not done much night work. We got over the target area at about 8000 ft with an undercast up to 7000ft.. The wx man had told me that the ceiling would be 2000 ft, so we did the best we could to locate our position by radio and then I started a slow turning descent in the soup. We broke out at about 1600 ft and did our target cover.

At about this time, in early 1967, Jon Heritage flew his first RF-4C mission up north. Assigned to the 16th TRS at Tan Son Nhut. Although new to the Phantom in the theatre, Jon was not new to Vietnam. He had flown a four month tour on F-102s in 1964. He recalls that first mission:

> I was assigned to photograph a strip of road about 10 miles long with photoflash just past the southern entrance of the Mu Ghia pass where the Ho Chi Minh trail entered Laos from North Vietnam. There were two passes into Laos from North Vietnam and this was one. We were aware that they had 12.7mm, 37mm & 57 mm radar directed guns. This was before the SAMs had gotten that far south. If you could see it on a topographical map you'd see the floor was about 5000 ft below the top and very narrow (less than a mile across at points) What saved my skin was what an old-timer told me before I went over. He said every one wanted to go as fast as they could and he advocated changing your speed or accelerating or decelerating which sounded like a good idea to me. When we were the new guys they usually teamed us with an old head in the back and vice-versa, so I had an experienced backseater. When we began our run in just after dark we weren't lined up just right. We hadn't been picking up much in the way of radar strobes and as we were 15 miles or so out we did a 360 and realigned. I was holding 420 kts, planning to accelerate just before starting the photo run. We went in nicely with very little radar and about a mile out I went to full military power, without afterburner, and began accelerating. When I entered the pass I was doing about 480 kts when the sky lit up like the 4 of July in Washington DC or Guy Fawkes' day in the UK. They were actually shooting down at me from both sides with the convergence zone right in front of me about 1/4 mile. They were probably firing manually rather than with radar control. I think they were keeping their radar off except for an occasional paint and anticipated I'd be doing 600 kts. In any event if I had been really moving they would have nailed me nicely. I had to do something pretty quickly or I'd be toast. Since I couldn't go lower or turn left or right I pulled the nicest 6g Immelman you've ever seen and said we'd try again another day.

In April, 1967, the EB-66s were assigned a new mission. Codenamed Tiny Tim this mission entailed flying ahead of SAC B-52 bombers to check for SAM threat. The mobility of the SAM systems had made it quite possible for a new site to be set up in an area within a half a day. Thus any area in the north could harbour a threat. Two EB-66s would fly the bombing route ahead of the B-52s and warn of any SAM activity. If the threat was particularly serious then the bombing mission was diverted or cancelled. On the 27 April, 1967, an EB-66 'Blade 01' was flying a Tiny Tim mission when it intercepted signals from a SAM site apparently in the DMZ between North and South Vietnam. Plotting of the signal revealed the site to be located in the eastern portion of the zone. Blade 01 immediately notified the B-52s of the threat. On the 29 April the site was positively identified and destroyed.

Commencing in early 1967 the number of EB-66s designated to support a strike mission was increased. As many as fourteen aircraft were used, flying three separate orbits. The effect on the North Vietnamese radars was significant and the downgrading of their capability enabled the strikes to be more effective. This, in turn, prompted the North Vietnamese to deploy new SAMs to force the EB-66s further away from the centre of activity around Hanoi. Simultaneously the USAF reduced the number of fighters it was prepared to use to escort the '66s. Within a matter of weeks the increase in the effectiveness of the jamming created by the use of multiple aircraft decreased very significantly. Fire control radars in particular were untouched by the EB-66s flying their new orbits and the pods carried by the fighters themselves were the only defence against these. The EB-66s concentrated on jamming and downgrading the Early Warning, GCI and acquisition radars with some degree of success.

The Voodoo was getting old and many of the aircraft were showing signs of that age and of the intense use they had been put to in south-east Asia. There were operational accidents and there were often novel solutions to keeping the aircraft in the air. Don Karges:

> Someone ran off a slick runway and sheared the nose gear. It sat in the 'too hard to fix' hanger for several months until Ed Greer took a near miss by a SAM. It shredded the tail but he got it home. You can guess the rest. Took a good nose and a good tail section and made one good bird. My job was to be the test hop guy. I forget how many hops it took before we could get it to fly with the ball in the middle. Kept wanting to fly in 5 degrees of bank or lots of rudder. But the maintenance guys got it fixed.

In spite of the problems and the operational losses incurred by the RF-101 squadrons they soldiered on. In January, 1967, some experimental photo recce missions were flown out of Udorn by the 20th TRS. Two RF-101s flying at 14,000 ft, would be escorted by four F-4s equipped with pod-mounted jamming equipment. The first mission was to photograph the Phuc Yen airfield and a railroad north-east of Hanoi. It was deemed a success. Only one SAM was launched and that didn't come close to the formation. The second mission was to cover three targets including the Mig airfield at Kep near Hanoi. This mission was not so fortunate as the first. The flight met with a heavy reaction from the defences, both AAA and SAMs. One of the escorting F-4s was hit by flak and went down. The pilot baled out and was captured. It was his 100th Mission. The third mission targeted the Thai Nguyen steel plant near Hanoi. It was heavily defended. Lieutenant Jim Brickel leading the flight, performed his photo run on one engine and, in spite of taking multiple hits, he succeeded in getting his stricken RF-101 back to Udorn. Notwithstanding the risks, these escorted flights continued.

Many of the experienced Voodoo pilots were making their way home to their families during the latter part of 1966 and 1967; their 100 missions completed. They were replaced by new younger pilots with no combat experience. These pilots were to fly aircraft with operational deficiencies. New pilots with the 45th TRS at Tan Son Nhut flew with a chase aircraft flown by an Instructor pilot on their first two missions over South Vietnam. Following this they then flew ten missions over the South before they were eligible to fly over Laos or North Vietnam. They

Aircraft RB-57E 55-4264 flown by Gene Durden and Ernie Perkins. This aircraft was shot down in October, 1968. (USAF)

were 'chased' by an IP on their first sortie over Laos or North Vietnam and on their first aerial refuelling mission.

In July, 1967, the Phyliss Ann programme was renamed Compass Dart. By this time all squadrons were up to or approaching their full complement of aircraft. The 360th TEWS had nineteen EC-47s assigned to Compass Dart and a further two assigned to the Sentinel Sara programme. Sentinel Sara was originally named Drill Press and involved the two aircraft staging out of Phu Bai. Theirs was not an ADRF mission but basically an airborne mission in cooperation with the 509th Radio Research Unit (RRU) at Phu Bai; the mission being to copy all enemy high frequency and VHF radio transmissions.

This RF-101 has just returned to Udorn from a mission over North Vietnam. (George Cowgill)

Fifteen minutes after landing these Voodoos were ready for another photo recce mission (George Cowgill)

Wearing the tail code AH this 45th TRS RF-101C was photographed at TSN (Phil Rowe)

   Most of the Compass Dart missions also carried leaflets to deceive the enemy if they were unfortunate enough to be brought down in enemy held territory. This in itself posed a massive logistics problem because of the sheer number of leaflets which it was necessary to make available to the squadrons on a daily basis! In a three month period the 360th alone dropped approximately 33 million leaflets.

   In August, 1967, the 45th TRS operated a detachment of aircraft from Phu Cat Air Base; the first mission from the base being flown on 3 September. The rationale behind this decision was to accelerate the delivery of photographs and shorten response time. Photo processing trailers and support facilities were sent to Phu Cat and the detachment was fully operational by September,

1967. The advantage of Phu Cat was that it was close to army units. Phu Cat was also important as a stop over for the RF-4Cs operating out of Tan Son Nhut. At this time the 12th and 16th TRS divided the days up for mission purposes. One squadron would take the midnight to noon shift and the other the noon to midnight shift. The squadron aircraft flying the midnight to noon schedule would recover at Phu Cat after the first mission over the north or Laos. This provided the opportunity to refuel and change the camera film. The film would be downloaded and processed in the labs at the base. The aircrews would have the time to breakfast, rest, view their film and plan their next mission which would be a daylight one on the way home to Tan Son Nhut.

By mid 1967 in-flight targeting had become routine for the RF-4C squadrons. As a means of avoiding ineffective missions it was invaluable. A natural extension to this was the airborne alert over North Vietnam and Laos which was instigated in October 1967. The reason for this was to gain instant BDA of strikes.

Operation Neutralize in September involved the RF-101s in photography designed to locate North Vietnamese artillery batteries which were inflicting considerable damage on the US Marine positions south of the DMZ. RF-4Cs had attempted to find the guns but their small format photographs were inadequate for the task. The large format KA-1 cameras of the RF-101s were more than adequate and many of the emplacements were found and attacked. The Voodoos flew the BDA missions after the strikes. Regrettably the BDA photos failed to verify that any of the artillery pieces had been destroyed. On the 26th September two aircraft undertook a low altitude mission searching for enemy positions. Previously undetected emplacements were discovered and plotted. For the RF-101s the rediscovered role of low level target acquisition was to be developed further.

On 12 August, 1967, two RF-4Cs of the 11th TRS took off from Udorn on a routine mission to conduct BDA photographic reconnaissance of the area north-east of the city of Gia Lam. The No. 2 aircraft detected the launch of a SAM at the aircraft as they began their photo run. Subsequently this aircraft witnessed a SAM pass underneath their RF-4C and head straight for the lead aircraft crewed by Captain Edwin Atterberry and Captain Thomas Parrot. The missile detonated in close proximity to the RF-4 and the resultant shrapnel struck the Phantom causing it to disintegrate. Atterberry and Parrot ejected and were taken prisoner by the North Vietnamese. Parrot was released some five and a half years later. Captain Atterberry died in captivity after being recaptured following an escape attempt.

On 30 August the EB-66E aircraft arrived at Takhli. Originally built as RB-66B photo recce and B-66 bombers, these aircraft had been taken out of desert storage at Davis Monthan and converted to ECM aircraft. Their arrival in south-east Asia coincided with the attachment of the 41st and 42nd TEWS to the 355th TFW at Takhli and the redistribution of Destroyers between these units. The 41st had fourteen EB-66B and EB-66E aircraft and six EB-66Cs. The 42nd had fifteen EB-66B and EB-66Es and six EB-66Cs.

To a very great extent the closing months of 1967 saw a significant decrease in the effectiveness of the EB-66s. Because of their vulnerability to both Migs and SAMs the aircraft rarely entered areas of high threat and when they did it was with an escort for protection against the Migs and suppression of the SAMs.

On 16 September, 1967, the first RF-101 to go down to the Mig 21 was 56-180 of the 20th TRS. Pilot Bobby Bagley was taken prisoner and spent the rest of the war in the Hanoi Hilton. The next day on the 17th September, Bob Patterson flying 56-181 also went down to a Mig. He was rescued.

The KA-1 camera carried by the RF-101 was a significant factor in the aircraft remaining in south-east Asia when the RF-4C Phantom squadrons had been fully operational for two years. The large format photographs produced much sharper images even at low level and the RF-101 was the preferred photo recce vehicle for certain targets. The Phantom, though a much more sophisticated aircraft in many respects simply could not provide satisfactory photography in certain circumstances. Commencing in August, 1967, the RF-101s were tasked with regular KA-

RB-57E 55-4264 was damaged in a Viet Cong attack on Tan Son Nhut in April, 1966. Such was the urgency in keeping the Patricia Lynn aircraft flying that the aircraft performed many missions in its state of temporary repair before being sent to Japan for a more permanent fix.

1 photography of the 'electronic barrier': a system of sensors which had been set up along the Ho Chi Minh Trail and in Laos to detect the passage of vehicles or people.

In October, 1967, the last RF-101 available was delivered to the 45th TRS. On 31 October, the 20th TRS at Udorn was deactivated and its remaining aircraft passed to the 45th at Tan Son Nhut. Maintenance and supply problems did not lessen however and in late 1967 a clerical error succeeded in getting much needed replacement parts returned to the USA. In order to keep the remaining aircraft flying some of the less airworthy ones were cannibalized to keep others flying. Also in this month the 14th TRS arrived at Udorn flying RF-4C Phantoms.

Small arms fire was far less of a threat to the RF-101s than were the SAMs and AAA. Nonetheless it could still be deadly as Nick Pishvanov found out whilst on a mission over Laos on the 18 October 1967:

> Corporate memory failed the mission planners in Saigon that week. Previously tactics had been changed to avoid low-altitude route recces because the Viets had field telephones and would call ahead when a recce bird was on its way. We had a new man at Hq, and he felt we should do this the same way we did in Europe – 200 or 500 ft and 480kts would do it fine. We were untouchable! I was happy not to get one of those high-altitude 'Magnet Ass' missions. I did have a couple of targets for counters up north which I was going to pick up after finishing this one. But that mission gave me some beautiful photos – hated to see them go up in smoke! But, I was one lucky guy.

In September, 1967, Hank Holden, a navigator with the Patricia Lynn detachment was one of those assigned to a task force to look at the problem of night interdiction on targets along the Ho Chi Minh trail; particularly the Mu Ghia Pass, the Tchepone pass and the Ashua Valley. The main issue was not how to locate the target but how best to guide the fighter bombers to the target and show them where to drop their ordnance. After much deliberation Combat Skyspot, as the programme was designated, was ready for testing. A date was set for late November 1967. Hank Holden:

John Harris and Phil Walker return to Tan Son Nhut after the completion of Phil's 100th mission in 1968. Aircraft 55-4245 has acquired some nose art by this time. (John Harris)

The programme called for the use of the Strategic Air Command's TSQ-81 bomb scoring radar to guide attack aircraft to predetermined target coordinates for ordanance release. The difference between this and other combat test programmes, was that the target for the mission did not require identification immediately prior to the strike. The target was determined based on reconnaissance flown several nights in progression before the actual attack. The other difference in the programme was that bomb damage assessment would be conducted immediately following the attack – before the enemy could remove evidence of the relative

Phil walker enjoys his traditional soaking after his 100th Mission. Phil was the navigator in Pat Lynn's aircraft 4264 when it was shot down in October, 1968. (John Harris)

Friedmans Follies was the name of EB-66 crew 41-30 of the 41st TRS out of Takhli from June 66 to Feb 67. Pilot was Don Friedman. Their undaunted exploits included flying down the middle of NVN and dropping a speed break full of signed empty beer cans. (Lous Herry)

success or failure of the mission. The assessment was to be done using infra-red reconnaissance. The responsibility for this assessment was assigned to the 460th Tactical Reconnaissance Wing.

The target area selected for the combat test was the region in north-east Laos known by MACV planners as 'Steel Tiger.' This was the area where The Trail exited North Vietnam through the Mu Ghia Pass and wound its way down through the mountains to various entry points into South Vietnam – beginning with the Tchepone Pass and then to the Ashau Valley.

The mission was flown as scheduled. F-4Cs were guided to the target area in the Tchepone Pass and delivered their ordnance. An RF-4C of the 16th TRS was to fly BDA two minutes after the strike. A Pat Lynn RB-57 flown by Holden and Reeder would be a back up to the RF-4 if something went wrong. The target was a truck park just west of the pass. An EB-66 of the 42nd TEWS was to provide stand-off radar jamming. In the event the Phantom had to abort and the RB-57E flew the BDA through a wall of AAA and small arms fire.

The North Vietnamese offensive against Khe Sanh in late 1967 and early 1968 diverted the RF-101s, RB-57s and RF-4Cs from many of their regular and routine targets. The marines under siege at Khe Sanh faced numerically superior odds but elected to defend rather than retreat. In the event, this decision was to prove the correct one. In fact the resistance of the marines was such that the considerable North Vietnamese force deployed against them was frustrated in every attempt to overcome them. The reconnaissance aircraft flew the Khe Sanh valley many times a day and brought back many hundreds of photographs which provided those tasked with the relief of the outpost with a tactical advantage. This recce effort was codenamed Niagara. The weather was such that the missions were often only partially successful, but under the circumstances this was acceptable. The targets were fragged 'best access and best scale' and this allowed for the RF-101s with their KA-1 cameras to repeat their successes of Operation Neutralize and fly low level missions consistent with the escalating weather.

The frustrated North Vietnamese and Viet Cong forces launched attacks against South Vietnamese cities and military bases. On 31 January 1968, at Tan Son Nhut, rockets and mortars damaged several aircraft. There was a brief period when reconnaissance missions had to be flown with limited aircraft; several having been damaged in the attacks. One of the regular missions flown at this time was photography of a North Vietnam army division retreating from Khe Sanh; a labour of love! On 18 February another rocket attack on Tan Son Nhut damaged eight RF-101s and destroyed one. This prompted yet another mission requirement for the Voodoos codenamed Operation Tan Son Nhut which was to fly regular photo missions in the Saigon area looking for and monitoring suspected rocket and mortar launch sites.

In January, 1968, one of five EB-66s supporting a strike in RP V was shot down by an Atoll missile fired from one of two Mig 21s out of Phuc Yen. The '66 was unescorted and was orbiting near the Laotian border. All seven crew members ejected successfully, three of them landing on a mountain and four in the valley where they were immediately picked up by North Vietnamese soldiers and spent the remainder of the war as PoWs. The three 'mountaineers' were rescued by friendly forces. This prompted a banning of all EB-66 flights over North Vietnam. Ned Colburn flew in the EB-66s out of Takhli as an EWO and recalls the circumstances of the shootdown:

> Rivet Top (EC-121 Constellation Aircraft) had just arrived in theatre for Operational Suitability Testing and was so successful that it remained in south-east Asia rather than return to the U.S. for modification. Rivet Top had electronic intercept gear that reportedly did the impossible of showing on a PPI Radar Scope exactly what the North Vietnamese radar controllers saw on their ground scopes.
>
> On or about 12 January 1968, Rivet Top observed and reported to Saigon what they correctly deemed was preparation to shoot down a B-66, since we were the first on station preceding a bomb strike and flew unescorted without fighter cover. The B-66 always got its share of attention since there was time for one or more MIg sweeps into the B-66 orbit area, before the Fighter Bombers arrived.
>
> Following the completion of Rolling Thunder operations for the afternoon and after all USAF & USN activity ceased over North Vietnam, Rivet Top observed Migs taxi and take-off without any radio transmissions whatsoever during the entire flight profile. Prior to this time, the usual radio calls were made to Ground Control, Tower and GCI as the Migs called for taxi and take-off, with IFF on and the mission controlled by GCI Radar Operators.
>
> The Migs taxied out, took-off and flew with their IFF transponders off, tracked 240 from Hanoi and then started a climbing turn into the orbit area and altitude that the B-66s flew West of Hanoi. Rivet Top passed the information to Saigon with the correct analysis that a B-66 shoot-down was being rehearsed – with not a peep from Saigon relayed as a warning to Takhli.
>
> On 14 January, 1968, an EB-66C, Tail Number 55-388 (Preview 01) from the 41st Tactical Electronic Warfare Squadron, Takhli Airbase, Thailand was shot down south-west of Hanoi by a Mig-21. Major Pollard H. [Sonny] Mercer was the pilot, Major Attilio [Pete] Pedroli [Instructor Navigator], Major Irby D. Terrell [Navigator], with Electronic Warfare Officers [EWO] Major Thomas W. Sumpter, First Lieutenant Ronald M. Lebert, Captain Hubert C. Walker and First Lieutenant James E. Thompson.
>
> All seven crew members ejected, but Sonny Mercer's legs were broken in the ejection. Jim Thompson was the only EWO rescued. The other three EWOs were captured and spent the rest of the war as POWs. Mercer, Pedroli and Thompson were rescued several days after the shoot-down. Mercer was air-evacuated to the Philippines where he died in

the hospital from a blood clot to the brain. Pete Pedroli and Jim Thompson went on to complete their required 100 combat tours at Takhli.

It is astonishing that four days later, on 18 January, Ned Colburn and the crew of EB-66 54-468 were tasked to fly an identical mission to that flown by 388 and had received no indication of the warning that Rivet Top had passed on. Colburn:

> We had just made our first orbit when Raven 3 detected a Mig-21 AI Radar in Acquisition Mode painting our aircraft, followed by the dreaded high-pitched steady lock-on that meant missiles would be forthcoming in 5 seconds or less. Raven 3 called "Mig, Mig – break left" twice, responded to by "Say Again" from the Aircraft Commander, before the warning was finally understood the third time. Just as we broke left, the missiles and Mig-21 passed harmlessly on our right hand side. Needless to say, during the communications break-down, we felt doomed for certain.

The assaults against Tan Son Nhut continued into the early part of 1968. In April and May they intensified in preparation for what was anticipated to be a second offensive. In order to guarantee the safety of its RF-101s and their mission, five aircraft were detached to Phu Cat AB every night and returned to Tan Son Nhut in the morning. When the North Vietnamese launched a rocket attack on Phu Cat on the 11th May and damaged two Voodoos the nightly flights were discontinued. The anticipated second offensive was slow to materialize and the flights over the area of Saigon by the recce aircraft diminished. The increased activity on the Ho Chi Minh trail which began after the end of the Monsoon season however led to a marked increase in the RF-101 and RF-4 flights in Laos. Pre-strike and BDA photographic reconnaissance kept the two aircraft extremely busy.

The success of the ARDF mission of the three EC-47 squadrons of the 460th TRW was outstanding. 90 per cent of the real time intelligence used by the tactical forces in the field was obtained by ARDF. An example of this was the intelligence obtained by a crew of a 360th EC-47 on 30 June, 1968. Acting on information gained from this intelligence a patrol was sent out in the Delta region and discovered that the 265th NVA Battalion had moved there. ARDF was also partially responsible for detecting targets for B-52 bombing missions. On the 29 July a B-52 raid was made on the Boi Loi woods after an aircraft of the 360th had intercepted and fixed transmissions over the previous two days.

Meanwhile the 362nd TEWS operating out of Pleiku was awaiting the arrival of ten replacement aircraft with upgraded, more powerful R-2000 engines. The rugged terrain and mountainous around the base was making it difficult for the squadron satisfactorily to complete its mission with standard engined aircraft.

The recce suites and camera configurations of all the photo reconnaissance aircraft was constantly changing and developing. This had some marked advantages but the one major disadvantage was the effect that this had on the in-commission rate of the available aircraft when cameras, sensors etc were being changed. This was particularly acute for the RF-101 squadron where replacement aircraft were in extremely short supply, if not non-existent. The RB-57Es of Det 1 of the 460th TRW at Tan Son Nhut received regular updates. Aircraft 55-4264 received two new cameras: the 12 in focal length KA-82 and the 24 in KA-83 high resolution panoramic cameras These cameras had been developed for the high altitude SR-71. Roger Wilkes flew with Patricia Lynn from September 1968 to September 1969 as Operations Officer and says of the cameras:

> Those cameras came out with super detail, but you had to fly slow to keep the image motion compensation and to provide a 60 per cent overlap. I didn't like the idea of flying slow at 4000 ft above the ground, flying at 200 kts, so I went to the intelligence people and said "Do you really need 60 per cent overlap/ Why don't you designate and on some of these flights I can go at 400 kts and get you 20 per cent overlap and that makes it a hell of a lot better for me as far as ground fire is concerned.

Roger was also responsible for developing another of the systems used in the RB-57E:

> I visited an army unit and they had a night scope which was about 4 1/2 in in diameter and it was about 2 ft long. They used it in the helicopters and so on and it made night almost day. I got specs from that and I corresponded with Air Development Depot and they gave me a short version and I was able to put it where the gunsight of the B-57 normally was, but the E model of course did not have a gunsight. The only thing I didn't like with it was when somebody would be up popping flares from an airplane. You had to close your eyes. But it did make it easier to see that you were on your flight line that you drew on the map that night.

Det 1 began flying Moon River missions in mid 1968. These were night missions using the RS-10A infra-red scanner and the VR-7 real time viewer. And the purpose of the missions was to detect illegal sampan and other Viet Cong activity along the waterways in the Rung Sat area. Moon River missions were in cooperation with the Navy. The accent was on real time recce and real time response.

Unfortunately aircraft 4264 was shot down in October 1968. Phil Walker was the navigator on that mission:

> Our call sign was Moonglow 11. All Det. 1 missions used the call sign Moonglow. The first mission of the day would start with 11, then 12, etc. I think we might have gone to 21, 22, etc for night missions. Crew consisted of Pilot: Captain James J. Johnson, and Nav: Maj. Phil Walker. We departed Tan Son Nhut at about 10.00 for a series of recce strips (along canals) and area covers over suspected areas of VC activity. The first target was a 10 or 15 km strip along a canal about 30 miles north-west of Saigon. The camera was the KA-56 lo-pan. At the time all our missions were restricted to no lower than 4500 ft AGL (to avoid small arms fire). The weather was overcast at about 5000 ft, with the ceiling decreasing as we progressed down the target run. Everything seemed to be going well as we pulled off the target to the right and started climbing out to our next target. The Pat Lynn aircraft had the flight controls removed from the rear cockpit, and as a result the backseater had nothing much else to do except operate his equipment, most of the time. At the time my head was in the cockpit and I was checking out the camera to be used on the next run. In what must have been a very short time, JJ asked me to check No. 2 engine for fire or smoke (I looked and could see none, but then even from the rear seat I could only see part of the engine). He then said, "Get ready to bale out, bale out". Between the 'get ready' and 'bale out', I remember thinking, 'Dammit JJ, stop goofing around, I'm having trouble getting this camera to operate properly – Oh Shit!!! JJ doesn't goof around in the airplane, this must be for real'. I then put on my gloves and after trying to remember the proper ejection procedure for the RB-57, decided to use the procedure for the Nav seat of the RB-66 which I had flown previously. Fortunately the procedures are the same, pretty much. Anyway, I closed my eyes, pulled up the left handle, the right handle and squeezed the trigger. I heard a lot of noise, felt the chute open and opened my eyes, wondering what the hell I was doing there. I heard and felt the airplane go in and explode, and saw JJ in a chute very close to mine. I asked him if he was OK, he couldn't hear me and took off his helmet, so I figured he was OK, and motioned 'never mind' to him.
>
> Looking down, I saw that I was going to land in a small round pond, so I tried all the sideslip parachute tactics I had ever been shown and simply managed to rotate myself 360 degrees and landed in the pond, at the very edge, where my chute flopped over onto a large bush. I was in about 3–4 ft of water, and in a mild state of shock. I eventually took off my helmet, which sank into the pond, listened to one of my two survival radios, and then realized that I had to disable my own seat beeper. After doing that I tried a call or two on the radio, and got no response, so used my signal mirror on a passing aircraft.
>
> Sometime during the 45 minutes to an hour we were on the ground, I heard an AK-47 shooting at something but saw no bullet impacts. My only thought then was, 'Boy, JJ is in

deep trouble'. He later told me that he heard the shots also, and seeing no bullets impacting near him, thought, 'Boy, Walker is in deep trouble'. We never did find out who was shooting at whom, nor did it ever occur to me to unholster the .38 revolver I was carrying.

Anyway we got picked up by an Army Huey, and carried to their camp (Cu Chi, I think), were fed, saw a medic and changed clothes.

After we got to Cu Chi, I found out that the airplane had been in a hard uncontrolled roll to the right with a fire warning light and other indications of bad things happening out there in the right wing. The final finding (best guess, actually, since there was no physical evidence to view – the aircraft impact was in VC territory and the only crash site investigation was to bomb the wreckage to ensure no evidence of the cameras we carried survived) was that the right wing had taken a small arms hit, caught fire and burned through the torque tube which controlled the right aileron.

Two of the RF-4Cs of the 12th TRS were equipped with T-11 mapping cameras. In July, 1968 these aircraft were tasked with a photographic mapping of the Saigon area for the purpose of detecting enemy rocket launching sites.

On 31 October 1968 President Lyndon Johnson ordered an immediate cessation of the bombing of North Vietnam. Reconnaissance flights however were to continue for the time being. Initially these recce flights north of the DMZ were only flown by RF-4Cs. Voodoo flights commenced in December 1968 but were kept to a minimum of daylight missions.

In the latter months of 1968 the TEWS squadrons of the 460th TRW were assigned three new areas on the borders with Cambodia. The border searches were initially carried out by select crews but by the end of the year most crews had flown the missions. The missions were flown with instructions to stay close to the border, to keep the shadow of the airplane in Cambodia. This was fraught with danger for the EC-47s, not least was the threat from 37mm anti-aircraft guns. Two tactics were used to minimize this danger: a detailed pre-mission briefing so that every effort could be made to skirt possible gun sites and a minimum mission altitude of 5000 ft .

In early 1969 the 45th TRS standardized the camera configuration of the Voodoos. A 12 in KS-72 was carried in the nose oblique position. Behind this were a 3 in panoramic camera and two KS-72As in a split vertical mount. In the rear camera compartment were two 36 in KA-1s, also in split vertical configuration. From 20 June 1969 one escorted mission per day was undertaken to search for SAM sites, truck parks, new roads and other targets. The Voodoos were accompanied by F-4Es and F-105s. The fighters would attack any targets of opportunity which presented themselves.

The RF-4Cs and RB-57s were heavily involved in low level searches for infiltrating Viet Cong in Southern Laos and the south of North Vietnam. Colonel Don Nash:

> Our low level target runs were between 1500 and 2500 ft. If we had AAA fire, we would make a hard break and leave. One of the rules of survival was to not fly over a 'hot' target more than once, because those that did got fired upon because the enemy was alerted. On flights into the southern part of North Vietnam, we would plan our target runs from west to east so that we could make it to the Gulf of Tonkin should we take a hit. The B-52s had made the DMZ look like swiss cheese so the threat to us was not as great as in Laos. Several of our planes had AAA holes from flying the Laos Ho Chi Minh Trail routes. One plane had a hole in the wing so big that the pilot had his picture taken afterwards standing on the ramp with his upper body through the hole.

Phil Rowe flew with the 12th TRS out of TSN in 1968 and 1969. He recalls what was scheduled to be a routine mission:

> Another recce flight to be remembered, took us east of Saigon one clear and starry night. The mission called for a low-level area coverage using our infra-red (IR) sensors. That meant completely photographing, with our downward-looking IR scanner, an area of about

10 by 10 miles. A dozen or more north-south flight lines were required, spaced less than a mile apart.

The terrain was not a problem. It wasn't particularly mountainous, so flying that night was relatively easy. There was no moon, but stars provided good illumination. We could see the terrain and even a few landmarks, especially streams and distant hills.

What startled us after about the fourth pass across the area was artillery and small arms fire. Tracers left brilliant tell-tale streaks above us. The shelling wasn't aimed as us, rather it arched over us, from the east and west. Two opposing forces were exchanging fire and we were in the middle. It was like being under a 4 July fireworks show, not in imminent danger, but well aware of what was taking place. We hoped they wouldn't alter their gun elevation angles.

We completed the ten lines of coverage, zipping back and forth at 480 kts, going from line to line at 400 feet, until we had the whole area on film. Our navigation lights were turned off, so as not to make it any easier for the enemy to target us, but in this case we knew not which guns were the enemy's and which were friendly. If we'd gotten hit, it probably wouldn't have mattered.

In May, 1969 a Visual Reconnaissance programme was initiated for the RF-4C squadrons known as RECCE/FAC. The mission was to observe roads and waterways in Southern Laos for enemy activity and, in cooperation with FAC aircraft and crews, to report observations for immediate response. In order to avoid unnecessary danger these mission were to be flown at a minimum altitude of 4500 ft and a ground speed of 450 kts.

Also instigated at this time were night missions into the Mu Ghia and Ban Loboy areas of Laos to photograph selected interdiction points along the main roads in these areas. These missions were very hazardous due to the mountainous terrain and the proliferation of anti-aircraft weapons. To go some way towards ensuring aircrew safety the following restrictions were imposed on the mission aircraft: the missions were to be flown at a minimum height of 4500 ft or 500 ft or lower! After two aircraft received hits below 500 ft only the minimum 4500 ft remained. During the period April to June 1969 three aircraft of the 12th TRS received battle damage while flying these missions.

The RB-57E Moon River missions continued into 1969 and were confined primarily to the Rung Sat area south of Saigon. This area was chosen because it was considered a major water traffic supply route for hostile forces and because it was flat and the land/water contrast facilitated good navigation. RB-57E Real Time reconnaissance operations were problematic. The aircraft needed an up to date computerized navigational system with quick read out capability in order for the system to work effectively. The necessity for the navigator to divide his time between navigation and scope viewing meant that there was only ever partial coverage of the area, and although there were some good results with the system it was felt that it could be better.

In April, 1969, the 460th TRW activated Det 2 at Nakhom Phanom airport in Thailand. This was to accommodate regular ARDF missions over Laos and the north of the Republic of Vietnam. Six EC-47s and four combat crews were detached to the base. Meanwhile the EC-47 fleet in south-east Asia began to upgrade to a computerized ARDF system. The first AIR 35 system was installed in aircraft No. 260 in June, the first mission being flown on the 14th of that month.

1969 and early 1970 witnessed a gradual rundown of reconnaissance forces in south-east Asia. In spite of a pair of RF-101s arriving from Shaw in March of 1969, the Voodoo force continued to suffer losses due to operational factors which clearly diminished its ability to fulfil its assigned role. In addition to this an economy drive back in the USA severely restricted the air-to-air refuelling capacity of all the USAF units in the theatre. In addition the detachment at Phu Cat was disbanded and all facilities returned to Tan Son Nhut.

On 31st October, 1969, the 41st TEWS was deactivated. All the EB-66Bs were returned to the US and placed in mothballs at Davis Monthan. The 42nd TEWS had six EB-66Cs and fourteen EB-66Es. Excess EB-66Es were assigned to the 19th TEWS resident at Kadena.

The continued demand for the large format KA-1 photos which still only the Voodoos could provide ensured that there was enough work for the 45th TRS. These cameras with a 36 in focal length and a 9×18 in plate gave the airplane a 36 in wide coverage at a very good scale at high altitude. Commando Hunt III, began in October, 1969. This interdiction campaign was directed at North Vietnamese and Viet Cong targets in Laos. The KA-1s ensured that the RF-101s flew the bulk of the BDA missions. Only these large photos were considered sharp and clear enough to provide the evidence of a successful strike. Both the RF-101s and the RF-4Cs were involved in some innovatory reconnaissance procedures during the course of Commando Hunt III. A limited number of both aircraft were designated to orbit at specific points until ordered to photograph areas that the fighter bombers had attacked. The speed with which the recce planes could do this from their orbits prevented the Viet Cong from concealing the effect of the strikes. Thus the BDA became more accurate. Similarly, after night interdiction missions against trucks, the recce aircraft would photograph at first light before the enemy had had the opportunity to remove or conceal the damaged vehicles.

In spite of the apparent run down in recce resources in the theatre, however, the RF-4Cs remained very much in business. Tactics continued to be developed and skills honed. Often it was left to the individual crews to decide the best way of approaching a particular mission. Some crews preferred to fly high out of the way of small arms fire and take their chances with missiles, while others preferred to stay low, taking advantage of the element of surprise. Night reconnaissance missions usually employed the tactic of coming out of the mountains at low altitude and remaining low until almost on the target. During January to June 1969 the 11th TRS flew 2051 missions.

In March, 1970, the 16th TRS was deactivated at Tan Son Nhut. This immediately placed a heavier daytime workload on the RF-101s. They continued to fly missions into North Vietnam into Route Package 1, but this area too was becoming dangerous. The North Vietnamese were increasingly using mobile SAM launchers and these could be put into operation in a very short time. The Mig 21 had control of the skies over the panhandle. The answer to these threats was to allow the Voodoos to fly their photo sorties as low as 400 ft. At this height the aircraft became more vulnerable to automatic fire. The North Vietnamese increased the complement of automatic weapons in the region.

In early 1970 the interdiction campaigns into Laos spread into Cambodia. Richard Nixon authorized strikes into Cambodia to attack enemy supply routes into South Vietnam. Reconnaissance in support of this campaign was carried out by RF-4Cs and RF-101s flying out of Tan Son Nhut. These missions reached a peak for the Voodoos during June of 1970. After this the weather turned bad and the RF-4Cs and RB-57s became solely responsible for all recce operations into the area.

Despite the popularity of its large format KA-1 camera the last remaining RF-101 unit in south-east Asia, Detachment 1 of the 45th TRS was deactivated on 16th November 1970. All the Voodoos were returned to the US to National Guard units. Just prior to this in October of 1970 the 11th TRS had left Udorn with their RF-4Cs. Tactical photo reconnaissance units now left in the theatre were the RF-4Cs of the 12th TRS at Tan Son Nhut and the 14th TRS at Udorn; and the Patricia Lynn RB-57Es of Detachment 1 of the 406th TRW at Tan Son Nhut.

On 30 September, 1970, the 42nd TEWS moved from Takhli to Korat in Thailand with eight EB-66Es and five EB-66Cs and became part of the 388th Tactical Fighter Wing. The reduction in the number of assigned aircraft had a debilitating effect on the operations, in particular the loss of one EB-66C to the 363rd at Shaw. The EB-66C was the only aircraft in the theatre which was capable of gathering ELINT data. Fortunately, the 42nd recovered some of its strength when in May, 1971, the squadron received nine EB-66s from Shaw. The Commando Hunt excursions into Laos had intensified during this period and the allocation of these additional aircraft was essential to the 42nd carrying out its assigned mission satisfactorily. Nonetheless, operations over Laos were augmented by Navy and Marine Corps EA-6 aircraft. The main business of the Electronic Warfare assets of both the USAF and the Navy and Marine Corps in the interdiction campaign over Laos and Cambodia was the location and identification of enemy Fire Control Radars.

Throughout the early 1970s there were several factors which mitigated against EB-66 success in south-east Asia. Significant among these were the limitations on air-to-air refuelling imposed by the Air Force. There were simply not enough KC-135s to go around and because the EB-66s probe and drogue refuelling method was not widely used by other air force aircraft the number of tanker aircraft which could be dedicated to this work was extremely limited. Mission cancellations resulted. Yet another serious factor was the limited number of aircraft at Shaw available for EWO training. EWOs were arriving at Korat with little or no experience in the EB-66. The shortage of available EB-66Cs in the theatre further exacerbated the situation. There were enormous maintenance problems experienced by the 42nd TEWS. This was particularly acute in the EB-66C models. The EB-66B and EB-66E aircraft relied on the data provided by the ELINT EB-66C in order to perform their jamming mission successfully. Every time an EB-66C was lost to the squadron, either temporarily or permanently, the capability of the jammer aircraft was compromised. It is a tribute to the crews of all EB-66s that the mission of ELINT and Countermeasures was carried out with the success that it was. Very often these men used their initiative and dedication to turn possible failure into outstanding success. Joe Canady flew missions with the EB-66C in 1965:

> Our problem as Chief Raven (EWO) that I had to contend with was the newly installed jammers. I had never seen them before this day. The check list called for leaving ECM equipment off until after take-off. I cheated here and turned it on during taxi out. I was warmed up and operating by the time we were airborne. I then started reading dials on the jammers and trying them out while watching the jammer output on my receivers. They were labelled pretty well and I had them figured by the time we reached North Vietnam. I promptly set the jammers to the frequencies I had figured out *en route* and took out all the

RF-4C pilot Bob Sweet of the 14th TRS at Udorn. Bob Sweet began his career in recce in the Korean War flying T-6 Harvards with the 6147th Tactical Control Group. He then flew RF-51 Mustangs with the 45th TRS, then the RF-80, RF-84 and RF-101C in Europe and the USA. (Bob Sweet)

RF-4C pilots of the 14th TRS celebrate their 100 missions over North Vietnam. Bob Sweet stands to the right. (Bob Sweet)

RF-4C 66-0396 of the 14th TRS, 432nd TRW at Udorn. (Bob Sweet)

fire control bands as we ingressed and did our chaff corridor. The mission went as smooth as glass and it was the first time the fighter pilots had not seen lots of anti-aircraft fire as they were inbound at higher altitudes with their bombs.

The RF-4Cs of the 12th and 14th TRS were regularly flying their dangerous but necessary missions into the North, into Route Package VI. Charles Munroe flew with the 14th TRS out of Udorn and relates a typical mission in 1972:

> I was flying out of Udorn AB in northern Thailand sometime during 1972 at a peak period of the Vietnam War. My mission was 'weather-recce' to be flown to RP [Route Pack]- VI in North Vietnam (around Hanoi) to determine if and when the wx was good enough to launch a large tactical strike-package. Sometimes, we'd look at a designated target area, find the wx poor, go get some JP-4 from a tanker, and return for another look. Occasionally, we'd do that multiple times, since the wx was volatile and timing for strike mission launches was very critical. We flew weather-recce flights with an RF-4C, because it was equipped with an HF radio that F-4 fighters lacked. Usually, we flew alone, but when going into a very high threat area we'd take along a flight of two to four fighters for protection; usually, just two.
>
> On this particular day, we flew significantly into NVA. up near to Hanoi. I popped up several thousand feet, and saw that the wx poor around most of the targets. So, we went to a tanker for more fuel and returned; several times. At any rate, one time as we turned south near the Red River and were heading south towards the Black River and Laos, Red Crown (a USN surveillance ship off the NVA coast) alerted me that a pair of MiG-21s were heading our way with about a 45-degree cut-off angle. Their range was roughly 25 miles and they were accelerating. We dropped our centreline fuel tanks (600-gal tanks), which were empty, and I accelerated the flight from about 450 kts IAS to 500 kts IAS. (NOTE: At high indicated airspeeds the 600-gal centreline fuel tank limited allowable manoeuvring and Gs.)
>
> Much quicker than anticipated, Red Crown advised that the MiGs had closed to 15 nm; same 45-degree angle-off, which was why they were closing so rapidly. Obviously, they were being vectored by a GCI facility. We accelerated to 600 kts. Next, Red Crown advised that the Migs were also accelerating and arming their air-to-air missiles (Red Crown was monitoring the Mig's radio transmissions). We dropped down to 4-5,000 ft MSL; as low as I thought we could go and still maintain contact with Red Crown. There was a broken cloud ceiling below us and we'd entered the mountainous region of NVA near the boarder with Laos. Soon, Red Crown called, "Migs at 10 miles…8 miles…5 miles…3 miles!" Then, I told my fighters, "Good bye! I'm going down. You two can play with the Migs!" I was going to drop down into the valleys, below, and use TFR (Terrain Following radar) as necessary to fly low-level in the weather.
>
> I jettisoned my wing tanks, pushed the throttles to Military (100 per cent) power and nosed the plane towards a valley about 3,000 ft below. As I levelled off, I glanced at the IAS and was astonished to see it reading 930 kts! That was 200+ kts over published redline (Max-Q limiting airspeed) for the RF-4C. Immediately, I got the airspeed back under control and stayed down low for about 5 minutes. When I popped back up through the clouds, I found myself to be a mile behind my fighter 'escort'! God only knows how fast they'd been going! By then, we'd all tremendously out distanced the Migs, who were probably wondering what the hell had happened to the F/RF-4s they were 'sneaking' up on! Immediately, it was obvious that my escorts had decided to stay with me, rather than break off for a fight with the Migs. I can't fault them for that!"

In August, 1971, the 460th TRW at Tan Son Nhut was inactivated and the RB-57s of Detachment 1 and the RF-4s of the 12th TRS returned home. In December, 1973, the EB-66 flew its last mission in south-east Asia. The RF-4Cs of the 14th TRS were to remain at Udorn until 1975 when the squadron was inactivated and the Phantoms returned to the USA.

APPENDIX I

The Aircraft

The RF-51 Mustang
The RF-51D was developed from the most prolific and successful of all the Mustang variants: the P-51D. Originally designated the F-6D, the reconnaissance version of this most famous fighter first entered service with the USAAF in 1944 and saw action in the war. The F-6D could carry two cameras in the rear fuselage: a K-17 and a K-22. One was placed in the horizontal position and one in the vertical oblique position. The aircraft retained the six 50 calibre machine guns of the fighter.

After the war the F-6Ds served with some tac recce units in both the regular air force and the newly established Air National Guard. In June 1950, at the onset of hostilities in Korea, many brand new aircraft, which had been held in storage since 1945, were taken out and assigned to air force units, most notably to the 45th TRS, newly activated at Komaki, Japan.

The main mission of the RF-51 was Visual Reconnaissance. The cameras were used as a means of confirming a visual report. For the purposes of Visual Reconnaissance the Mustang had the advantage of being able to stay airborne for a long time. Its marked disadvantage was that it had a liquid-cooled engine and was extremely vulnerable to ground fire, a small hole in the cooling system would disable the aircraft. For the purposes of reporting, the RF-51D was

RF-51D Mustang 44-84847 of the 45th TRS at Taegu in 1952. (via Bob Archibald)

equipped with an AN/AMQ-1A wire recorder which enabled the pilot to record his sightings for playback later.

In an attempt to supplement the number of photo Mustangs in the 45th TRS in Korea an attempt was made to develop a camera pod for the F-51 fighter. The project was abandoned when it became apparent that it was unsafe. The aircraft were less manoeuvrable, slower by 30 mph and there was a marked increase in pilot fatigue. These factors increased the airplanes vulnerability to ground fire.

In the early 1950s all RF-51Ds in the USAF were phased out; the ANG units being the last to relinquish the aircraft. It had, however, been a highly successful aircraft in spite of its drawbacks and had served with distinction for a number of years.

The RF-80A

On 8 January 1944 the prototype of the United States' first jet fighter, the Lockheed P-80 flew for the first time. Development had begun in 1943 in response to an Army Air Force requirement for a jet propelled airplane using the British de Havilland Halford engine. Lockheed produced the XP-80 in no less than 145 days, well within schedule. The Halford was replaced in the YP-80A by the General Electric J33-11 engine. On 18 September the Army Air Force accepted the first of the YP-80A prototypes. By the end of February, 1945, all of these aircraft had left the Lockheed plant and were engaged in development operations.

The first production P-80A was received by the Air Force in February, 1945, and the following month was in quantity production. The view at this time was that the aircraft was going to be needed for combat operations in both the Far East and the European theatre. The Germans were using the ME 262, and the P-80 initially received the same high priority production schedule as the B-29. In spite of this, however, what kept the P-80 out of the Second World War, apart from a brief appearance in Italy, was primarily a shortage of spares and engines.

The P-80 went into squadron service in the Spring of 1946. Eventually, after further problems had been overcome, the F-80 Shooting Star in it's later models, the F-80B and F-80C, became one of the successes of the Korean War and was deployed by the United States Air Force to its squadrons all over the world. When production of the F-80C ceased in 1950, 1731 of the aircraft had been produced and delivered to the Air Force.

The second YP-80A prototype, 44-84988, was completed in 1944 as the XF-14: a reconnaissance version of the basic fighter. It had a redesigned nose that rotated forward for servicing and carried only vertical seeing cameras. It was unarmed. The F-14A followed the XF-14 and was a direct modification of the standard P-80 airframe. Of the first of these aircraft, 44-85260, little is known of it's configuration. However, the second F-14A, 44-84998, was designed to carry oblique and forward looking cameras in addition to the vertical. The nose hinged forward to facilitate access to the cameras. The camera ports were, on the port side, a trapezoid shaped window; on the starboard side a smaller square window; and under the fuselage three flat windows forward of the nose wheel bay. The F-14A was followed by the XFP-80A. Aircraft 44-85201 refined the configuration and the photographic suite and became the definitive prototype of the reconnaissance 'Shooting Star.'

Thirty-eight of the initial 917 P-80As were scheduled for conversion to FP-80A models. Subsequently 112 aircraft were ordered and built as FP-80As. In 1948 the aircraft were redesignated RF-80A. In 1951 sixty-six of the F-80As were converted to the reconnaissance type and, to fit them better for Korea, were given improved photographic equipment. These converted aircraft are distinguishable by a humped nose antennae cover. A later modification was the installation of a wire recorder for use on visual recce missions. The initial powerplants for the RF-80A were the Allison J-33-A-9A, J-33-GE-11A and the J-33-A-17 in the RF-80A-5-LO, and the J-33-A-9B, J-33-GE-11B, J-33-A-17A and −21 in the RF-80A-10-LO. In 1953, ninety-eight RF-80As exchanged their J33-A-11 engines for the upgraded and more powerful J33-A-35s of 5400lb of thrust, the powerplant of the T-33. These aircraft were designated RF-80A-15-LO.

An RF-80A of the 302nd TRS at Goose Bay *en route* to Sembach in 1953. (Ed Stoltz)

With over 1400 hours logged in the RF-80A I consider it on of the best jet fighter type airplanes produced by the US aviation industry. The P-80 was the pioneer jet for the USAAF/USAF and when viewed in that context must be considered a fabulous airplane. It served well as a fighter interceptor, fighter-bomber and as a trainer. When operated within the prescribed limits of the airframe and engine it was very dependable and a dream to fly. Those who are critical of the shortcomings of the early P/F-80 have forgotten, or are unaware of, the problems encountered with early versions of the F-84, F-100 and the F-104, to name a few.

Ed Stoltz 8th/15th/303rd TRS

I thoroughly enjoyed flying the old RF-80A and had copious amounts of time in the craft. It was a fine recce aircraft for its day albeit it was slow. I never flew it in combat but methinks it's planform at 400 kts wouldn't be too hard to hit with AAA. Nonetheless, if we had been equipped with other than focal plane shutters on our cameras and some pretty poor IMC devices, we could have done some better photography with the jet. It was fine for mosaics and strips and of course super for dicing shots but who in his right mind would fly a mosaic over defended enemy terrain at any altitude that would give you good enough scale to provide the PIs with some target information. We learned over the years the advantage of speed when challenged by ground stabilized guns. We learned how to jink to defeat radar controlled AAA too but in the vintage years of the RF-80A a lot of that skill hadn't been exercised, hence we took losses in Korea.

The idiosyncrasies in the RF-80A were numerous when compared to the modern aircraft that we've flown since. The aileron buzz after you passed 0.83 mach and the stiffening of the ailerons beyond the capability for the aileron boost to help you was always a bother. Lost a friend who lost his boost altogether in a high speed dive at Shaw and he pranged into a field and went home in a body bag of small parts and fluids. Frank Geitlinger was his name and he was a class mate of mine in flying school at Webb AFB. The high adventure of flying precision instruments in Japanese weather (solid gurk from ground to over 60,000 ft which is well above our highest cruising altitudes) on suction gauges (artificial horizon and directional gyro) was always an attention getter, especially with ITOs during the winter months.

Bill Goldfein 15th TRS

There was a long standing debate on how long you could keep an RF-80 airborne. On 19th November, 1954, Bob Kilpatrick and I in a two ship formation stayed airborne for an honest 4:00. We must have flown from the North Sea to Munich a half dozen times and I near froze to death. We also received a glorious ass chewing since we had filed out a local clearance showing 2:45 fuel on board!

I believe anyone who flew the RF-80 had a soft spot in his heart for the aircraft in spite of its negative characteristics. Cockpit pressurization was usually missing. Another problem was cockpit heat. If climbing to altitude and one neglected to push the heat control lever full forward it would stick and you were stuck with a very, very cold cockpit. The '80A did not have a fuel counter and a pilot could keep track of internal fuel by allowing the fuselage tank to drop to a predetermined level, then select a wing tank to refill the fuselage tank, turn off the wing tank and keep repeating the procedure.

Bob Sweet 302nd TRS

The RF-84F Thunderflash
It was with the development of the swept wing F-84F Thunderstreak that the story of the Thunderflash begins. The F-84F was developed as a low cost response to an air force revision of the General Operational Requirement of September 1944 that had led to the development of the original F-84. Republic claimed that its new aircraft would be a development of the F-84E and that as a consequence 55 per cent of current tooling could be used in production and subsequent air force maintenance. On the basis of this the air force allocated one F-84E for the company to build a prototype. This was in December 1949.

In the event innumerable problems with the power plant and the airframe effectively delayed the programme and the Thunderstreak did not enter operational service until January 1954.

The RF-84F Thunderflash was developed virtually in tandem with the F-84F and was a response to Tactical Air Command's requirement for a state of the art reconnaissance platform to replace its ageing Lockheed RF-80, which, although it had acquitted itself well in Korea, had many shortcomings which only a new, custom built reconnaissance aircraft could overcome. Although similar to the Thunderstreak the RF-84F had many differences. The intake ducts were located in the wing roots instead of the nose. The latter was elongated and enclosed to contain the impressive array of cameras and visual reconnaissance equipment.

The Thunderflash could potentially carry fifteen cameras: six forward facing, eight in vertical and oblique positions and the Trimetrogen camera. The systems also incorporated a computerized control system. Based on light speed and altitude it adjusted camera settings to produce pictures with greater delineation. A wire recorder was fitted as standard allied to a vertical view finder with a periscopic presentation on the cockpit panel. The pilot could, by speaking into the recorder, describe ground movements that might not appear on still pictures. Some less sophisticated wire recorder systems had been fitted retrospectively to the RF-84's predecessor, the RF-80, but in the Thunderflash they were designed in from the outset. The aircraft also carried two 0.5 in Colt Browning M-3 machine guns mounted in the lower lip of each intake. The RF-84F was night mission capable by using magnesium flares carried under its wings in flash ejector cartridges.

The RF-84F did not escape the development problems of its stablemate, and delivery to the air force did not commence until January 1954. During its career the aircraft served with the 67th Tactical Reconnaissance Wing, the 363rd Tactical Reconnaissance Wing, the 432nd Tactical Reconnaissance Wing, the 10th Tactical Reconnaissance Wing and the 66th Tactical Reconnaissance Wing. Many Air National Guard units flew the aircraft, and it also saw service with Allied air forces and Strategic Air Command; in the latter case as the RF-84K.

Reaction to the Thunderflash of the pilots who flew it was mixed. While all agreed that the aircraft was heavy and underpowered, not all found its other characteristics difficult to live with.

Aircraft RF-84F 52-7366 was one of the last Thunderflashes used by the regular Air Force. (via George Cowgill)

It was a tough airplane, being built by the 'Republic Aircraft and Battleship Company, Parts Interchangeable'. It was heavy, underpowered, but very reliable. How Tough? I was stationed at Spangdahlem, Germany in 1956 and 1957. One day, one of the 32nd pilots had to 'belly in' due to a hydraulic leak and he couldn't get the gear down. He put down on the drop tanks and slid to a stop. This occurred in the morning. The ground crew picked the bird up, tossed the drop tanks, fixed the leak and the airplane made the afternoon schedule.

Dick Vaughters, 32nd TRS

The RF-84, like all Republic products ever built, was known to be a hardy piece of equipment. But, like some Republic products, its thrust-to-weight ratio left a lot to be desired. Take-off roll calculations were absolutely required, and a slight mistake in those calculations could produce exciting moments. But it was a tough airplane, like the F-84G at Luke was, and the P47 was, and the F105 proved later to be. It was an easy airplane to fly, although frustrating when the Canadians in their Mark VI Sabres would bounce us from 45,000 ft perch positions while we're struggling to stay at 35,000 on a cross country flight (happened constantly- the Canucks were at Gros Tenquin, Zweibrucken and Marville, all near the routes we always took to go south from Sembach. They waited for the turkeys to appear, then had target practice for 15 minutes while we sat there with clenched teeth, because, as I said, we were just trying to remain airborne at that altitude).

Paul Hodges, 303rd TRS

The day that I reported to the 17th TRS in 1955 two RF-84Fs were lost because of engine failure due to shrinkage of the shroud ring around the compressor blades while flying in 'visible moisture' (clouds). One pilot was killed and the other ejected safely. Because of this problem, all F-84s were prohibited from flying in any clouds. We just thought that we had an all-weather air force. The fix for this problem was to shave the compressor blades to provide adequate clearance. Unfortunately, this fix further reduced the engine thrust of an already under powered flying machine. There were still hydraulic problems and long take-off rolls. On one very hot July day, At Kirtland AFB in Albuquerque, N.M. (field elevation- 4000 ft) I experienced a take-off roll of approximately 11,000 ft. That was dicey.

Scotty Schoolfield, 17th TRS

RF-SID, 45th TRS, KOREA, 1951.

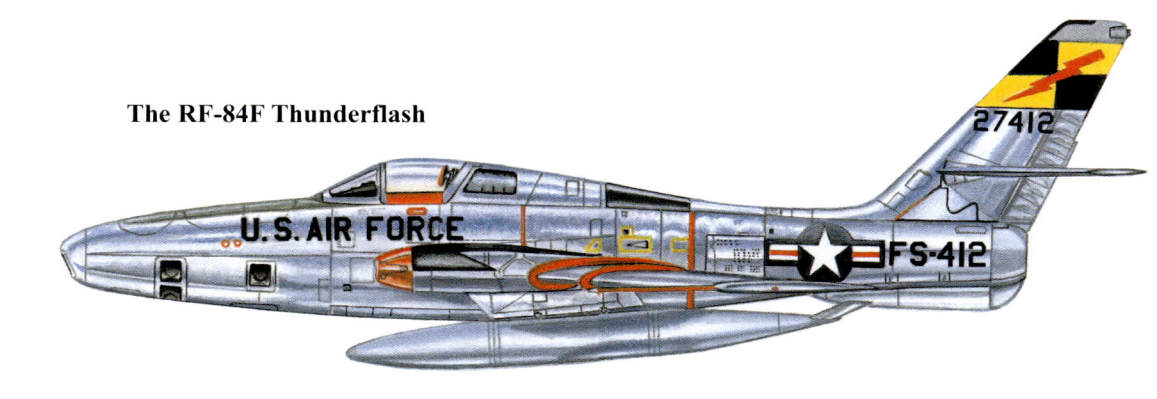

The RF-80A

The RF-84F Thunderflash

RF-84K, 45th TRS

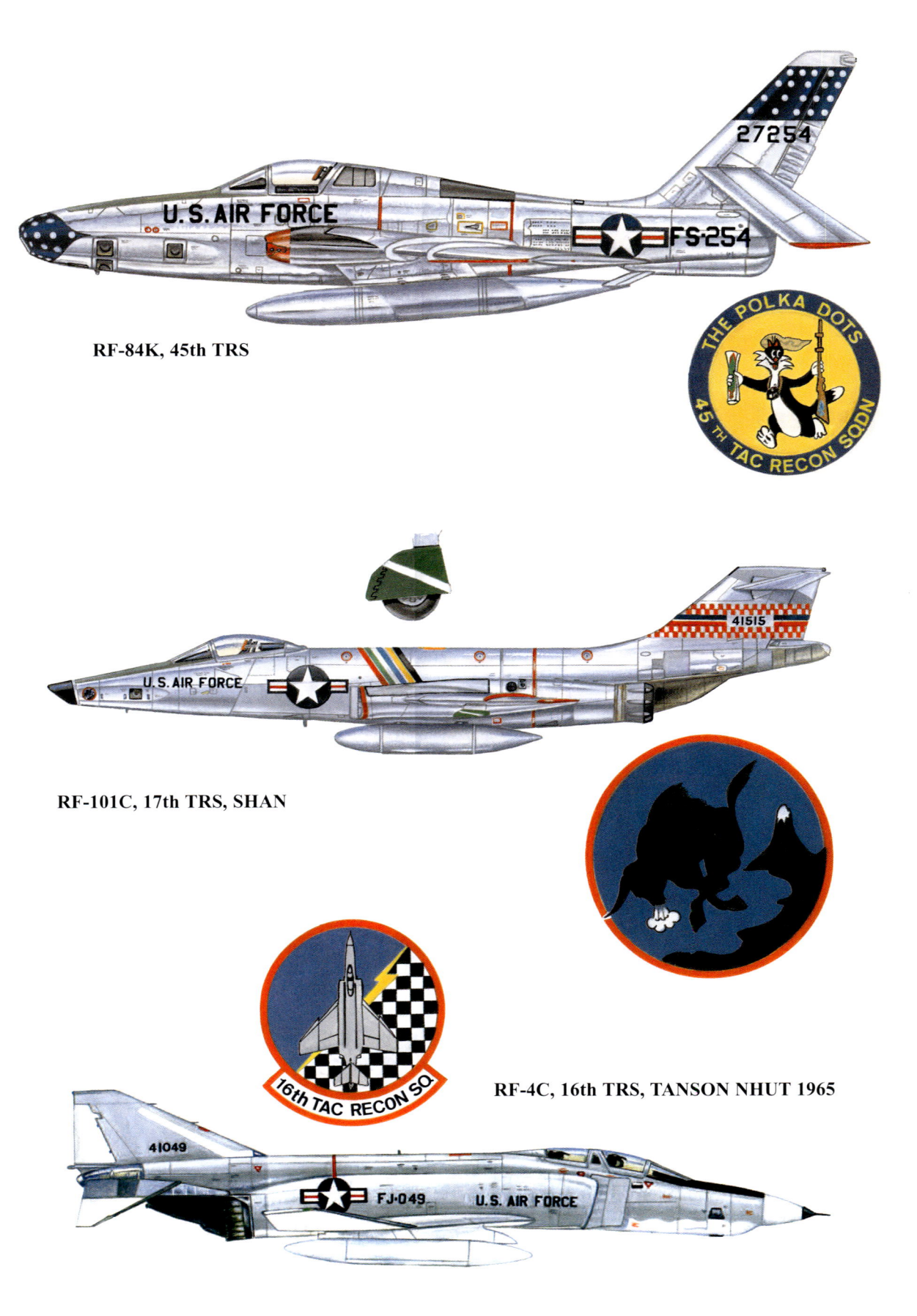

RF-101C, 17th TRS, SHAN

RF-4C, 16th TRS, TANSON NHUT 1965

The bird had room for four 50 cal guns in the wing roots. When I got back from Nellis and the gunnery school we tried air-to-ground on the Poinsett range near Shaw. I shot a 40 per cent on my first missions and 15 per cent on the second one. Keeping the guns harmonized was difficult. After I left for college I was told that the squadron tried to shoot air-to-air off the coast but didn't hit a thing. The gunsight was a fixed sight and I am sure they did not compensate enough for bullet jump, angle off, lead etc. I know I would not have liked to fly the tow bird.

Larry Garrison, 17th TRS

The RF-84F was a stable, rugged aircraft but needed an additional 2000 lb. of thrust. During conversion from the RF-80A to the RF-84F several pilots complained that the 84 required far more runway for take-off then stated in the Technical Manual. Not true. It did require a lot of runway but it would meet the TO performance when flown correctly. On one occasion a pilot flying a fully loaded RF-84F staggered from the runway and sank into the valley at the east-end of the Sembach runway. On returning from his flight he complained the airplane simply would not fly. To prove that it would fly I selected the oldest aircraft in the squadron, one equipped with an engine producing 600 lb. less thrust, and with the same fuel load demonstrated the airplane would fly at the exact distance specified by the T.O. A problem with converting from the straight wing F-80 was convincing the pilots to rotate to the correct attitude, at the correct speed for take-off. The F-84F, as with most swept wing fighters, would continue forever on three wheels unless the take-off attitude was attained. On the other hand, lift the nose beyond the take-off attitude and it would never fly.

Ed Stoltz, 303rd TRS

The RF-84F had excellent range and cruise performance. The engines never came close to matching the airframe. A couple of thousand pounds of added thrust would have made it a great aircraft. That was never to be. The RF-84F was transonic in a clean configuration and in a dive. Rate of roll was very fast. Certainly no one worried about pulling the wings off. The cockpit was roomy and comfortable. All in all it was a nice aircraft to fly but not one you would choose to enter combat with if there were any degree of air opposition.

Bob Sweet, 302nd TRS

In the winter we used to have most of the USAFE fighters in Morocco at Nouasseur doing their bit for God and country while flying in the sun. Lots of strange stuff went on down there in those days. RF-84F aircraft used to be towed out to the end of the runway and plugged into a fuel truck and power unit so they could top off after their run up and hopefully make the trip back to France without having to land and refuel, assuming they could take off in 14,500 ft with the fuel load. They started from the end of the overrun with the barrier down at the departure end.

Nick Pishvanov, 18th TRS

I checked out in the '84 in May 56 and we did refuelling, probe and drogue, with the KB-50. Yes, we took every inch of runway that Nouasseur had to offer and when runway temp started to go over 90 we would only put 300 gallons in the drops. The machine initially had 7300 lb of thrust but was later modified with the W-7 engine which gave us a thundering 7800 lb. It still took a lot of runway to get airborne. You can imagine how my first take-off in the 101 felt when I lit the burners and felt the push of 30,000 lb. Awesome!!! I transitioned into the 101 at Shaw and then went to Phalsbourg, France and back to the Hog. Got the 101 there about six months later and transitioned the squadron at Nouasseur. That was really a great time to be flying. (Chuck Lustig 32nd TRS)

We had some of the RF-84K models in the 45th at Misawa when I got there in late '57. I recall that the hook system developed some hydraulic leaks on occasion even though it was inactivated. Other than that I don't remember much different about that model – still took every inch of the runway (8000 ft) to get that sucker in the air with full tanks in summer. I was told during check-out that if someone built a runway that went all the way round the world, Republic would build an airplane that used every foot of it to get airborne. I believe it.

I don't recall that the 84 had short legs, however. It seems that we went between Misawa and Kadena with the usual reserve for primary alternates which were Yokota and Itazuki, respectively (an additional 300 nautical miles or so). I distinctly remember one flight for that distance. In formation, on Abe Tanaka's wing, in the weather and 'upside down'. Even my sweat was running 'up' on my face and mask. Perhaps my memory is faulty, but like the Voodoo, that hog would get great gas mileage when the fuel was low. It was just hard to get it in the air.

Dewey Hemphill 45th TRS

The RF-101C Voodoo
The F-101 Voodoo was developed from the XF-88 strategic penetration fighter which first flew on 20 October, 1948, and which was cancelled by the air force in August, 1950, just months after the second prototype's first flight. Reasons for the cancellation were many: the increased finance put into the large bombers such as the B-36, the production debut of the F-84 which could satisfy immediate demands for a penetration fighter and not least the quite poor performance of the XF-88 in meeting the requirements placed upon it.

However, Strategic Air Command (SAC) in January, 1951, outlined the minimum characteristics it required of an escort fighter to accompany its long range B-36s, and a new reconnaissance variant. General Operations Requirements 101 (GOR 101) was published in February, 1951, and although there were many contenders for the contract, McDonnell's newly configured F-88 won the day, although production was not to go ahead until October, 1951.

Originally intended as an interim fighter, it soon became clear that the Voodoo could be developed to satisfy the Air Force's requirements for a long range fighter. Fiscal Year 1952 funds previously allocated to the F-84 and F-86F were released to get the F-88 into production without delay. Because of the quite significant difference in configuration between the original XF-88 and the new aircraft, the Air Force Council directed a new designation of F-101 on 30 November, 1951.

The time from designation to first flight of the F-101 was almost three years. On 29 September, 1954, the aircraft was flown at Edwards Air Force Base with encouraging results. Mach 1.07 was achieved in a dive and the programmed test profile was completed satisfactorily. Before the end of the year three further F-101s were accepted by the Air Force.

From then on the programme proceeded fitfully and was fraught with problems. By mid 1956 the twenty-nine F-101s accepted by the Air Force were experiencing structural, propulsion, aerodynamic and armament problems. A production halt was ordered by the Air Force in May, 1956, and, although short-lived, was indicative of the concern felt at that time.

Development of the reconnaissance RF-101A was proceeding alongside the fighter version and was experiencing the same problems; not least of which was the inability to match GOR 1s requirement for an aircraft capable of surviving forces of 7.33g. Initial F-101s were only capable of loads of 6.33g. The Air Force reluctantly accepted the downgrading of capability in the initial aircraft, but stipulated that the 7.33g requirement must be adhered to in the subsequent model Voodoo which it designated F-101C. This aircraft would be internally strengthened to meet GOR 1 requirements. The RF-101C would be developed according to the same structural principles and would retain the RF-101As 'special weapons' delivery capability.

RB-26, TRS

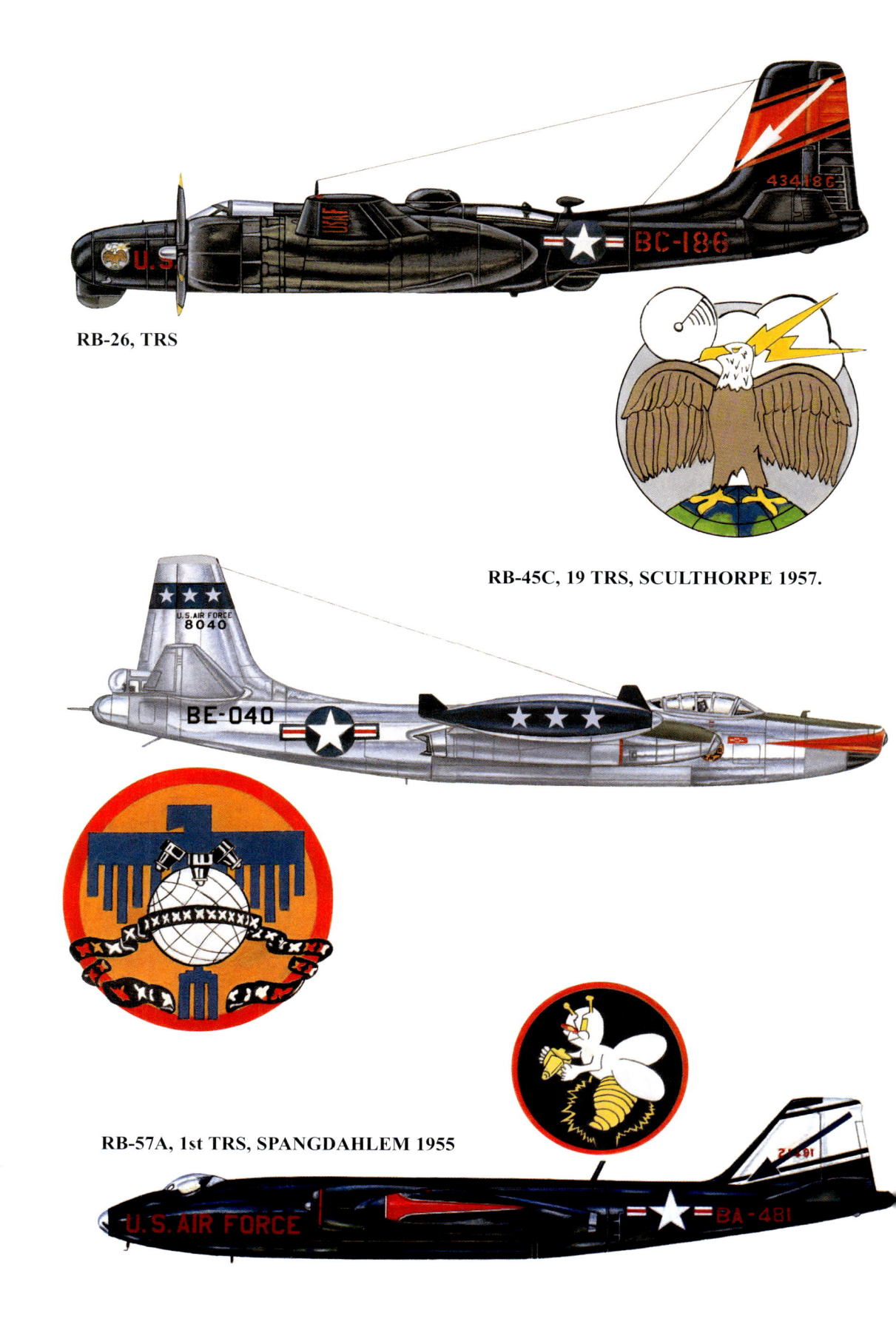

RB-45C, 19 TRS, SCULTHORPE 1957.

RB-57A, 1st TRS, SPANGDAHLEM 1955

RB-57E DET #1 460 TRW, TAN SON NHUT, 1967

RB-66B, 9th TRS, SHAW 1952

RF-100A, 7407th SS, BITBURG 1955

RF-100A, 7407th SS, BITBURG 1955

One of the most significant of the Voodoo's dangerous idiosyncrasies was the tendency to 'pitch-up.' The 'T' tail configuration of the airframe was responsible for this phenomenon. At high angles of attack and high G manoeuvring the wing blocked or disrupted the airflow causing the stabilitors to become ineffective, thus causing the nose to pitch-up at a high degree creating dramatic loss of air speed and subsequent stall and spin. The problem of pitch-up kept recurring throughout the Voodoo's service career. The pitch-up inhibitor system was not foolproof and certainly not always effective. The pitch-up phenomenon became apparent very early on in the RF-101s USAFE career. In June 1960, Don Stuck, the chief test pilot with McDonnell visited Phalsbourg and conducted an indoctrination programme on RF-101 pitch-up recovery. Concurrent with this, safety personnel constantly tried to develop procedures for calibrating the pitch-up warning system.

Solving the pitch-up problem had to be a top priority before the Voodoo could enter squadron service. Eventually an inhibitor system was developed by McDonnell which provided the pilot with an audible warning as pitch-up was approached, thus enabling evasive action to be taken. Although the device satisfied the Air Force it did not eliminate pitch-up occurring in emergency or unexpected circumstances.

The RF-101A reconnaissance version of the Voodoo was soon succeeded in production by the RF-101C. The Air Force had also decided in December, 1956, to limit production of the F-101A/C and convert to reconnaissance configuration the last ninety-six aircraft under contract. The first flight of the RF-101C took place on 12 July, 1957, and the aircraft entered service with the 432nd Tactical Reconnaissance Wing in September, 1957.

In late 1964 a substantial upgrade was initiated in the RF-101Cs reconnaissance equipment. Because it was planned to continue the aircraft in operational service before being phased into the Air National Guard, it was essential that something was done to upgrade a suite that was very dated and had outlived it's usefulness. Modification 1181 was designed to give the Voodoo an improved high-speed low-altitude capability, a night capability, in flight processing, cassette ejection and an increase in sensor reliability due to automatic exposure control. The centrepiece of the modification was the Hycon KS-72A framing camera being developed for the McDonnell RF-4C Phantom. Initially there were problems. The 66th TRW in 1964 reported many failures of the system and spares deficiencies. These problems were ironed out, however, and in the final analysis the upgrade did all that was intended for it, and, indeed, enabled the RF-101C to serve with distinction in south-east Asia.

RF-101C, 56-0210, 66th TRW at Bentwaters Open House, 1967. (Alan Johnson)

In 1957, the 17th began to transition into the RF101A. In fact, the entire squadron accomplished the check outs in just two aircraft, 41503 and 41504. The Voodoo had growing pains much like any new bird. Hydraulics were the primary problems. We learned to respect the infamous pitch-up characteristics and worked around them. The pitch-up trait was brought to reality during the operational testing at Eglin AFB, Fla. Lonnie Moore (I think), was killed when he pitched up on take off. Since he was a Korean War ace, the feelings among the higher ups were that if a test pilot could do it what were the garden variety jocks going to do? What we garden variety pilots did was to read the flight handbook and fly the aircraft like the book said!

Scotty Schoolfield, 17th TRS, 1957

Once we had the angle of attack indicator installed pitch-up was no longer a worry. We were able to fly the airplane right up to its limits with no problem. Actually, if the pilot was smooth on the controls and paid close attention to the nose of the aircraft and the forces on the stick, he could avoid pitch-up but that is difficult to do in the heat of the moment. I was a test pilot in the Voodoo for four years and one of the test objectives was to calibrate the angle of attack indicator – a very dicey procedure requiring smooth control inputs and close attention to what the aircraft was doing.

Don Karges, 38th TRS, 20th TRS

Then, there's the RF-101A/C, which was a hot airplane in every sense of the word. It wouldn't turn worth a hoot … still, the airplane had a lot of good points. It was fast (Mach1.57 indicated and it could do it), and carrying 14620 lb of fuel internally, it had long legs. Normal fuel flow at cruise speed would be 6000 lb per hour or a little less…..I was with the Phalsbourg AB group that went to Nouasseur in 1958 to check out in the RF-101. Everybody took their first hop in good old 56-0221, with no drop tanks. To impress you, the first take-off and climb out was made with afterburners. As I recall, the first words I ever spoke in a '101 (very rapidly passing 40,000 feet) was 'How do you slow this son of a buck down?'

Dick Vaughters, 32nd TRS

We switched to RF-101Cs in the Spring of 1959. It felt good to have a plane with plenty of power. On hot summer days at Larson we would often figure a take off-roll over 9000 ft on a 10,000 ft runway. They would lower the barrier at the end of the runway so we couldn't snag our gear on take-off. The 101 with afterburners would make you feel you were strapped to a rocket. Great plane but it couldn't turn. The T tail would be blanked out if you pulled too many Gs or if you got too high an angle of attack.

Donald Watt 38th TRS

Barnard, 17th Ops Officer, brought the first RF-101A into Shaw, 6 May, 1957. Shortly afterwards he took a flight of four out to Clovis, NM for the dedication of Cannon AFB. During the briefing conducted by the F-100 Fighter Group commander, he indicated how the aircraft would line up depending up on the wind. He asked Barney how much of a tail wind the 101s could take and was informed anything up to 40 kts. That produced the desired effect from the fighter jocks in whose dust we had trailed for so long. The remark wasn't too far off the mark except for time limitations. I think we were limited to as few as two or three flights when carrying two 450 external tanks, between tyre changes.

Bob Sweet 17th TRS

I had been selected as one of the spare aircrews for 'Mobile Zebra.' On all our simulated practise flights to Hawaii, someone had always aborted and I joined in. So, I just assumed I would make the trip. But on the day we were to leave George AFB for the long awaited trip 15 Nov, 1957), it was I who aborted. There was a failure in the power block and I could not get external power for starting. (The planes were later modified so we could make starts using battery power.) On my return to Shaw, I stopped at Laughlin AFB (Del Rio, Texas.), for refuelling and an enjoyable weekend with some friends. Monday morning was nice. Weather for the flight to Shaw was OK except for a line of thunderstorms over Mississippi. But since I was leaving early, I should be able to overfly them. Sure enough I found a line of thunderstorms as I approached Mississippi, I began a slow climb. I was listening to a low frequency radio station weather report and began to get the clue that these storms were serious: Severe winds, heavy hail and funnel clouds seem to get your attention. I considered returning to Laughlin, but it looked like I was about to get past them, so I pressed on. As I attempted to get Meridian Radio for a position report, I noticed the clouds just below me were really boiling up. (It was beautiful, but scary site.) I had plenty of fuel, so I pushed up the throttles but they were already at 100 per cent and I'm at 47,000 ft. I attempted to light the afterburners, without success. It was time to get on the gauges and hang on. Suddenly, the left engine begins a compressor stall and the overheat light comes on. I shut it down and started a descent. Then bang, I hit one of those boiling clouds and I'm flipped for a 'loop.' I look at the airspeed indicator and it reads '0.' (That is the scariest thing I've ever seen while flying.) The artificial horizon, that was guaranteed not to tumble was spinning like crazy. So was the altimeter and I know where it headed. Obviously, I have 'pitched-up' and must take some immediate action. I initiate pitch-up recovery: stick full forward and deploy the drag chute. I can tell the plane is flying, but the instruments are still whirling like crazy. I consider baling out and then remember the weather report and decide that would be a fatal error. It was then that I got control of myself, and began to get control of the aircraft using basic training and basic instruments. Needle, ball and airspeed really do work.   Finally, things get under control. I get the plane back on the straight and level, and then all of a sudden, pop out of the side of the storm and I'm in the clear at 17,000 ft. I have lost 30,000 ft in this experience. The plane is flying in trim with one engine shut down. Sometime during this experience, I trimmed for the dead engine. Credit that to training in the simulator. I didn't remember doing it and certainly would not have noticed the difference in the thunderstorm. I restarted the left engine, called Atlanta Center and got a vector direct to Shaw. I shook all the way home. Fortunately, the aircraft and I both survived.

Bob Gould 17th TRS Shaw, 1957

The RF-4C Phantom
The McDonnell Douglas RF-4C Phantom was developed in response to Special Operations Requirement 196 (SOR 196) which called for an all weather reconnaissance version of the F-4C fighter bomber. SOR 196 was published on the 29 May, 1962, and in addition to the reconnaissance requirement it also requested a nuclear delivery role. The mock-up inspection took place on 29 October, 1962, and demanded 150 configuration changes. Most of these were designed to ease maintenance of the aircrafts systems and components such as better access to cameras, infra-red sensors and side looking radar sensors. The air force also endorsed a less sophisticated forward looking radar system.

The first flight of the RF-4C, actually a reconfigured navy F-4B (62-12200), took place on the 8 August, 1963. Subsequently, McDonnell test pilots undertook extensive testing of the airplane's reconnaissance systems prior to the delivery of the first production model to the Air Force which took place in September, 1964, at Shaw AFB to the 33rd Tactical Reconnaissance Training Squadron (TRTS). All initial production aircraft were delivered to this unit. In 1965 they were transferred to the first operational RF-4C squadron the 16th TRS. The first aircraft arriving on the 30 April, 1965.

Initially the 16th TRS experienced problems with safety aspects of the new aircraft. The RF-4C suffered significant flight and directional control problems while taking off from wet runways.

An RF-4C 64-1077 at Alconbury in 1966 wearing the gull grey and white colour scheme that all early recce Phantoms wore. (Author's collection)

The war in south-east Asia demanded that the 16th TRS become combat ready in the RF-4C in a very short period of time. On the 31 July the first Forward Looking Radars, APQ-99 were delivered to the squadron. On the 27 October, 1965, the first element of the squadron deployed to Tan Son Nhut with nine aircraft and two spares. The second element deployed on the 28 December.

Also in 1965 the RF-4C began deployment to USAFE with the 10th TRW and the 32nd and 38th TRS of the 26th TRW. The PACAF squadron, the 15th TRS then assigned to the 18th TFW received their first Phantoms in 1967 and saw action in south-east Asia.

The regular Air Force service career of the RF-4C spanned almost 30 years and during that time the aircraft underwent many system changes and developments. As well as SE Asia the aircraft saw action in The Gulf war.

> The RF-4 was really set up for day and night recce. We had good terrain following avoidance and navigation radar plus inertial navigation. More than 50 per cent of our missions were flown at night. Performance wise it was the best fighter I'd flown (F-86, F-102, T-33 and T-38). It was very stable and, as long as you didn't push the stall, very easy to fly. The worst thing was the seat, which was as hard as a rock. We usually carried two 300 gallon drop tanks. For sensors we had infra red, side looking radar, various cameras including forward oblique, a really great low panoramic, medium or high vertical, or split vert.
>
> Captain Jon Heritage, 16th TRS TSN 1967

> The RF-4C had dual controls in the rear seat; whereas the navy's RF-4B did not. The USAF decided initially to place young pilots just out of flying school in the rear cockpit to act as Weapons Systems Officers (WSOs). It was felt that the Phantom was too complicated for young pilots to handle. This, in my opinion, was not the case. I always believed that it was so simple and easy to fly that it could have been used as a basic training aircraft, although the cost to equip and operate would have been excessively high.
>
> Scotty Schoolfield 16th TRS TSN, 1966

> Overall the plane was excellent. It was extremely fast, capable of attaining very high altitudes, and it was very stable in addition to being very fast in a low altitude

environment. It had excellent acceleration, along with more than enough power for its mission.

Another aspect of the RF-4C that everyone appreciated was having two powerful and highly reliable J-79 engines with afterburners. We could sustain a lot of battle damage, lose an engine and still outrun an enemy and make it back home.

IR and photo sensor arrays on the RF-4C were superior. They worked very well at high, medium and low altitudes. Photo-flash at night was OK at low altitudes in a low-threat areas, but hardly desirable otherwise. In high-threat areas the IR was first choice, especially, for night missions.

Charles K. Munroe 14th TRS Udorn 1972

RF-4C versus the RF-101

The RF-101 was a single seater so the pilot did the flying, navigating and camera activations. Those that transitioned to the RF-4C initially thought the WSO was 'non-essential' to mission success. Bad weather and the lack of range (fuel) were drawbacks for the RF-101. There success at night was strictly visual so if there weren't some flares or lights, then they were limited. The RF-4C's radar allowed penetration through bad weather but still required a break-out under the clouds to get photographs or infrared film. Target acquisition at night was the big differentiator between the two aircraft. The RF-101 did not have the infra-red capability nor the side-looking radar for capturing intelligence. They also did not have the ECM (Electronic Counter Measures) jamming pods like the RF-4C. This saved many from getting shot down by the SAM (Surface-to-Air Missiles, SA-4s & SA-6s) supplied by and trained by the Russians.

Captain Don Nash 16th TRS Tan Son Nhut

The Douglas RB-26 Invader

The Douglas Invader, original designation A-26, was designed to fulfil a United States Army Air Force requirement for an attack bomber to replace the B-26 Marauder, the B-25 Mitchell and the A-20 Havoc. The first prototype flew in July 1942 and the first delivery to operational units began in December 1943. By the end of the Second World War, production of the Invader had ceased and it would have been reasonable to assume that the life span of the aircraft was limited from then on, particularly bearing in mind the advent of the jet engine and all that that implied in terms of the future development of combat aircraft. In fact the aircraft was to soldier on in one guise or another right up to and beyond the Vietnam War.

In 1948 the Martin Marauder was finally retired from service and the Invader took over the B-26 designation. Two principal sub types were in operation at this time: the B-26B and the B26C. The B26B had a solid nose containing it's main armament of six 0.5 inch Browning machine guns and the remotely controlled dorsal and ventral turrets, each mounting two similar guns. The B-26C had a transparent nose.

Throughout the 1950s the B-26 operated with the USAF as a light bomber, target tug and as a tactical reconnaissance aircraft. In all these roles it saw service in all the major theatres of operation. The RB-26 was used for night photo-reconnaissance, weather reconnaissance and electronic reconnaissance. It was always considered a stop gap between the recce aircraft of the Second World War and any future developments. In the event it served in its recce role until the mid 1950s and in the electronic reconnaissance role for longer than this.

There were a variety of modifications that were made to the basic B-26 airframe in order to equip the aircraft for the night photo role. IFF equipment was installed. Armour plate was placed inside the bomb-bay doors to protect the highly explosive flash bombs from small arms fire and flak. Guns and turrets were removed. Additional cockpit lights were installed. Collector rings were installed around both engines with finger type exhaust stacks at the bottom of the engine to

RB-26 44-35262 of the 1st TRS, 10th TRW based at Spangdahlem in 1954. (Bob Webster)

reduce glare during night operations. The aircraft were painted black. Night-photo recce aircraft carried a pilot and two navigators: one in the nose position and one in the rear compartment who was responsible for operating the electronic navigation equipment and changing the film magazines. RB-26 aircraft equipped for weather reconnaissance carried a crew of a pilot, navigator, weather observer and radio operator. A variety of specialist equipment was carried including a ventilator, psychrometer and a dropsonde.

Electronic RB-26s carried an extensive range of equipment which developed considerably over the period of time that the aircraft was in service.

> Our crews, as with the Interdiction people, consisted of three men. However, the guy in the back (GIB) was also a navigator or bombardier/navigator the same as the guy in the nose (GIN). He replaced the gunner on interdiction aircraft. Of course the pilot was in the cockpit making the third crew member. The GIN was really the 'Eyes' of the crew. He noted all sighting during the mission to brief the intelligence people at home base. The pilot of course had his hands full with flying the aircraft and the view from the rear compartment was limited to a small window in the side entry-way door and two window strips at the top of compartment, each measuring about 1 ft × 4 ft. The exit door in the rear was actually the best way out for bale-out. In fact, in the afore mentioned runway crash, the GIB, not hearing anything from the front of the aircraft, jumped out on the runway while it was still going forward on the two main gear and the nose. He broke his arm and was the only one hurt.
>
> Jere Moulton 12th TRS 1953

> Every time a plane started its engines, there had to be a person with a fire extinguisher standing by. There where several extinguishers on carts by the planes. One of the pilot's told one of the shop guys to grab the extinguisher and stand by. This guy asked us what he was supposed to do. We told him to take the extinguisher and stand by the plane so that the pilot could see you. When the pilot hollered "Clear", you had to let go of the extinguisher and run like hell. Well, he did just that. The pilot stood up in his seat with his head out the top of the plane scratching his head. There was a modification to the radio system that we had to retrofit. The radios had eight channels with eight frequency crystals. The modification was an adapter that fit into the slot where the eight crystals plugged in. We had to fasten this adapter so it would stay in place, then add sixteen crystals and then check out the radios. We kept the spare crystals in a cabinet in the shop. We were responsible for these crystals and had to make sure that the radios always worked on all sixteen channels.
>
> Ron Lang 30th TRS Shaw 1952

A mission required us to follow certain prescribed routes observing the weather and reporting back by radio. There were three different routes every day. Mission 1 took off at midnight and flew to Seoul, Pyongyang, a point near the Yalu at about the midpoint of the Korea/Chinese border, thence to Hungnam, a major port on the north-east coast, and then back to K-2 via the east coast. One night when I was flying night intruders with the 3rd Bomb Group, I got involved in adjusting gunfire for the Navy into Hungnam. Mission 2 took off at 4 a.m. and flew to the bomb line and thence to whatever sector was the most active or to a sector we might be planning some sort of offensive action. The parachute drop sometime that spring is an example (March 1951 – the 187th Airborne Regimental Combat Team was airdropped on Munsan-ni in an operation called Operation Tomahawk). I remember it was a big one and there were no other big ones. Mission 3 took off at noon and flew about 100 miles north of K-14 then directly east to a midpoint between Korea and China then south to a point about 50 miles south of the Korean south coast then to Cheju-Do then north to K-2.

John Auer 6166th Weather Flight, Taegu, Korea 1952

North American RB-45C Tornado
Towards the end of the Second World War, in April, 1944, the US Army Air Force issued a requirement for a jet bomber with a speed of 500 miles per hour, a radius of 1000 miles and a bomb load of 8000 lb. In response to this requirement North American proposed the XB-45; Convair, the XB-46; and Martin, the XB-48. In the event three prototypes of the XB-45 were ordered in December, 1944. The first flight took place on the 17th March, 1947, at Muroc. The B-45A bomber entered service with the 47th Bombardment Group at Biggs AFB, Texas, in November, 1948.

The RB-45C reconnaissance version of the aircraft was the final production model. The B-45C on which it was based, was cancelled by the Air Force after only ten aircraft had been built. The reconnaissance Tornado differed from the bomber version in many respects. The transparent nose of the aircraft was completely covered and a forward oblique camera installed. Two 214 gallon drop tanks were carried underneath the nacelles. These carried water for the water injection system employed to increase the take-off thrust of the J-47 engines. Wing-tip tanks, each carrying 1200 gallons of fuel, considerably increased the range of the aircraft. The RB-45C was also capable of air-to-air refuelling. A total of twelve cameras were carried. In addition to the forward oblique in the nose, there were four in the vertical position in the rear compartment, four split verticals, and a trimetrogen mounted on a pallet centrally. The bomb bay was retained and contained extra fuel tanks and twenty-five M-122 photo flash bombs.

The first RB-45C flew in April, 1950, and the first delivery to the Air Force took place on 26 August to the 91st Strategic Reconnaissance Wing at Barksdale AFB, Louisiana. All the RB-45Cs were destined for SAC and the 91st. By the end of 1950 twenty-seven aircraft had been assigned. This figure rose to the full complement of thirty-three in early 1951.

The early service career of the RB-45C was fraught with difficulty, due in no small part to the rush to get it into production and into service. Of the thirty-three aircraft assigned to the 91st SRW, eleven had been written off by the end of 1952. One of these had been shot down by Migs in Korea. The others had perished as a result of flying accidents. This was almost a wartime attrition rate, not a peacetime one.

Nevertheless the Tornado went on to serve for several more years in the Air Force. The 91st had detachments in the Far East, at Yokota and, in Europe at RAF Sculthorpe. It was from Sculthorpe that several overflights were undertaken in the aircraft by RAF crews in RB-45s painted in RAF colours.

In 1953, as the RB-47 entered the SAC inventory, the RB-45Cs were transferred to Tactical Air Command. Aircraft in Yokota were assigned to the 6021st Reconnaissance Squadron. Those at Sculthorpe were assigned to the 47th Bombardment Wing, which, at that time flew the B-45A in the nuclear attack role. In May, 1954, the 19th TRS was assigned to the 47th BW and took over control of the RB-45Cs. In 1957 the 19th TRS became assigned to the 66th TRW.

> We also pushed it through Mach 1 more than once. Our group lost eight airplanes in that first year. One of the first we lost, we think the guy went through the Mach trying to get down, trying to see what the airplane would do. I went through the Mach with it – rough as hell going through, rougher coming back out. The one that crashed had the tail come off. He was south-east of Barksdale at 43,000 ft when it happened. That's the altitude where I pushed mine through, the only time I ever pushed it through. We lost other aircraft going through the Mach before anyone survived to tell us what happened. An aeronautical engineer finally explained to us that the rigid wing passed the vibrations encountered going through the Mach to the tail section. Unfortunately, the airplane wasn't designed to handle such stress. It was basically a Second World War airplane powered by jet engines.
>
> The cockpit of the RB-45 was laid out like that of a fighter. The visibility was excellent. The air refuelling receptacle was behind the canopy, so the airplane ended up right under the KB-29 tanker and didn't feel the prop wash as much as one did in the newer B-47, with its receptacle in front of the canopy. By 1952 we had resolved our engine problems. We didn't fix them, mind you, except for the crossover problem. We learned to manage the engines. A great pilot's airplane.
>
> Colonel Hal Austin 324th SRS, 91st SRW*

Two of our birds were equipped with 100-in focal-length cameras (9 × 18 in film) mounted in the bomb bay in a side-oblique configuration. We used these for peripheral photograph flying along the coastline of the USSR and North Korea. The crew to which I was assigned as co-pilot consisted of Lieutenant Colonel Leonard Kaufmann (AC), Major William Meikle (nav) and Staff Sergeant Quick (gunner). Our crew was never threatened with enemy action on these missions. Two other crews were. While photographing North Korea, they were attacked by North Korean

An RB-45C Tornado. The recce version of the USAF's first jet bomber served with both SAC and TAC. The aircraft undertook many clandestine over-flights of Communist countries during the Cold War. (via George Cowgill)

---

* As quoted in 'I always wanted to fly' Wolfgang Samuel, University Press of Mississippi 2001.

Mig 15s. They were escorted by F-86s of the 4th Fighter Wing. In at least one action, a Mig was shot down. The RB-45's gun camera showed it's tracers going into the intake of the Mig. But the 4th Fighters got the credit, of course.

Bob Gould 6021st RS Yokota, 1954

The RB-57 Canberra

On the 26 February, 1951, at Andrews Air Force Base in Maryland, the USAF, urgently looking for a replacement for its B-26 Invader aircraft, arranged a comparative display and included in the fly-off two aircraft designed and built in foreign countries: the English Electric Canberra and the Avro CF-100 Canuck from Canada. Roland 'Bee' Beaumont, chief test pilot for the English Electric Company had the task of presenting the Canberra.

The Invader, a veteran of the Second World War, was proving to be relatively ineffective at night in Korea. In the immediate post-war period the USAF. had concentrated on building up its nuclear forces and had rather neglected its conventional capability. There was not the capacity effectively to mount night interdictor missions. In spite of the best efforts of the B-26's the North Koreans were able to operate their supply lines at night without more than an irritating interference. The Invaders were also proving to be vulnerable to ground anti-aircraft fire. If the nocturnal missions of the USAF were to be effective they must quickly acquire a state of the art light bomber capable of night attack. It was necessary to buy 'off the shelf.' as speed was of the essence. A group of officers was tasked with the job of examining the alternatives and coming up with the right aircraft. Their research and deliberation led to the fly-off that winter day. This involved, in addition to the foreigners, the North American B-45 Tornado, the North American AJ-1 Savage and the Martin XB-51.

In spite of promising performances by the Savage and the Canuck the Canberra carried the day and proved itself the undoubted winner. However, it was not until the United States had procured manufacturing rights, that the decision to adopt the Canberra was finally made. The order for 250 licence-built Canberras was awarded to the Martin company, partly in compensation for the rejection of their XB-51. Subsequent to the successful competition at Andrews, Beaumont flew the Canberra, WD932, to the Martin facility at Middle River and demonstrated the aircraft to 15,000 Martin employees. The Canberra was to be designated B-57.

It is an interesting footnote to these events that the B-26 Invader, which the Canberra was procured to replace, soldiered on in USAF service for many more years achieving some distinction in Vietnam as a night interdictor!

The first B.2 was delivered to Martin in March, 1951, and a second in August. Much testing and evaluation work was done and as a result of this Martin suggested some modifications to the basic design which were put into effect. The first production B-57A rolled off the production line on the 20 July 1953 and flew at once.

The B-57A differed from the B.2 in having a two man crew instead of a three. The navigators window was deleted from the port side of the forward fuselage and on the starboard it was repositioned. The engine nacelles were slightly redesigned to accommodate the Wright YJ65-W-1 jet engines and the bomb bay was shortened. Regrettably the aircraft did not perform as well as had been expected and the USA. encouraged a further redesign to create the tactical reconnaissance dedicated RB-57A. Production of the B-57A ceased after eight aircraft had come off the line and production was switched to the RB-57. Altogether some sixty-seven of these aircraft were produced and saw service with the USAF and the Air National Guard into the 1960s.

After the RB-57A the Canberra was redesigned quite dramatically and all future variants were to have the now familiar tandem cockpit and bubble canopy. The B-57B was designed as a light bomber and one of the special features that Martin introduced on this model, which it also retrospectively fitted to some of the RB-57As, was the rotating bomb bay. This had been one of the revolutionary features on the ill fated XB-51 aircraft. The B-57B was followed by the B-57C dual trainer version, and subsequently by a host of highly successful variants, including the

RB-57A 52-1421 of the 1st TRS, 10th TRW in 1956. (Bob Webster)

B-57E which was developed into the RB-57E which flew recce in south-east Asia.

Initially, two B-57Es were modified for recce and sent to Tan Son Nhut. as RB-57Es. The number of aircraft eventually rose to six and two were lost in combat. The sensor suites of the RB-57E were changed and modified regularly. One of the most important aspects of the Patricia Lynn mission was the testing and development of new reconnaissance equipment.

> A very nice stable airplane. We got the first in 16 squadron; brand new ones when they first came in. The navigators back there were very nervous about being able to get out of that thing. The ejection seat had a bunch of explosive bolts to blow out of the way. They decided to put on a big show for the crews to make the navigators feel better. We jury-rigged a thing up in the hangar with a pulley going up over the hangar door. They brought it down and hooked it on this door that's supposed to blow off and then they got a pick-up truck. The whole Wing was there to see this demonstration of the wonders of the ejection seat for the navigator. They put a manikin from one of the stores and strapped it in the seat. The countdown started. We had a lanyard that pulled the ejection seat. The pick-up truck had to try and catch the seat before it fell back down on the ground. It went fine except for one thing. The countdown went, the truck started moving, the lanyard got pulled, the thing blew; but when they went back out there the manikin had been beheaded by the explosive bolts!
>
> Howard Peckham RB-57A.16th TRS Shaw 1955

> Great airplane, the 57, when we could keep it in the air. We lost several aircraft and crews, due to the electric stab trim inadvertently running away, nose down! The results caused lengthy groundings until Martin finally engineered a hydraulic boost mod which allowed the pilot to override a runaway.
>
> The Canberra was a stranger to most Air Force bases so when you dropped in somewhere for an overnight, you had to be sure the tower personnel knew that during engine start multitudes of pitch-black smoke poured out of the 'shotgun starters.' Otherwise you might have one of the base crash trucks sitting by your nose, ready to effect your rescue from the burning aircraft!
>
> Ed Gorman RB-57A 43rd TRS Shaw 1956

The Heart Throb Canberra was simple enough and didn't require any special depth of mechanical, electronic or hydraulic knowledge. The aircraft control system was mechanical push-pull rods. Gear, flaps and spoilers were the only hydraulics. There were no speed boards as on the B models. Fundamentally it was a Second World War genre with two simple J65 Curtis Wright axial flow jet engines. Simple two way radio, and no navigation equipment except an Automatic Direction Finder (ADF) radio receiver. I can't remember if it was equipped with a VOR nav-receiver. I only remember ADF let downs and hand-off to GCA. I don't remember much of VOR navigation. I'm sure we were ILS equipped, only because a couple were logged in my records. I also remember the ADF receiver because it had a nasty habit of hanging up in the cable drive component, and we had to remove the emergency hydraulic handle from its storage and bang on the cable transmission box to break it loose. The procedure came in handy and was used often enough. I can't recall when this was fixed or modified. I got accustomed to the procedure after a while. But it does help you remember the ADF radio.

Navigation was pilotage aided by the optical viewfinder, instrument landings were by ADF tear drop let down and hand off to Ground Control Approach (GCA) for final approach. Tip tanks were not used except to ferry the aircraft to Europe. Air defense radar was available for vectors when the mission was on unclassified operations.

Gerry Cooke 'Heart Throb' pilot 7407th Support Squadron Rhein-Main 1955

The RB-66 Destroyer

The Douglas RB-66 evolved out of a response to a requirement published by the Air Force in 1951 for a Reconnaissance/Light Tactical Bomber Experimental. RBL-X. A long term replacement for the B/RB-26 was needed. The RB-57 would be fulfilling the role in the interim. The expectation was that the new aircraft would be in service by 1954. To meet this requirement Douglas submitted a revised version of their A3D Skywarrior. Other designs submitted were modified versions of the Boeing B-47 Stratojet, the Martin 'Super Canberra', the Martin XB-51 and the North American B-45 Tornado. A British design, the Vickers Valiant, was also tendered.

In the event the Douglas proposal carried the day and the order for five pre-production RB-66As was placed in February, 1952. In many ways externally similar to the Skywarrior, the RB-66 was a substantially different airplane. In addition to shedding some of the uniquely naval equipment such as arrestor hooks and strengthened undercarriage, some 400 alterations were made to the basic design. These included the use of anti-icing technology to enable an all-weather and night capability, and modifications which recognized the low level, high speed mission, such as upward exiting ejection seats and strengthening of the airframe. To accommodate alterations in the cockpit layout this had become wider and longer. The nose had been widened to accommodation the 45 inch radar dish which had been required in order to give the aircraft a greater radar range. The wing had been redesigned and altered in appearance from the Navy aircraft. In spite of considerable difficulties, not least in the selection of the powerplant for the RB-66, the first aircraft flew on 28 June, 1954. Following this flight, subsequent test flights revealed more problems with the aircraft, many related to control and stability. These were mostly ironed out by the time the aircraft reached the squadrons, although, as we have seen in the preceding narrative, the early service life of the RB-66 was often fraught with difficulties.

The first RB-66B flew in December, 1954, and the first aircraft entered service with the 16th TRS at Shaw in January 1956, replacing that units RB-26 Invaders. Over the succeeding two years the RB-66 reached USAFE and PACAF squadrons as well as three more at Shaw. In 1966 some RB-66B aircraft were redesignated EB-66E in recognition of their change of equipment and role in the south-east Asia war.

The B-66B first flew in January, 1955, and served with the 17th and 47th Bombardment Wings. In May, 1959, thirteen B-66Bs were modified as 'Brown Cradle' aircraft for use by USAFE.

An RB-66B takes its first flight from Long Beach in August, 1955. (via George Cowgill)

These aircraft were redesignated EB-66Bs in 1966 and were deployed to south-east Asia.

The RB-66C was designed from the outset as an electronic version of the aircraft. It differed from the RB-66B in that, the bomb bay, which in the RB-66B accommodated the cameras, became a pressurized compartment with space for four ECM operators and their equipment. The RB-66C was redesignated EB-66C in 1966.

The WB-66D was designed as a weather reconnaissance aircraft. It was the last variant of the aircraft to fly; initially doing so in May 1957. Similar to the RB-66C the bomb bay compartment was occupied by two weather observers and their equipment.

> Having worked on contract proposals for the F-12, a passenger version of the B-57, and the submarine launched ballistic missile as a civilian, the thing that impressed me most about the B-66 design was the main landing gear. Not only could you see completely through the fuselage, but watching it's gyrations during retraction or extension was a sight to behold. On the negative sight, in a heavy cross wind and at lower speeds when the ailerons were ineffective there was a decided tilt to the aircraft. I often wondered if this time it would remain tilted or just fall over.
>
> Dick Johnson 1st TRS 1963

> The B-66 was a pleasure to navigate when all the equipment was in and things were going right, but at times 'The Old Gal' could really turn on a crew. This happened to Clyde Trent, Roth Owens and their engineer on a trip from Shaw AFB across the Atlantic. I do not recall the model of the airplane but it was a three man crew. The route was Shaw, Bermuda via Charleston SC and Lajes Azores. Air refuelling was successfully accomplished in the ESSO BRAVO refuelling area some 400 nautical miles ENE of Bermuda. After refuelling navigation deteriorated due to suspected compass malfunction. The crew had no way of detecting this insidious malfunction. Precession was to the right. No contact was made with the Ocean Station Vessel on station midway between Bermuda and Lajes. The crew ejected when they ran out of fuel. Fortunately they had spotted a ship, a Norwegian freighter, just as the fuel gave out. Unfortunately, the ejection occurred during evening twilight and rescue had to wait until morning. The engineer was lost, but Clyde and Roth

survived. A Jet Nav chart used for the Lajes portion of the trip was recovered by the crew of the Norwegian ship. It was later presented to the Flying Evaluation Board. Lieutenant Owens had ticked his position in latitude when he crossed each meridian of longitude along with the time. His navigation equipment had the aircraft on course. As the crew was out of radar and radio range, there was little they could do but believe their Doppler, which in turn relied on N-1 compass input.

Kermit Helmke 9th TRS Shaw, 1955–1961

The RF-100A Super Sabre
The F-100 was originally conceived as a private development by North American of their F-86, and was originally designated Sabre 45 because of the aircraft's 45 degrees of wing sweepback. In October, 1951, the Air Force Council gave the go ahead to develop the aircraft in accord with a requirement published in August 1951 which called for an air superiority weapon to be operational, preferably by 1955, and not later than 1957. The mock-up of the Sabre 45 took place on 7 November, 1951, and more than a hundred configuration requests were made. On 30 November the revised Sabre 45 was renamed the F-100. In January, 1952, two prototypes were ordered and on 11 February an order for twenty-three F-100As was placed.

The F-100A mock up took place on 21 March, 1952, and the Air Force subsequently placed an order for an additional 250 aircraft. The first prototype first flew on 25 May, 1953, seven months ahead of schedule and the second on 14 October. Some major flight control and stability deficiencies were found and during the flights of the two prototypes attempts were made to rectify these. The first production aircraft flew on 29 October, 1953.

During a stringent flight testing programme the F-100A was put through its paces and its high speed was demonstrated when it reached Mach 1.34 in level flight.

In December 1953 a programme change took place when TAC recommended a production of a day fighter with a fighter-bomber capability. The reasons for this were twofold. There had been a slippage in F-84F production and there was also a requirement from those countries covered by the Mutual Development Assistance Program (MDAP).

The modifications made to the F-100A included black boxes incorporated in the yaw and pitch control axis of the aircraft to eliminate stability and control deficiencies at certain speeds. North American recommended the installation of integral fuel wings to increase the operational radius, and TAC sought to give the F-100 a nuclear as well as a conventional capability.

The F-100A was accepted into the USAF inventory in September, 1954. These initial seventy aircraft differed from the prototype in having a shorter fin and rudder of increased chord. However, continuing control problems led to a further change in design of the vertical tail surfaces though these were not incorporated into the initial aircraft which joined the 479th Fighter Day Wing (FDW) at George AFB in late September.

Six major accidents caused by unsatisfactory yaw characteristics and malfunctions in the flight control systems hydraulics caused the F-100As to be grounded and factory production to be put on hold from November 1954 to April 1955.

At the same time as the F-100A was entering its troubled service with the 479th FDW, North American was developing the F-100C, F-100D and the two seater F-100F models. These aircraft were to prove the saviour of the Super Sabre programme and would serve with distinction with the Air Force until 1972 when many were transferred to the ANG.

In September, 1954, North American received a contract to modify six F-100As to a reconnaissance configuration. They were to be used in the clandestine overflight programme. Three were to be sent to Europe and three to Asia. It was considered that the superior speed of the Super Sabre would make it an efficient and secure overflight aircraft.

The F-100s were modified to carry five cameras: Three K-17s were placed in a trimetrogen arrangement and two K-38s with 36 in cones in the split vertical. The K-38s were the main

RF-100A 53-1551 takes off. Aircraft 551 was one of the six aircraft assigned to the Slick Chick project. (USAF)

intelligence gathering cameras. It was intended to use the RF-100 for high-altitude photo reconnaissance. The K-38s were ideally suited to this purpose. In the split vertical configuration they provided photos of a sufficiently large scale to provide acceptable intelligence information. Modifications to the forward fuselage of the F-100s was necessary in order to accommodate the photographic equipment. The 20mm cannon and ammunition bays were removed. The two K-17 oblique cameras required the fuselage below the cockpit to be blistered in order to accommodate them. The two K-38s were mounted horizontally and shot their photos through a mirror which was designed to be an integral part of the camera in order to reduce the vibration that had been such a frustrating aspect of early RF-86 photography. One of the reasons that the F-100 was such a problematic aircraft to modify for photo recce was the presence of the large air duct which opened in the nose of the aircraft and passed under the cockpit. This proved particularly troublesome in the installation of the viewfinder. In the event the system evolved used a mirror which was situated at the bottom of the air duct which picked up the ground image. This image was picked up through a clear glass plate at the top of the duct and viewed by the pilot through the viewfinder.

The RF-100As undertook their secret missions until mid 1956. One of the European aircraft crashed and the remaining two returned to the USA from Europe in 1958. In late 1961 four RF-100s were sent to the Chinese Nationalist Air Force in Taiwan and it is thought that these were used for flights over China.

> There was short delay in Slick Chick because of a problem with the F-100A. The rudder of the vertical stabilizer was too small to maintain directional stability at maximum speed. North American's chief test pilot, George S Welch, a P-38 Squadron Commander in New Guinea during the Second World War was killed in his F-100 when the aircraft yawed to one side at maximum speed and broke apart. Also many in-service F-100A models were lost in what pilots called the JC, or 'Jesus Christ!' manoeuvre. At low altitude, when the airplane experienced turbulence, or when the pilot would select afterburner, the nose of the airplane would begin an up and down movement that increased in intensity until the pilot began to lose control.
>
> Because the RF-100A was not equipped with anti-skid brakes, we all concentrated on short field landings with heavy braking. We wanted to know how much braking power we had and could use before a tyre would skid or blowout. I had the aircraft crew chief watch my landings and he would tell me if he saw any smoke from my tyres. The aircraft landed at 150 kts, the pilot then deployed the drag chute, and used the brakes to stop. If the drag chute failed to open, or you landed on a short field, the maximum brake pressure was

required. We learned early about landing the RF-100A and we never had any landing problems thereafter. This was in sharp contrast to our counterparts in the F-100 fighter units.
Captain Cecil H. Rigsby Det No. 1 7407th Support Squadron, 1954–1958

The RF-86A/F Sabre

In May, 1945, the Army Air Force published a GOR which called for a day fighter of medium range that could work as an escort fighter and dive bomber. There was an emphasis on speed: a minimum speed of 600 mph was stipulated.

North American had been in the process of developing the XFJ-1 Fury for the navy; a straight wing jet fighter. In November, 1945, they proposed to the AAF that the design of the Fury be modified with a swept wing. They had already proved that this would lead to a significant increase in speed. On 2 June, 1946, an order for three prototypes was placed. Before the prototypes had flown a production order was placed for thirty-three P-86s.

The first flight of the prototype took place on 1 October, 1947. This aircraft was powered by a General Electric J35-C-3 turbojet engine. This was replaced shortly after by a more powerful J47-GE-3. The first production Sabre first flew on 20 May, 1948, and in the following month the designation was changed to F-86A. In February, 1949, the F-86A entered service with the 94th Fighter Squadron of the 1st Fighter Group at March Field, California.

In November, 1950, the first F-86As were urgently deployed to Korea with the 4th Fighter Interceptor Wing (FIW). The success of the F-86A in Korea is legendary. Within weeks the units had established air superiority over the Mig. This was due more to the skill of the pilots than the inherent superiority of the aircraft, which, in reality, probably had only a marginal performance advantage over the Mig 15.

There were three variants of the RF-86. All flew with the 15th TRS which was initially based at Kimpo in Korea and subsequently at Komaki in Japan. The two RF-86A Honeybucket aircraft, 48-217 and 48-187 were designed and modified in the field at K-14 using two 4th Fighter Wing aircraft destined to be returned to the USA. The modifications consisted of installing a camera, a K-20, on its side by taking out the gun and taking vertical photos through a mirror mounted at a 45 degree angle. Subsequently five RF-86As were specially modified with a suite designed by the now converted FEAMCOM and North American which comprised a K-22 nose oblique camera and a K-22 vertical camera with a 36 in cone installed with the axis of the cone paralleled to the axis of the wing; the photo obtained by shooting through a 45 degree mirror. The project was renamed Ashtray. Aircraft converted, in addition to the two Honeybucket aircraft, were 48-195, 48-246, 48-257, and 48-196.

In February, 1953, the first of two RF-86Fs arrived for the 15th TRS. The camera configuration for these aircraft was essentially the same as for the Ashtray RF-86As and they were known by the same codename. They replaced the RF-86As, although at any one time the 15th TRS had no more than three at its disposal.

In March, 1954, after the Korean conflict was over the 15th TRS moved to Komaki and received eight RF-86F Haymaker aircraft. The Haymaker was specially equipped for high altitude vertical photographic reconnaissance, carrying two K-22 cameras with 40 in cones. In order to accommodate the camera and the film magazines, distinctive bulges appeared on the sides of the forward fuselage, and the nickname 'Mae West' was bestowed on the aircraft! It was these cheek bulges which had so obviously altered the appearance of the RF-86 so that it could not be based in Korea under the terms of the armistice. The United Nations Inspection Teams, or NITS as they were known, were very active at this time.

The RF-86 Haymaker served with the 15th TRS and subsequently, the 6021st Reconnaissance Squadron, until 1956. Subsequently they went on to serve in Korea and Taiwan with these respective air forces.

It was fast. It accelerated well, and you could dive it with impunity as long as you didn't exceed 0.90 Mach which was our redline. To join the Mach Busters club we had a clean F-86F that we took up to do our Mach run which was straight down with full power on. I didn't find the pictures from the RF-86 to be to any better at all than the photos we took in the RF-80A. It was just a better flying aircraft all the way round

Bill Goldfein 15th TRS, Komaki, 1955

Although we continued to fly the RF-80A, the reconnaissance version of the F-80 fighter, the new RF-86Fs (Haymakers) were dynamite ships, the hottest our country had in regular service. They had about ten hours on the airframe and they even smelled new.... The service ceiling on a standard F-86 was about 42,000 ft. When we reached an altitude of 54,000 ft with the RF-86, handling the plane became very touchy. At that rarefied level it was almost like riding the edge of a stall. The aircraft also attained a distinct nose up attitude. To correct the attitude, we cracked the wing flaps about one or one and a half inches which resulted in the nose coming down while giving the pilot greater visibility.*

Jerry Depew 15th TRS Komaki, 1955

We knew that maximum thrust was obtained in the RF-86 at 690 degrees Celsius at full military revolutions-per-minute. This was usually set for take-off considering that this was the most essential time for achieving maximum thrust. But for the RF-86 pilots, getting airborne with relatively long runways was not the problem. We wanted maximum speed at the highest possible altitude.

From then on we estimated the temperatures at altitudes above 40,000 ft, and placed a number of rats and mice (small pieces of aluminium) in the tail pipes to ensure achieving 690 degrees Celsius exhaust tail-pipe temperature at full military power at altitudes above 40,000 ft. Our dash one stated that full military thrust should not be maintained for more than thirty minutes. Our 'tech rep' said that exceeding that time at full thrust would not have a deleterious effect on engine performance on any given flight, but it would drastically reduce overall engine life. That was the answer we wanted to hear. We then planned our missions for maximum thrust throughout the entire flight envelope. We wanted maximum speed and maximum altitude to avoid interception by Soviet and Chinese Mig aircraft.

Samuel T. Dickens 15th TRS Komaki, 1955

An RF-86A 196 at Kimpo. One of the original Honeybuckets. (Clyde Voss)

---

* As quoted in '*Early Cold War Overflights Symposium Proceedings*' Ed. Cargill Hall and clayton Laurie. The National Reconnaissance Office. 2003

APPENDIX II

Aerial Photography

Vertical Photography
Vertical Photography was, arguably, the most widely used type of aerial photography in the Air Force during the period covered by this book. It has the virtue of being capable of accurate scaling, has minimum distortion and is relatively easy to interpret. It is a photograph taken with the camera axis vertical, or as nearly vertical as possible. Vertical reconnaissance photography is usually accomplished in strips. Strip Vertical photography consists of taking a series of photographs in a strip to cover the target. This type of photography would be used, for example to photograph roads,

A mosaic is compiled from two or more vertical photos. It is usually used for mapping. The average mosaic can be composed of as many as seventy overlapping photos. (USAF)

A split vertical camera installation in an RB-26 in the early 1950s. Two overlapping photos are produced covering a large area. Night Split verticals can only be taken at low altitude. (USAF)

rivers and railways. Where an individual target is identified for reconnaissance cover, for example a bridge or building, the number of photographs taken in a strip is limited to those required to bracket and include the target, usually five. This type of target is called Pinpoint. The Mosaic is a series of photo strips side by side with at least a 20% side overlap. Mosaics are usually used for mapping and for covering large targets such as the front line areas for the ground forces or a large city. The Split Vertical format mounted two cameras side by side. The cameras would be tripped simultaneously. This camera installation would produce two overlapping photographs covering a wide ground area.

Oblique Photography
The Side Oblique is a photograph taken with the cone of the camera depressed downward from the lateral axis of the aircraft. There are two types: the High Oblique and the Low Oblique. In the former the camera cone is depressed 15 degrees from the lateral axis. In this photo the horizon can be seen. The horizon cannot be seen in the Low Oblique where the camera cone is depressed 30 degrees. The techniques for accomplishing Side Oblique Photography are similar to those used in Vertical photography, either pinpoint or strip. They have the advantage over the vertical in that they provide an image which is easily recognisable to the photo interpreter. The disadvantage is that the images further from the aircraft tend to be unclear and distorted and because of the lack of scale measurements are not possible. Often the Oblique will be taken to complement or clarify the intelligence from a vertical photograph.

The Forward Oblique photograph is taken with a camera mounted in the nose of the aircraft, pointing forward, often called the 'Dicing' camera. All standard cameras were used from the 12 in to the 40 in cone and were, with the exception of the 12 in mounted parallel to the longitudinal axis of the aircraft. The 12 in was depressed 12 degrees. Dicing shots are usually taken at low altitude with the pilot aiming the aircraft at the building or some other important individual target. A dicing run would consist of taking a strip with the forward oblique of a road or an airfield to cover troop or vehicle movements or aircraft. Forward photographs have the advantage of being very clear but were considered the most dangerous of all for the pilots, approaching the target as they did through areas which were invariably heavily defended.

It is difficult to be precise about the origin of the term 'dicing' It has been suggested that the term came from the British in the Second World War who would throw dice to decide who took on these rather 'hairy' missions.

This vertical was taken by an RB-26 at night during an exercise. The flashes have illuminated something under camouflage nets which the Photo Interpreter has marked on the photo. (USAF)

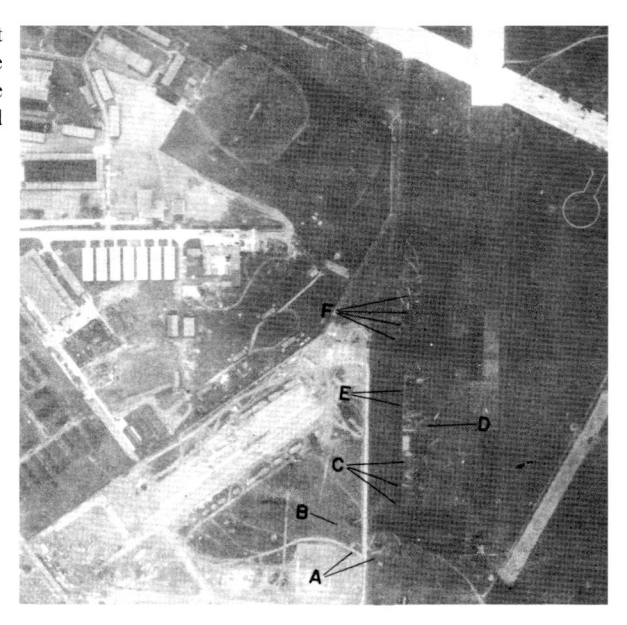

Following the night mission of the RB-26, during the following day an RF-80 was sent for a closer look and made a low dicing run. The aircraft under the nets can be clearly seen. (USAF)

Panoramic Photography.

Panoramic photography is photography obtained by swinging or 'panning' an aerial camera to photograph the terrain from horizon to horizon. Actually the camera is not swung. A dove prism is rotated in front of the camera lens and the result is as though the camera were swung.

Sonne Strip Photography
The Sonne Strip camera is designed to take a continuous strip photograph the entire length of the film if necessary. Its advantage is that it enables clear photographs to be taken at low altitudes at speeds from 150 mph to transonic. The strip camera employs the moving film principle (film synchronized with image movement) to obtain continuous aerial strip photography. The movement of the film across the focal plane behind a variable-width slit is synchronized with the speed of the aircraft over the ground.

The Sonne camera tended to fall into disuse after the Korean war, but its use was revived in some of the RF-101 aircraft which flew missions over Cuba in 1962.

Trimetrogen Photography
This type of photography enables the mapping of large areas in a short time, which may be necessary in a combat situation. Three cameras are used. One is mounted vertically and the other

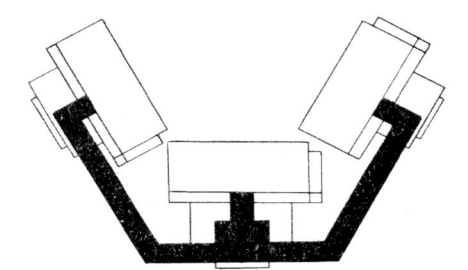

THREE K-17 CAMERAS IN FIXED TRI-METROGON MOUNT. WIDE ANGLE LENS OF SIX INCH FOCAL LENGTH USED.

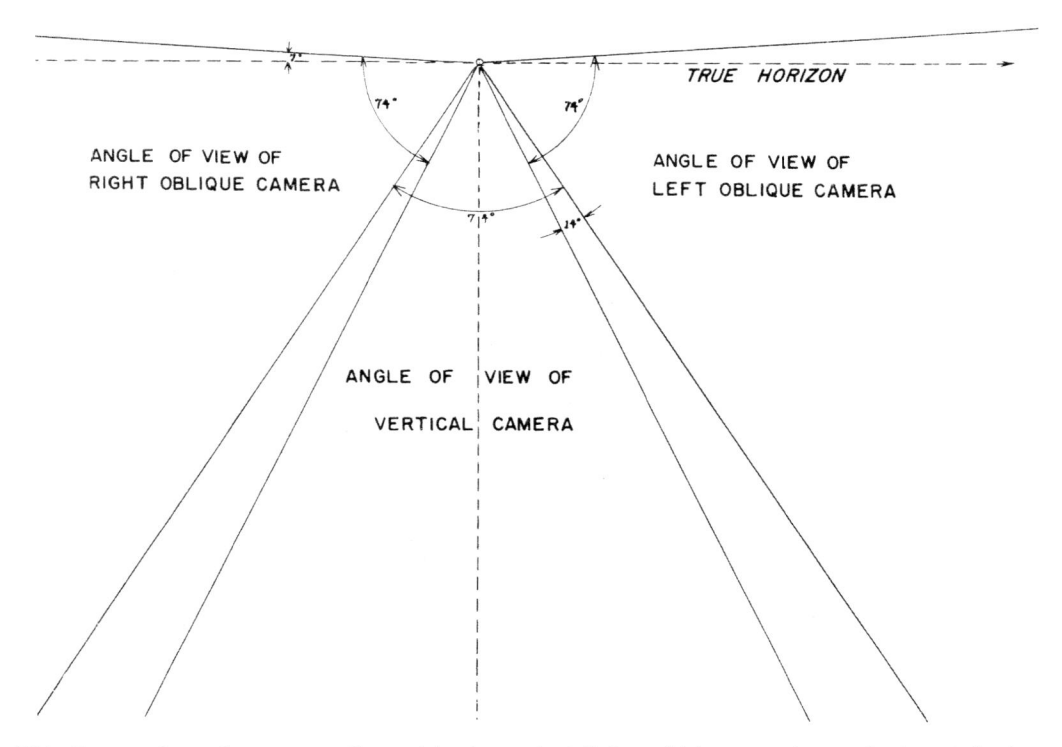

This diagram shows the coverage from a trimetrogen installation which can produce an horizon-to-horizon photograph. (USAF)

two are mounted in the Left and Right Oblique positions, each depressed 30 degrees from the lateral axis of the aircraft. In this way the terrain is covered from horizon-to-horizon.

Movie Photography
At no time was the 16 or 35mm movie camera a standard fit in recce aircraft. However, there were times when such cameras were installed. For example, in Korea both the RF-80 and the RF-86 at one time carried a 35 mm camera to record the results of fighter bomber sorties. In the case of the RF-80 the camera was installed in the nose forward position. In the case of the RF-86 in an underwing tank.

The importance of Scale
Scale is a prerequisite of any photographic coverage. It is determined at the planning stage of a mission and will determine the cameras used, their focal length and the altitude of the mission to be flown as far as is practicable. For example, a photograph taken at 10,000 ft with a 6 in wide angle lens will produce a scale of 1:20,000. With a 12 in lens the scale would be 1:10,000 and

These three photographs demonstrate the importance of scale. All three photographs were taken at 10,000 ft: a) with a six in lens, b) with a 12 in lens and c) with a 24 in lens. (USAF)

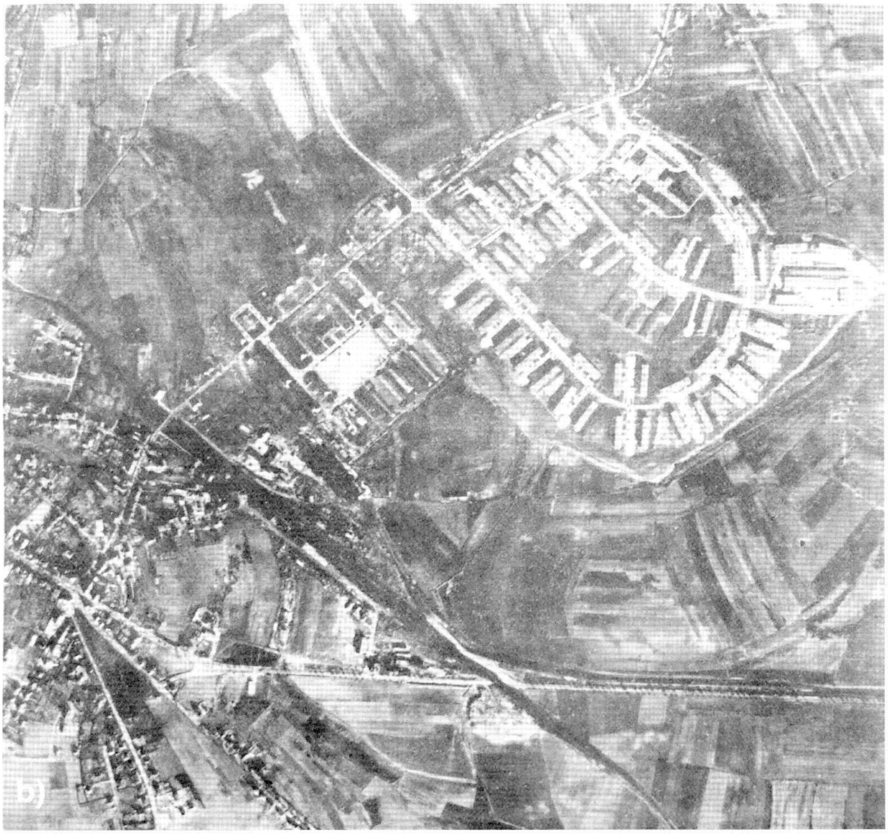
b)

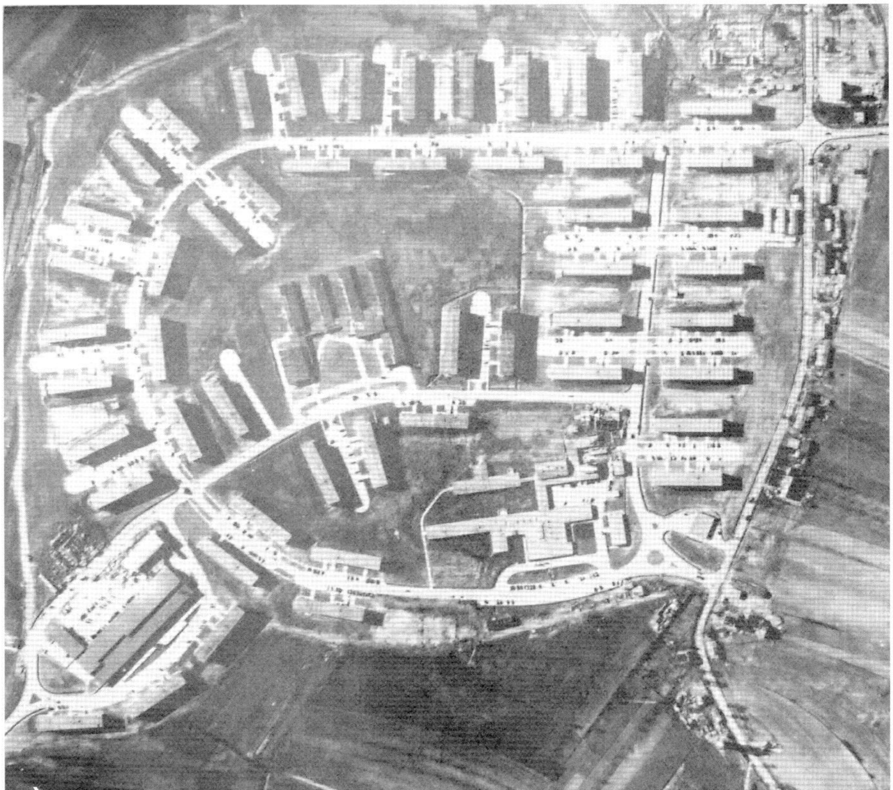
c)

with a 24 in lens 1:5,000. For the pilot the size of the scale determines the height at which he must fly. For the photo interpreter the scale is crucial in that it facilitates the analysis of a photo and the amount and accuracy of the information that can be gleaned from it. The nature of the target to be photographed determines the scale at which the photograph should be taken to enable a good and detailed interpretation. For example, photos of airfields provide for best interpretation at a scale of 1:15,000; machine gun positions at 1:5,000. However, for the former a scale of 1:30,000 will usually enable the interpreter to identify the airfield and at 1:15,000, the machine gun position should just about be recognizable. One of the reasons the RF-101 endured so long in south-east Asia was its continued use of the KA-1 camera with a 36 in focal length. The scale was good at high altitude and, in addition, the KA-1 used a 9 × 18 inch plate. Good quality large format photos were in much demand.

An RF-86 Haymaker aircraft on a mission on the 19th February, 1955, took photos over Khabarovsk with its K-22 camera with 40 in cones at a height of 42,000 ft. This gave a scale to the photos of 1:12,600. This scale gave the interpreters at the 548th Reconnaissance Technical Squadron the opportunity to identify all but the smallest objects.

Night Photo Reconnaissance
During the Second World War and up to and including the Korean War, the role of the Night Photo squadrons was primarily one of Visual Reconnaissance. For example a mere 15 per cent of the mission of the RB-26s, in Korea, the Continental United States and Europe, was photographic. The RB-26C used the K-19B camera with the M-46 flash bomb and the M-112 photo flash cartridge. Most night photo missions in the RB-26 were vertical missions flown at medium altitude between 7000 and 8000 ft.

With the development of more sophisticated sensors, the night photo aircraft became more efficient and this is exemplified in the RB-57Es and RF-4Cs in south-east Asia. Both these aircraft relied on

These two photographs were taken by an RF-101C in south-east Asia. The first, A, is a pre-strike photograph of a POL depot near Hanoi. B, is a BDA photo taken shortly after a strike on the POL by USAF F-105s. (USAF via George Cowgill))

high resolution infra-red systems to bring home the intelligence, but both were also equipped with photo flash cartridges and cameras for forward and side oblique and vertical photography.

Requesting Agencies
The two primary requesting agencies for photographic reconnaissance are the ground forces and the air forces. Photography for the ground forces are mainly of three types. Basic Cover can be defined as photographic coverage of an area the width of the front line extending some 100 miles into enemy territory. Front Line Cover is daily vertical coverage of an army area the width of the battle line and extending to a desired depth. Special Cover missions are 'one off' requests for specific photographic coverage of specific targets such as bridges, buildings and airfields.

Photography for the Air forces would be Battle Damage Assessment (BDA), Pre-Strike photography, Target Folder photography and Interdiction Cover Photography. Interdiction Cover is used by the Air Force to plan strikes and the coverage will extend along the front line and as far as the range of the reconnaissance aircraft will allow. It can be one time coverage or recurring coverage. Target Folder Photography serves as an aid to navigation and identification of targets by air crew members. It is easier, for example, for fighter bomber pilots to identify and plan their approach to their targets if they have a photo rather than a map as an aid to planning. Target folder photography by its nature is usually oblique.

The Cameras
The three decades covered by this book witnessed a rapid development, not only in reconnaissance aircraft, but also in the cameras that they carried. In 1946 the F-6D Mustang carried two cameras, the K-17 and/or the K-22. In the early 1970s the RF-4C could carry as many as eight different cameras in a variety of configurations, in addition to a number of infra-red, laser

This RB-26 belongs to the 1st TRS. The RB-26 could carry both flash bombs and cartridges for night photography.(USAF via Bob Webster)

Above: The Lockheed RF-80A with its array of cameras. The K-22 36 in, below, was often carried in the Forward Oblique position in Korea. (USAF)

APPENDIX II 305

An RF-84F of the 10th TRW at Spangdahlem demonstrates the extent of its camera capability. (10th TRW Historical Office)

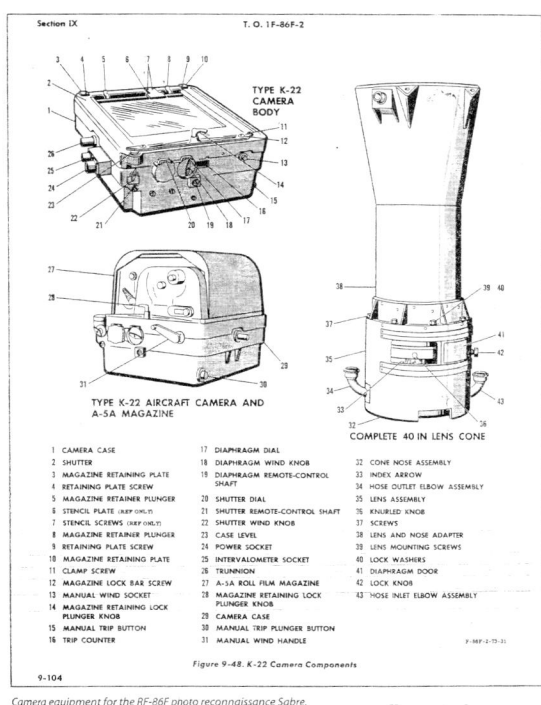

and radar sensors.

The standard cameras used by the Air Force at the time of Korea were all Second World War cameras. They were the K-17, K-18, K-22, K-19B and K-37; all designed by Fairchild. The K-19B and K-37 were carried by the RB-26 for night photography in conjunction with a photo electric cell which automatically synchronized the camera exposure with the flash bomb illumination. The K-17, K-18, and K-22 were for day photography. The K-17 was capable of carrying lenses from 6 in to 24 in. The K-22 could carry lenses from 6 inches to 40 in. All the above cameras produced negatives in 9 × 9 in format. The K-18 was a 9 × 18 in format camera and the body and lens were designed as a single unit. The RF-80 could carry all the

Camera equipment for the RF-86F photo reconnaissance Sabre.

The K-22 camera as carried by the RF-86F on its clandestine missions over China and the Soviet Union. Note the long 40 in lens. (USAF via Bob Archibald)

The RB-26 was replaced in the night recce units by the RB-57A. This example is from the 1st TRS at Spangdahlem. (USAF)

above day photographic cameras in a variety of configurations utilizing up to four cameras at a time.

The K-17C and K-22A cameras were used in the successor to the RF-80A, the RF-84. The RF-84 could carry up to six cameras in variety of configurations. In addition to the K-17 and the K-22, the K-37 and K-38 were also used. The K-38 was developed from the K-18 and was used in the prime vertical station in the rear of the camera compartment. With its 9 × 18 in format and its capability of utilizing a 24 and a 36 in lens it was a very effective vertical camera.

The K-38 was used in the RB-57A along with the K-17 and the K-37. It was also used as the main intelligence gathering camera in the RF-100A.

The RB-66B which was configured for night reconnaissance utilized the K-37 and the K-46 cameras in the forward and central portion of the bomb bay.

The K-38 was developed into the KA-1 camera. This camera were used in the RF-101, the RB-57E, and, to a limited extent, the RF-4C. The early configuration of the RF-101 utilized a pair of KA-1s in the split vertical position. Fairchild KA-2s which shot in the 9 × 9 inch format were installed in the forward and side oblique stations. During its long career the camera suite of the Voodoo underwent many developments and upgrades, including Modification 1181, which sought to take full advantage of the rapid developments in camera technology which were taking place at this time.

Panoramic cameras, in particular were developing fast. The development in satellite optical technology did have a pay-off for the tac recce aircraft. The KA-56 low altitude panoramic, the KA-82 and KA-83 medium altitude panoramic cameras and the KA-55 high altitude panoramic camera were in regular use in the war in south-east Asia. They were installed in the Patricia Lynn RB-57Es at

The K-17 camera with a 12in lens. Next to it is the intervalometer which automatically trips the camera at predetermined intervals.(USAF)

The RF-101C carried a considerable variety of cameras during its long career with the USAF, undergoing several modifications and upgrades. (USAF)

An RF-4C forward oblique pre-strike photo taken in south-east Asia. The object of possible attack is the ford across the river. It has been marked by the photo interpreter. (USAF)

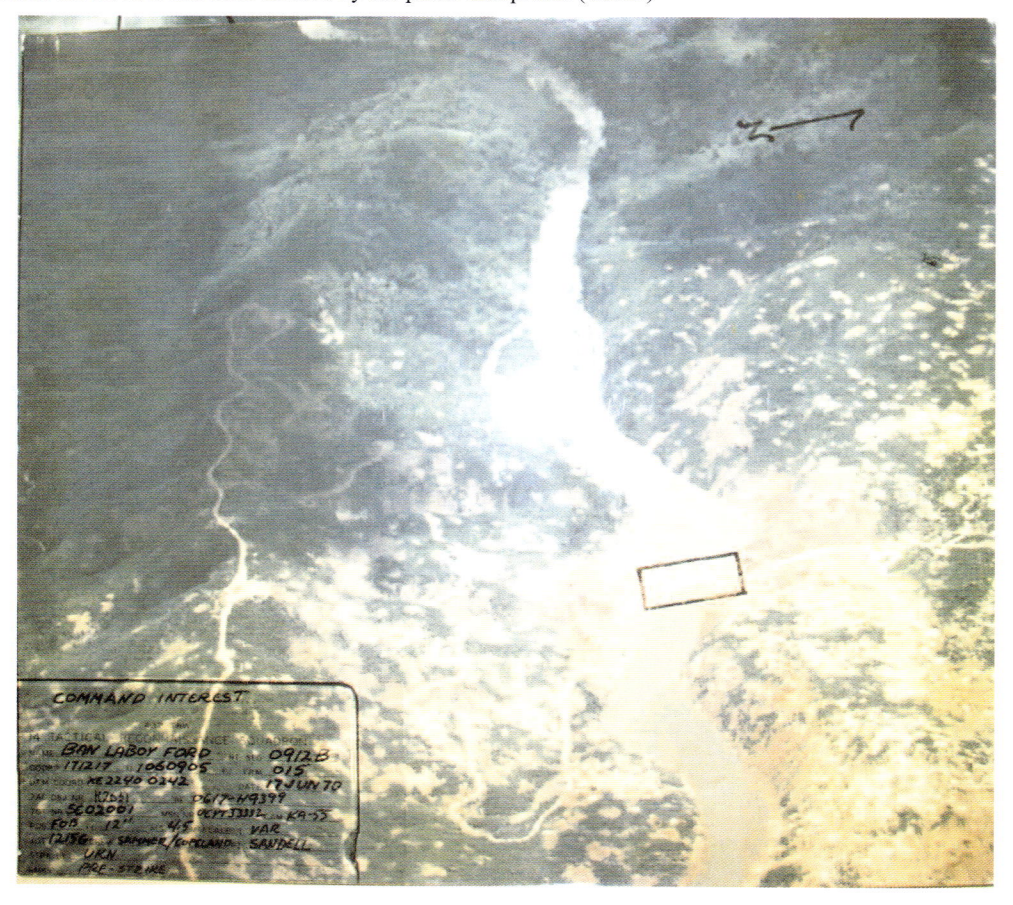

USAFE Happy Snap. Canterbury Cathedral 1955. RF-80A 38th TRS (USAF via Ron Colpron)

USAFE happy Snap. Hohernzoller Castle Germany, RF-80A 38th TRS 1955. (USAF via Ron Colpron)

USAFE Happy Snap. An RAF Meteor flies over Cologne, RF-80A 302nd TRS 1953. (USAF via Bob Sweet)

USAFE Happy Snap. Sacre Coeur Paris, RF-84F 38th TRS 1956. (USAF via Ron Colpron)

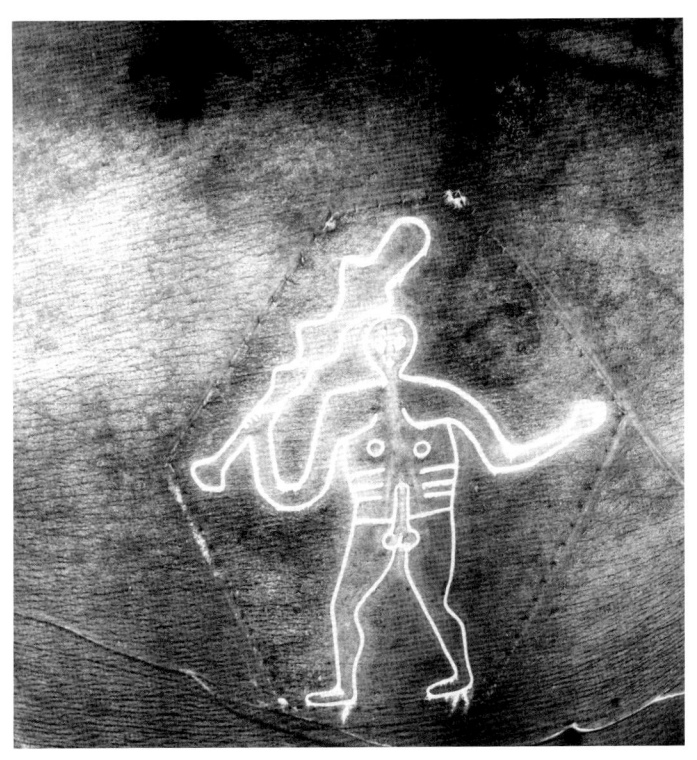

USAFE Happy Snap. The Cerne Abbas Giant, RF-101C 18th TRS 1967. (USAF via Nick Pishvanov)

USAFE Happy Snap. The Uffington Horse, RF-101C 18th TRS 1967. (USAF via Nick Pishvanov)

USAFE Happy Snap. The Wide Barrel at Bad Durkheim, RF-4C 38th TRS 1966. (USAF via Fred Muesegaes)

Tan Son Nhut. The KA-55 and KA-56 were also used by the RF-4C. The low altitude KS-87 was used in the RF-4C and the RF-101.

The progress of time witnessed a huge development in the number and variety of sensors that could be carried and used in reconnaissance aircraft. In its long service life the RF-4Cs reconnaissance capabilities were enhanced to a degree never imagined when the aircraft first joined the squadrons in 1965, including the HIAC-1 LOROP camera and the RCA AN/UXD-1 podded electronic camera system.

The development of podded integrated systems heralded the end of the purpose designed reconnaissance aircraft. Now all the reconnaissance equipment could be carried underneath a standard fighter, or indeed in a remotely controlled pilotless reconnaissance vehicle.

APPENDIX III

Glossary of Abbreviations

AAA	Anti-Aircraft Artillery
AAR	Air-to-Air refuelling
AB	Air Base
AFB	Air Force Base
AGL	Above Ground Level
ANG	Air National Guard
ARDF	Airborne Radio Direction Finding
ATAF	Allied Tactical Air Force
BDA	Battle Damage Assessment
CASF	Composite Air Strike Force
CCTG	Combat Crew Training Group
CCTS	Combat Crew Training Squadron
CONUS	Continental United States
DR	Dead Reckoning
ECM	Electronic Countermeasures
ELINT	Electronic Intelligence
EWO	Electronic Warfare Officer
FAC	Forward Air Controller
FEAF	Far East Air Force
FEAMCOM	Far East Air Material Command
FIW	Fighter Interceptor Wing
FLR	Flight Refuelling
FOD	Foreign Object Damage
GCA	Ground Control Approach
GCI	Ground Control Intercept
GIB	Guy in the Back
GOR	General Operational Requirement
ICC	International Control Commission
IFF	Identification Friend or Foe
IFR	Instrument Flight Rules
IP	Instructor Pilot
IR	Infra-Red
KJOC	Korean Joint Operations Center
Kts	Knots
MAAG	Military Assistance Advisory Group
NORAD	North American Air Defense Command
NVA	North Vietnam
ORI	Operational Readiness Inspection
PACAF	Pacific Air Forces
PI	Photo Interpreter

POL	Petrol Oil and Lubricant Depot
PPC	Photo Processing Centre
PRS	Photo Reconnaissance Squadron
RCTS	Reconnaissance Crew Training Squadron
RP	Route Package
RTAFB	Royal Thai Air Base
RTF	Reconnaissance Task Force
RTU	Replacement Training Unit
RVN	Republic of Vietnam
SAM	Surface to Air Missile
SLAR	Side Looking Airborne Radar
SLR	Side Looking Radar
SOR	Specific Operational Requirements
SRW	Strategic Reconnaissance Wing
TACAN	Tactical Air Navigation
TDY	Temporary Duty
TEWS	Tactical Electronic Warfare Squadron
TFR	Terrain Following Radar
TFS	Tactical Fighter Squadron
TFW	Tactical Fighter Wing
TRG(p)	Tactical Reconnaissance Group
TRS	Tactical Reconnaissance Squadron
TRTS	Tactical Reconnaissance Training Squadron
TSN	Tan Son Nhut
USAAF	United States Army Air Force
USAF	United States Air Force
USAFE	United States Air Forces in Europe
USN	United States Navy
VFR	Visual Flight Rules
WSO	Weapons Systems Officer
Wx	Weather

Bibliography

Early Cold War Overflights Symposium Proceedings Ed. Cargill Hall and Clayton Laurie. The National Reconnaissance Office. 2003

Sparks Over Vietnam. The EB-66 and the Early Struggle of Tactical Electronic Warfare. Captain Giles Van Nederveen. Airpower Research Institute. 2000

Air Force Combat Wings Charles A Ravenstein. Office of Air Force History. 1984

Combat Squadrons of the Air Force. Maurer Maurer. Office of Air force History. 1982

US Aircraft and Missile Systems: Post World War II Fighters Marcelle Size Knaak. Office of Air Force History. 1978

The Air Force in Southeast Asia: The RF-101 VOODOO, 1961-1970. USAF Historical Studies, No. 149.' William H. Greenhalgh, Jr. Air Force Historical Research Agency, Maxwell AFB.

Modern Military Aircraft Voodoo Lou Drendel & Paul Stevens, Squadron Signal 1985

Douglas B-66 Destroyer. Rene Francillon & Mick Roth. Aerofax 1988

McDonnell RF-4 Variants Jay Miller. Aerofax 1984

Republic F-84 Swept Wing Variants Kevin Keaveney. Aerofax. 1987.

Before Centuries MSgt David W. Menard. 1999. Airlife.

McDonnell Douglas F-101 Voodoo. Bunrin-Do. 1975

Famous Airplanes of the World, F-4C/D. Bunrin Do. 1981

B-57 Canberra in Action Jim Mesco. Squadron Signal. 1986

I always wanted to fly. American's Cold War Airmen W.E. Samuel University Press of Mississippi. 2001

A Pictorial History of the USAF David Mondey. Ian Allen. 1971

Moonglow a novel about Patricia Lynn operations in SE Asia. Hank Holden, Books By Bookends 2004. email: Dave Logan booksbybookends@verizon.net

Swift Justice, Nigel Walpole. Pen and Sword. 2004

Web Sites
There are a number of web sites, the webmasters of which have kindly assisted with information and photographs.

http://b66info Paul Duplessis
http://philrowe.net/rf4stuf2 Phil Rowe
http://ransomsroots.com/anotherlife Kirk Ransom
http://www.b-57canberra.org Mark Witt
http://www.cottonpickers.org John Duquette

Index

GENERAL INDEX

Able Mable 184, 219–265
Air America 216
Antung, Korea 24, 26, 29, 39
Archibald, Bob 126
Ashtray, Project 38, 56
Auer, John 10, 286
Austin, Hal 287

Bergstrom AFB., 150, 167, 188, 189
Berlin 127
Birdseye, Project 10, **11**
Bissett, Bill 47, **48**
Bitburg AB, Germany 68, 69, 98, 114
Brooks, Wes 131
Brothers, Wes **157**
Brown Cradle 124, 130, 236, 247
Bruenner, Willi 130
Bryant, Jim 57, 62, 64
Bultman, Dick 129
Burkhart, Bob 171

Cameron, Mort **21**
Canady, Joe 266
Carrodus, Paul 119, 126
Carte Blanche, Exercise 92
Caseaux, France 104, 112
Caudry, Bob 214, 216–219
Chambley, France 140
Coghlan, Jack **99**
Colburn, Ned 260, 261
Compass Dart 254
Cooke, Gerry 61, 65, 289
Cooper, David 202
Cowgill, George **235**, 237
Cuban Missile Crisis 129, 179
Czechoslovakia 65, 72, 122, 198

Daly, Joe 28, 32
Darien, China 51
Depew, Jerry 51, 295
Desert Storm 151
Dickens, Sam 47, **48**, 295
Display Determination, Exercise 150
Don Muang Airport Thailand 219
Dunn, Frank 204, **205**
Duquette, Norman 25, 29

East, Clyde 15, 19, 20, 24, 25, 103, 126
Eindhoven, The Netherlands

Ellis, Edward
Ezell, Henry E. 24

Field Goal, Project 214–219
Fosdick, Jim 37
Furstenfeldbruck AB, Germany 72

Gafford, Bill 57
Garrison, Larry 47, 48, 53, 162, 243, 276
Garrison, Pete 47, 48
Goldfein, Bill 195, 271, 295
Gorman, Ed 289
Gould, Bob 142, 194, 281, 287
Grant, Hal 90, 94, 104, 113
Gray, Ruffin 28, 32
Green Dragon, Project 123
Green Python 231–265
Griffin, LaVerne 41, 46, 47
Gulf of Tonkin 227, 234, 246
Guthrie, Joe 57, 59, 61

Halfhill, Tom 13
Harbin, China 37, 41
Hawkeye, Project 192, 199–201
Haymaker 44–47
Heart Throb 44, 57–67
Helmke, Kermit 90, 177, 292
Hemphill, Dewey 277
Heritage, Jon 252, 283
Hines, Bob 57, 65, 67
Hodges, Paul 104, **124,** 273
Holbury, Bob 63
Holden, Hank **247**, 257
Holland, David 131
Honeybucket, Project 32, 33, 36
Howell, James 40
Howell, Philip 40
Hungary 65, 67

Ilyushin Il 28 37
Itami AB, Japan 192–213
Itazuke AB, Japan 15

Johnson, Dick 291
June Primer, Exercise 75

Kadena AB Okinawa 188, 197, 214, 264
Karges, Don 121, 127, **132**, 133, **240**, 241, 253, 281
Khabarovsk, USSR 53

Kilpatrick, Bob 92, 171
Kimpo K14, Korea 25–43, 192
Klatt, Gus 91, 171
Komaki AB, Japan 15, 45, 192
Korat RTAB, Thailand 230

Lake, Robin 144, **145**
Lang, Ron 285
Langley AFB 19, 152–156
Laon AB, France 111, 117–140, 175
Lebanon 117, 175

Madrishin, John 164
Martz, Bill 28
McMurray, Bill 29, 31
Meyer, Frank 32, 79, 82
Mig Alley 21, 28
Mikoyan Mig 15 21, 24, 25, 28, 29, 38, 47, 85, 227
Mikoyan Mig 17 50, 53, 66, 91, 126, 127, 180, 227, 237
Mikoyan Mig 19 65, 129, 132
Mikoyan Mig 21 180, 245, 256, 260, 261, 268
Miller, Jerry **220**, **224**, **239**
Misawa AB, Japan 189, 192, 195–213, 214
Mobile Zebra 171, 203, 219
Moon River 262, 264
Morrison, Red 53
Mosher, Brad 130
Moulton, Jere 28, 285
Mountain Home AFB. 139, 185
Muesegaes, Fred 180, 181, 214, 216–219, 221, 222
Mukden, China 24, 37
Munroe, Charles 'Chuck' 188, 268, 283
Myers, Horace 17

Nakhom Phanom, Thailand 264
Namsi, Korea 25
Nash, Don 236, 263, 283
Neubiberg AB, Germany 74
North Field 164
Nouasseur, Morocco 76, 115, 118, 126

O' Grady, Joe 179
Osan K55, Korea 47, 55, 188, 204

Patricia Lynn 225, 228, 257, 261
Peckham, Howard 289
Pell, John 33
Phalsbourg AB, France 113,
Phu Cat, S. Vietnam 255, 261, 264
Phyliss Ann 250, 254
Picciano, Lou 57, 64, 67
Pierrelatte, France 133–138
Pipe Stem 220–223

Pishvanov, Nick 123, 131, 132, 257, 276
Pleiku, S. Vietnam 252, 261
Polifka, Karl 'Pop' 19, 20, 23, 24
Port Arthur, China 52

RAF Alconbury 121–185
RAF Bentwaters 93
RAF Bruntingthorpe 121–131
RAF Chelveston 121–131, 178
RAF Sculthorpe 107, 110, 111
RAF Upper Heyford 140, 188
RAM 88 151
Ramstein AB, Germany 128, 142, **144**
Red Berry, Operation 165, 174
Reeder, Bill 247, 252
Reeder, Johnnie 129
Rhein-Main, Germany, 57, 59
Rhodarmer, Roger 10, 69
Rigsby, Cecil 18, 26, 36, 68, **69**, 72, 294
Robertson, John 'Robbie' 104, 114
Rolling Thunder 230, 260
Ross, Mike 'Squid Bait' 150
Rowe, Phil 189, 263
Royal Flush, Exercise 88, 104, 114, 117, **121**, 123, 124, 126, 131, 140

Sakhalin, USSR 61
Satterfield, Ed 140
Saylor, George **46**, **47**
Schoolfield, 'Scotty' 117, 273, 281, 283
Schrecengost, Ray 15, 24, 131, 171
Sembach AB, Germany 79–117, 162
Semonin, Bill 55
Shaw AFB 14, 19, 67, 57, 79, 91, 118, 152–191
Sidi Slimane, Morocco 76, 95, 98
Sinuiju, Korea 25, **57**
Skinner, Lee 119
Slick Chick 44, 67–73
Smith, Joe 133–138
Space cadet, 116
Spangdahlem AB, Germany 79–121, 144
Stairstep, Exercise 178
Stamm, Bob 197
Stoltz, Ed 21, 23, 83, **84**, 89, 155, 156, 164, 271, 276
Suez Crisis 67
Suippes, France 131
Sun Run, Operation 171
Swamp Fox 125, **176**, 178, 179
Sweet, Bob **16**, 18, 81, 91, 93, 167, 171, **174** 175, 266, **267**, 272, 276, 281

Taechon, Korea 75
Taegu K2, Korea 15–25, 213
Taiwan 175, 195
Takhli RTAB, Thailand 140, 184, 230, 232–268

Tan Son Nhut, Saigon 184, 189, 220–268
Tansey, James 'Russ' 92, **93**, 103
Taxi Cab, Exercise 120, 122, 247
Taylor, Arthur 'Kibby' 248
Tchepone 222
Toul-Rosiere AB, France 74, 124, 125, 131, 139, 140
Tupolev TU-104 204
Tupolev TU-4 **53**

Udorn RTAB, Thailand 185, 188, 214–219, 230–268
Uiju, Korea 25
USS Pueblo 188

Vaughters, Dick 123, 273, 281
Vladivostok, USSR 23, 28, 47, **49**, 53, 65
Vojdovich, Mele 38
Voss, Clyde 37

Walker, Bob **241**, 245
Walker, Phil **258**, 262
Waltz, Burt 228
Watkins, Benny **144**, 145
Weatherby, Jack 219, **221,** 233
Webster, Bob 89
Weisbaden AB, Germany 63, 74, 76, 91
Wheelus, Libya 90, 112, 114. 125
Whipsaw, Exercise 104
White, Don 41
Wilkes, Roger 261
William Tell 131
Williams, Jack 36, 37
Woodyard, John 15, 21, 24, 25, 80, 152, 153

Yalu 28, 29, 38
Yankee Team 225
Yokota AB, Japan 15, 57, 59, 68, 197
Zweibrucken AB, Germany 142, 150, 144, 150

INDEX to USAF Tactical Reconnaissance Squadrons
1st Balloon Squadron 9
1st TRS 75–150
2nd Balloon Squadron 9
4th TRS 10, 12, 188, 189, 213
8th TRS 10, 12, 14–18
9th TRS 124, 161–185, 188, 189, 232–237
10th TRS 185
11th TRS 10, 41, 185, 192–213, 248–268
12th Aero Squadron 9
12th TRS 10, 14, 19–43, 185, 192–213, 248–268
14th TRS 188, 213–268
15th TRS 18–43, 45–57, 192–268
16th TRS 150, 154, 236–265

17th TRS 118–150, 156–175, 219
18th TRS 14, 118–150, 156–175, 188
19th TRS 110–140
19th TEWS 185, 264
20th TRS 162–184, 236
22nd RS 10
22nd TRS 139, 185, 189
25th TRS 10, 13
29th TRS 162–188
30th TRS 79–150
31st TRTS 188
32nd TRS 75–150, 185
33rd TRS 189
38th TRS 75–151
39th TRS 10
39th TEWS 144–150
39th TEWTS 188
41st TRS 162–175
41st TEWS 248–164
42nd TRS 86–140
42nd ECS 151
42nd TEWS 248, 256
43rd ECS 151
43rd TRS 162–175
45th RS 10
45th TRS 10, 15– 43, 188, 189, 192–213, 214–265
62nd TRS 189
82nd RS 10
91st TRS 188, 189
106th TRS 150
112th TRS 74, 75
157th TRS 74, 75
160th TRS 10, 74, 75, 152–153
161st RS 10
161st TRS 14, 152
162nd RS 10
162nd TRS 15, 152–156
302nd TRS 79–118
303rd TRS 79–118
360th RS 250
360th TEWS 252, 254
361st RS 250
361st TEWS 252
362nd RS 252
362nd TEWS 252, 261
4400th CCTS 154
4414th CCTS 176, 188
4415th CCTS 176
4416th CCTS 185
4417th CCTS 185
4426th RCTS 160
6021st RS 57, 193
6166th Weather Flight 15
6460th TEWS 140, 257
7407th Support Squadron 59–73